Elementary Education
A Basic Text

Fredricka K. Reisman
Drexel University

Beverly D. Payne
University of Georgia

Merrill Publishing Company
A Bell & Howell Information Company
Columbus Toronto London Melbourne

To Ben and Sam
　　F.K.R.

To David, for his unfailing love and wisdom
　　B.D.P.

Cover photo: David S. Strickler/Strix Pix

Published by Merrill Publishing Company
A Bell & Howell Information Company
Columbus, Ohio 43216

This book was set in Garamond.

Administrative Editor: Jeff Johnston
Production Coordinator: Linda Hillis Bayma
Cover Designer: Cathy Watterson

Photo Credits: All photos copyrighted by individuals or companies listed. Bell & Howell, p. 289; Paul Conklin, pp. 35, 197, 265; Vivienne della Grotta, p. 287; Merrill Publishing, p. 5, Ben Chandler, p. 95, Kevin Fitzsimons, p. 127, Jean Greenwald, pp. 133, 154, 225, 248, Mary Hagler, pp. 101, 158, 170, Larry Hamill, p. 83, Bruce Johnson, pp. 50, 71, 143, 212, Lloyd Lemmerman, p. 249; David C. Phillips, p. 261; Michael Siluk, pp. 3, 21, 39, 120, 182; David S. Strickler/Strix Pix, pp. 18, 111, 149, 176; University of Minnesota, Student Support Services, Publication Center, p. 79.

Copyright © 1987 by Merrill Publishing Company. All rights reserved. No part of this book may be reproduced in any form, electronic or mechanical, including photocopy, recording, or any information storage and retrieval system, without permission in writing from the publisher. "Merrill Publishing Company" and "Merrill" are registered trademarks of Merrill Publishing Company.

Library of Congress Catalog Card Number: 86-63611
International Standard Book Number: 0-675-20407-0
Printed in the United States of America
1 2 3 4 5 6 7 8 9—91 90 89 88 87

Preface

This book was designed for teachers of kindergarten through the eighth grade. Much of the material presented is generic in nature and thus equally applicable to learning, instruction, and assessment through the twelfth grade. Some may wish to expand use of this book to secondary education or use it in conjunction with a secondary education content or methods text; for this purpose, we have provided an appendix that extends the principles of the book to secondary education.

We have not organized our discussion around specific elementary-school curriculum areas such as mathematics, reading, language arts, science, physical education, social studies, art, music, and foreign language. That approach often is prescriptive and would run counter to the philosophy of teacher preparation espoused here—that of preparing teachers to cope with change, and to become creative problem solvers. We believe teachers should be able to adapt instruction to learner idiosyncrasies and to deal with rapidly changing curriculum due to the onslaught of new information. They should be able to engage in thinking about what it is they are doing (employ cognitive monitoring) in order to provide the best possible learning opportunities for students, and they should use and encourage their students to use technology as a tool—not as yet another "subject."

The book is organized into three parts. Part 1, including chapters 1 through 8, espouses a spirit of teaching that encourages lifelong learning on the teacher's part. Teachers are more and more becoming instructional designers: that is, designers of learning environments that accommodate the complex natures of learners and that address curricular changes as new knowledge constantly emerges. Part 1 begins with an introduction in chapter 1 which discusses the state of the teaching profession, offering recommendations and suggestions for the future of teacher preparation. Chapters 2 and 3 cover generic influences on learning and their implications for designing instruction. Chapters 4 and 5 provide basic information on instructional goals and objectives and how they are used to plan lessons. Chapter 6 defines instructional design while chapter 7 discusses integration of computing into instruction. Chapter 8 describes various strategies for improving classroom communication through questioning. Part 2 provides an in-depth discussion of educational assessment, since we believe that educational evaluation is essential to diagnostic teaching and should be integrated with instruction. Part 3 is designed to tie up loose ends and to serve as a catalyst to start readers on their paths to becoming teachers. Thought questions in each chapter help students engage their creativity in the issues being considered. A glossary of terms is provided at the text's conclusion.

Many people have contributed to the completion of this text and we thank them wholeheartedly for their wisdom and their willingness to share in its preparation. We would like to thank the reviewers for their constructive comments, including George Wetmore, State University of New York College at Oneonta; Elizabeth Stimson, Bowling Green State University; Dale Harp, Western Oregon State College; Franklin D. Carlson, Central Washington University; Johnny Purvis, The University of Southern Mississippi; and Frank Hughes, Belmont College. Thanks are also extended to the editorial staff at Merrill Publishing: Linda Bayma, production editor, and Jeffrey Johnston, executive editor. Thanks are due Larry Keiser, Behrouz Hazany, and Carlos Lazzari for their help in researching the instructional design and computing chapters. We owe a particular debt to copyeditor Margaret Conable, who provided the editorial skills so necessary to make the book read consistently. Our colleagues at Drexel University and The University of Georgia counseled and shared with us. We are also indebted to our students for their suggestions and responses to our class presentations. Lisa Paski, Martha Roach, and Paulette Bone, thank you for your patience and skill in transforming our numerous drafts into a polished, typed manuscript.

Fredricka Reisman
Beverly Payne

Contents

Part 1
Introduction to Teaching

1. Introduction / 2
2. Observation and analysis of school-related behavior / 17
3. Applying observations and inferences to school-related tasks / 29
4. Instructional goals and objectives / 48
5. Lesson planning / 78
6. Becoming an instructional designer / 91
7. Integrating computing into elementary school instruction / 110
8. Questions and classroom communication / 125

Part 2
Assessment of Student Progress

9. Educational measurement, evaluation, and testing / 142
10. Methods for assessing student achievement / 151
11. Getting ready to build your test / 169
12. Constructing test items / 181
13. Summarizing, analyzing, and reporting student achievement data / 209

Part 3
Pulling It All Together

14. Classroom management and discipline / 238
15. Applying what I've learned / 256
16. How do I cope? / 278

Appendix: Suggestions for bridging to secondary education / 294

Glossary / 315

Index / 323

Part 1 Introduction to Teaching

1 *Introduction*

The basic premises of this book are (1) that people recognize the importance of a good education; (2) that teaching is an honorable profession; and (3) that there will be a teacher shortage in the magnitude of 100,000 by 1990, since more students will be entering school at the same time that more teachers will be retiring, while the number of potential teacher replacements is declining (Branscomb et al. 1986). The first premise is usually accepted; the second took a nosedive during the late seventies and early eighties, and efforts to improve the image of the teaching profession are drawing attention; the third has led educators and others throughout the nation to begin brainstorming for ways to attract talented people into teaching. Their resulting ideas include a teaching peace corps, full tuition benefits, and industry-school collaboratives.

A report by the Rand Corporation, *Beyond the Commission Reports,* articulates the crisis in education and addresses the following problems (Darling-Hammond 1984):

The motivation to enter teaching.
The data paint a rather gloomy picture of the teaching profession. But many studies suggest that people are attracted to teaching for altruistic reasons . . . the primary rewards of teaching are the intrinsic, non-pecuniary satisfactions. . . .

The reasons for the high attrition rate of teachers, especially the most academically qualified.
. . . satisfactions [with teaching] have been declining as the nature of teaching work has changed. Teachers express increasing dissatisfaction with the conditions under which they work and the policies that define their classroom activities.

For several decades, the National Education Association has polled several thousand teachers annually about their teaching condition and views. One question asked in each poll is, if you could go back and start all over again, would you still become a teacher? . . . Between 1971 and 1981, the proportion of re-

Most rewards of teaching are intrinsic ones.

spondents saying they would not teach again more than tripled, rising from about 10 percent to nearly 40 percent. Less than half of the present teaching force say they plan to continue teaching until retirement.

The shortage of subject-matter qualified teachers, especially in science and mathematics.

. . . of a total teaching force of about 200,000 mathematics and science teachers, 9 percent left in 1982–83, 30 percent are not fully qualified for the subjects they are teaching, and over 40 percent will retire within the next decade.

The Rand Report discusses professionalism, diagnoses trouble spots in teacher education, and proposes concrete steps to "re-professionalize" teaching. The report states that the primary reasons for the high level of dissatisfaction, especially among the best-educated teachers, are a lack of support services and, more important, teachers' belief that they are not treated as professionals.

The report emphasizes that competency-based education, minimum competency testing, and other efforts to develop a teacherproof curriculum were imposed in the belief that if teachers do exactly as they are told, students will learn exactly as they are supposed to. The teacherproof curriculum is designed around an objective of minimal competency. According to the Rand Report, such standardized practice is malpractice. The need to diagnose individual situations and judge appropriate strategies and tactics is what defines a profession.

The report identifies five characteristics of a profession that ensure and allow competent performance:

- Rigorous entry requirements
- Supervised induction
- Autonomous performance
- Peer-defined standards of excellence
- Increased responsibility with increased competence

The strong teacher preparation program will incorporate these characteristics. It will have rigorous entry requirements and will supervise entry into classroom practice so that students will be prepared to perform autonomously upon graduation. Collaboration with master teachers in field placements will help enable teacher education graduates to set high professional standards in their careers. Field placements must be selective so that novice teachers have good models. In terms of increased responsibility, the Carnegie Forum on Education and the Economy (Branscomb et al. 1986, 55) calls for "restructure of the teaching force" with Lead Teachers who can make administrative decisions.

The Rand Report suggests, then, that teachers should be problem-solvers with in-depth knowledge of their students and subject matter. They should be diagnostic teachers who can identify students' learning strengths and weaknesses, locate missing links in learning, and use appropriate instructional strategies. This chapter will suggest components of a teacher preparation program that can help new teachers to develop these abilities.

Recommendations for Teacher Preparation

The following suggestions address requirements of today's teacher preparation. The emphasis is on expecting teachers to be responsible to students and parents "for making and defending sound educational decisions . . . rather than expecting teachers and principals to be *accountable* to a bureaucracy for carrying out someone else's decisions in a manner to be mechanically assessed" (Duckworth 1984, 20).

Studies in Individual Differences and Cognitive Processes

Programs of study should include coursework and experiences that emphasize the importance of understanding how "people differ in a variety of physical, intellectual, and personality traits" (Romberg 1985, 11). An understanding of where our students have come from, and where they are going helps us assess and appreciate where they are.

The study of human development and cognitive processes provides an understanding of individualism as distinguished from individualization (Romberg 1985, 13):

Programs of "individualization" are based on assumptions about biological traits and associational learning. "Teacher-proof" materials are the outcome of most programs of individualization. The teacher is seen as the operator of a complex engineered system. "Individualism" on the other hand is based on assumptions related to constructive learning paradigms. The teacher is viewed as a guide who provides students a rich environment in which to grow and mature.

Teachers must continue their studies.

People reach milestones in their intellectual, physical, emotional, social, and psychomotor development at different times. Family pressures affect learning at all ages. Sexual pressures, too, must be expected and understood, especially by middle school teachers. Human interaction must be understood by teachers at all levels. Coursework in developmental changes and in cognitive processes should address these issues.

In addition to gaining a better understanding of their pupils, students enrolled in teacher education programs have an opportunity to gain insight into their own strengths and weaknesses. You, as an emerging teacher, will become aware that personal pressures and frustrations are human characteristics and that they sometimes interfere with daily routines. In learning to cope with these pressures, you will develop empathy for your students and an ability to look at situations from different perspectives. In gaining insight into yourself, you will refine your problem-solving skills and become aware of the excitement and well-being of knowing you have touched a student's life and in some way made it better.

The following courses may be included in teacher education programs to address issues of individualism, development, and cognitive processing:

Cognition and Learning

Cognitive Influences of Instructional Design

Educational Psychology

Writing as Inquiry

Perception

Group Dynamics and Interpersonal Relationships

Creativity: Theory, Assessment, and Development

Comparative Theories of Development

Concept Formation

Science and Values

Techniques in Human Relations

Family Dynamics

Diagnostic Teaching

Studies in Communication Skills

Two educators who were classroom teachers for several years before changing careers to include college teaching and supervisory work provide a view of teaching different from the depressing findings of the Rand Report and other commission reports. Elizabeth Haslam has employed writing as inquiry in a variety of settings with her students. Margaret Stumpf has led the development of a district-wide mathematics curriculum, described later in this chapter.

Haslam (1985) describes her approach as follows:

The focus on writing as a process of inquiry allows the student (the writer) to emerge as an observer of his or her own thinking and learning. These self-reflective writing activities can be in the form of journal responses, class journals or double-entry logs. For example, in a course which includes the research paper, an inquiry approach reverses the emphasis on product (the research paper), and puts the inquiring researcher at the heart of the research process.

She continues:

From what I had observed over the years, it appeared that the students' concepts of research and research writing were construed as trying to find a topic, spending hours in the library searching, and more hours splicing together a display of references and perspectives to end up with a passing research paper.... Students were not sure of differences between quantitative and qualitative modes of inquiry, or even between primary and secondary sources. Compounding their confusion, was the University-mandated use of online data bases, a potentially useful, but sophisticated tool for freshmen-level researchers.... Although students could master procedures for searches and documentation, they had little understanding of what the data represented in terms of inquiry and significance, and their papers were often without substance or even plagiarized.... What we teach and model as approaches to writing research papers was as important, if not more so, than the procedures to master the formats and procedures for researching.... The question, it seemed to me, was not, "What are your references?" but questions like, "How do we determine what is a fact?" "What is our epistemology?" "How do you determine what is appropriate or valid?" "What are my questions?" And so the course used an inquiry approach which stressed the active participation of the students in using primary sources of research across the disciplines, and keeping a **double-entry researcher log** (a model of journal writing written about by Ann Berthoff, 1981) in which they reflected on the nature of inquiry, writing, and learning.
    ... I had thought that maybe when students finished this course, they would reflect: "I did all kinds of research for this course, and I really learned how to write!" But that's not what happened. Instead, they wrote: "I did all kinds of writing in this course, and I really learned about research."*

Instruction in written communication skills is discussed further in chapter 15.

Studies in Computing

Another trend in teacher preparation programs involves computers. Many universities require freshmen to have a microcomputer for use in courses. Students learn computer applications including word processing, data

---

*From Elizabeth Haslam, "The Student as Participant-Observer in College Writing," paper presented at a meeting of the National Council of Teachers of English, Philadelphia, Nov. 23, 1985. Used by permission of the author.

management, spreadsheets, and graphics. Sandoval (1984) points out some of the problems of incorporating computing into teacher preparation:

As with all new areas that have been incorporated into an existing curriculum, computer training for teachers has had to overcome the perennial problems of an already crowded program, an inelastic amount of time, and the lack of qualified faculty. The result has been computer training for teachers which is not teacher oriented, taking place outside the schools of education, mostly at the inservice level, and little being done in undergraduate courses.

A general analysis of the computer courses offered in colleges of teacher education reveals their number to be meager and the content too heavily involved in programming, history of computers, and the output of business reports and mathematical/statistical applications of computers.

Traditionally, teacher training has two general components: (1) training in a content area such as social studies, math, reading, etc., and (2) training in the methodology of teaching that particular content. This second component is quite frequently the weakest in the training program, since it requires an instructional media center, projection equipment, facilities, materials, and instructors with expertise in the area—all of which require the expenditure of *money*.

In 1984, added to the many graduating teachers who were not taught to thread a projector, trouble-shoot a recorder, or even select or properly use media materials in their classes, are those who did not receive any training in computers or who received inadequate training in computer utilization.*

The integration of computing into instruction is discussed in chapters 7 and 16.

Studies in the Field

An important aspect of teacher education is the extensive use of field placements. Field experiences often begin in the freshman year with observation of pupil behavior in school classrooms. Instructional responsibility increases each year to full responsibility culminating in student teaching. Master classroom teachers in the public schools may provide instruction in **pedagogy** (methods of teaching). University faculty address theoretical issues dealing with elementary and middle school curriculum to complement field experiences in the freshman and sophomore years and student teaching in the senior year. One teacher preparation program, at Drexel University in Philadelphia, incorporates a six-month paid field placement or co-op experience in industry in the junior year to provide a real-world perspective to future teachers. The rationale is that a chemistry teacher who has worked as a chemist brings more credibility to the classroom. The same holds true for the other sciences and for mathematics.

---

*From Hugo F. Sandoval, "Teacher Training in Computer Skills," *Educational Technology* (Oct., 1984): 29–31. Reprinted by permission of the publisher.

Field experiences allow students to apply what they learn in their on-campus courses to their major area of teaching. Courses that might be taught by master classroom teachers include the following:

Personal and Interpersonal Dynamics
Introduction to Classroom Procedures
Instructional Planning
Classroom Management

Lesson Planning

There are many formats for writing lesson plans. Some instructors require students to specify everything: prepare long-term and short-term goals, translate these into detailed lists of objectives, set performance goals for each objective (pupil must get 80 percent of test items correct), describe procedures and materials to match each objective, schedule time for instruction, describe extended activities for reteaching, remediation, or enrichment, and set evaluation procedures. Objectives can become one-sentence paragraphs. To some extent, lesson plans in the detail required in pedagogy courses are not carried into the real world of teaching. In fact, they turn off teachers who are involved in the pressures of daily teaching. Preservice teachers having to write objectives of this type often comment:

- "Wait until I get out of here, I'll never write another of these mindless lesson plans again."
- "This is wasting my precious time—I should be spending this time improving my mind so that I could bring more to my students."
- "How do I know what procedures to use until I determine what materials or activities are available—at best defining procedures and materials should be an interactive process, not sequential."
- "Why can't I be given sample lesson plans to try out that have been developed by experts and found to be effective—it is ridiculous to expect that I can be an instant expert on what and how to teach—that's what I'm here to learn."

Dick and Carey (1978) present a systems approach model for lesson planning that provides a useful framework for designing instruction. The steps are as follows:

1. Identifying an instructional goal
2. Conducting an instructional analysis
3. Identifying entry behaviors and charatcristics
4. Writing performance objectives
5. Developing criterion-referenced tests
6. Developing an instructional strategy
7. Developing and selecting instruction

8. Designing and conducting the formative evaluation
9. Revising instruction
10. Conducting summative evaluation

Molnar (1985, vii–viii) points out differences in point of view between the professor of pedagogy and the classroom teacher. These different viewpoints may explain differences concerning the form and function of lesson plans:

1. To a great extent, academics and educational practitioners live in different worlds, respond to different pressures, must satisfy different audiences.
2. Academics and practitioners need each other because each occupies a territory necessary for the other to explore if they are to be effective in their work.
3. Academics are asked to be relevant to, but are rarely expected to learn from, practitioners.
4. Practitioners are told to value the theories of academics, but they are rarely offered help in identifying and thinking about how their own theories shape and direct the decisions they make.
5. Little help is offered in looking at how the theories that actually guide a professional's practice are developed and how they can be refined.
6. There is a gulf between academics and practitioners that results from a mutual irrelevance in each other's daily affairs. This gulf is reflected in academics who work in schools of education and who say that their work does not have to do with schools, and teachers who roll their eyes at the mention of the word *theory* and whose conception of professional training doesn't go beyond learning how to use the teacher's guide for the new reading program.

Molnar uses as an analogy for this gulf between academics and practitioners the relationship between two players in the game of Prisoner's Dilemma, described by Axelrod (1984, 6–9):

In the Prisoner's Dilemma game, there are two players. Each has two choices, namely cooperate or defect. Each must make the choice without knowing what the other will do. No matter what the other does, defection yields a higher payoff than cooperation. The dilemma is that if both defect, they do worse than if both had cooperated. . . .

The way the game works is shown in Figure 1. One player chooses a row, either cooperating or defecting. The other player simultaneously chooses a column, either cooperating or defecting. Together, these choices result in one of the four possible outcomes shown in the matrix. If both players cooperate, both do fairly well. Both get *R*, the *reward for mutual cooperation.* In the concrete illustration in Figure 1, the reward is three points. This number might, for example, be a payoff in dollars that each player gets for that outcome. If one player cooperates but the other player defects, the defecting player gets the *temptation to defect,* while the cooperating player gets the *"sucker's payoff."* In the example, these are five points and zero points respectively. If both defect, both get one point, the *punishment for mutual defection.* . . .

Figure 1
The Prisoner's Dilemma

		Column Player	
		Cooperate	**Defect**
Row Player	**Cooperate**	$R = 3, R = 3$ Reward for mutual cooperation	$S = 0, T = 5$ Sucker's payoff, and temptation to defect
	Defect	$T = 5, S = 0$ Temptation to defect and sucker's payoff	$P = 1, P = 1$ Punishment for mutual defection

Source: Quotation and figure reprinted by permission of the publisher from *The Evolution of Cooperation* by Robert Axelrod (New York: Basic Books, 1984), pp. 6–9.

Note: The payoffs to the row-chooser are listed first.

The Prisoner's Dilemma is simply an abstract formulation of some very common and very interesting situations in which what is best for each person individually leads to mutual defection, whereas everyone would have been better off with mutual cooperation.

What is needed, then, is cooperation: a plan for instruction that both the college professor and the classroom teacher will use. Lesson planning is discussed in detail in chapter 5.

District-wide Support for Teachers

Many school districts provide teachers, especially new ones, with system-wide curriculum guides that include detailed lesson plans. In some circumstances, school districts are able to provide summer compensation to teachers who develop such curriculum guides, which include instructional activities and available materials for each objective within a content area for each grade level. Then, these writing teams (sometimes with the help of consultants) provide a year-long induction of the curriculum guide with district teachers.

The Waycross, Georgia system is an example of a school district where practitioners (teachers and school administrators) and academicians (university professors) designed, produced, and integrated curriculum guides containing K–8 lesson plans for mathematics, science, and language arts. The collaborative design effectively brought together practitioners and academicians to bridge the usual gaps stemming from theory versus practice.

Newcomers to teaching need to be aware that such cells of excellence exist within the bodies of mediocrity and that future teacher-scholars must not be turned off by the commission reports. The reports served a purpose—they drew attention to serious problems that had crept into our educational environment. But people like Haslam and the Waycross, Georgia, team remind us of the professionalism and excellence that ought to be. They serve as models for future teacher-scholars.

The following scenario by a district mathematics supervisor, Margaret Stumpf, is another example of excellence now occurring in education:

Where does one begin to develop curriculum for a specific school district? This was my initial question when I was hired by the Bensalem Township School District to develop a district wide mathematics curriculum. I couldn't help but think of the shelves and shelves of curricula in teachers' classrooms all over the world in pristine condition under layers of dust! In most places the textbook series currently in use was the curriculum and the hours, weeks, months and years of the efforts of teachers, supervisors, and administrators to develop curricula seemed to have been nothing but exercises in futility—all the good ideas and creative planning of countless educators lying inert between the covers of so-called district wide curricula.

So, could I coordinate the efforts of the teachers and principals in our ten schools to develop a mathematics curriculum? No problem. BUT could I guarantee it would be used? That was the question—one I couldn't answer with a definite 'yes.' However, I love a challenge and plunged ahead determined to prove it could be done!

Being new in the school district and in Pennsylvania as well I began by investigating the resources available. The best educational resources anywhere are teachers and I started with them. I spent at least thrity minutes with every teacher in the district, sometimes in groups and sometimes individually. These interviews were open ended because I wanted to hear what concerns teachers had when they weren't prompted by specific questions. I made careful note of every comment, evaluation, criticism and concern and then prepared an item analysis which gave an overview of the strengths and weaknesses of the current mathematics program.

The major concern of teachers was that the problem solving sections of their textbooks did not challenge students to think but rather were exercises in certain operations; for example, a page of addition exercises was followed by word problems using addition so that children just put whatever numbers they found together and added without necessarily thinking about them.

Another concern was that even though some youngsters were doing computation at a grade or two above their level, they did not appear to have the concept of what they were doing. Teachers in the upper grades found this lack of understanding more than those at lower grade levels.

Other teachers expressed concern over a lack of manipulative materials, calculators, and other technology, especially computers for the elementary grades, as well as inservice programs to help them keep up with their professional obligations. A number of teachers felt that an articulation of grade level content and skills was needed in order that there would be no overlapping nor gap between grades.

The next step was to get a clear picture of what was actually in place in the district and teachers again provided the input for this by writing down exactly what they were doing at their grade levels that they considered essential for the average learner. This data provided a map of where we were and from this map a mathematics committee plotted the rest of the road.

The mathematics task force was made up of eleven teachers, one from each school and grade level with one representative from the high school. Their initial task was to tally the data from the teachers and analyze what was done in each grade across the district. Then armed with all the state and national norms and recommendations they worked out a program of the content and skills they believed should be attended to each grade level.

A decision was made to use The Pennsylvania Retrieval of Information for Managing Educational Systems (PRIMES). This is a list of mathematics concepts/skills for grades kindergarten through eight. This list consists of about 350 concepts and skills which have been compiled logically and sequenced under five major topics.

Some of the questions we had before making the decision to use PRIMES were readily answered by examining the materials explaining the system. PRIMES does not make any curricular decisions nor recommend what content should be used or sequence followed. It did provide us with a management system that fit very nicely into what we had already planned to do and it gave us an excellent format in which to present our mathematics curriculum.

After deciding on content/skills for each grade level, we sat down as a group representing kindergarten through eighth grade and made decisions on what priority each would have at individual grade levels, where each concept/skill would be introduced, developed, mastered or reviewed. This was a tedious job but one we felt had the greatest impact for our mathematics program.

Concept/skill pages were assembled and performance objectives were matched. All members of the task force field tested the mathematics curriculum for their own grade levels during the 1984–1985 school year. A number of other teachers also asked to be included. This was reviewed and revised in the spring.

Choosing a district wide textbook to supplement our curriculum was the next step and one I thought would be easy compared to the process we had already completed! All I had to do was send letters to publishing companies requesting examination copies, have a committee screen these, send the top 3 to 5 texts to teachers who would overwhelmingly choose one of them. I soon found out that the only easy part was requesting books!

The Mathematics Task Force met for a day in January to do the initial screening. Out of the fifteen series received, they chose five, which they felt appropriate to go out to all the teachers. I spent a day in each of the schools discussing the evaluation process. The teachers were given a copy of the scope and sequence for the district along with a copy of the content for their grade levels. We wanted everyone involved to base their evaluations on these, as well as what we considered the heart of our curriculum—a balance among concept development, computation and problem solving skills.

There was an almost one hundred percent response from teachers, and it was evident from written comments that teachers took this responsibility very seriously.

A lack of response was not the problem. The problem was that the teachers found almost all the books very satisfactory. I spent several weeks tallying, checking out teachers comments with textbooks and/or calling the companies for further information.

We felt we needed more information about each of the companies so we prepared a list of questions to ask each sales representative. We wanted to know the background of authors, how current research in mathematics was incorporated into their programs; we also wanted to know their philosophy of concept development and problem solving and how these were developed in their books. Another question we felt needed clarification was that of the services provided by each company. Each sales representative provided the information we requested and all seemed to have excellent programs, top notch authors, problem solving that developed thinking skills and concept development that was attended to at every level. Not only that, but almost all assured us that they would provide us with consultants for inservice in mathematics.

With this information, we reexamined the teachers' evaluation forms—this time giving more weight to the responses that dealt with concept development and problem solving. The responses were then rank ordered showing a preference for one of the series.

Much had been done but there was still a long way to go to implement the new program. Since I am the only supervisor for mathematics in the district, I decided I needed as much help as I could get. So in June of 1985 a Mathematics council was formed. This group was made up of a teacher from every grade level from every school—a total of 45 teachers. This group spent three days together preparing to work with the teachers at their own grade levels in their own schools coordinating the mathematics program.

This might sound as though we were at the end of our task of developing a new curriculum. Actually it is just the beginning. Teachers are being encouraged to see the curriculum as being in process and not as a finished product. Their input in the form of evaluation, recommendations, and ideas is being actively sought. Can I guarantee that this curriculum will be found in the hands of teachers and not on a shelf somewhere? Only if teachers see it as their curriculum—one that makes their teaching easier and more effective.*

Call for More Rigor

An in-depth knowledge of one's discipline is necessary to understand its pedagogy, including how to sequence topics, select instructional materials and strategies, respond to students' questions, and deal with students' misconceptions. In-depth study of a particular discipline, such as mathematics, science, language, or history, is recommended for elementary and middle-school teachers. On the other hand, more study about how humans learn, develop, and interact with one another would be appropriate for secondary teachers, who traditionally have more in-depth knowledge of a particular discipline.

Elementary programs must increase the rigor of content areas, especially mathematics, computing, science, and oral and written communication. Graduates of K–6 certification programs must be very knowledgeable in at least two of these areas and should use this strength to help alleviate the poor (or minimal) mathematics and science instruction in elementary schools and poor instruction in communication skills. That

---

*Margaret K. Stumpf, "Bensalem School District Mathematics Curriculum Development," letter to author, Aug. 24, 1985. Reprinted by permission of Margaret K. Stumpf.

teachers be exceptionally well-versed in one particular content area is crucial during this current and projected teacher shortage.

Thought Activity

1. Why are you becoming a teacher? Do any of these, honestly, apply:
   a. Because it is an easy major
   b. Because my parents encouraged me to enter teaching
   c. Because I like to interact with people
   d. Because learning fascinates me
   e. Because I like to control others' lives
   f. Because I like to deal with children
   g. Because I am bright and want to do something about the crisis in education
   h. Because a teacher helped my life and I want to help someone else
   i. Because . . . .
2. If you felt *a, b,* and/or *e* might be part of your reasons, are you sure you are in the right major?
3. How will you cope with the frustrations of teaching?
4. As you are becoming a teacher, how do you think you will cope with your college supervisor(s), supervising teacher(s), principal in your field placements, certification requirements? Upon what experience or evidence have you based this response?
5. Try the Prisoner's Dilemma game with peers and then with some elementary school children. Describe any differences in their behavior.
6. Do you effect change when change is needed or do you blend into the status quo?
7. Are you aware of your thinking as you proceed through a day?

References

Axelrod, R. 1984. *The evolution of cooperation.* New York: Basic Books.

Berthoff, A. 1981. *The making of meaning.* Montclair, N. J.: Boynton/Cook.

Branscomb, L. M., et al. 1986. *A nation prepared: Teachers for the 21st century.* New York: Carnegie.

Darling-Hammond, L. 1984. *Beyond the commission reports: The coming crisis in teaching.* Santa Monica, Calif.: Rand.

Dick, W., and L. Carey. 1978. *The systematic design of instruction.* Glenview, Ill.: Scott, Foresman.

Duckworth, E. 1984. What teachers know: The best knowledge base. In *Changing the schools: Issues facing teachers and administrators. Symposium on the year of the reports: Resources from the educational community,* 15–20. Cambridge, Mass.: Harvard Educational Review Monograph Series.

Haslam, E. 1985. The student as participant-observer in college writing. Paper presented as part of a National Council of Teachers of English panel entitled "How students' awareness of writing processes affects their writing," Philadelphia, Nov. 23.

Molnar, A. 1985. Introduction. In *Current thought on curriculum,* edited by A. Molnar. 1985 Yearbook, Association for Supervision and Curriculum Development. Alexandria, Va.: ASCD.

Romberg, T. A. 1985. *Toward effective schooling: The IGE experience.* Lanham, Md.: Univ. Press of America.

Sandoval, H. F. 1984. Teacher training in computer skills: A call for a redefinition. *Educational Technology* (Oct.): 29–31.

Stumpf, M. K. 1985. Bensalem School District mathematics curriculum development. Letter to author, Aug. 24.

2 *Observation and analysis of school-related behavior*

This chapter will give you an awareness of the importance of being a good observer. Then, having practiced the skills involved, you will use this ability for the benefit of your students. The chapter will distinguish between **observation** and **inference** so that you will avoid confusing these two very different functions. **Cognitive monitoring** skills will be introduced as an aid for developing awareness of your observations. **Generic** or core factors that influence learning will be presented as tools for aiding you in your observations of your students as they are engaged in school-related tasks.

Purpose of Observation

People "tend to infer, generalize, and predict too much, while observing too little" (Mischel 1979). Phinney (1982, 23–24) states the purpose of observation and analysis of school-related behavior as follows:

The ability to understand children through observation might be compared to the ability to judge fine art. We all respond to art—positively, negatively, indifferently—but the person with experience and training can better assess the aesthetic value of a work of art. Similarly, we all form impressions of children, but for the inexperienced observer, the impression may be inaccurate, biased, or limited in scope. As we gain more skill and experience, we know better how to look at children, what to look for, and how to interpret what we see. . . . With practice, the teacher or student will learn to use a variety of observation techniques to gain understanding of the particular combination of attitudes, abilities, and traits that make up the uniqueness of each child.

Difference between Observation and Inference

How many times have you heard a teacher say things like:

She's lazy.

He's LD.

She has math anxiety.

He has test anxiety.

She has visual perception problems.

He's spoiled.

Observation enhances one's ability to understand children.

The criterion for determining if these are observations or inferences is whether the statements describe actions you can actually see. What does lazy look like? or LD? or anxious? or spoiled? What do visual perception problems look like? These words are generalizations that describe clusters of observable characteristics. They imply that the individual described will behave in a certain manner.

Role play is a useful technique for distinguishing between observations and inferences. Four or five volunteers can act out a scene where all of their behavior is different but their motives are the same. For example, one student might throw spit balls across the room, another wave his hands wildly to answer a question, a third sit quietly at her desk staring intently at a boy in front of her, another might rock back and forth in his chair, and still another draw cartoons of her classmates and show the drawings around.

What is a common feature underlying all of these observations? It would be reasonable to say that each of these students was trying to get attention for one reason or another. However, more information would be needed to verify this inference. This need for verification points up another important difference between observations and inferences. Inferences are generalizations derived from clusters of observations. In order to check out the validity of an inference you may need to make further observations in similar or related circumstances.

Another role play situation that may be used in class is to have students portray the same observable behavior but have different underlying motives. One scenario might involve four "actors," one of whom came to class with his leg encased in a plaster cast that went from his heel to his upper thigh. The instructor asks the volunteer actors to meet with her for a few minutes outside of the lecture hall to set the stage for the following role play episode. The students simulate a front row in an elementary school classroom. The instructor asks a question and not one of the students makes any noticeable effort to answer the question. The instructor tries in several ways to elicit a response, but the students do not budge. This situation may continue for about three minutes or until an air of discomfort begins to pervade the classroom.

At this point the instructor asks the class to **infer** or hypothesize what was going on. Responses may include the following:

They don't understand the question.

They are behavior-disordered.

I don't know about the others, but the one with the cast looks bored.

The one who always looks down is bashful.

After a number of other hypotheses are offered, the instructor asks the role players to explain their motives for their lack of any response. The class may be surprised at how wrong they were in their inferences of the students' behavior. Some of the observers may have considered the responses of the role players as all stemming from the same motive simply because the overt behavior appeared the same for all. They may have fallen into the trap of making stereotyped interpretations, such as assuming no response means a discipline problem or bashfulness.

The role players can then explain their motives for their lack of any response. The student with the broken leg was in pain and therefore was afraid he would burst out crying if he tried to answer. A second student said her parents had had a family argument at breakfast that morning and that she was worried about a possible breakup of her family. A third student did not understand the question and was ashamed to admit this. And the fourth student said he did not like the teacher and would do anything to annoy her. Thus, there were four different **covert** (hidden) motives for the same **overt** (observable) behavior.

Cognitive Monitoring or Metacognition

Owings et al. (1980) provide evidence that when students can monitor and regulate learning strategies, they are more successful than those who cannot. Flavell (1979) terms the ability to think about one's thinking **metacognition**. He points out that metacognition, also called **cognitive monitoring**, refers to a number of processes that involve conscious monitoring. These processes include paying attention, perceiving, imagining, problem solving, memorizing, and getting motivated. They involve cognition about cognition.

How does cognitive monitoring relate to observation and analysis of school-related behavior? It does little good to be an observer if you are not aware of what you observe. The teacher who observes but does not register what is observed is analogous to the person who looks but does not see. When you *think* as you observe, you are more able to identify **salient** (important) features of a situation.

A teacher is like a detective. In order to notice characteristics of a student or of a situation the teacher must be sensitive to his own observations. An awareness of the nuances of observations provides the crucial ingredients for solving the mystery of a troubled child or for solving the murder by some teachers of a student's quest for learning.

The quality of inferences depends upon the sensitivity and correctness of observations. For example, the teacher who observes that a student does not pay attention to the color of blocks when the objective of the lesson is to select all of the red blocks from a group of red, blue, and yellow blocks is making an important observation. Thus it is proof of some very important detective work if the teacher notices that this same child does not attend to shape when the objective of a task is to select the round blocks from a set of wooden cubes and cylinders, or that the child picks the toy airplane from a set of trucks, cars, and boats

Selection of appropriate tasks aids observation.

when the task is to pick a mode of transportation that is used to cross a river. The teacher may infer from these observations that the child does not identify the salient aspects of a learning situation.

Selection of appropriate instructional materials and instructional strategies can help a student to notice what the task demands. **Cues** such as the use of color to highlight letters in a word or of textured material to emphasize shapes have been effective in teaching students to attend to salient dimensions of a learning task. But the teacher must first be aware that a difficulty is present. The teacher has to observe in a number of different situations over a period of time that the student has a pattern of not attending to salient aspects of a situation.

Attending to salient aspects of a situation is a **generic influence on learning**. One might make the following comparison: *Observations are to inferences as generic influences on learning are to categorical labeling of students.*

There are other generic factors that affect learning. These will be discussed next.

Generic Influences on Learning

Reisman and Kauffman (1980) have proposed that there are generic or core factors that influence learning. They group these generic factors into four categories: cognitive, psychomotor, physical and sensory, social and emotional. The generic factors provide a framework that is functional for teachers. It moves us away from a medical model of categorizing students as "LD," retarded, gifted, etc., which are inferences. Instead, this approach presents a framework for observing and analyzing learners' strengths and weaknesses in school-related tasks. Designing instruction thus comes to mean enhancing learners' strengths instead of emphasizing their weaknesses. This approach is relevant whether you are designing a single lesson or an entire unit, writing a textbook, developing instructional software for computing, or evaluating any of the preceding.

Cognitive influences on learning include the following (Reisman and Kauffman 1980, 3):

Rate and amount of learning compared to age peers
Speed of learning related to specific content
Ability to retain information
Need for repetition
Verbal skills
Ability to learn symbol systems and arbitrary associations
Size of vocabulary compared to peers
Ability to form relationships, concepts, and generalizations
Ability to attend to salient aspects of a situation
Use of problem-solving strategies
Ability to make decisions and judgments
Ability to draw inferences and conclusions and to hypothesize
Ability in general to abstract and to cope with complexity

Psychomotor influences (or motor effects of mental processes) on learning (Reisman and Kauffman 1980, 20) include the following:

Visual perception
Visual discrimination
Visual field dependence/field independence
Visual form constancy

Visual-sequential memory
Auditory perception
Auditory discrimination
Auditory field dependence/field independence
Auditory form constancy
Auditory-sequential memory
Ability to form rules (phonological, morphological, syntactical, semantic)

Physical and sensory factors that influence learning (Reisman and Kauffman 1980, 30–33) include the following:

Physical impairments
Low vitality and fatigue
Sensory limitation

Social factors that influence learning (Reisman and Kauffman 1980, 37) include the following:

Rules of conduct, moral codes, values, customs
Modeling others' behavior
Being aware of cues in the environment
Relating to and interacting with other people
Using diplomacy
Understanding another's point of view
Empathizing
Enjoying company of others
Including the desires and intentions of others in one's decisions
Accepting needed help, forming a balance between autonomy and dependency

Emotional factors that influence learning (Reisman and Kauffman 1980, 37) include the following:

Feeling afraid, anxious, frustrated, joyous, angry, surprised
Becoming overly upset, moody, sad, happy

Using these generic influences on learning as a guide for observing students provides a structure for understanding their strengths and weaknesses as they engage in the work of learning. The generic influences may be clustered into a profile of observations that form a foundation for understanding an individual student. In the extreme, these generic factors that influence learning represent handicaps or talents. Observing the impact on learning of one or more of these generic influences provides important information for instruction.

Reisman and Kauffman (1980) explain the generic influences on learning as follows:

Cognitive Generic Influences on Learning

Rate and Amount of Learning Compared to Age Peers refers to the length of time taken to learn a given amount of material in relationship to other members of a similar age group.

Speed of Learning Related to Specific Content involves consideration of a student's strengths and weaknesses in particular learning tasks such as verbal comprehension (e.g., reading and listening), perceptual organization (e.g., puzzles, geometry, spelling), numerical reasoning (e.g., mathematics).

Ability to Retain Information refers to tasks that utilize memory such as repeating digits, obeying simple commands, role counting, or naming the days of the week.

Need for Repetition refers to the amount of practice necessary for mastery.

Verbal Skills involve tasks such as comprehending and producing written and spoken words and sentences.

Ability to Learn Symbol Systems and Arbitrary Associations refers to communication of thoughts through a conventional system of signs or symbols that simultaneously are understood by the sender and the receiver.

Size of Vocabulary Compared to Peers refers to the number of words a student understands and uses as well as the number of different meanings and nuances for a given word.

Ability to Form Relationships, Concepts, and Generalizations refers to the psychological nature of the content that is being learned. For example, constructing one-to-one correspondence is forming a relationship; abstracting the number property *three* from a set of three objects forms a concept; and putting two or more concepts together into some kind of relationship forms a generalization (e.g., combine the concepts *two* and *three* into an *addition* relationship).

Ability to Attend to Salient Aspects of a Situation refers to the ability to notice the important and most relevant aspect(s) or attribute(s) of a situation and simultaneously disregard extraneous cues; the ability to attend to detail and to differentiate the essential from the nonessential (e.g., to select the attribute of thickness of blocks when given blocks of various color, shape, size, and thickness when asked to pick out the thinner blocks).

Use of Problem-solving Strategies refers to a systematic organized approach to tasks as compared to those who flounder randomly, never moving beyond a trial and error approach.

Ability to Make Decisions and Judgments involves recognizing salient aspects of a situation, using important information given, being aware of missing information, abstracting essential from nonessential details, evaluating relationships embedded in a situation, and making choices among alternatives.

Ability to Draw Inferences and Conclusions and to Hypotehsize involves generating a set of possible alternatives, dealing with future ideas, and making judgments according to a set of criteria.

Ability in General to Abstract and to Cope with Complexity includes classifying objects or ideas, finding logical relationships or analogies, performing simple operations of logical deductions, and using similes and metaphors.

Psychomotor Generic Influences on Learning

Visual Perception involves the child's understanding the world through visual experience—through what he or she sees.

Visual Discrimination refers to the ability to perceive the difference between two similar visual symbols (e.g., + and × ; − and ÷ ; 6 and 9; □ and △; 3 and E; Σ and E).

Visual Field Dependence/Field Independence refers to the ability to separate figure from background, i.e., to screen out irrelevant visual stimuli.

Visual Form Constancy involves the ability to recognize a visual stimulus when it appears in different spatial positions or in slightly different form (e.g., the digit 5 placed around the classroom in different size or color representations).

Visual-sequential Memory involves the ability to process or recall a series of visual stimuli in sequential memory (e.g., saying alphabet or digits 0–9 in a counting order).

Auditory Perception involves the child's understanding the world through auditory experience—through what he or she hears.

Auditory Discrimination refers to the ability to perceive the difference between two similar auditory symbols (e.g., child with a problem in this area might draw *hair* instead of a *chair*, or child gets *in* instead of *on* a box).

Auditory Field Dependence/Field Independence refers to the ability to screen out irrelevant auditory stimuli and focus upon the primary auditory message (e.g., child with a problem in this area cannot concentrate on what teacher is saying in the classroom because of noises outside).

Auditory Form Constancy is the ability to recognize sounds spoken by different people or presented in different environments (e.g., recognizing the sound of a train on a recording, understanding language when spoken with a dialect different from what the student is accustomed to).

Auditory-Sequential Memory involves the ability to process or recall a series of auditory events in order (e.g., repeat telephone number, retell a story, name the days of the week in order).

Ability to Form Rules (Phonological, Morphological, Syntactical, Semantic) involves interpretation and expression of combinations of sounds, inflectional endings, word order, and word meaning.

Physical and Sensory Generic Influences on Learning

Physical Impairments include cardiac conditions, diabetes, epilepsy, rheumatic fever, cerebral palsy, muscular dystrophy, etc.

Low Vitality and Fatigue may result from chronic medical problems and from effects of medication.

Sensory Limitation includes blindness and hearing and speech impairment.

Social Generic Influences on Learning

Rules of Conduct, Moral Codes, Values, Customs involve being able to relate well to peers and adults.

Modeling Others' Behavior can be positive if acceptable behavior is modeled.

Being Aware of Cues in the Environment involves knowing when to quiet down, when to speak up, responding appropriately to others' behavior.

Relating to and Interacting with Other People includes cooperation and consideration.

Using Diplomacy includes tactfulness.

Understanding Another's Point of View and Empathizing includes having an emotional as well as a cognitive view of another's needs.

Including the Desires and Intentions of Others in One's Decisions involves being able to discern the wishes of others.

Accepting Needed Help, Forming a Balance Between Autonomy and Dependency involves ability to take responsibility, displaying initiative, while being aware of one's limitations.

Emotional Generic Influences on Learning

Feeling Afraid, Anxious, Frustrated, Joyous, Angry, Surprised involve conscious experience that can be communicated to another person.

Becoming Overly Upset, Moody, Sad, Happy represent extremes of cmotion that one learns to control under normative development.

How May Observations Aid Instructional Decisions?

In a previous section of this chapter you read about the distinction between observation and inference. The main difference is that observable behavior refers to actions you can see, hear or note with your senses without necessarily applying any evaluation or interpretation to the observations. The correctness of your observations will affect the validity of your inferences.

Observations and the inferences drawn from them may be categorized in a variety of ways. Generic influences on learning, presented earlier in this chapter, provide a structure for observations (Reisman and Kauffman 1980).* Two additional schemes useful for interpreting students' behavior are Bannatyne's (1974) grouping of subtests on the Wechsler Intelligence Scale for Children (WISC) and Guilford's (1967) Structure of the Intellect (SOI).

Bannatyne clusters tasks on the WISC into four areas as follows: **Spatial Ability** (Picture Completion, Block Design, Object Assembly), **Conceptualizing Ability** (Comprehension, Similarities, Vocabulary), **Sequencing Ability** (Digit Span, Picture Arrangement, Coding), **Ability to Acquire Knowledge** (Information, Arithmetic, Vocabulary). This scheme is also applicable to the revised Wechsler test, the WISC–R. Bannatyne points out that four of the tasks rely on one's ability to plan. Planning ability is involved in Picture Arrangement, Block Design, Object Assembly, and Mazes.

The SOI is also helpful as a framework for making inferences based on observations. Examples of some of the SOI interpretations are Figural Relations (e.g., Block Design, Object Assembly, Mazes), Figural Transformations (e.g., Object Assembly), Semantic Relations (e.g., Information, Picture Arrangement, Similarities), Semantic Comprehension (e.g., Information, Arithmetic, Vocabulary, Comprehension), and Memory of Sym-

---

*For further study, other schemes for categorizing observations in the cognitive domain include Carroll (1976), Jensen (1980), and Meeker (1969, 1982).

bolic Information (e.g., Picture Completion, Information, Coding, Digit Span, Arithmetic).

All three schemes allow teachers to gather information about how students learn. The teacher may observe the way a student plans, uses judgment, pays attention, concentrates, and remembers.

The next chapter describes school-related tasks and discusses behavioral observations relying on the three schemes—generic influences on learning, Bannatyne's categories, and the SOI. Student profiles developed from generic influences on learning may be used as a basis to translate observation data into design of instructional procedures and instructional materials. Since this book concerns elementary school teaching, examples of how observations aid instructional decisions will apply to that age range of students.

Thought Activity

1. Can you think of an instance when you interpreted someone's actions toward you in one way and later found that you were wrong? How did you get clarification? Did you ask the person? Did another friend help in clarifying the situation?
2. How can you apply what you learned from that incident to an elementary classroom situation?
3. Are you aware of your thinking as you answer these questions? What insights into your own ways of observing do you now have?
4. Do you usually think about your thinking? Ask your friends and others if they are aware of their thinking in various situations. Keep a log of instances when you become aware that you are thinking about your thinking.
5. Describe a situation where you are conscious of your strategies for solving problems, for remembering things that you need to remember, for analyzing tasks and then selecting appropriate rules or shortcuts to success.
6. Do you monitor your thinking as you sequence your thoughts or actions to complete a task? Write the sequence of thoughts or actions you proceed through as you complete a task.
7. Do you check the effectiveness of strategies you are using as you solve problems? If you engage in these cognitive activities you are involved in **cognitive monitoring** or **metacognition**.
8. Discuss the advantages and disadvantages of the **generic function model** as compared to the medical model of categorizing students.

References

Bannatyne, A. 1974. Diagnosis: A note on recategorization of the WISC scaled scores. *Journal of Learning Disabilities* 7: 272–74.

Carroll, J. B. 1976. Psychometric tests as cognitive tasks: A new "Structure of the Intellect." In *The Nature of intelligence*, edited by L. E. Resnick. Hillsdale, N.J.: Lawrence Erlbaum Associates, 1979.

3 Applying observations and inferences to school-related tasks

School-related Tasks Involving Spatial Ability

Picture Completion

A picture completion task provides a series of pictures of familiar objects with a part missing: a face in profile with an eyebrow missing, a mirror image lacking some part of the reflection in the mirror, a ladder with a rung gone, etc. The student is to identify what is missing. Some students will name the missing part, while others will merely point to where it should be. Picture completion, according to Bannatyne (1974), involves the following:

It is a test of simple visual detail

It calls upon previous experience or familiarity with objects in the individual's environment, although some may have been seen only in books

It calls upon the individual to generalize a previous experience; e.g., in the picture that shows a person's head with only one ear, the student must know that people have two ears

It requires a recognition of asymmetry, e.g., only one side of a nose is completed

It tests attention to detail and observation of visual clues

The child must know how an object works or moves to discover the missing piece of the pictured object, e.g., the screw is missing from a scissors*

The Structure of the Intellect interpretation (Meeker 1969) of the picture completion task gives three factors:

Ability to remember the order of symbolic information

Ability to perceive or recognize figural entities

Ability to evaluate a system of figural units that were grouped in some manner*

In summary, a picture completion task involves recognizing the picture, noticing where it is incomplete, and figuring out the missing part. The student must distinguish essential from nonessential details. Concentration, visual organization, and visual memory are involved. Experience with similar objects in one's surroundings may well affect performance on this type of task.

Thought Activity

1. What should you observe as a student or group of students is engaged in identifying what is missing from a particular picture?
2. Is there evidence that the task is understood?
3. What is the students' manner of operation? Do they say the first thing that comes to mind or search consciously for the correct answer? If a student gives an incorrect answer and knows it, does he blame himself or find fault with the picture? Does the age of the student affect the observations?
4. Does the student merely point to the missing part or does she name it?
5. If the task is timed, does the student's performance change? In what ways?
6. How do data about a student's performance in a picture completion task help you understand the following elementary school situations?
    a. A kindergarten student learning to recognize letters and digits.
    b. A primary grades student learning to read.
    c. An intermediate grades student doing a science experiment.

---

*Analyses of school-related tasks throughout this chapter are adapted from A. Bannatyne, "Diagnosis: A Note on Recategorization of the WISC Scaled Scores," *Journal of Learning Disabilities* 7 (1974): 272–74, by permission of the publisher; and from M. N. Meeker, *The Structure of the Intellect* (Columbus, Ohio: Charles E. Merrill, 1969), by permission of the publisher.

7. What generic influences on learning are most related to a picture completion task? Construct a profile, as shown below, of a child whom you have assessed in terms of ability to complete a familiar picture that has a missing part. Note that 1 represents a deficit and 5 a strength.

Picture Completion Task Profile

1. Ability to attend to salient aspects of a situation

− •―――――•―――――•―――――•―――――• +
   1   2   3   4   5

2. Ability to learn symbol systems and arbitrary associations

•―――――•―――――•―――――•―――――•
1   2   3   4   5

3. Size of vocabulary compared to peers'

•―――――•―――――•―――――•―――――•
1   2   3   4   5

4. Ability to form relationships, concepts, and generalizations

•―――――•―――――•―――――•―――――•
1   2   3   4   5

5. Ability to retain information

•―――――•―――――•―――――•―――――•
1   2   3   4   5

6. Ability to make decisions and judgments

•―――――•―――――•―――――•―――――•
1   2   3   4   5

7. Ability to draw inferences and conclusions and to hypothesize

•―――――•―――――•―――――•―――――•
1   2   3   4   5

8. Visual discrimination skills

•―――――•―――――•―――――•―――――•
1   2   3   4   5

9. Visual field independence

•―――――•―――――•―――――•―――――•
1   2   3   4   5

10. Visual form constancy

•―――――•―――――•―――――•―――――•
1   2   3   4   5

Block Design   A second school-related activity that assesses spatial ability requires constructing with small blocks a series of geometric designs that are represented to the student in picture form. Since this is a copying task, memory is not an issue. Block design, according to Bannatyne (1974), involves the following:

The task does not depend upon information gathered from experience

The task requires the student to analyze each design into its parts and then synthesize them into a whole that is identical to the model picture

The task provides information on the student's ability to learn from training in spatial relations as evidenced by increased facility with the task by some as they progress through the series of designs

The Structure of the Intellect interpretation (Meeker 1969) of the block design task gives the following factors:

Ability to recognize figural relations between forms

Ability to choose a form based on the evaluation of what the relations are between the figures or forms in the sequence

A task of this nature measures perceptual and spatial organization ability, abstract conceptualizing ability, and the ability to generalize. Printed designs must first be perceived, then analyzed, and then broken up into a number of squares that are transposed to blocks. Identifying the blocks involves a number of transpositions from the printed design cards, including differences in size, texture (wood or plastic), and manipulative qualities. Block design tasks measure the reproductive aspect of visual-motor coordination. Tasks of this type are good measures for observing methods of working. For example, if a student is careless and hurries through the task this may indicate impulsiveness. Is the student persistent or does he give up easily when faced with possible failure? Excessive fumbling or failure to check patterns may reveal anxiety on the part of the student. Since the task is timed on the WISC–R, the rate of motor activity is assessed. It should be noted that poor performance on this task may not mean inadequate visual form and pattern perception. Ability to discriminate designs may be intact even though ability to reproduce the designs is impaired. To check this the teacher might modify the task from one of production to one of recognition. That is, instead of requiring the student to copy the pictured design with blocks, the teacher might show the picture and three arrangements with blocks and ask the student to point to the set of blocks that has the same design as the picture shown. This modification allows students who may have production problems to show what they can do when the weakness is circumvented.

Thought Activity

1. What should you observe as students are engaging in block design tasks?

2. What observations on this task would indicate to you that a student is a planner? For example, does she study the designs first?
3. What observations on this task would indicate to you that a student is **reflective** or **impulsive** in approaching tasks? For example, is he quick or slow, patient, orderly, overmeticulous, erratic? Reflective students study a task for a period of time and then proceed to solve it. Such students would study the design first. On the other hand, those who are impulsive would immediately begin to copy the design.* Usually, reflective students are more accurate in their performance. How is performance on a timed test affected by reflective or impulsive behavior?
4. What observations on this task would lead you to infer that a student was flexible in approaching problems? Does the student continue in one kind of approach throughout the task, or alter the approach as the need arises?
5. How might the block design task relate to spelling performance for a first grader? A fourth grader? A sixth grader?
6. What generic influences on learning are most related to a block design task? What domains would you include (cognitive, psychomotor, physical and sensory, social, emotional)?
7. Following is a sample profile of a third grade boy who did well on the simple designs but who could not copy the more complex designs. What would you, as the teacher, tell the boy's parents about his problem-solving strategies?

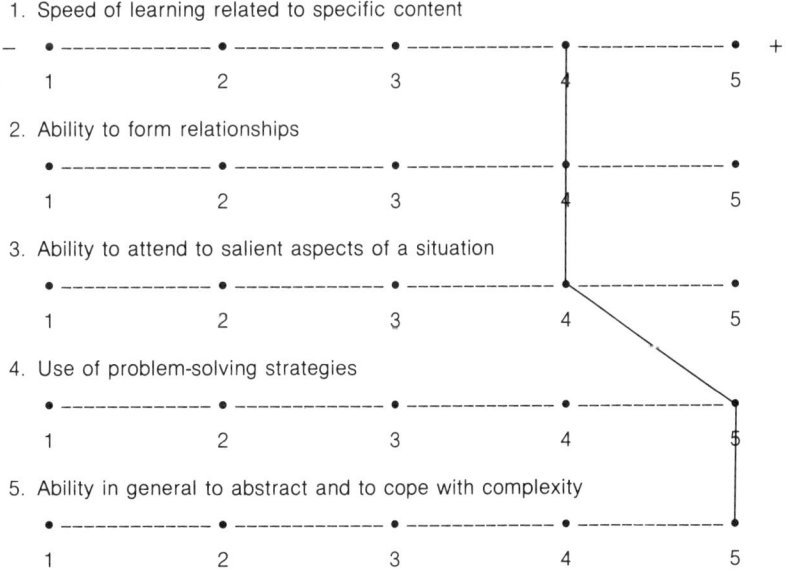

Block Design Task Profile

---

*For further study of reflection and impulsivity see Kagan, Moss, and Sigel (1963).

Flavell, J. H. 1979. Metacognition and cognitive monitoring: A new area of cognitive developmental inquiry. *American Psychologist* 10: 906–11.

Guilford, J. P. 1967. *The nature of human intelligence.* New York: McGraw Hill.

Jensen, A. R. 1980. *Bias in mental testing.* New York: Free Press.

Kagan, J., H. A. Moss, and I. Sigel. 1963, Psychological significance of styles of conceptualization. In *Basic cognitive processes in children*, edited by J. C. Wright and J. Kagan. *Monographs of the Society for Research in Child Development* 28 (2, serial no. 86).

Meeker, M. N. 1969. *The structure of the intellect.* Columbus, Ohio: Charles E. Merrill.

———. 1982. *Relationship of structure of intellect (SOI) abilities to school curriculum programming.* El Segundo, Calif.: SOI Institute.

Mischel, W. 1979. On the interface of cognition and personality: Beyond the person-situation debate. *American Psychologist* 34: 740–754.

Owings, R. A., G. A. Petersen, J. D. Bransford, C. D. Morris, and B. S. Stein. 1980. Spontaneous monitoring and regulations of learning: A comparison of successful and less successful fifth-graders. *Journal of Educational Psychology* 72: 250–56.

Phinney, S. 1982. Observing children: Ideas for teachers. *Young Children* 37 (5): 16–24.

Reisman, F. K., and S. H. Kauffman, 1980. *Teaching mathematics to children with special needs.* Columbus, Ohio: Charles E. Merrill.

6. Visual discrimination skills

```
•--------------•--------------•--------------•--------------•
1              2              3              4              5
```

7. Visual field independence

```
•--------------•--------------•--------------•--------------•
1              2              3              4              5
```

8. Feeling anxious

```
•--------------•--------------•--------------•--------------•
5              4              3              2              1
```

9. Becoming overly upset

```
•--------------•--------------•--------------•--------------•
5              4              3              2              1
```

Note that the scale is reversed for 8 and 9; i.e., a low score is positive.

Object Assembly   This task involves putting puzzle parts together to form an object. Bannatyne (1974) describes a task of this nature as follows:

The task involves organizing parts into a meaningful whole.

The task depends upon past experience since the objects to be constructed are real and should be familiar to the student.

The student must recognize each part as a section of the whole.

Object constancy or the ability to recognize spatial transformations is involved—especially when the completed object is seen from an unusual angle or perspective.

Experience with puzzles improves performance on this task.

Rigidity of thought affects performance, i.e., the less rigid child who is able to experiment freely has an advantage.

Visual memory contributes to success.

Perseveration inhibits performance, i.e., the inability to take a totally new approach to the task.

The Structure of the Intellect interpretation (Meeker 1969) of the object assembly task is as follows:

Ability to comprehend arrangements and positions of visual objects in space

Ability to visualize how a given figure or object will appear after transformations (changes) such as folding, flipping, or rotating

Ability to choose a form based on the evaluation of what the relations are among the parts

Object assembly requires many abilities.

In summary, object assembly involves producing something out of parts that are not immediately recognizable. Puzzle assembly tasks of this type measure perceptual organization that requires visual-motor coordination. The student must anticipate relationships among the individual parts of the puzzle.

Thought Activity

1. What should you observe as students are assembling objects or puzzles?
2. In what ways do you think a student's ideas about the final figure will enhance or impede his solution?
3. What observations on this task would be indicative of good planning? For example, does the student use trial and error methods, especially if the final object is not evident? How does she respond to errors? Does the student appear to anticipate the final figure?
4. Construct a profile of a child you have observed performing an object assembly task that you have made. This time select the generic influences on learning yourself. Will you use only the cognitive domain? Psychomotor? Physical? Social? Emotional?
5. Discuss the profile you have created with one or two colleagues. Ascertain whether their interpretation of your observations is similar to yours.
6. How do the three school-related tasks (picture completion, block design, object assembly) that involve spatial ability help you to understand students' strengths and weaknesses in elementary school subjects?
7. What are the similarities and differences among these spatial tasks in terms of generic influences on learning?

School-related Tasks Involving Conceptual Ability

Comprehension

Comprehension tasks measure judgment, common sense, ability to use practical information, and awareness of interpersonal and societal relations. A comprehension task, according to Bannatyne (1974), involves the following:

A comprehension task depends upon experience.

A task of this kind involves problem solving skills.

It shows one's ability to work out or appreciate common sense reasons for a situation.

The Structure of the Intellect interpretation (Meeker 1969) of comprehension tasks notes the following factor:

Ability to judge the adequacy of information

Comprehension tasks depend on the ability to deal successfully with interpersonal interactions, including social activities. One must be able to evaluate and use past experience in order to comprehend the salient aspects of situations—whether in real life or in pictured or written form. This is why it is so crucial to provide students with concrete experiences of situations that they are to read about. If a story describes a velvet gown or a sour lemon, students should know about the soft smoothness of velvet and the sourness of lemons, grapefruits, or gooseberries.

Thought Activity

1. What inferences would you draw about students' comprehension by assessing their performance according to the following questions:
   a. Does a student fail a question through misunderstanding the meaning of a word or the implication of a particular group of words?
   b. Does the student give an answer or just repeat part of a particular phrase?
   c. Does the student respond to part or all of the question?
   d. Do responses suggest that the student wants to appear independent and self-sufficient?
   e. Does the student view all various possibilities objectively and then choose the best way to solve a task?
2. Look at the task profile of a sixth grade student who is having difficulty with reading comprehension in science but does well in reading for pleasure. How will you explain your hypotheses for this situation to your colleague?

Comprehension Task Profile

1. Rate and amount of learning compared to age-peers

   − • -------------- • -------------- • -------------- • -------------- • +
      1   2   3   4   5

2. Ability to learn symbol systems and arbitrary associations

      1   2   3   4   5

3. Size of vocabulary compared to peers'

      1   2   3   4   5

4. Ability to form relationships, concepts, and generalizations

      1   2   3   4   5

5. Ability in general to abstract

      1   2   3   4   5

6. Awareness of cues in the environment

      1   2   3   4   5

38 Chapter 3

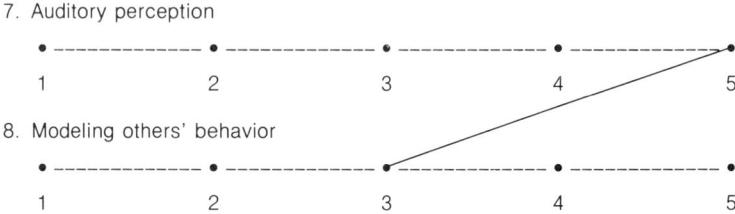

7. Auditory perception

8. Modeling others' behavior

Similarities

Similarity tasks assess ability to abstract a generic category from two related situations. Similarity tasks depend on oral vocabulary responses. For example, you might ask in what ways a potato and an apple are alike. In order to abstract any of the generic features (e.g., that they are both round, both have skin, or both are food—but not fruit), students need concrete experiences and attentive listening and reading to acquire the words that form the abstract similarity. Bannatyne (1974) describes a similarities task as follows:

It is a task that verbally depends on sophisticated oral vocabulary responses.

It is a task that requires attentive listening and a great deal of reading for constructing abstract words, e.g, *motherhood, patriotism, satisfaction.*

The Structure of the Intellect interpretation (Meeker 1969) of similarities tasks includes the following factors:

Ability to see relations between ideas or between meanings of words
Ability to see potential changes of interpretations of objects and situations
Ability to see relations between items of symbolic information

Similarity tasks assess one's ability to abstract a common theme from two or more situations. This activity is at the heart of forming concepts. Identifying what is similar among objects or situations underlies tasks in geometry, spelling, word identification, set theory, and identification of color, shape, size, and texture.

Thought Activity

1. What tasks would you design to assess a student's ability to see relations between ideas or between meanings of words?
2. What generic influences on learning have the greatest impact on similarity tasks?
3. How do data about a student's performance on similarity tasks help you understand the following elementary school situations?

A teacher points out similarities.

    a. A kingergarten or first grade student learning the cardinal number property of sets of objects.
    b. A third grader's spelling lesson.
    c. A fifth grader learning to recognize that many rules of conduct in sports also apply to classroom behavior.

4. Construct a profile using generic influences on learning to portray a student who is having difficulty in similarity tasks.

5. Construct a profile using generic influences on learning to portray a student in the same class who is successful on similarity tasks.

6. What are the similarities and differences between the two profiles you constructed in activities 4 and 5?

Vocabulary

Vocabulary tasks test word knowledge and measure verbal comprehension. A vocabulary task assesses the following abilities needed for the use of words, according to Bannatyne (1974):

It requires understanding word meanings.

It involves ability to associate auditory labels with **referents.**

It involves ability to remember auditory labels.

The more verbally able student will use verbal memory rather than visual memory.

The Structure of the Intellect interpretation (Meeker 1969) of vocabulary tests emphasizes the ability to comprehend meanings of words or ideas. Vocabulary tasks permeate all subject areas of the elementary school curriculum. They assess the ability to comprehend meanings of both written and spoken communication.

Thought Activity

1. What inferences would you draw about students' vocabulary skills by assessing their performance according to the followng questions:
   a. Does showing the printed word help the student recognize the word?
   b. Does the student repeat the word correctly, or is there a possible hearing disorder?
   c. Does the student find it easy or difficult to say what he means?
   d. Does the student have difficulties getting words said properly or seem uncertain about how best to express what she thinks? Does she use gestures to help illustrate statements? Does the student depend upon gestures almost exclusively?
   e. Does the student have a specific or a general (global) familiarity with a particular word? Are explanations precise and brief or does the student embark on lengthy explanations?
   f. Does the student guess, say "I don't know," try to avoid further demands? Is he puzzled?
2. What activities will you use to assess knowledge of vocabulary? Will they involve meaningless drill? Copying definitions? Essays about field trips? Do you have access to computer activities?
3. What generic influences on learning are most related to vocabulary tasks? Complete the following profile to show your observations of a student whose vocabulary skills you have assessed.

Vocabulary Task Profile

1. Rate and amount of learning compared to age-peers

   − •------------•------------•------------•------------• +
      1   2   3   4   5

2. Ability to learn symbol systems and arbitrary associations

     •------------•------------•------------•------------•
      1   2   3   4   5

3. Size of vocabulary compared to peers'

•--------------•--------------•--------------•--------------•
1   2   3   4   5

4. Ability to form relationships, concepts, and generalizations

•--------------•--------------•--------------•--------------•
1   2   3   4   5

5. Ability in general to abstract

•--------------•--------------•--------------•--------------•
1   2   3   4   5

6. Awareness of cues in the environment

•--------------•--------------•--------------•--------------•
1   2   3   4   5

7. Auditory perception

•--------------•--------------•--------------•--------------•
1   2   3   4   5

8. Modeling others' behavior

•--------------•--------------•--------------•--------------•
1   2   3   4   5

School-Related Tasks Involving Sequencing Ability

Digit Span

The digit span task involves asking the student to repeat a series from three to nine digits. The task assesses one's immediate memory for auditory sequences. It requires the ability to recall separate items of sound that have no meaning as a group. It measures attention, freedom from distraction, short-term memory, and concentration. The student may be asked to say the digits backwards. This changes the original task because it involves transformation, manipulation of data, or reorganization of input. According to Bannatyne (1974), digit span involves the following:

It assesses immediate memory for auditory sequences.

It tests ability to remember a specific sequence through time.

The Structure of the Intellect interpretation cites the ability to remember the order of symbolic information (Meeker 1969).

Sequencing tasks require the student both to remember the order of a series and to judge units of information as being similar or different. Repeating a series in a given order (e.g., a telephone number or the alphabet) assesses memory. We shall see next, in picture arrangement, a task that assesses the judgment aspect of sequencing.

Thought Activity

1. Listen as someone reads you the following sets of numbers, one at a time, and repeat them from memory: 746   3859   37219   214365   7946128   58923451   387961425
2. Did you notice a particular pattern in one of the series? Does being aware of the pattern facilitate the task?
3. Did you visualize the digits as a cue? Say them to yourself as a cue? Use no cue?
4. Administer a digit span task to a student and notice the following:
    a. Does the student find the task boring? Interesting? Difficult?
    b. As the series proceeds, does the student become stimulated and encouraged, or discouraged, tense, and anxious with increasing length?
    c. Does the student give up or continue to try?
    d. When the student makes errors, does she notice them, or think the answers are correct?
    e. Does the student make the same or different types of errors in the digit backward as compared to the digit forward task?

Picture Arrangement

The picture arrangement task involves understanding events as temporal sequences. The student must be aware of the conventions of storytelling. Familiarity with comic strips and their conventions for integrating several separate events as a whole story facilitates this type of task. The task requires reading comic strips in a left-to-right sequence but with the option of scanning back and forth for more information. Picture arrangement measures planning ability and perceptual organization and is considered a nonverbal reasoning test; it also requires interpretation of social situations. The task measures comprehension of a story as told in pictures. The student must be able to size up and comprehend a total situation, organize it visually, and predict the consequences of initial acts or situations. Bannatyne (1974) describes the picture arrangement task as follows:

It assesses understanding of events as a temporal sequence.

It assesses ability to synthesize separate events into a story.

It is a measure of verbal comprehension.

It incorporates extraneous clues that must be ignored.

It involves left-right sequencing.

The Structure of the Intellect interpretation cites the evaluation of semantic relations and the ability to make choices (Meeker 1969).

The picture arrangement task measures the ability to organize information that is out of logical sequence. It is useful to compare performance on picture arrangement tasks with performance on block design and object assembly tasks to ascertain whether the student uses consistent patterns in search of solutions to the various tasks.

Thought Activity	1. What should you observe as a student or group of students is engaged in arranging the pictures to tell a story?
	2. Administer a picture arrangement task to a student and notice the following:
	   a. Are stories logical, fanciful, bizarre, original, conventional?
	   b. Are incorrect picture arrangements due to incorrect perceptions of details in the pictures or to failure to consider some details?
	   c. Were all relationships in the pictures considered?
	   d. What did you notice about the student's behavior? Persistence? Trial and error patterns? Discouragement? Impulsiveness? Reflection? Rigidity? Flexibility?
	   e. Did the student employ consistent patterns in search of solutions?
	   f. Did the student appear to become fatigued as the task progressed?

Coding	The coding task presents designs that are to be coded as numbers. This task assesses the ability to memorize symbols and judge designs as being similar or different. Since the activity is timed, it is a test of motor proficiency, eye-motor coordination, fine motor coordination, and the ability to return one's eyes quickly to the appropriate place on the guide key. This is an important skill in reading. Coding rests on the capacity to sustain concentrated attention and effort on a meaningless routine timed task. The task assesses one's ability to make rapid decisions about arbitrarily associated sets of letters or numbers. Skill with paper and pencil will affect task performance, and the perfectionist will be at a disadvantage because of the importance of speed. The intensity of the task can be fatiguing.
	    Bannatyne (1974) describes the abilities measured in coding as follows:
	
	Ability to memorize symbols
	
	Ability to understand that it is possible to memorize symbols
	
	Ability to memorize arbitrary associations at speed
	
	Ability to interpret designs meaningfully
	
	    The Structure of the Intellect interpretation of coding notes the following factors (Meeker 1969):
	
	The convergent production of figural units
	
	Ability to judge units of figural information as being similar or different
	
	Convergent production of symbolic units
	
	Ability to make rapid decisions regarding the identification of letter or number sets

Thought Activity	1. Design your own coding task, administer it to a student, and notice the following:

a. Does the student skip around, filling like shapes or numbers first? If so, tell him to proceed in order.
   b. Study the student's working habits. For example, is she impulsive or meticulous? Is there a tremor evident—a shaky hand?
   c. Notice the pace of the performance. Does the students speed increase or decrease? An increase in speed over the course of the task plus correct copying of the symbols is indicative of good ability to adjust to the task. On the other hand, a decrease in speed plus correct copying of the symbols may indicate fatigue.
   d. Notice whether the student has attention difficulties in this task.
   e. Are the marks well done, just recognizable, or wrong? Is the student penalized for lack of speed? For inaccuracy? Both?
   f. Does the student understand the task?
   g. Does the student check each figure with the sample designs, or try to remember the samples?
   h. Does the student pick out one figure only and skip others?
   i. Does the student work smoothly or become confused as the task progresses?
2. Children may do better on performance tests such as coding if encouraged to think aloud. For example, as students proceed in the coding task they might talk their way through by saying the digit that represents a design. Ask students in school psychology or special education who have been trained to administer the WISC–R whether they found this to be true. Is this more often the case for block design or picture arrangement? How are these observations related to cognitive monitoring?

School-Related Tasks Involving Ability to Acquire Knowledge

Information

Information tasks test general information acquired through experience. For example, you might ask a first grader what the thumb is called by holding up your thumb and asking, What is this? You might ask a third grader, What do we call a baby horse? and ask a sixth grader to name the month that comes after July. Bannatyne (1974) concluded that an information task:

Depends on acquired knowledge, educational experience, and cultural factors

The Structure of the Intellect interpretation of information tasks (Meeker 1969) includes:

Ability to comprehend the meaning of ideas or words

Ability to remember spatial order or placement of given visual information or to remember rhythm or melody

Ability to remember the order of symbolic information

Ability to remember isolated ideas or word meanings

Ability to remember meaningful connections between items of verbal information

Ability to remember meaningful ordered verbal information

Ability to remember arbitrary connections between pairs of meaningful elements of information

Ability to make choices among semantic relationships based on the similarity and consistency of the meanings

Ability to converge on the appropriate name, or summarizing word, for any given information

Ability to deduce the implicit meaning in given information

In short, information tasks require memory and measures both verbal comprehension and verbal expression.

Thought Activity

1. You can make up your own information tasks. Extract appropriate information for your students' textbooks, including their basal reading books and their subject matter texts, or ask the school librarian for help in selecting general reading matter for a particular student.
2. What generic influences on learning most affect performance on information tasks? Create your own profile and evaluate your own performance on information tasks.
3. In light of generic influences on learning and the Structure of the Intellect interpretation of this task, discuss the difference between the following two information items:
   a. How many nickels are in a quarter?
   b. What does the heart do?
4. Pretend that you are the teacher of a fifth grade boy and interpret the following profile of this student to the boy's parents. Then take the position of the parent and imagine how you would react.

Information Task Profile

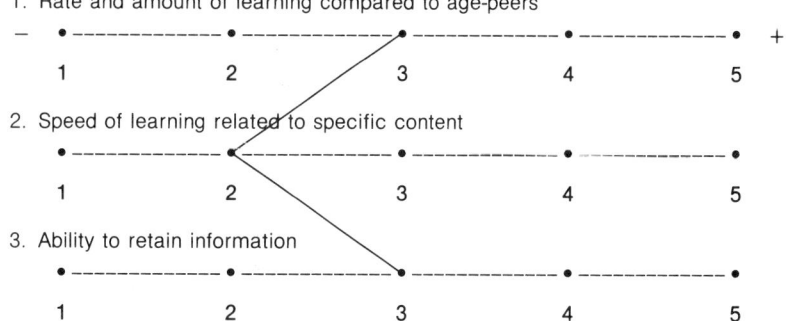

4. Need for repetition

    •--------------•--------------•--------------•--------------•
    1   2   3   4   5

5. Ability to learn symbol systems and arbitrary associations

    •--------------•--------------•--------------•--------------•
    1   2   3   4   5

6. Size of vocabulary compared to peers'

    •--------------•--------------•--------------•--------------•
    1   2   3   4   5

7. Ability to form relationships, concepts, and generalizations

    •--------------•--------------•--------------•--------------•
    1   2   3   4   5

8. Ability to attend to salient aspects of a situation

    •--------------•--------------•--------------•--------------•
    1   2   3   4   5

9. Ability to draw inferences

    •--------------•--------------•--------------•--------------•
    1   2   3   4   5

10. Awarness of cues in the environment

    •--------------•--------------•--------------•--------------•
    1   2   3   4   5

11. Relating to and interaction with other people

    •--------------•--------------•--------------•--------------•
    1   2   3   4   5

12. Understanding others' points of view

    •--------------•--------------•--------------•--------------•
    1   2   3   4   5

13. Modeling others' behavior

    •--------------•--------------•--------------•--------------•
    1   2   3   4   5

14. Becoming overly upset

    •--------------•--------------•--------------•--------------•
    5   4   3   2   1

Note that the scale is reversed for 14; i.e., a low score is positive.

References   Bannatyne, A. 1974. Diagnosis: A note on recategorization of the WISC scaled scores. *Journal of Learning Disabilities* 7: 272–74.

Kagan, J., H. A. Moss, and I. Sigel. 1963. Psychological significance of styles of conceptualization. In *Basic cognitive processes in children,* edited by J. C. Wright and J. Kagan, Monographs of the Society for Research in Child Development 28 (2, serial no. 86).

Meeker, M. N. 1969. *The structure of the intellect.* Columbus, Ohio: Charles E. Merrill.

4 *Instructional goals and objectives*

Educational goals are broad, long-term statements of what one strives to teach. One way of defining goals for education is to specify what the learner will need to know as a member of society. Another focus for goal selection is what the learner will need to know as a member of a discipline—as a mathematician, scientist, writer, musician, artist, carpenter, or printer. Objectives translate goals into accomplishable tasks; thus, they are stated in terms of behavior and content.

Sources of Goals for Education

A variety of groups—Presidential commissions on higher education, the American Council on Education, the Educational Policies Commission of the Education Association, and others—have provided guidelines for developing educational goals. For example, the American Council on Education's *A Design for General Education* (1944) presented ten broad goals translated into clearly defined objectives for student behavior and subject-matter content.

Educational goals have been phrased in broad descriptive terms such as those of the historic *Cardinal Principles of Secondary Education* (Commission on the Reorganization of Secondary Education 1918):

1. Good health.
2. Command of fundamental processes.
3. Worthy home membership.
4. Vocational efficiency.
5. Good citizenship.
6. Worthy use of leisure time.
7. Ethical character.

The Educational Policies Commission of the National Education Association provided socially oriented (1938) and cognitively oriented (1961) sets of objectives:

Social Objectives
1. Self-realization
2. Human relationship
3. Economic efficiency
4. Civic responsibility

Cognitive Objectives
1. Recalling and imagining
2. Classifying and generalizing
3. Comparing and evaluating
4. Analyzing and synthesizing
5. Deducing and inferring

Complete and detailed objectives have been formulated for elementary schools by the Mid-Century Committee on Outcomes in Elementary Education (Kearney 1953) and for secondary schools by French et al. (1957). While neither report provides an overall rationale for its objectives, each represents the combined wisdom of numerous subcommittees and groups. The objectives for elementary education are categorized as (a) knowledge and understanding, (b) skills and competencies, (c) attitudes and interests, and (d) action patterns. These four general categories extend to ethical behavior, standards, and values at one extreme and to quantitative relationships at the other. Secondary-school goals include self-realization, interpersonal relationships, large-group memberships and leaderships, intellectual development, cultural integration, physical and mental health, and economic competency.

Goals differ according to degree of emphasis on individual or on societal needs. A list of individual-oriented goals might resemble Havighurst's list of developmental tasks (1953, 25–41):

1. Learning physical skills necessary for ordinary games.
2. Building wholesome attitudes toward oneself as a growing organism.
3. Learning to get along with age-mates.
4. Developing fundamental skills in reading, writing, and calculating.
5. Developing conscience, morality, and a scale of values.
6. Developing attitudes toward groups and institutions.

Children learn to get along with others.

A more society-oriented view of education might elicit a set of goals like those of Hand, Hoppock, and Zlatchin (1948, 425–31):

1. To keep the population healthy.
2. To conserve natural resources and use them wisely.
3. To provide the opportunity for people to make a living.
4. To enable the population to realize aesthetic and spiritual values.
5. To provide a sufficient body of commonly held beliefs and aspirations to guarantee social integration.
6. To organize and govern in harmony with beliefs and aspirations.

While statements by official bodies and committees and analyses by talented individuals are extremely helpful, often an individual or group wishes to make independent choices or to develop its own goals. Tyler (1964) proposes a process for developing and selecting goals that has proven very effective and has been used to develop more specific objectives as well. Tyler names three sources of objectives that should be routinely considered in the process of developing goals: (a) studies of the needs of individuals in the society, (b) studies of the needs of the society the school must serve, and (c) statements by those trained in specific subject matter, about the contributions of their specialty to the area of education under consideration.

Choice of Objectives

Many more objectives will be proposed by interested parties and derived from general objectives than the school will be able to achieve. The final selection of objectives will be dictated in part by the school's intended function, the assigned role of the portion of the curriculum being developed, a realistic appraisal of what can be accomplished, and the degree of abstraction appropriate to the curriculum level. Tyler (1964) discusses two main criteria for the choice of objectives: (a) the educational philosophy of the person or institution making the selection, and (b) the extent to which the objectives accord with psychological realities affecting what can be taught to students at the given age and state of preparation in the time available.

Is the objective consistent with the school's philosophy of education? This criterion engages the values emphasized in a given school situation. Selection will draw on such concerns as the school's view of the satisfying and effective life for an individual in our society. What are the most important values? What is the proper relation between the individual and society? What are the proper relations between individuals? Should different kinds of education be provided for different segments of society? Answers to these and similar questions of educational philosophy clearly influence what is ruled out, what is chosen, and what is emphasized.

Is the objective consistent with accepted knowledge and theories about learning, instruction, and the discipline? Theories of learning and instruction will assist in determining whether given objectives are appropriate to particular grades or learning sequences. Theory can help one to choose objectives realistically for short- and long-term behavior and to distinguish teachable objectives from those that are not suited to the instructional process.

Instructional Objectives

One of the most important aspects of teaching is to determine what students are to learn and to make sure that the students know the aim of each task. A teacher must have a clear idea at the beginning of a lesson, a unit, or a course of what students should know when instruction is completed. Often, little attention is given to how students can demonstrate what they have learned. Specifying objectives for instruction helps correct this problem.

Instructional objectives are statements that describe what students may be expected to do after completing a prescribed unit of instruction. An objective represents the teacher's judgment of what is important for students to learn.

In another sense, objectives represent a standard to be attained by the student. Some teachers rebel at the notion of "setting standards," but who is in a better position than the teacher to make judgments about what students should learn? It is part of a teacher's responsibility to delineate learning objectives and activities for instruction, monitor student learning progress, and select or construct appropriate evaluation procedures.

Table 4.1
Dressel's Classification of Educational Objectives

Dressel's Categories	Main Characteristic	Example
1. achievable unachievable	attainable not attainable	To jump rope. To jump over the moon.
2. explicit implicit	apparent hidden	To write a job application letter. To learn appropriate writing skills.
3. intrinsic transcendental	internal external	To detect main ideas of an argument. To derive hypotheses from data.
4. individual societal	personal group-oriented	To recognize a friend. To elect classroom monitors.
5. ultimate immediate	future present	To state consequences of a law. To follow a rule.
6. general specific	broad narrow	To apply rules of grammar. To insert commas where necessary.

Source: Items in column 1 are from P. L. Dressel, "Evaluation as Instruction," in *Proceedings of the 1953 Invitational Conference on Testing Problems* (Princeton, N.J.: Educational Testing Service, 1954).

Types of Instructional Objectives

Many systems are available for classifying instructional objectives. Dressel (1954) characterizes objectives as (1) achievable or unachievable, (2) explicit or implicit, (3) intrinsic or transcendental, (4) individual or societal, (5) ultimate or immediate, and (6) general or specific. Table 4.1 summarizes these types of objectives.

Instructional objectives can also be described as **performance objectives** or **behavioral objectives.** These two terms describe objectives that inform students of "performances" or "behaviors" (e.g., construct a birdhouse, add with renaming) they are expected to demonstrate as evidence of learning.

Writing Instructional Objectives

Instructional (behavioral) objectives are statements that describe tasks students should be able to do after completing instruction that they could not do before instruction. Mager (1962) identifies the following three essential elements of behavioral objectives:

1. The *terminal behavior* is a description of the observable behavior the student is asked to employ as demonstrating mastery of the objective (e.g., "to write," "to list," "to solve").
2. The *testing condition* is a description of the relevant condition under which the student will be expected to demonstrate achievement of the objective (e.g., materials or equipment that will be available, materials or equipment that will *not* be allowed, or special instructions).
3. The *performance standard or criterion* is used to evaluate the success of the performance or the product (e.g., "90 percent correct,"

"three out of four correct," "no spelling errors," or "complete the task in ten minutes").

Each of the three essential elements is identified in the instructional objective shown below. The number of each component is identified above the appropriate portion of the objective.

Given a list of thirty spelling words [2], student will correctly spell [1] 80 percent of the words [3].

Mager's three essentials, if broadly interpreted, form a sound foundation for writing instructional objectives. Using words that express observable behavior, considering testing conditions, and deciding ahead of time what level of performance is satisfactory are steps essential to writing objectives.

Since "terminal behavior" has come to mean the "end of the line" in some instances, let us reinterpret Mager's phrase as **products of instruction.** The product of instruction is the observable or measurable behavior expected after a lesson has been taught—that is, following some kind of instruction.

The Terminal Behavior

The most important element of an instructional objective is the specific term describing the observable or measurable behavior that the learner is to perform. This statement of how learning is to be demonstrated at the end of an instructional episode helps students become aware of how they will be tested. An objective describing only an internal state of the student does not provide a means to show that learning has occurred. In the objective "The student will know the names of the four most recent presidents of the United States," for example, "knowing" is an internal mental condition that cannot be directly observed or measured and is open to many interpretations. To make the objective behavioral the teacher must change the unobservable "know" to an observable behavior such as "list" or "name" that demonstrates "knowing." This observable behavior is usually described in an **action verb.** Listed below are examples of verb phrases. Some are ambiguous and allow for many interpretations; others are precise and open to few interpretations.

Ambiguous

to know
to appreciate
to understand
to become familiar with
to think about
to learn

Precise

to state
to choose
to define
to describe
to discuss
to use

The phrases in the left-hand column do not define the behavior needed to demonstrate that learning has occurred. Knowing or appreciating means different things to different people. The words in the right-hand column identify behavior that can be observed or measured when instruction has been completed.

Here are some examples of statements containing observable behavior:

The student will write a complete sentence.
The student will draw a map of the United States.
The student will name the first ten prime numbers.

The Testing Condition

There are various ways of looking at testing conditions beyond Mager's interpretation. What is the physical environment of the testing situation? Is it comfortable? Is it familiar to the student? What about the physical and emotional characteristics of the student? Does he feel well? Is he anxious about the test?

Pretest conditions should also be considered. Did the student study for the test? Did she feel well the night before? Sleep well? Eat something? Was there a family argument at breakfast? Was the student bullied on the way to school?

Consider instruction related conditions of the testing situation. Does the test address what was taught? Do test items require at least some responses from the student that were also required during instruction? For example, a classroom procedure to check progress during spelling instruction includes oral spelling bees. However, the usual testing condition is written. The progress check during instruction (see chaps. 5 and 9 for discussion of formative evaluation) might better have included written spelling bees, in which the students from each team in turn write the word on the board rather than spelling it aloud. The point is that behavior required during testing should also have been required during instruction.

Mager's use of the term "testing conditions" implies that one should specify the conditions under which the expected student behavior will be observed. What materials will students be given and what limitations or restrictions will be imposed on them when they are demonstrating the end behavior? Here are some phrases that contain statements of testing conditions:

Given a list of . . .
Given a ruler . . .
Given a map . . .
Referring to the periodic chart . . .
Without the use of references . . .
Without the aid of tools . . .

A common error is to confuse conditions that involve instructional activities with those surrounding the testing situation. For example, "given forty hours of instruction" is a condition that describes instruction rather than testing. In summary, two important assumptions are necessary in order to test for the presence or absence of an instructional objective: (1) that instruction has been effective, and (2) that the conditions under which behavior is related to the objective have been specified.

The Performance Standard or Criterion

Mager proposed that instructional objectives should also delineate time or error limits. In the instructional objective, the standard or criterion is the basis given for evaluating the end product of instruction. What minimal level of acceptable performance will identify those learners who have "mastered" a task? Mager (1962) states that specifying the minimum acceptable performance level for each objective provides a standard to use in assessing instructional programs and in determining the success of instruction. The following phrases are examples of criteria or standards of performance:

Without an error . . .
At least five out of six . . .
Within ten minutes . . .
All four steps . . .
List 80 percent of the nouns . . .
Must be correct to the nearest percent . . .
Must include three of the four reasons. . .
The customer must be satisfied . . .

Some performance standards can be stated objectively, while others are more subjective; in either case, they define minimal acceptable performance.

Consider the following sample instructional objective for teaching students the correct use of commas in writing: "Given a set of rules for the use of commas and a set of sentences that require comma insertion, the student will place each comma properly without any errors."

In summary, an instructional objective describes what students should be able to do after completing a prescribed unit of instruction. For Mager, the objective should contain three components, stating (1) terminal behavior, (2) testing conditions, and (3) performance standards or criteria. Objectives serve two major functions. First, they communicate the teacher's instructional intentions to students, to instructors who teach related lessons that precede and follow, and to those responsible for planning and evaluating curricula, such as writers and test developers. Second, they are used by teachers to assist in designing and evaluating their instruction (Kibler et al. 1970, 1).

The Taxonomy of Educational Objectives

One attempt to provide a framework for the entire panorama of educational objectives is the *Taxonomy of Educational Objectives,* so called because it is a hierarchical classification scheme. Since the Taxonomy's authors were much concerned with the holistic nature of learning, educational objectives are divided solely for the purposes of convenience into three domains—cognitive, affective, and psychomotor. Most objectives for conventional courses are in the cognitive and affective domains, and a framework has been developed for each of these (Bloom 1956; Krathwohl, Bloom, and Masia 1964). Tentative frameworks for the psychomotor domain have been developed (Harrow 1972; Simpson 1966). All these frameworks are hierarchical in nature; that is, the lowest level of behavior in the hierarchy is believed to be the least complex, and its achievement is presumed to be the key to successful achievement at the next higher level in the structure.

The structure proposed in the Taxonomy is consistent with the logic of education and with psychology. The categories in the Taxonomy reflect the concerns of teachers who must develop objectives and select learning experiences for attaining them. The categories are precisely defined and can be subdivided logically. The Taxonomy presents a system for analyzing and organizing curriculum in relation to cognitive, affective and psychomotor objectives.

The Cognitive Domain

The *Taxonomy of Educational Objectives, Handbook I: Cognitive Domain* (1965) was developed by a committee of college and university examiners under the leadership of Benjamin S. Bloom. The cognitive domain is composed of categories graded from simple to complex and from concrete to abstract. Objectives classified as cognitive emphasize intellectual learning and problem solving. Commonly referred to as *Bloom's Taxonomy,* the handbook gives six hierarchically ordered levels of instructional outcomes: knowledge, comprehension, application, analysis, synthesis, and evaluation. Each category is assumed to require behavior more complex and abstract than for the previous category. Thus, an objective classified as *analysis* requires knowledge, comprehension, and application of information in the course of its completion. The six major levels are subdivided, and each subdivision describes the kind of behavior it classifies. A synopsis of the taxonomy for the cognitive domain is presented in table 4.2.

A brief description and illustration of each major category follows:

Knowledge. Recall or recognition in an appropriate context of specific facts, universal principles, methods, process patterns, structures, or set-

Table 4.2
Synopsis of the Taxonomy of Educational Objectives: Cognitive Domain

Knowledge

1.00 *Knowledge.* Recall of information.
1.10 Knowledge of specifics. Emphasis is on symbols with concrete referents.
    1.11 Knowledge of terminology.
    1.12 Knowledge of specific facts.
1.20 Knowledge of ways and means of dealing with specifics. Includes methods of inquiry, chronological sequences, standards of judgment, patterns or organization within a field.
    1.21 Knowledge of conventions: accepted usage, correct style etc.
    1.22 Knowledge of trends and sequences.
    1.23 Knowledge of classifications and categories.
    1.24 Knowledge of criteria.
    1.25 Knowledge of methodology for investigating particular problems.
1.30 Knowledge of the universals and abstractions in a field. Patterns and schemes by which phenomena and ideas are organized.
    1.31 Knowledge of principles and generalizations.
    1.32 Knowledge of theories and structures (as a connected body of principles, generalizations, and interrelations).

Intellectual Skills and Abilities

2.00 *Comprehension.* Understanding of material being communicated, without necessarily relating it to other material.
    2.10 Translation. From one set of symbols to another.
    2.20 Interpretations. Summarization or explanation of a communication.
3.00 *Application.* The use of abstractions in particular, concrete situations.
4.00 *Analysis.* Breaking a communication into its parts so that organization of ideas is clear.
    4.10 Analysis of elements. E.g., recognizing assumptions.
    4.20 Analysis of relationships. Content or mechanical factors.
    4.30 Analysis of organizational principles. What holds the communication together?
5.00 *Synthesis.* Putting elements into a whole.
    5.10 Production of a unique communication.
    5.20 Production of a plan for operations.
    5.30 Derivation of a set of abstract relations.
6.00 *Evaluation.* Judging the value of material for a given purpose.
    6.10 Judgments in terms of internal evidence. E.g., logical consistency.
    6.20 Judgments in terms of external evidence. E.g., consistency with facts developed elsewhere.

Source: After L. J. Cronbach, *Essentials of Psychological Testing,* 2d ed. (New York: Harper & Row, 1960), p. 376. Reprinted by permission of the publisher. Material in this table is taken from *Taxonomy of Educational Objectives: Handbook I, Cognitive Domain,* edited by B. S. Bloom (New York: McKay, 1956).

tings. Little is required beyond bringing to mind previously learned information.

To say the letters of the alphabet in order.

To point to all of the *e*'s in a word.

To state the definition of the word *mammal.*

Comprehension. The lowest level of what is commonly called "understanding," requiring that students be able to paraphrase knowledge accurately, explain or summarize in their own words, or make logical extensions to implications or corollaries.

To translate a simple word sentence to a simple number sentence.

To summarize the main ideas of a paragraph.

To predict the ending of a story.

Application. The ability to use a given abstraction (idea, rule, procedure, or generalized method) appropriate to a new situation and apply it correctly.

To follow safety rules when the fire drill bell rings.

To make cookies using a recipe.

To compose a paragraph using proper usage and good sentence structure.

Analysis. The ability to break down a communication or concept into its constituent elements in order to illustrate the hierarchy or other internal relations of ideas, show the basis for its organization, and indicate how it conveys its effects.

To recognize statements of fact and opinion in a short story.

To underline the main ideas in a letter.

To identify the parts of a sentence.

Synthesis. The arrangement of units, parts, or elements in such a way as to create a new pattern or structure.

To create geometric shapes using only circles, squares, and triangles.

To write a poem.

To construct a collage.

Evaluation. The making of judgments about the value, for some purpose, of ideas, works, solutions, methods, materials, etc. The criteria for evaluation may be determined by the student or the teacher, and the judgments may be qualitative or quantitative.

To write a critique of a short story.

To draw a conclusion based on data.

There have been numerous attempts to validate the hierarchical theory of the taxonomy—namely, that achievement at a higher level of behavior is dependent on achievement at a previous level. Empirical evidence from numerous studies gives at least mild support to the order of the first four categories of the cognitive domain (Ayers 1966; Kropp, Stoker, and Bashaw 1968; Miller 1965). The order of the more complex categories has found little support in the same studies. All of the investigators encountered problems in developing measures, particularly objective ones, at the most complex end of the continuum.

A further consideration if one attempts to use the cognitive domain taxonomy for classifying instructional objectives is the experience of the learner with the particular objective. A metaphor might be two elevators, side by side. Elevator A represents a learner, elevator B the cognitive domain taxonomy. Consider the objective: To solve a simple word problem by addition with renaming.

| | *Elevator A:* | | *Elevator B:* |
| | *Learner* | | *Cognitive domain taxonomy* |
Floors	(Experience of pupils)	Floors	(Types of learning)
6	grade six	6	evaluation
5	grade five	5	synthesis
4	grade four	4	analysis
3	grade three	3	application
2	grade two	2	comprehension
1	grade one	1	knowledge

For the second grader, the task of adding with renaming may be new, and thus the second grader has to produce a plan for operations (synthesis, 5.0). For the average fifth grader, this task has been reduced to a relatively automatic recall of information (knowledge, 1.0). That is, the second grader must go all the way to the fifth floor to perform what is only a first-floor task for the fifth grader. Thus, the same objective is at a different level depending on the level and characteristics of the learner.

Terms to Help Write Objectives in the Cognitive Domain Taxonomy

Objectives may be stated, as we have seen, at a variety of levels of specificity. Metfessel, Michael, and Kirsner (1969) provide a series of verbal guidelines useful in operationalizing specific levels of the taxonomy. That portion of their guidelines dealing with the cognitive domain is summarized in table 4.3. Their lists of sample infinitives and direct objects should facilitate the writing of instructional objectives that, although keyed to the taxonomy, are closer to being behavioral statements.

The Usefulness of the Cognitive Domain Taxonomy

The comprehensiveness of the Taxonomy has made it useful in determining whether or not objectives were included at all levels appropriate to the curriculum under consideration. The Taxonomy, like a periodic chart of elements or a check-off shopping list, displays the range of possible objectives. In particular, it provides many examples of complex objectives that are frequently omitted or insufficiently emphasized.

Table 4.3
Instrumentation of the Taxonomy of Educational Objectives: Cognitive Domain

Taxonomy Classification	Key Words	
	Examples of Infinitives	Examples of Direct Objects
1.00 *Knowledge*		
1.10 Knowledge of Specifics		
1.11 Knowledge of Terminology	to define, to distinguish, to acquire, to identify, to recall, to recognize	vocabulary terms, terminology, meaning(s), definitions, referents, elements
1.12 Knowledge of Specific Facts	to recall, to recognize, to acquire, to identify	facts, factual information (sources, names, dates, events, persons, places, time periods), properties, examples, phenomena
1.20 Knowledge of Ways and Means of Dealing with Specifics		
1.21 Knowledge of Conventions	to recall, to identify, to recognize, to acquire	form(s), conventions, uses, usage, rules, ways, devices, symbols, representations, style(s), format(s)
1.22 Knowledge of Trends	to recall, to recognize, to acquire, to identify	action(s), processes, movement(s), continuity, development(s), trend(s), sequence(s), causes, relationship(s), forces, influences
1.23 Knowledge of Classfication and Categories	to recall, to recognize	area(s), type(s), feature(s), class(es), set(s), division(s), arrangement(s), classification(s), category/categories
1.24 Knowledge of Criteria	to recall, to recognize, to acquire, to identify	criteria, basics, elements
1.25 Knowledge of Methodology	to recall, to recognize, to acquire, to identify	methods, techniques, approaches, uses, procedures, treatments
1.30 Knowledge of the Universals and Abstractions in a Field		
1.31 Knowledge of Principles and Generalizations	to recall, to recognize, to acquire, to identify	principle(s), generalization(s), proposition(s), fundamentals, laws, principal elements, implication(s)
1.32 Knowledge of Theories and Structures	to recall, to recognize, to acquire, to identify	theories, bases, interrelations, structure(s), organization(s), formulation(s)
2.00 *Comprehension*		
2.10 Translation	to translate, to transform, to give in own words, to illustrate, to prepare, to read, to represent, to change, to rephrase, to restate	meaning(s), sample(s), definitions, abstractions, representations, words, phrases
2.20 Interpretation	to interpret, to reorder, to rearrange, to differentiate, to distinguish, to make, to draw, to explain, to demonstrate	relevancies, relationships, essentials, aspects, new view(s), qualifications, conclusions, methods, theories, abstractions

Table 4.3 continued

		Key Words	
	Taxonomy Classification	Examples of Infinitives	Examples of Direct Objects
	2.30 Extrapolation	to estimate, to infer, to conclude, to predict, to differentiate, to determine, to extend, to interpolate	consequences, implications, conclusions, factors, ramifications, meanings, corollaries, effects, probabilities
	3.00 *Application*	to apply, to generalize, to relate, to choose, to develop, to organize, to use, to employ, to transfer, to restructure, to classify	principles, laws, conclusions, effects, methods, theories, abstractions, situations, generalizations, processes, phenomena, procedures
	4.00 *Analysis*		
	4.10 Analysis of Elements	to distinguish, to detect, to identify, to classify, to discriminate, to recognize, to categorize	elements, hypothesis/hypotheses, conclusions, assumptions, statements (of fact), statements (of intent), arguments, particulars
	4.20 Analysis of Relationships	to analyze, to contrast, to compare, to distinguish, to deduce	relationships, interrelations, relevance, relevancies, themes, evidence, fallacies, arguments, cause-effect(s), consistency, consistencies, parts, ideas, assumptions
	4.30 Analysis of Organizational Principles	to analyze, to distinguish, to detect, to deduce	form(s), pattern(s), purpose(s), point(s) of view(s), techniques, bias(es), structure(s), theme(s), arrangement(s), organization(s)
	5.00 *Synthesis*		
	5.10 Production of a Unique Communication	to write, to tell, to relate, to produce, to constitute, to transmit, to originate, to modify, to document	structure(s), pattern(s), product(s), performance(s), design(s), work(s), communications, effort(s), specifics, composition(s)
	5.20 Production of a Plan or Proposed Set of Operations	to propose, to plan, to produce, to design, to modify, to specify	plan(s), objectives, specification(s), schematic(s), operation(s), way(s), solution(s), mean(s)
	5.30 Derivation of a Set of Abstract Relations	to produce, to derive, to develop, to combine, to organize, to synthesize, to classify, to deduce, to develop, to formulate, to modify	phenomena, taxonomies, concept(s), scheme(s), theories, relationships, abstractions, generalizations, hypothesis/hypotheses, perceptions, ways, discoveries
	6.00 *Evaluation*		
	6.10 Judgments in Terms of Internal Evidence	to judge, to argue, to validate, to assess, to decide	accuracy/accuracies, consistency/consistencies, fallacies, reliability flaws, errors, precision, exactness
	6.20 Judgments in of External Criteria	to judge, to argue, to consider, to compare, to contrast, to standardize, to appraise	ends, means, efficiency, economy/economies, utility, alternatives, course of action, standards, theories, generalizations

Source: W. S. Metfessel, W. B. Michael, and D. A. Kirsner, "Instrumentation of Bloom's and Krathwohl's Taxonomies for the Writing of Educational Objectives," *Psychology in the Schools* 6 (1969): 227–31. Reprinted by permission of Clinical Psychology Pub. Co.

The Taxonomy has also been used in analysis of examinations and teaching practices to compare the emphases in course objectives with those in test questions and instruction (McGuire 1963; Scannell and Stellwagen 1960). As might be expected, the balance between factual knowledge and thinking called for in the statement of objectives frequently fails to be actualized in the test items. Heavy emphasis on memorization indicates a disproportionate use of the *knowledge* category, which often outweighs the other categories combined. It is not unusual to find 50 to 90 percent of the total instruction time guided by knowledge-level objectives.

Evaluating the Effectiveness of Cognitive Instructional Objectives

While many consider the explicit formulation of instructional objectives for teaching, evaluation, and curriculum development a very useful approach, that attitude is not universal. Some teachers fear that objectives create a lock-step instructional setting that blocks spontaneity and creativity. Admittedly, such a mechanical approach to instruction is a danger, but clear objectives provide the advantages of clarifying intent and of helping teachers to select content, behavior to be changed, and instructional materials.

The teacher's instructional intent must be communicated to the student. The following anecdote, reported by Yelon and Scott (1970, 5) illustrates a possible result of failure to communicate:

At a parent-teacher conference the teacher complained to Mr. Bird about the foul language of his children. Mr. Bird decided to correct this behavior. At breakfast he asked his oldest son, "What will you have for breakfast?" The boy replied, "Gimme some of those damn cornflakes." Immediately Mr. Bird smashed the boy on the mouth. The boy's chair tumbled over and the boy rolled up against the wall. The father then turned to his second son and politely inquired, "What would you like for breakfast?" The boy hesitated, then said, "I don't know but I sure as hell don't want any of those damn cornflakes!"

Moral: If you want students to change their behavior, tell them your goals.

Many controversies about instructional objectives stem either from philosophical differences about the nature of education or from questions about how instructional objectives are applied to certain areas of education, such as the fine arts and humanities. Popham (1969) has summarized major objections to the use of instructional objectives and responded to each. The following parallel lists (adapted from Wynn 1973) summarize the pros and cons of instructional objectives:

Instructional Goals and Objectives

Objection to Behavioral Objectives	Rebuttal to Objection
1. Trival behaviors are easiest to operationalize. Really important outcomes will be underemphasized.	1. Explicit objectives more readily focus attention on important goals.
2. Specification prevents the teacher from acting on unexpected instructional opportunities.	2. Ends do not necessarily specify means. Serendipity is always welcome.
3. Other types of educational outcomes are also important, e.g., for for parents, staff, community.	3. Schools can't do everything. Their primary responsibility is to pupils.
4. Objectively, mechanistically measured behaviors are dehumanizing.	4. The broadened concept of evaluation includes "human" elements.
5. Precise, unpreplanned behavior is undemocratic.	5. Society knows what it wants. Instruction is naturally undemocratic.
6. In certain areas—e.g., fine arts and humanities—it is more difficult to measure behaviors.	6. Sure it's tough—but it is still a responsibility.
7. General statements appear more worthwhile to outsiders.	7. We must abandon the ploy of "obfuscation by generality."
8. Measurability implies accountability. Teachers might be judged solely on ability to produce particular results.	8. Teachers should be held accountable for producing changes.
9. It is more difficult to generate precise objectives than to talk about them in vague terms.	9. We should allocate the necessary resources to accomplish the task.
10. Unanticipated results are often more important. Specification may cause inattentiveness.	10. Dramatic unanticipated outcomes cannot be overlooked. Keep your eyes open.

Role of Content and Form in Writing Objectives

Two major factors that must be considered in writing educational objectives are content and form. Content is the curricular material, the objective's subject matter; form is the way in which the subject matter is treated. These two interrelated dimensions can significantly affect the utility of objectives. The following characteristics in the content and form of objectives are desirable:

Content

1. Objectives should be at an appropriate level of difficulty based on prior learning. If the Taxonomy were used as a guide, objectives at all six major levels might be stated for a college-level course but only the first three levels used for a second grade science course.
2. Objectives should be "real," in the sense that they describe goals the teacher intends to act on in the classroom situation. Frequently teachers will state that they intend to bring about changes in the "attitudes" and "appreciations" of their students, but plan no specific learning experiences to achieve these objectives. This is not to say that such goals are not useful or desirable, but that stated objectives must be followed up. If an objective is not part of the actual instructional program, do not evaluate it.
3. A useful objective will describe both the content and the mental process or behavior required for an appropriate response. A set of objectives should not become a "table of contents"—a list of topics to be covered in class. Instead, it should describe the overt behavior expected and the instructional procedure that will be used to bring about change.
4. The content of the objectives should be reponsive to the needs of both the individual and society.
5. A variety of behavior should be called for, since students need to develop skills other than "recall." Only recently have we made a concerted effort to abandon the stifling emphasis on memorizing facts. Classroom practice has lagged behind the relevant research, whose results have been available for some time. Tyler (1933), for example, has shown that knowledge of specific information is not a lasting outcome of instruction. The higher-order mental abilities and skills (e.g., application and interpretation) show much greater stability.

Form

1. Instructional objectives should be stated in the form of expected student behavior, not in terms of teacher behavior. Instructional objectives should specify what the learners will be able to do if they have learned. The list of phrases below will demonstrate the difference:

Inappropriate	*Appropriate*
To demonstrate to students...	The student will show...
To instruct...	The student will tell...
To acquaint the student...	The student will describe...
To point out...	The student will explain...

2. Instructional objectives should state the desired learning product rather than a learning process or activity. The following two phrases clarify this difference. Which one states an instructional outcome?
   a. Identify the causes of the Civil War.
   b. Acquire knowledge of the causes of the Civil War.

   If you selected the first phrase, you are correct. This phrase tells the teacher what the student should be able to do after instruction. The second phrase does not state a learning outcome, but describes a learning process or activity (the acquisition of knowledge).
3. Instructional objectives should be stated in behavioral or performance terms. Mager (1962) points out that words such as "identify," "differentiate," "solve," "construct," "list," "compare," and "contrast" communicate in a precise and efficient manner. In general, the broad class of words called "action verbs" is preferable. Objectives must be stated operationally if we are to evaluate proposed learning.
4. Instructional objectives should be stated singly. Compound objectives are likely to lead to inconsistent measurement. For example, the objective "The student will recognize the twenty-six letters of the alphabet and write them on a piece of paper" contains two processes, a cognitive process of recalling information and a psychomotor process of physically producing the letters. When the time comes to measure the achievement of this objective, either of the two behaviors might be measured; the one selected may or may not be measured in proportion to the emphasis given it in class.
5. Instructional objectives should be concise. They are easier to use when trimmed of excess verbiage.
6. Instructional objectives should be grouped logically, so that they help teachers determine units of instruction and evaluation.

Affective Objectives

Affective learning is the term used to refer to likes and dislikes, attitudes, values, and beliefs. If students tell us they "really like to play racquetball," they are implying they have learned to value the sport. This statement is much different from one like, "I can play racquetball." Playing racquetball is a psychomotor skill. Enjoying or valuing a particular sport involves affective learning.

Affective Domain Objectives

Some objectives for the affective domain follow. Refer to the list of affective domain categories in table 4.5 for the specific classification of each objective.

1.3 Listens for nuances in a musical selection.

2.2 Volunteers to be in a play.

3.2 Helps a friend with a project.

4.2 Organizes time to complete a task.

5.1 Changes behavior to improve relationships with classmates.

Behavior associated with affective objectives is more difficult to define than that associated with cognitive objectives because learners do not always show their attitudes, values, and beliefs. Furthermore, consensus as to what an objective means may be difficult to reach. For example, one teacher might define "appreciation of art" in terms of the number of times a student visits a museum during the semester; another teacher might translate this objective into the degree of student participation during music class. Both of these activities represent the objective, although the observable behavior differs.

Structure and Categories of the Affective Domain

The cognitive domain taxonomy (Bloom et al. 1956) was structured on "simple-to-complex" and "concrete-to-abstract" continua; the affective domain taxonomy is based on a hierarchical structure of internalization. Internalization is a process where positive values emerge from within the individual. Inner growth occurs as the individual becomes aware of and then adopts attitudes and principles that eventually guide his or her conduct. At first, the new values may appear only in isolated instances; gradually they come to dominate the person's thinking and motivation until actions are consistent with stated values. Affective domain categories are delineated in the *Taxonomy of Educational Objectives, Handbook II: Affective Domain* (Krathwohl, Bloom, and Masia 1964, 34–35), as shown in table 4.4.

Examples of objectives are provided for each category. The most basic behavior in the affective domain taxonomy is awareness of stimuli that

Table 4.4 Synopsis of the Taxonomy of Educational Objectives: Affective Domain

1.0 Receiving (attending)
   1.1 Awareness
   1.2 Willingness to receive
   1.3 Controlled or selected attention
2.0 Responding
   2.1 Acquiescence in responding
   2.2 Willingness to respond
   2.3 Satisfaction in response
3.0 Valuing
   3.1 Acceptance of a value
   3.2 Preference for a value
   3.3 Commitment (conviction)
4.0 Organization
   4.1 Conceptualization of a value
   4.2 Organization of a value system
5.0 Characterization by a value or a value complex
   5.1 Generalized set
   5.2 Characterization

Source: From *Taxonomy of Educational Objectives, Book 2: Affective Domain,* by Benjamin S. Bloom, David R. Krathwohl, and Bertram B. Masia. Copyright © 1964 by Longman Inc. All Rights Reserved.

elicit affective behavior, or *Receiving* (1.0). It is subdivided into three categories:

1.1 *Awareness.* Attending to the stimulus: To differentiate sounds.
1.2 *Willingness to receive.* Being willing to give attention: To accumulate examples from nature of geometric shapes.
1.3 *Controlled or selected attention.* Actively attending to stimuli despite competing and distracting stimuli: To respond to rhythms.

A the next level, *Responding* (2.0), the student responds regularly or becomes committed to affective stimuli.

2.1 *Acquiescence in responding.* Complying with expectations: To obey traffic lights.
2.2 *Willingness to respond.* Increasing response to inner compulsion: To volunteer to answer questions in class.
2.3 *Satisfaction in response.* Feeling satisfaction or enjoyment: To spend free time reading.

Up to this point, the focus has been on distinguishing among stimuli; now emphasis is on seeking them out and attaching emotional significance to them. The next level, *Valuing* (3.0), describes increasing internalization as the student's behavior becomes sufficiently consistent to desire and hold a value.

3.1 *Acceptance of a value.* Endorsing a basic proposition or assumption: To specify friendships.
3.2 *Preference for a value.* Expressing a willingness to be identified with a value: To support a viewpoint.
3.3 *Commitment.* Expressing a strongly held value or conviction: To protest an umpire's call.

As the student successively internalizes values he encounters situations in which more than one value is relevant. These situations require *Organization* (4.0) of two or more values in a system.

4.1 *Conceptualization of a value.* Understanding how a value relates to values already held: To discuss scores on examinations.
4.2 *Organization of a value system.* Bringing together a complex of values, possibly disparate values, into a harmonious ordered relationship: To organize ideas to form an opinion.

Finally, the internalization and organization processes reach a point at which the individual responds very consistently to value laden situations based on an interrelated set of values and a structured view of the world. This is *Characterization by a Value or Value Complex* (5.0).

5.1 *Generalized set.* Exhibiting a predisposition to act in a certain way: To revise plans in light of teacher feedback.

5.2 *Characterization set.* Developing a consistent philosophy of life: To be rated high by peers in maturity.

In summary, the major steps in the affective domain hierarchy are: (1) increasing the emotional quality of responses; (2) increasing the automaticity of responses; (3) increasing willingness to attend to specific stimuli; (4) organizing values into a system; and (5) developing integration of a value pattern at the upper levels of the continuum.

Behavioral Affective Categories for the Taxonomy of Educational Objectives

One of the criticisms frequently leveled at the Taxonomy is that it is not couched in behavioral terms. Metfessel, Michael, and Kirsner (1969) have made a very practical contribution by listing infinitives and direct objects that can be used to operationalize the Taxonomy. Table 4.5 may suggest many important objectives and can help teachers translate affective domain objectives into measurable terms.

Popham's Strategy for Specifying Affective Objectives

In addition to Metfessel, Michael, and Kirsner's examples of infinitives and direct objects, Popham's strategy is also useful in identifying and specifying affective outcomes. Its intent is to describe observable student behaviors that reflect attainment or nonattainment of affective objectives. The procedure has five steps (Popham 1969):

1. Begin with a general statement of the broad affective objectives.
   Example: At the end of this year, students will have more favorable attitudes toward science.
2. Next, imagine applying the objective to a typical student who possesses the specific attitude. The intent is to describe the behavior likely to be exhibited.
   Example: A student who has a positive attitude toward science is more likely to read scientific articles in popular magazines, attend science fiction movies and select science book titles.
3. Third, imagine applying the objective to a typical student who does not possess the attitude in question or has a negative attitude toward the stimulus.
   Example: A student who has a negative attitude toward science will not read magazine articles dealing with science, will not enjoy courses in science, and will not choose to visit a science museum.
4. Describe real or hypothetical situations that elicit different behavior from one who possesses the given attribute and from one who does not.

Table 4.5 *Instrumentation of the Taxonomy of Educational Objectives: Affective Domain*

Taxonomy Classification		Key Words	
		Examples of Infinitives	Examples of Direct Objects
1.0	Receiving		
1.1	Awareness	to differentiate, to separate, to set apart, to share	sights, sounds, events, designs, arrangements
1.2	Willingness to Receive	to accumulate, to select, to combine, to accept	models, examples, shapes, sizes, meters, cadences
1.3	Controlled or Selected Attention	to select, to posturally respond to, to listen (for), to control	alternatives, answers, rhythms, nuances
2.0	Responding		
2.1	Acquiescence in Responding	to comply (with), to follow, to commend, to approve	directions, instructions, laws, policies
2.2	Willingness to Respond	to volunteer, to discuss, to practice, to play	instruments, games, dramatic works, charades, burlesques
2.3	Satisfaction in Response	to applaud, to acclaim, to spend leisure time in, to argue	speeches, plays, presentations, writings
3.0	Valuing		
3.1	Acceptance of a Value	to increase measured proficiency in, to increase numbers of, to relinquish, to specify	group membership(s), artistic production(s), musical productions, personal friendships
3.2	Preference for a Value	to assist, to subsidize, to help, to support	artists, projects, viewpoints, arguments
3.3	Commitment	to deny, to protest, to debate, to argue	deceptions, irrelevancies, abdications, irrationalities
4.0	Organization		
4.1	Conceptualization of a Value	to discuss, to theorize (on), to abstract, to compare	parameters, codes, standards, goals
4.2	Organization of a Value System	to balance, to organize, to define, to formulate	systems, approaches, criteria, limits
5.0	Characterization by Value or Value Complex		
5.1	Generalized Set	to revise, to change, to complete, to require	plans, behavior methods, effort(s)
5.2	Characterization	to be rated high by peers in, to be rated high by superiors in, and to be rated high by subordinates in,	humanitarianism, ethics, integrity, maturity
		to avoid, to manage, to resolve, to resist	extravagance(s), excesses, conflicts, exorbitancy/exorbitancies

Source: W. S. Metfessel, W. B. Michael, and D. A. Kirsner, "Instrumentation of Bloom's and Krathwohl's Taxonomies for the Writing of Educational Objectives," *Psychology in the Schools* 6 (1969): 227–31. Reprinted by permission of Clinical Psychology Pub. Co.

Example: When put in a forced-choice situation, students who enjoy science will select more book titles dealing with scientific topics than will those who do not enjoy science.

It is important that the situation chosen be free of cues that might elicit certain behavior. There should be no external pressure to respond in a particular way. For example, you would not ask for a show of hands to indicate interest, or request that students sign a survey of attitudes toward a course. You may, however, wish to work out a code with students that will help you keep track of individual progress toward selected affective objectives.

5. Select those difference-producing situations that most effectively, efficiently, and practically define the intended outcomes.

Objectives in the Psychomotor Domain

The psychomotor domain is the realm of physical development of motor skills. Motor skills are movement abilities such as running, walking, eye-hand coordination, perceptual ability, strength, and endurance.

Several attempts have been made to specify elements of a psychomotor taxonomy (Dave 1970; Harrow 1972; Kibler et al. 1970; Ragsdale 1950; Simpson 1966). The models proposed by Simpson and Harrow attempt to organize the behaviors into a sequential hierarchy. The other three systems present classifications that are not hierarchical.

Each of the classification schemes in table 4.6 provides an organization for writing behavioral objectives in the psychomotor domain. Some examples from each system follow:

Simpson
1. To select red objects from a set of colored blocks.
2. To get in a ready position to run.
3. To coach a friend in swimming.
4. To trace the digits 0 through 9.
5. To jump rope.

Table 4.6 Alternative Ways to Conceptualize Categories for Classifying Psychomotor Behaviors	Simpson (1966)	Dave (1970)	Ragsdale (1950)	Kibler et al. (1970)
	1. Perception (interpreting)	1. Imitation	1. Object Motor (manipulating or acting with direct reference to an object)	1. Gross Body Movements (locomotor and axile)
	2. Sets (preparing)	2. Manipulation		2. Finely Coordinated Movement (maniuplation and visual motor coordination)
	3. Guided Response (learning)	3. Precision		
	4. Mechanism (habituating)	4. Articulation	2. Language Motor (movements of speech, sight, handwriting)	
	5. Complex Overt Response (performing)		3. Feeling Motor (movements communicating feelings and attitudes)	3. Nonverbal Communication Behavior (communication of feelings and attitudes)
	6. Adaptation (modifying)			4. Speech
	7. Origination (creating)			

6. To ride a bicycle up a steep incline.
7. To make up rules for a relay race.

Dave

1. To play follow the leader.
2. To complete a simple puzzle.
3. To thread a needle.
4. To demonstrate hopscotch.

Ragsdale

1. To throw a ball.
2. To write the digits 0 through 9.
3. To walk like a scared rabbit.

Kibler et al.

1. To imitate walking like an elephant.
2. To play the violin.
3. To use facial expressions to show a happy rabbit, a sad rabbit.
4. To recite the letters of the alphabet.

The most comprehensive system developed to date for classifying psychomotor behaviors is Harrow's (1972). This system assumes that psychomotor behavior operationalizes cognitive and affective intentions. The components of the system are arranged along a continuum as shown in table 4.7 from a low level of observable movement to a highly integrated level of complex movement.

Consider the psychomotor domain in selecting instructional goals.

Selected objectives adapted from Harrow's (1972) psychomotor taxonomy follow:

1.00 *Reflex Movements.* Due to the autonomic nature of this classification, no objectives need be developed by teachers.

2.10 *Locomotor Movement.* The student will do a two-footed jump.

3.40 *Tactile Discrimination.* The student will distinguish between a penny, a nickel, a dime, and a quarter solely by touch.

4.20 *Strength.* The student will show grip strength of at least five pounds as measured by a dynamometer.

5.10 *Simple Adaptive Skill.* The student will type at least thirty words per minute during a five-minute typing test with no more than five errors.

Table 4.7
Harrow's Taxonomy of the Psychomotor Domain

```
1.00  Reflex Movements
      1.10  Segmental Reflexes
            1.11  Flexion Reflex
            1.12  Myotatic Reflex
            1.13  Extensor Reflex
            1.14  Crossed Extensor Reactions
      1.20  Intersegmental Reflexes
            1.21  Cooperative Reflex
            1.22  Competitive Reflex
            1.23  Successive Induction
            1.24  Reflex Figure
      1.30  Suprasegmental Reflexes
            1.31  Extensor Rigidity
            1.32  Plasticity Reactions
            1.33  Postural Reflexes
                  1.331  Supporting Reactions
                  1.332  Shifting Reactions
                  1.333  Tonic-Attitudinal Reflexes
                  1.334  Righting Reaction
                  1.335  Grasp Reflex
                  1.336  Placing and Hopping Reactions
2.00  Basic-Fundamental Movements
      2.10  Locomotor Movements
      2.20  Non-Locomotor Movements
      2.30  Manipulative Movements
            2.31  Prehension
            2.32  Dexterity
3.00  Perceptual Abilities
      3.10  Kinesthetic Discrimination
            3.11  Body Awareness
                  3.111  Bilaterality
                  3.112  Laterality
                  3.113  Sidedness
                  3.114  Balance
            3.12  Body Image
            3.13  Body Relationship to Surrounding Objectives in Space
      3.20  Visual Discrimination
            3.21  Visual Acuity
            3.22  Visual Tracking
            3.23  Visual Memory
            3.24  Figure-Ground Differentiation
            3.25  Perceptual Consistency
      3.30  Auditory Discrimination
            3.31  Auditory Acuity
```

                3.32 Auditory Tracking
                3.33 Auditory Memory
        3.40 Tactile Discrimination
        3.50 Coordinated Abilities
                3.51 Eye-Hand Coordination
                3.52 Eye-Foot Coordination
4.00 Physical Abilities
        4.10 Endurance
                4.11 Muscular Endurance
                4.12 Cardiovascular Endurance
        4.20 Strength
        4.30 Flexibility
        4.40 Agility
                4.41 Change Direction
                4.42 Stops and Starts
                4.43 Reaction-Response Time
                4.44 Dexterity
5.00 Skilled Movements
        5.10 Simple Adaptive Skill
                5.11 Beginner
                5.12 Intermediate
                5.13 Advanced
                5.14 Highly Skilled
        5.20 Compound Adaptive Skill
                5.21 Beginner
                5.22 Intermediate
                5.23 Advanced
                5.24 Highly Skilled
        5.30 Complex Adaptive Skill
                5.31 Beginner
                5.32 Intermediate
                5.33 Advanced
                5.34 Highly Skilled
6.00 Non-Discursive Communication
        6.10 Expressive Movement
                6.11 Posture and Carriage
                6.12 Gestures
                6.13 Facial Expression
        6.20 Interpretive Movement
                6.21 Aesthetic Movement
                6.22 Creative Movement

Source: From *A Taxonomy of the Psychomotor Domain* by Anita J. Harrow. Copyright © 1972 by Longman Inc. Reprinted by permission of the publisher. All rights reserved.

6.20 *Interpretive Movement.* The student will produce a recognizable rhythmic pattern for at least thirty seconds.

Summary

In some schools, teachers are provided with curriculum guides that include topical outlines and objectives. But in many other situations, teachers will want to develop their own objectives.

Educational endeavors are guided by goals and objectives. General goals are broad statements that establish the purposes of instruction. Instructional objectives describe the activities students are expected to perform after instruction to demonstrate learning. Objectives translate goals into accomplished tasks.

Instructional objectives specify three important elements of the instruction process: the testing condition, the terminal behavior, and the performance standard or criterion. Objectives should communicate the teacher's instructional intentions to students and assist teachers in planning and evaluating their instruction.

Writing instructional objectives should not be burdensome. The point to be kept in mind is that teachers should know specifically what is expected of students and how they are going to evaluate it.

Suggested learning outcomes for objectives may be obtained from the taxonomy of educational objectives for the cognitive and affective domains. The psychomoter area covers objectives relating to manual and motor skills, and several models are available for specifying the elements of a psychomotor taxonomy.

Thought Activity

1. State the difference between educational goals and objectives.
2. Describe how you will use Dressel's classification scheme (see table 4.1) for writing instructional objectives. What are the strengths and weaknesses of this classification system from your own perspective as an instructional designer? (See chap. 6 for a definition of the role of teacher as instructional designer.)
3. Describe how you will use Mager's three essential elements for writing instructional objectives. What are the strengths and weaknesses of Mager's suggestions (see pp. 52–55) from your own perspective as an instructional designer?
4. Categorize the following instructional objectives according to the taxonomy of educational objectives for the cognitive domain (see pp. 55–58 Cog. Domain):
   a. To identify main ideas in an essay.
   b. To say the base ten digits in order.
   c. To paint a picture.
   d. To predict the next musical note in a series of notes.
   e. To sit on a panel whose purpose is to critique the way in which student teachers are evaluated.
   f. To follow directions on a computer.
5. Using the work of Metfessel, Michael, and Kirsner (1969) regarding the cognitive domain, shown in table 4.3, write instructional objectives that serve as the structure for a lesson plan. If possible, teach the lesson and note if there is internal consistency among the objectives, procedures, materials, and your means of evaluating whether or not you accomplished the goal(s) of the lesson.
6. Write an evaluation of Popham's objections to instructional objectives (see pp. 62–63) and share your thoughts with a colleague for the purpose of obtaining another perspective on your written evaluation.
7. State how content and form of educational objectives are interrelated.

Instructional Goals and Objectives

8. Using the work of Metfessel, Michael, and Kirsner (1969) regarding the affective domain, shown in table 4.5, write instructional objectives that serve as the structure for a lesson plan. If possible, teach the lesson and note if there is internal consistency among the objectives, procedures, materials, and your means of evaluating whether or not you accomplished the goal(s) of the lesson.
9. Write instructional objectives in the psychomotor domain using as a guide tables 4.6 and 4.7.
10. Classify the following objectives into the appropriate domain and taxonomy level according to the following scheme:

C = Cognitive	A = Affective	P = Psychomotor
1 = Knowledge	1 = Receiving	1 = Perceptual abilities
2 = Comprehension	2 = Responding	
3 = Application	3 = Valuing	2 = Physical abilities
4 = Analysis	4 = Organization	
5 = Synthesis	5 = Characterization	3 = Skilled movement
6 = Evaluation		

C-1 List states and their capitals with 60 percent accuracy.

_____ a. Given a description of a particular situation, the student will construct a three-part diagram that accurately reflects the structure of the situation.
_____ b. Members will demonstrate a committed interest to a project by becoming active participants.
_____ c. Pupils will write from memory the basic ideas in an essay.
_____ d. Using appropriate literary criteria, the student will describe in writing the style used in an essay and explain the response.
_____ e. The student will show an understanding of a mathematical relation by drawing a diagram.
_____ f. The student will run 200 yards in 26 seconds.
_____ g. The student will demonstrate understanding of a written passage by paraphrasing it.
_____ h. Without referring to the text, the student will list the factors that led up to World War I.
_____ i. Students will show respect for each other by listening while peers speak.

Key: a) C-2   b) A-3   c) C-1   d) C-6   e) C-2   f) P-2   g) C-2
       h) C-1   i) A-2

References

American Council on Education. 1944. *A design for general education.* Washington, D. C.: Author.

Ayers, J. D. 1966. Justification of Bloom's taxonomy by factor analysis. Paper presented at the annual meeting of the American Educational Research Association, Chicago.

Bloom, B. S., ed. 1956. *Taxonomy of educational objectives, handbook I: Cognitive domain.* New York: McKay.

Bloom, B. S., D. R. Krathwohl, and B. B. Masia. 1964. *Taxonomy of educational objectives, handbook II: Affective domain.* New York: McKay.

Commission on the Reorganization of Secondary Education (appointed by the National Education Association, Department of the Interior, Bureau of Education). 1918. *Cardinal principles of secondary education: A report of the Commission on the Reorganization of Secondary Education.* Bulletin 1918, 35. Washington, D. C.: GPO.

Cronbach, L. J. 1960. *Essentials of psychological testing.* 2d ed. New York: Harper & Row.

Educational Policies Commission. 1938. *The purpose of education in American democracy.* Washington, D. C.: National Education Association and American Association of School Administrators.

Dalis, G. T. 1970. Effect of precise objectives upon student achievement in health education. *Journal of Experimental Education* 39, 20–23.

Daines, D. 1982. Teachers' oral questions and subsequent verbal behavior of teachers and students. Provo, Utah: Brigham Young University (EDRS/ERIC ED 225 979).

Dave, R. H. 1970. Psychomotor levels. In *Developing and writing behavioral objectives,* edited by R. J. Armstrong, T. D. Cornell, R. E. Kraner, and E. W. Roberson. Tucson, Ariz.: Educational Innovators Press.

Dressel, P. L. 1954. Evaluation as instruction. In *Proceedings of the 1953 invitational conference on testing problems.* Princeton, N.J.: Educational Testing Service.

Educational Policies Commission. 1961. *The central purpose of American education.* Washington: National Education Association of School Administrators.

French, J. W., et al. 1957. *Behavioral goals of general education in high school.* New York: Russell Sage Foundation.

Hand, T., R. Hoppock, and P. J. Zlatchin. Job satisfaction: Researchers of 1944 and 1945. *Occupations* 26: 425–31.

Havighurst, R. J. 1953. *Human development and education.* New York: David McKay.

Harrow, A. J. 1972. *A taxonomy of the psychomotor domain.* New York: David McKay.

Hunkins, F. 1976. *Involving students in questioning.* Boston: Allyn & Bacon.

Jenkins, J. R., and S. L. Deno. 1971. Influence on knowledge and type of objectives on subject-matter learning. *Journal of Educational Psychology* 62: 67–70.

Kearney, N. C. 1953. *Elementary school objectives.* New York: Russell Sage Foundation.

Kibler, R. J., L. L. Barber, and D. T. Milen. 1970. *Behavioral objectives and instruction.* Boston: Allyn & Bacon.

Kropp, R. P., H. W. Stoker, and W. L. Bashaw. 1968. The validation of the taxonomy of educational objectives. *Journal of Experimental Education* 34: 69–76.

Lee, B. N., and M. D. Merrill. 1972. *Writing complete objectives: A short course.* Belmont, Calif.: Wadsworth.

McGuire, C. 1963. A process of approach to the construction and analysis of medical examinations. *Journal of Medical Education* 1: 556–63.

McNeil, J. D. 1967. Concomitants of using behavioral objectives in the assessment of teacher effectiveness. *Journal of Experimental Education* 36: 69–74.

Mager, R. F. 1962. *Preparing instructional objectives.* Palo Alto, Calif.: Ferson.

Metfessel, W. S., W. B. Michael, and D. A. Kirsner. 1969. Instrumentation of Bloom's and Krathwohl's taxonomies for the writing of educational objectives. *Psychology in the Schools* 6: 227–31.

Miller, R. I. 1972. *Evaluating faculty performance.* San Francisco: Jossey-Bass.

Popham, W. J. 1968. Probing the validity of arguments against behavioral goals. Paper presented at the annual meeting of the American Educational Research Association, Chicago, Feb.

Popham, W. J. 1969. *Identifying affective objectives.* Filmstrip. Los Angles: Vimcet/Instructional Objectives Exchange.

Popham, W. J. 1969. Objectives and instruction. In *Instructional Objectives,* edited by W. J. Popham, 32–52. Chicago: Rand McNally.

Ragsdale, C. E. 1950. How children learn motor types of activities. In *Forty-Ninth Yearbook of the National Society for the Study of Education,* 69–91. Chicago: University of Chicago Press.

Sanders, N. 1966. *Classroom questions: What kinds.* New York: Harper & Row.

Scannell, D. P., and W. R. Stellwagen. 1960. Teaching and testing for degrees of understanding. *California Journal of Instructional Improvement* 3(1): 8–14.

Simpson, E. J. 1966. The classification of educational objectives: Psychomotor domain. *Illinois Teacher of Home Economics* 10: 110–14.

Tyler, R. W. 1933. Permanence of learning. *Journal of Higher Education* 4: 203–4.

Tyler, R. W. 1964. Some persistent questions on the defining of objectives. In *Defining educational objectives,* edited by C. M. Lindwall, 77–83. Pittsburg: University of Pittsburgh Press.

Wynn, C. 1973. Pros and cons of behavioral objectives. *Georgia Educator* 3: 12–14.

Yelon, S. L., and R. O. Scott. 1970. *A strategy in writing objectives.* Dubuque, Iowa: Kendall/Hunt.

5 *Lesson planning*

Teachers synthesize all the information they have about the students, the curriculum, and the learning resources and environment when they develop comprehensive plans. Planning lessons and evaluating student performance are two of the most crucial skills you can acquire as a teacher. These skills fit into a cyclical process that includes planning for instruction, implementing lesson plans, and evaluating student progress.

Planning for Teaching

This chapter will offer specific guidelines and suggestions for the development of lesson plans. It is important that teachers learn to think about what they are doing and not try to "wing it" with meager or nonexistent plans. While careful planning does not by itself make a creative, enthusiastic, and effective teacher or ensure student learning, it does increase the likelihood of success and provide an organized framework consistent with the teacher's purposes.

Lesson Planning

Planning is one of the most difficult and time-consuming parts of the whole teaching process. During the teacher preparation period, it is extremely important that you learn the elements of effective planning. Pre-service and beginning teachers usually need to plan in more detail than do experienced teachers to achieve similar results.

Many school districts provide teachers, especially new ones, with system-wide curriculum guides. At best, school districts provide summer compensation to teachers for developing the guides, which include instructional activities and available materials for each objective within a content area for each grade level. Then these writing teams (sometimes with the help of consultants) supervise a year-long induction of the curriculum guide for district teachers.

All teachers, however—pre-service, beginning and experienced—should realize that curriuclum guides, teacher manuals, and textbooks are good resources but no substitutes for their planning. Carefully developed plans by all teachers mean less time is wasted, provide better for individual and group needs, and improve chances for success in the classroom.

Levels of Planning

Sometimes the beginning teacher is confused by the kinds and levels of planning. Teachers should consider at least four levels of planning: (1)

Group planning enhances instruction.

curriculum guides, (2) resource units, (3) teaching units, and (4) lesson plans. **Curriculum guides** are usually developed by curriculum consultants and administrators in cooperation with teachers in the city, county, or state. The guides set goals for the program or subject area and may or may not include instructional objectives and learning activities. A curriculum guide, which may cover the whole range from kindergarten through twelfth grade, provides a large structure within which teachers can organize their own units and lessons. **Resource units** are sample units developed for a hypothetical group of students and may cover instructional periods of weeks or months. Resource units give much attention to pupil activities and instructional materials. They are sometimes part of curriculum guides and often aid teachers in planning classroom experiences. The **teaching unit** is created by a teacher for a specific group of students. It is more detailed than the resource unit and usually covers two to six weeks. From the teaching unit the teacher develops specific **lesson plans.** A lesson plan is usually developed for one to five days of a particular class.

Lesson planning thus moves from very general to very specific:

- Curriculum guides (very general)
- Resource units (general)
- Teaching units (specific)
- Lesson plans (very specific)

Classroom teachers are directly responsible for both the teaching unit and the lesson plan.

Plans differ widely, because they are written by individual teachers for their own students. A good plan also has many elements, some written down and some simply thought through in the teacher's mind and implied in the plan. Even though the planning process is individual by nature, certain components should be included in all teachers' plans. Your plans will be very detailed at first, but as you gain teaching experience and your planning skills improve, you will need less time for the process. We suggest the following minimal format:

I. Objectives
II. Procedures
III. Evaluation

Our purpose here is to provide guidelines for preparing lesson plans for daily instruction. Remember, however, that a lesson plan is simply an expanded portion of a unit plan. A number of lesson plans combine to form a unit of instruction. On Monday, for example, students may identify characteristics of reptiles. Tuesday, they may identify characteristics of mammals. Wednesday, they may compare and contrast the characterisics of reptiles and mammals. Thursday, they may study the offspring of these animals. All of these daily lessons make up a unit of instruction on animals.

Table 5.1
A Model Lesson Plan Format

Unit Title: _____

Goals: _____

Objectives: _____

Procedures

    Rationale: _____

    Materials: _____

    Motivation: _____

    Content (Topic to be covered): _____

    Closure: _____

    Evaluation: _____

    Critique: _____

Lesson Plan Components

Because teachers differ and varied modes of instruction are possible, there is no one best form for a lesson plan. The level of specificity depends upon the teacher's needs for the particular purpose at the time. For now, be sure to plan for each of the following components. Table 5.1 presents a model lesson plan format (Jacobsen et al. 1985; Orlich et al. 1985). A description of each component follows. A sample lesson plan on the topic of advertising will be presented in table 5.2.

Unit Title

To prepare this portion of the lesson plan it is only necessary that you identify in a word or sentence the larger unit of instruction to which the individual lesson pertains. For example, units might be entitled: "Community Helpers," "Uses of Land in My Community," "The Five Senses," and "Animal Identification."

Instructional Goals and Objectives

In chapter 4 we discussed the preparation of instructional goals and objectives. These goals and objectives form an integral part of the planning process.

Unit goals are cast as outcomes students should achieve after completing a unit of instruction. They are usually stated in broad, nonbehavioral terms and provide direction and organization to the lesson:

1. The students will understand the services performed by community helpers.
2. The students will understand the positive effects community helpers have on the people who live in the community.

Unit goals represent the teacher's aims for the instruction and are translated into objectives for pupil behavior (instructional objectives) that demonstrate student attainment of the goal.

Before beginning instruction a teacher must have a clear idea of what students should know once the lesson is completed. To accomplish this, translate instructional goals into instructional objectives or accomplishable tasks. Instructional objectives describe what students may be expected to do after completing a prescribed unit of instruction. Unlike unit goals, instructional objectives are stated in specific, observable terms:

1. The student will draw pictures of five community helpers, illustrating a service that each performs.
2. The student will state orally the three positive effects that policemen have on the community.

Pre-service and beginning teachers often wonder how many objectives should be included in a single lesson. It has been our experience that novice teachers tend to plan too lengthy lessons containing too many objectives. Daily lessons should probably focus on one or two objectives and should not exceed twenty or thirty minutes.

The choice of objectives is possibly the most important decision teachers make because of its subsequent impact on the choice of content, learning experiences, instructional methods and materials, and evaluation procedures.

Experienced classroom teachers rarely spend time writing out goals and objectives on daily plans, but good teachers still think them through and are aware of them. Pre-service and beginning teachers, on the other hand, have little or no expeirence to rely on and need to include goals and objectives in their plans. This practice will help you to keep in mind the reasons for what you are teaching.

Instructional Procedures and Components

Rationale. What is the purpose for the instruction? To prepare this part of your lesson you might think about a person visiting your classroom and asking, "Why are you teaching this lesson?" You should be able to

Use a lesson plan format that is precise and helpful.

state your view of the subject and its importance to the curriculum and to the students. If you cannot think of a good reason for teaching the lesson, perhaps you should not teach it at all.

Including a rationale in your formal planning is helpful for a number of reasons. First, it helps to focus attention on the goals and objectives of the lesson, separating significant from trivial outcomes. Second, if you know both what you are going to teach (instructional objectives) and why you are going to teach it (rationale), your lesson will more likely be relevant to the students in your class. Finally, discussing the purpose(s) of the unit or lesson with your students will help prepare them to learn.

Materials. The teacher's plans should also include any learning materials and aids which will help students achieve the instructional objectives. Anything you intend to use to supplement your lesson should be considered a material. For example, materials can include audiovisual equipment, slides, films, charts, graphs, books, pictures, crayons, pencils, the chalkboard, handouts, microcomputers, and software. It is important to list the materials you will need, both for the student's use and for your own use. The list can be quickly checked before you begin the lesson and will go a long way in keeping you from forgetting a necessary portion of your lesson.

A word of advice is offered here. In addition to listing your materials, always preview any films, slides, software, etc., and make sure all equipment is in working order before the lesson.

Motivation. Capturing students' attention, interest, and curiosity at the beginning of every lesson is extremely important. When students are motivated to learn, they are better prepared for subsequent work and more likely to become actively involved in their own learning. Carefully consider how you can get lessons off to an exciting start. Some ways might include using a colorful bulletin board, reading a riddle, story, or poem, relating the concept to an analogy, bringing a resource person to the room, taking a field trip, discussing an unusual, puzzling, or confusing dimension of the topic, showing a film followed by a discussion, and doing a dramatic presentation.

Getting your students interested in the lesson depends not only on what you say but on how you say it: the manner in which you present the material. Enthusiasm is contagious!

Teaching Strategies. A wide variety of methods and strategies is available for teacher use. The choice is influenced by the learning task, students' experiences, teachers' strengths and preferences, physical environment, and learning resources available. Teaching can be didactic or expository, can use discovery or discussion. Teaching strategies are discussed in more detail in chapter 6.

Content. The content component of the lesson plan refers to what you are going to teach—the facts, generalizations, and theories of a particular subject or content area. Usually this section outlines what you intend to say to students in the order that you plan to teach it.

To help the teacher to select content, Hunkins (1980) has provided the following criteria:

1. *Significance.* The importance of the content to be learned is the first criterion. The content is significant only if it contributes to basic ideas, principles, or generalizations. Significance also depends on how the content helps students develop particular learning abilities, skills, processes, and attitudes. It relates, too, to the degree to which content will last over time. Significant content will have both contemporary and future value and interest for students.

   Pre-service teachers are often unsure how much detail should be given in the content section of the lesson plan. No simple answer exists to this question. Factors such as individual needs, subject matter, teaching method used, and age of students influence the amount of detail present in the plan. The important point to be kept in mind is the organization of the material to be presented.

2. *Validity.* The second criterion is the authenticity of the content. Validity means whether the content selected is sound in relation to a unit's objectives. We should apply this test when we first select content, and we should continue to apply it at regular intervals during the instruction.

3. *Interest.* When using this criterion, the teacher can answer these questions: Is the content potentially interesting to students? Are students' current interests of long lasting educational value? Will this content expand the range of students' concerns? Consider also the students' maturity, their level of schooling, their prior experiences, and the educational and social value of their interests.

4. *Utility.* Students frequently want to know why they should learn certain information. In some cases, content can be applied immediately in activities like reading or cooperative games. Content useful for laying the foundations of later learning, however, is usually more difficult for students to appreciate.

5. *Learnability.* The content selected should be learnable. Students have various learning styles that make some content and its organization more difficult to learn than others. When we consider learnability, we are asking ourselves if the unit material is appropriate for our student audience.

6. *Feasibility.* This criterion addresses the constraints of time, available resources, expertise of the curriculum staff, political climate in the community, current legislation, and funds available for the program.

Closure. Summarizing or culminating activities should conclude the lesson, but these are too often rushed or completely neglected. How a lesson or unit ends is actually as important as how it is introduced, because the ending helps students to synthesize and summarize the values, understandings, and concepts they have acquired during the lesson.

It is often beneficial to have students participate actively in culminating activities such as

1. making a scrapbook;
2. summarizing in a group discussion the major points of the lesson;
3. participating in an original play or skit;
4. creating murals or pictures depicting lesson activities;
5. exhibiting materials developed in the unit.

Evaluation

Decisions about student performance on stated objectives are based on information gathered through formative and summative evaluation. Various techniques and procedures should be used throughout the lesson and/or unit by teacher and pupils to assess progress toward the objectives. This ongoing or **formative** evaluation keeps students on task and provides them with immediate feedback on their work.

Post-evaluation assessment, or **summative** evaluation, enables the teacher to determine whether a student has mastered a skill or concept at the completion of instruction. The summative evaluation should measure the student's performance of tasks specified in the instructional objectives. In other words, whatever behavior is called for in the objectives should be assessed at the end of instruction. It is very important that the teacher's instructional objectives, learning activities, and evaluation procedures correspond with each other. For example, consider a fourth grade unit entitled, "The North Central Region and Rocky Mountains":

Objective: Given a map of the U.S., the student will circle all the states of the North Central Region.

Selected Procedures:
1. Display large map of United States with North Central Region outlined.
2. Teacher points out each state within the region.
3. Students and teachers discuss physical characteristics of each state.
4. Teacher, using large map, points to states and asks class to name them.

Evaluation: On a map, students are to circle all the states in the North Central Region.

It would be very unfair if, given the objective above, the teacher evaluated the students by asking them to draw a map of the United States and label the states in the North Central Region.

You should recall from chapter 4 that testing conditions are specified in instructional objectives. These conditions are to be imposed during the testing situation. In addition, the test should require at least some responses from the student that were also required during instruction. The student should have had some experience or practice with the behavior called for in the testing situation.

A system of evaluation enables the teacher to determine whether a student has mastered the skill or concept set forth in a given instructional objective. With this information the teacher can decide whether the skill or concept should be retaught using different materials and/or strategies, whether the teacher should backtrack and teach prerequisite skills, or whether the student can progress to the next skill. Evaluation, the final component of the planning process, turns it into a cycle through which students pass.

Critique

Evaluation of students should not be confused with the evaluation teachers conduct of their own teaching performance. We will refer to this evaluation as a **critique.** During and after instruction teachers should ask themselves questions such as these:

Were my objectives appropriate?
Were my directions easy to follow?
Were my students able to complete their assignments on their own?
What parts of the lesson could be improved?
What parts of the lesson were particularly successful?

As a guide for lesson development, a sample lesson plan on the topic of advertising is shown in table 5.2.

Table 5.2
A Sample Second Grade Lesson Plan

Unit Title:	Advertising/Creative Writing
Goal:	Students will gain an understanding of some of the ploys of advertising and the creativity involved in advertising.
Objectives:	1. Given a product, quicksand, the student will write and illustrate an original commercial employing at least one advertising ploy. 2. Given an audience, the student will recite the commercial with animation and proper voice.
Procedures Rationale:	Teacher begins: Today we are going to talk about ways advertisers try to sell us products and how oftentimes these advertisements can be very misleading. Sometimes the gimmicks or strategies used to advertise the product have little or nothing to do with the purpose or the quality of the product. They are used only to get your attention and to make you want to buy the product. After talking about ways advertisers try to sell us products, we are going to try to sell our own products.
Materials:	Posters, paper, pencils, crayons, cardboard TV, tape recorder, tape.
Motivation:	Begin by playing an audio tape of commercials. Then ask the students, "What are you listening to?" Next ask, "Do you have a favorite commercial?" "Why?"
Content:	Advertising ploys of repitition, humor, famous live characters, and fictitious heroes are a few used to sell products. Repetition is.... An example is.... Humor in advertising is.... An example is.... Famous live characters being used are.... An example is Bob Hope selling clothes made in the USA; Wonder Woman selling Maybelline. Fictitious heroes being used are.... An example is the Pink Panther selling Dow Insulation.

Table 5.2
continued

Activities:	1. Each ploy will be listed on a poster and a familiar example will be presented by the teacher. Discuss techniques used to sell a product. Show posters and discuss their techniques. 2. Present students with a product, quicksand. Tell them to come up with a way to use it. If they appear to be having trouble, brainstorm ideas as a group. 3. Ask students to write a commerical for quicksand using an advertising phrase or ploy. 4. Tell them, when they finish, to practice saying the commerical aloud to themselves. They need to raise their voice when an idea is important. They need to try using facial expressions or movements to liven up their commercial. Mention the example of "The man who has a cold" commercial. 5. Have them pair up and practice their commercial. Mention that they are going to share their commercial with the group. The group will choose one to produce. 6. Have them present their commercials one by one to the whole group. 7. Take a vote to decide the group's favorite. Then discuss ways to illustrate it. Mention that it will be done frame by frame. Help them come up with an appropriate sequence and then assign a child or two to each scene. Let them draw. 8. Put the scenes on the rollers in the cardboard television. Then let the child who wrote the commercial read it into the tape recorder. 9. Then have a run-through or two, practicing turning the sticks so that the pictures follow the words. 10. Finally, return to the classroom and let the students share their commercial with the rest of the class.
Closure:	Gather up all the commercials. using phrases from them, ask what type of ploy is being used. Mix in some examples from TV ads. Discuss which way appears to be the best for selling quicksand. Praise the efforts of the students.
Evaluation Objective 1:	Teacher assessment of students' illustrations of the commercial based on logical relevance to the commercial's story line, and teacher assessment of students' ability to work together to get a logical finished product.
Objective 2:	Teacher assessment of student's recitation of his commercial based on student's animation and voice appropriateness.
Critique:	Was my lesson too long? Was this lesson too complicated for second graders? What needs to be changed for this particular group of students? What parts of the lesson were particularly successful?

Source: This lesson plan was written by Teresa Schretter, an undergraduate Elementary Education major at the University of Georgia.

Summary

Planning should be considered a tool to assist teachers in guiding the many decisions they must make to provide students with the best possible opportunities for learning. Experienced teachers do not always write out detailed plans for each and every lesson they teach. Nevertheless, competent teachers realize the importance of careful planning, especially when presenting new learnings.

To summarize the importance of planning, Hoover and Hollingsworth (1975, 159–60) offer guidelines for efficient use of unit and lesson planning:

1. Plans serve as useful guides or blueprints for teaching. They must be flexible enough to permit modification or revision as the occasion may demand.
2. Pupils appropriately play a part in planning classroom experiences. This does not imply that the teacher waits until she enters the classroom before she begins to plan. The prepared teacher has set up general goals, some definite activities, and some specific sources of materials that may be used.
3. Unit planning is designed to emphasize important patterns or relationships. Such an arrangement facilitates transfer of training to out-of-school situations.
4. Through adequate planning the teacher's attention tends to be directed to important problems of motivation and individual differences.
5. The lesson plan provides a handy reference to important statistics, illustrations, difficult work, special procedures, and the like.
6. Planning increases the teacher's own understanding of the problems involved.
7. Planning brings into proper balance and focus goals, subject matter, activities, and evaluation.
8. Adequate planning provides a basis for future teaching experiences. By making use of marginal notes the teacher easily can make substantial improvements in succeeding years.
9. Unit and lesson plans may be used more than once. It make good sense to capitalize the next year on a highly successful experience. A word of caution is in order here, however. The responsible teacher does not permit his teaching to become staid—going through the same motions year after year. Prior to each experience he asks himself what improvements, changes, or substitutions might be in order. Continuous experimentation provides a basis for improved teaching.
10. Planning is a personal invention. The thoroughness and nature of unit and lesson planning will depend on the needs of each individual teacher involved.

Thought Activity

1. On pages 79 and 80 we talked about curriculum guides and resource units. Plan to visit a curriculum library in a local school or school district office and review some of these materials.
2. Visit the classrooms of a first-year teacher and an experienced teacher. Talk with both teachers about how they plan for instruction. How do their methods differ? Why?
3. Discuss the differences between daily lesson plans and unit plans.
4. State the advantages of careful lesson planning for a new classroom teacher.
5. Hunkins provides us with criteria (see list on p. 85) that will assist teachers in the selection of content. Define each of these criteria: *significance, validity, interest, utility, learnability, feasibility.*
6. Write a definition for each of the lesson plan components in table 5.1.
7. Develop a daily lesson plan in a curriculum area such as science, language arts, mathematics, or social studies.

References

Hoover, K. H., and P. M. Hollingsworth. 1975. *Learning and teaching in the elementary school.* 2nd ed. Boston: Allyn & Bacon.

Hunkins, F. P. 1980. *Curriculum development: Program improvement.* Columbus, Ohio: Charles E. Merrill.

Jacobsen, D., P. Eggen, D. Kauchak, and C. Dulaney. 1985. *Methods for teaching: A skills approach.* 2d ed. Columbus, Ohio: Charles E. Merrill.

Orlich, S., R. Harder, R. Callahan, C. Kravas, D. Kauchak, R. Pendergrass, and A. Keogh. 1985. *Teaching strategies: A guide to better instruction.* Lexington; Mass.: D. C. Heath.

6 *Becoming an instructional designer*

Defining Instructional Design

An instructional designer is a creator of learning environments. Learning environments in the broad sense may be identified from birth through the life span. For infants they may include the hospital, home, day care center, nursery, preschool, and kindergarten; for older children, elementary and secondary classrooms, scout troops, summer camp; for adults, higher education including colleges and universities, inservice and continuing education, corporate classrooms; for accident and stroke victims, rehabilitation such as physical therpay and computer-based stimulation. Instructional materials take many forms: rattles, toys, books, film, audio tape, video tape, interactive videodisc systems that integrate computers and video tape monitors, closed circuit TV, and computer software. A designer of instruction must understand how people develop, how they learn, how technology can enhance education, how to select the medium or technology that best suits the instructional goal, and how to help learners acquire and manage information.

Cognitive Processing and Instructional Design

Developing students' ability to obtain and manage information should be a primary goal of instruction. We encounter so much information daily that it is impossible to read and digest everything that might be relevant or interesting. Students must be taught to select and sift through the information available to them. The need is already so obvious that some businesses are hiring educators to help their employees learn to cope with the information overload. Instructional programs that help clients identify their learning strengths and weaknesses and that use computer technology in instruction are replacing speed reading courses and tachistoscopes. These programs integrate two previously separate disciplines: the study of individual differences and the psychology of learning.

Chipman and Segal (1985) point out that it is difficult to predict what knowledge students will need or what problems will have to be addressed in twenty years due to our rapidly changing technological environment. Thus, students need to learn how to learn. Teachers must understand and foster the skills of general thinking and learning: (1) acquisition of knowledge, (2) problem solving, and (3) basic cognitive skills, such as approaching tasks in an organized way and drawing logical conclusions from information.

These three skills have common features. For example, Brown (1980) describes the key cognitive characteristics for acquiring knowledge as: knowing when you know, knowing what you know, knowing what you need to know, and knowing how to change your state of knowledge.

Problem solving skills include analyzing the problem, searching related knowledge, planning attempts at a solution, keeping track of progress, and checking results against the overall goal or subgoals. (Problem solving is discussed in detail in chap. 15.)

The third area of general thinking and learning, basic cognitive skills such as organizing tasks and drawing logical conclusions, draws on self-control, self-management, and metacognition (see chap. 2).

Glaser (1985, 83) notes that "in recent years, cognitive psychologists have begun to investigate, from a common theoretical base, measures of individual differences in aptitude and the cognitive processes that lead to learning." The new approach, he says, "should contribute to better understanding of the relations between a wide range of human capacities and the design of various learning environments.

Glaser proposes a theoretical base for instructional design similar to Piaget's notion of **schemata.** A schema is a

modifiable information structure that represents generic concepts stored in memory. Schemata represent knowledge of what we experience—interrelationships between objects, situations, events, and sequences of events that normally occur.... Like a theory, a schema allows prediction, enabling individuals to make assumptions about common patterns of events so that the knowledge they infer goes beyond the observations made in any one instance.... People continually try to understand and think about the new in terms of this information. . . . Then it seems best to anchor teaching to the knowledge domains in which an individual has some competence. Abilities to make inferences and to generate new information can be fostered by ensuring maximum contact with prior knowledge, which can be restructured and further developed.

It should be noted here as an **advance organizer** that the meshing of new learning to what the learner already knows is at the heart of diagnostic teaching (Reisman 1982), which is described below as an instructional design model.

What Is the Instructional Design of This Text?

This text is designed to help you become an instructional designer who is aware of learners' needs, understands curriculum needs, and can bridge the two through appropriate instruction. Reisman (1982, 4) has labeled this bridging process *diagnostic teaching*. The systematic integration of learner and content to be learned is a type of systems approach to instruction that also incorporates a humanistic focus. Dick and Carey (1978, 2–3) explain the humanistic and systems approaches to instruction:

> Educators who consider themselves in the humanistic camp have a genuine interest in the total development of individual children. They recognize the importance of individual differences and believe that the essence of outstanding education is to show genuine care and concern for students as they attempt to define those areas of learning which are important and relevant to them. . . . Many teacher-training programs can also be viewed as humanistic, since they focus upon the importance of the interactive relationship between the teacher and the student and emphasize such aspects of the educational process as flexibility and adaptability, methods of learning, self-actualization, discovery methods, and promotion of each student's individuality. In essence, humanistically oriented teachers believe that there is no best way to manage a classroom or to organize a learning experience. They believe there is no single formula for good teaching, but rather a number of approaches, one or more being appropriate for the needs of a particular student.
>
> Some teachers prefer a behavioral approach to teaching. These individuals tend to view the teacher as one responsible for instruction in cultural heritage, social responsibilities, and specific subject matter. They believe that these matters cannot be left to the individual interests of the students alone. This type of teacher emphasizes a carefully prepared lesson plan, logically organized material, and specific educational objectives and tends to emphasize "getting the correct answer." In essence, these teachers prefer a systematic approach which utilizes research knowledge on the conditions of learning required for students to achieve clearly defined outcomes. The systematic approach to instruction . . . emphasizes the importance of a precise definition of what it is that the student will learn and the importance of careful structuring of instructional materials.*

---

*From *The Systematic Design of Instruction* by W. Dick and R. Carey. Copyright © 1978 by Scott, Foresman and Company. Reprinted by permission.

Diagnostic teaching is described by Wilson (1982, iii–iv) as follows:

Teaching that is diagnostic in nature attempts to identify the child's level of performance and all the relevant information that contributes to that performance. Then the material to be learned is analyzed into its component parts. Finally, an instructional sequence is implemented for the child that blends the child's cognitive and emotional status with the proper part of the task to be learned. It is important to recognize that these principles of the diagnostic teaching cycle apply to group instruction just as naturally as to individual instruction. . . . Diagnostic teaching can be used to anticipate and avoid learning difficulties. The matching of the current level of performance and the material to be learned is certainly appropriate for instruction with every child, not just those with a learning difficulty. . . . Diagnostic teaching . . . [involves] an understanding of the child, an understanding of the subject matter and the blending of the two during instruction.

Reisman and Kauffman (1980, 4–8) integrate curriculum and learning issues into the diagnostic model for instructional design as follows:

Diagnostic teaching . . . involves guiding a child to learn a portion of the curriculum. . . . First, the developmental level at which a child is performing cognitively must be identified. Second, the task to be learned must be analyzed in order to determine how many components of the task the child has already acquired. . . . Diagnosis involves looking at both the curriculum to be taught and the method of instruction. It may involve asking the following questions: *Is the curriculum that I am attempting to teach this child appropriate to his or her needs, both present and future? Is the concept to be taught appropriate to his or her level of cognitive functioning? Is a learning discrepancy or learning disability preventing the child from learning? Has the child acquired the necessary prerequisites in order to learn this curriculum? What is the most appropriate method of istruction that I can use for the learner to facilitate acquisition of this knowledge? Why has this student not acquired this portion of curriculum, or why is he or she not able to perform this task?*

Example of How Results of a Task Analysis Affect Instruction

As a result of diagnostically analyzing mathematics tasks in relation to learner concerns, Reisman and Kauffman (1980, 254–257) point out the following learning "trouble spots" in the primary grades mathematics curriculum and their implications for design (or redesign) of instruction:

Counting objects employing one-to-one correspondence between the number name and the object to be counted is not the same as counting jumps or spaces between objects—as in telling time on a clock face, which is a circular number line. This discrepancy causes children to count one too many minutes after the hour, as they start counting the minute marks at the twelve.

A youngster counts objects at the concrete level.

There is a discrepancy between the physical representation of zero and its digital representation. When representing the number zero concretely or with pictures, no objects or pictures are used. However, at the symbol level, the digit *0* is used. This discrepancy is apparent in place-value notation, when the digit zero must be used to represent none of a place. Zero is the only digit which has this discrepancy. All of the other digits 1 through 9 may be represented in the real world by *something*.

The numbers resulting from *one ten (1 × 10), ten ones (10 × 1), ten tens (10 × 10), ten hundreds (10 × 100),* and so on are products. A product is the result of performing the binary operation of multiplication on two numbers; product is the term used for the answer to a multiplication problem. Place value is a product. When we generate place value (*units, tens, hundreds, thousands,* etc.), we are mutiplying the number system's base by the value of the previous place: *10 × 10 × 10 × 1 >> 10 × 10 × 1 >> 10 × 1 >> 1*. Yet when is place value taught? (In first grade.) And when is multiplication taught? (Usually at the end of grade two or in grade three.) Unless the prerequisite of multiplication is taught prior to or simultaneously with place value, only a rote learning will occur.

The value of a multi-digit number is the sum of the products found when multiplying the face value of the number's digits times their respective place-values. For example, the value of number 32 is found by the following algorithm: (3 × 10) + (2 × 1) = 30 + 2 = 32. This trouble spot also relates to the late formal introduction of multiplication into the instructional sequence after topics are taught for which multiplication is a prerequisite.

The *bundling-of-tens* is not a valid physical representation for counting in sequence beyond the number nine, although this is often the activity used to teach this instructional goal. Writing numbers greater than nine in sequence is not the same as making a ten-for-one exchange. The ten-for-one exchange is a multiplication relationship, while counting in sequence is additive in nature. Children count aloud before they write numerals. When a child says *nine* and then *ten* in the early stages, he or she uses *ten, eleven,* and so on as the same type of label as *nine*. *Nine* triggers *ten* in the *add-one* sequence, just as *eight* was the stimulus for *nine*. The same thought processes are involved as the child begins to record this sequence with numerals. He or she may be aware that two digits are used to record ten, but has probably learned this by rote with no thought to the notational principle of place value. The sequence model recognizes that the learner focuses on only two consecutive numbers at a time; it involves a stimulus-response learning series. The bridge from writing *9* to *10* involves the idea of "nine and one more is ten" rather than the many-to-one relation underlying the bundling-by-tens or *exchange* model.

We should be teaching time to the minute first, and initial instruction should just deal with so *many minutes after* the hour to maintain the forward sequence (Reisman 1971). Children learn to count by ones first, not last. The traditional sequence introduces the more difficult parts of the task before the necessary prerequisites are established (e.g., counting by fives, telling time in terms of so many minutes *before* the next hour).

Multiplication should be formally pointed out as early as kindergarten, but certainly in first grade. Simple expressions of the multiplication operations are apparent in the early childhood environment:

I have three pieces of gum. (3×1)
I have four sisters. (4×1)
I ate two hot dogs. (2×1)
I have two bags of marbles and there's three in a bag. (2×3)

The child's language expresses multiplication long before the operation is pointed out formally. Being aware of multiplication relations is prerequisite to understanding place-value. The developmental nature of the mathematics curriculum is violated when multiplication is not even introduced until two years after topics based upon it are taught.

There is a discrepancy between writing and reading the vertical multiplication algorithm. The algorithm is usually written from top to bottom as follows for the example *three times forty-two*:

Step 1	*Step 2*	*Step 3*	*Step 4*
42	42	42	42
	3	× 3	× 3

The completed algorithm is read in an upward direction, stating the multiplier (*3*) first and then the multiplicand (*42*). Although the resulting product is the same, this discrepancy is confusing when one wishes to distinguish between *three* forty-twos and *forty-two* threes. Somtimes merely pointing out the discrepancy is sufficient for helping a confused student. For a student with learning problems it helps to suggest writing the algorithm in the same direction as subvocalizing or stating the problem—*forty-two three times* for the sequence of the algorithm written above, or the following sequence for the oral expression *three times forty-two equals*:

Step 1	Step 2	Step 3	Step 4
		42	42
3	× 3	× 3	× 3

There is a discrepancy between interpreting place-values and integer values (. . . −3, −2, −1, 0, 1, 2, 3, . . .) when using a number line for instruction. Place-values increase in a *right-to-left* direction; values of integers on the x axis increase in a *left-to-right* direction. This is not a trivial matter because if confusion persists, it can interfere with understanding exponential place-value notation in later grades when negative integers are used as superscript numerals to indicate smaller place values to the right.

Also confusing is the fact that the fulcrum of our place value notational system is the *units (ones)* place, while *zero* is the fulcrum when representing negative and positive integers on a number line. Perhaps using a vertical number line for counting would help children distinguish this difference.

Learning Tasks and Their Characteristics

We have just seen how characteristics of learning tasks can facilitate or inhibit instruction for the learner. You can identify the characteristics of learning tasks by asking yourself questions such as the following (Jensen 1980, 327–28):

- Is the task *intentional?* Does the learning task involve cognitive awareness as in reasoning, analyzing, synthesizing; or do the task requirements involve passive repetition of simple material with little need for "thinking"?
- Does the learning task depend upon prerequisite knowledge or skills? Is it *hierarchical* in nature?
- Does the learning task have *meaning* for the learner? How is the task related to other knowledge or experience?
- Does the learning task permit *transfer* from somewhat different but related past learning? Does this transferred learning facilitate or inhibit learning the new task?
- What is the degree of *complexity* or difficulty embedded in the task? If a learning task is too complex for an individual, the tendency is to flounder and fall back on simpler processes such as trial and error and rote association. Complexity refers to the number of elements that the learner must synthesize; difficulty refers to the amount of material to be learned.

- Does the learning task involve "catching on" or "getting the idea"? This type of *insightful* learning is sometimes called "aha" learning.
- Is the amount of *time* allotted for learning the task fixed for all students or may they learn at their own pace?
- Does the learning task rely on readiness or maturation? Is the material to be learned age-related? The concept of *learning readiness* refers to learning that is facilitated by maturation and correlates with age.
- Does the learning task involve learning something brand new or is practice for proficiency the objective? IQ is related more to rate of acquisition of new skills or knowledge than to rate of improvement or degree of proficiency at later stages of learning.*

Adaptive Education

The practice of adaptive instruction takes many forms. All versions, however, must incorporate direct instruction, provide some form of assessment and feedback, focus principally on cognitive learning, give some attention to developing self-direction, and involve learners in planning or managing their own progress. "Adaptive education, in brief, is intended to make learning more effective by suiting instruction to the needs of students" (Walberg 1985, 3). Clearly, adaptive instruction has much in common with the diagnostic teaching approach in instructional design described earlier in this chapter.

Adaptive education today matches instructional objectives and activities to the experiences, aptitudes, and interests of individual pupils (Bangert, Kulik, and Kulik 1983; Glaser 1977, 1983). "It is one of the more venerable practices in pedagogy" (Grinder and Nelsen 1985, 24):

Our forebears who taught children to draw hieroglyphics on the walls of caves, to hunt the prairies for their supper, to respect their elders, and so forth, surely taught according to children's individual abilities.

Plato, in his *Republic* (Jowett 1942), urged that children be directed toward philosopher, guardian, or artisan roles depending on whether they possessed "golden, silver, or brass" talents (p. 25).

Wang and Lindvall (1984) list seven features of adaptive education that distinguish it from nonadaptive education:

1. Instruction based on the assessed capabilities of each student.
2. Materials and procedures that permit each student to make progress in the mastery of instructional content at a pace suited to his or her abilities and interests.
3. Periodic evaluations of student progress that serve to inform the student concerning mastery.

---

*Adapted from A. R. Jensen, *Bias in Mental Testing* (New York: Free Press, 1980). Used by permission.

4. Student assumption of responsibility for diagnosing present needs and abilities, for planning individual learning activities, and for evaluating mastery.
5. Alternative activities and materials for aiding student acquisition of essential academic skills and content.
6. Student choice in selecting educational goals, outcomes, and activities.
7. Students' assistance of one another in pursuing individual goals and cooperation in achieving group goals.

Does the Adaptive Instruction Model Enhance Achievement?

There appear to be problems in determining whether adaptive instruction really makes a difference at this stage in its development. Berliner (1985, 306–7), critiquing the Adaptive Learning Environments Model (ALEM), which was supported by the University of Pittsburgh Learning Research and Development Center, notes that research data show that the ALEM, one of the most massive investigations on this topic to date, is "unrelated or negatively related to classroom processes that we know affect achievement, such as time-on-task, distraction, waiting for teacher help, and the like." Berliner further questions the model's instructional design, asking, "what is adaptive about the adaptive ALEM model?" In fact, Berliner argues, instead of the schools modifying their programs to meet the children's needs, the ALEM researchers appear to require the children to adapt to the schools' needs. Berliner (1985, 309) summarizes his observations as follows:

There is a lot of talk about accommodating to the students' diverse needs. I really cannot tell what diverse needs are being met besides the differences in students' rate of learning. It does look like there really is adaptation to rate of learning. But I do not see any evidence of clearly different instructional techniques for different kinds of students, or clearly different content for different kinds of student needs. Where is the concern for individual differences in anxiety, need for structure, intelligence (as opposed to speed), and so forth? I cannot even tell if the handicapped students are receiving a different program or not.

Some advocates of adaptive learning cite Bloom's "learning for mastery" concept (Bloom 1971) as an instance of adaptive instruction. Bloom himself does not agree. Berliner (1985) points out that some programs that purport to combine adaptive and mastery learning methods actually hold time constant in curriculum units, "destroying the one major adaptive feature that mastery has."

Tools of the Teacher's Trade

Designers of instructional environments must be aware of the following variables:

- generic factors that influence learning
- characteristics of learning tasks

- mode of representing curriculum
- sequencing of topics

They should understand that a mismatch between learner needs and delivery of the curriculum often causes learning difficulties.

Generic factors that influence learning were presented in chapter 2. You may wish to review them now. They were presented to help you begin to understand "the learning person." Gordon, DeStefano, and Shipman (1985, 55–59) remind us that factors other than cognition affect human learners:

Human learners are more than cognitive beings. Human behavior is also influenced by affect, by motivation, by identity, by environmental press, and, indeed, by various manifestations of status, for example, sex and gender, social and economic status, ethnicity and race, and language and culture.

Diagnostic teaching requires that the instructional designer understand learners from each of these perspectives and as whole persons. However, we must face the possibility that we still do not know enough about how these dimensions affect learning. Gordon et al. (1985, 55) discuss the dimensions of human diversity in learners and their relevance for the design and management of teaching and learning transactions:

- **Socioeconomic status** refers to income, style of life, prestige of birth, education, occupation, and the acquisition of corresponding life styles. Mercer (1973) and Wolf (1966) suggest that functional dimensions, not hierarchical social position, make differences in educational achievement, and socioeconomic status is not a reliable indicator of these dimensions.
- **Gender** and sex refer to social and biological roles, respectively. The educationally relevant attribute is gender, not sex. Socially assigned or adopted role functions influence how boys and girls are treated, what is expected of them, and what is allowed.
- **Ethnicity** refers to such attributes of a group as physical characteristics, genetic and cultural history, belief systems, and sometimes language. Ethnicity provides few leads for pedagogy.
- **Culture** refers to one's experiences of knowledge, belief, art, morals, customs; culture is the mores and life of a people. The culture of a school may be foreign to or complement one's culture. The ability to bridge cultures that differ is a key to education.
- **Motivation** is the ability to sustain effort when there is no extrinsic reward; it is a prompting force from within to move one to action.
- **Language** is a systematic means of communicating ideas or feelings through conventional symbol systems (e.g., sounds, gestures, or marks) that have understood meanings. Language competence is necessary for effective education, which requires congruence between the language of the school and of the learner.

- **Identity** refers to what is unique and apparent about a person and how the person perceives herself. Identity relates to self-concept and self-esteem.
- **Cognitive response tendency**, usually called **cognitive style**, is a consistent manner of perceiving, remembering, and thinking. Recognizable patterns include abstract/concrete and field independent/field dependent thinking. Gordon et al. suggest using the term *tendency* instead of *style* since style connotes a higher degree of stability than is demonstrated in the literature. *Affective response tendency*, or temperament (e.g., tempo, rhythmicity, adaptability, energy expenditure, mood, focus of attention), refers to consistency in emotional responses to a specific stimulus situation. Learning is thought to be facilitated when response tendencies match the task demands.

Cognitive style is simply another name for learning style, a person's characteristic ways of organizing and processing information. For example, **field dependent** learners, in perceptual tasks, do not tend to

Ability to bridge cultures is the key to a good learning environment.

keep an item separate from its surrounding context or *field*. If a text page is too busy or too colorful, they may have trouble isolating the task to be done. **Field independent** learners respond to their environment in analytical as opposed to global terms.

Other cognitive styles have been identified. **Convergent thinking** is closed and resembles Socratic teaching; **divergent thinking** is open and is exemplified by brainstorming. **Right brain dominance** uses intuitive and holistic thinking; **left brain dominance** is analytical and sequential. **Complex thinkers** tend to look at situations in multidimensional or abstract ways; **simple thinkers** look at situations in single-dimensional or concrete ways. The **reflective/impulsive** dichotomy of cognitive style indicates differences in speed and adequacy of generating alternatives and processing information. **Risk-taking/cautiousness** involves differences in willingness to take chances to achieve a desired goal. **Sensory modality preference** refers to differences in relative reliance on kinesthetic, visual, or auditory senses for receiving, processing, expressing, and remembering information. Do you need to see an unfamiliar name written in order to comprehend and remember it, or do you have to hear it? Or do you have to write it out or trace it?

- **Health and nutrition**, the biophysiological status of the individual, has an important effect on education, influencing attention, energy levels, and school attendance and consequent availability for instruction.
- **Environmental press** refers to what living and nonliving influences can do to and for the subject, in this case the human learner. It appears that the social and personal dimension may be salient to learning.

Emerging Role of the Teacher

Dick and Carey (1978, 4) suggest an augmented role for teachers in the instructional process:

It is our thesis that the primary role of the teacher is that of designer of instruction, with accompanying roles of implementor and evaluator of instruction.... If education is to meet the needs of individual students through provision of appropriate knowledge and training in important skills, there must be increased dependence upon well-designed, effective instruction. Teacher-dependent, group-paced instruction can no longer serve as the primary model for the teacher. Conversely, teachers have been, are, and will continue to be designers of at least some of their own instructional materials. Some of the best teachers have been doing this intuitively for years. However, it will become more important for teachers to have technical skills that will enable them to design *and* implement instruction in the classroom. In addition, they must be prepared to make wise decisions about the selection of materials developed elsewhere. Knowledge of instructional design techniques will greatly enhance each teacher's ability to select such materials wisely. Certainly, not all instruction will (or should) be based totally on the use of instructional materials.

There is a reduced need for the teacher to disseminate information. Obviously, the teacher must be concerned with the act of teaching. The expanded role includes monitoring the progress of students using individualized materials, tutoring and counseling students, conducting small-group discussions, assisting with special projects, and, when necessary, presenting major topics to an entire class. The teacher must also act as evaluator—not only of student success in the learning process, but also of the instructional process itself. Did the instruction work? For which students and to what extent? What components of the instruction failed? What aspects could be improved? Teachers should answer these questions systematically and use their answers to redesign the instruction for future use.

While the skills of implementation and evaluation of instruction are crucial to the teacher, an equally critical skill is that of instructional design. Principles that have been successfully applied by professional instructional designers can prove equally valuable to the instructor. One can apply them to the design of instruction or to the selection or modification of existing materials.*

Teaching Strategies

Just as adaptive instruction takes many forms, so do teaching strategies themselves vary widely. We will therefore provide an advance organizer by indicating what strategies we will discuss in this section: advance organizers, modes of representation, didactic instruction, discovery learning, and finally, tacit learning.

Advance Organizer

An **advance organizer** is introduced in advance of new learning tasks. When designing the advance organizer, take into account concepts (ideas) already existing in the cognitive structure of the learner. Advance organizers should be at a level more abstract, general, and inclusive than the material to be learned. They provide "ideational scaffolding" and a meaningful context for new learning.

The type of advance organizer to use depends on the learner's familiarity with the material to be learned. It is best to use an *expository* advance organizer when the material is completely new to the learner. A *comparative* organizer may be used when material to be learned is familiar or relatable to previously learned ideas. In either case, the short verbal or pictorial introduction helps the learner to construct a structure, a schema, for assimilating the new material.

Modes of Presentation

There are three basic modes for representing knowledge: *concretely, pictorially,* and with *symbols.* The concrete mode (*enactive,* in Piaget's language) involves hands-on experience. Objects for counting, field trips, laboratory experiments, and interactive learning simulations such as producing and acting in a stage play are examples of instructional activities in the concrete mode. This is the least abstract level of representation.

Pictures (*iconic representation,* for Piaget) bring a higher level of abstraction to the instructional setting. The more closely the image re-

---

*From *The Systematic Design of Instruction* by W. Dick and R. Carey. Copyright © 1978 by Scott, Foresman and Company. Reprinted by permission.

sembles the real world, the less abstract it is.

Symbols—oral and written words, mathematical symbols, scientific symbols—are the most abstract mode for representing material to be learned. You may see this level referred to as the "symbolic" level, but since all three modes are symbolic in that they are representational, we use the term "symbols mode."

It is important to consider using a combination of modes as you design instruction. For example, if you are teaching addition with renaming using an abacus, a place value chart, counting boards (see Reisman 1981), or counting sticks you might record the addition algorithm step by step. The learner would thus see the connection of the concrete activity to the end goal—the algorithm. Similarly, graphing with paper and pencil or on a computer might facilitate understanding of equations and formulae.

It is also important that you test in all three modes. Too often teachers diligently teach at all levels of representation and then test students only at the symbols level. The meshing of teaching and testing is particularly important for younger children.

Didactic Instruction

Didactic instruction is best exemplified by the lecture method, an approach particularly appropriate for delivering a great deal of information quickly. However, the nature of the content to be learned should be considered. Didactic instruction does not support instructional goals that seek to engage the learner in higher order reasoning, problem solving, or creative thinking. Didactic instruction is often referred to as expository and is used for recall, comprehension, and application tasks (see chap. 4).

Discovery Learning

Instruction designed to foster **discovery learning** focuses more on thought processes than on acquisition of data. Discovery learning is appropriate for tasks of analysis, synthesis, and evaluation, described in chapter 4. Feuerstein (1980) refers to this kind of learning as **mediated learning**, defined as

> the way in which stimuli emitted by the environment are transformed by a "mediating" agent, usually a parent, sibling, or other caregiver. This mediating agent, guided by his intentions, culture, and emotional investment, selects and organizes the world of stimuli for the child. The mediator selects stimuli that are most appropriate and then frames, filters, and schedules them; he determines the appearance or disappearance of certain stimuli and ignores others. Through this process of mediation, the cognitive structure of the child is affected. The child acquires behavior patterns and learning sets, which in turn become important ingredients of his capacity to become modified through direct exposure to stimuli.

Feuerstein argues that mediated experience is universal and is crucial in a child's cognitive development.

Tacit Learning

Tacit knowledge is "knowledge that usually is not openly expressed or stated" (*Oxford English Dictionary,* s.v. "tacit"). Sternberg and Wagner (1986) define tacit learning as "knowledge ... typically not directly taught or spoken about, in contrast to knowledge taught in classrooms."

A practical application of tacit knowledge occurs when an elementary school child sizes up and learns the ways of a classroom quickly and accurately and is therefore able to satisfy the teacher's expectations.

Current Instructional Programs

The following are programs currently being refined and evaluated that include instructional strategies for elementary age students. They are presented for your information and as topics for further study. Detailed descriptions of these instructional programs are presented by Segal, Chipman, and Glaser (1985) and Chipman, Segal, and Glaser (1985).

1. The *Instrumental Enrichment Program*, developed by Feuerstein (1980), is designed to help low socioeconomic status (SES) adolescents to function more effectively in school.
2. The *Philosophy for Children Program*, developed by Lipman (1985), focuses not only on teaching children how to think more effectively but also on fostering and valuing effective thinking.
3. The program entitled *Matrix Outlining and Analysis (MOAN)* (Amiran, Jones, and Fridell 1980; Jones, Amiran, and Katims 1985) teaches a new system of outlining using matrices as devices for remembering, analyzing, and reporting on comparative information.
4. The *Chicago Mastery Learning Reading Program with Learning Strategies (CMLR/LS)* is a set of reading strategies to be used in conjunction with a basal reader for grades K–8, developed by the Chicago Public Schools (Chicago Board of Education 1980).
5. Herber's (1978, 1985) *Teaching Reading in the Content Areas* is an instructional program for teaching reading and thinking skills as an integrated part of the various academic subjects.
6. Edward deBono's (1969, 1970, 1976, 1985) *CoRT Thinking Program* is based on deBono's ideas about the importance of perception in thinking. The learner constructs a representation of elements in a thinking situation and then applies logical processes to reach conclusions about the thinking situation.
7. The *Productive Thinking Program* (Covington, Crutchfield, Davies, and Olton 1974) is a course in learning to think for students in the upper elementary grades. The program comprises a series of complex problems for students to solve, requiring techniques for generating new ideas, techniques for discovering and formulating problems, and techniques for restructuring problem solving when previous strategies are not working.

Thought Activity

1. How do advance organizers of a comparative nature relate to the Piagetian notion of adaptation?
2. Tell where you believe computing falls within the three modes of representing curriculum to be learned. Is it a new level? Is it a combination of two?
3. Cover the grid that follows and do not look at it until you have followed these directions. Construct a 3 × 3 matrix and write the three modes of representing material to be learned along each of the two axes. Let the horizontal axis represent the mode(s) in which you will deliver a lesson; label this *Teaching Modes*. Let the vertical axis represent the mode(s) in which you will test to see if your students can demonstrate what you wanted them to learn. Label this axis *Testing Modes*. Mark cells within the grid that you will use to guide your design of instruction and testing activities (each cell represents the combination of a mode of teaching with a mode of testing).
4. Now look at the grid below. Did you construct yours the same way from the written directions? Which approach to communicating our directions was easier for you: written or graphic? What conclusions for representing tasks do you draw from your preference?
5. What might some appropriate instructional goals be for each of the filled-in cells in the teaching testing grid below? Select objectives from the variety of subjects an elementary teacher is responsible for teaching.

Teaching Modes

	Concrete	Pictures	Symbols	
Concrete	•			Testing
Pictures	••			Modes
Symbols		•••	••••	

6. Analyze a task you might teach to an elementary school student and see if you discover a better way of presenting the lesson. For example, you might select a task that teaches the following instructional objective: To sequence thoughts into a logical, interesting one-page story.
7. Using insights from the section in this chapter on characteristics of learning tasks, discuss the success or failure of a lesson you taught.
8. Write a list of components of your emerging nature as a teacher. As a guide for your thinking, use information from the section "Tools for the Teacher's Trade."

9. Select one of the instructional programs listed at the end of this chapter and research the instructional strategies employed. Compare information obtained with a peer who has studied the same program.
10. Compare the instructional strategies used in listed programs. Discuss similarities and differences with teachers and peers to decide which strategies will help you based on the characteristics of your students.

References

Amiran, M. R., B. F. Jones, and R. Fridell. 1980. *Matrix outlining and analysis.* Unpublished instructional materials. (Available from Beau Jones, Department of Curriculum, Chicago Public Schools, 1819 W. Pershing Rd., Chicago, Ill. 60609.)

Bangert, R. L., J. A. Kulik, and C. C. Kulik. 1983. Individualized systems of instruction in secondary schools. *Review of Educational Research* 53 (Summer): 143–58.

Berliner, D. 1985. Critique of the ALEM model. In *Adapting instruction to individual differences*, edited by M. C. Wang and H. J. Walberg. Berkeley, Calif.: McCutchan.

Bloom, B. F. 1971. Mastery learning. In *Mastery learning: Theory and practice*, edited by J. H. Block. New York: Holt, Rinehart & Winston.

Brown, A. L. 1980. Metacognitive development and reading. In *Theoretical issues in reading comprehension*, edited by R. J. Spiro, B. C. Bruce, and W. F. Brewer. Hillsdale, N.J.: Lawrence Erlbaum Associates.

Chicago Board of Education. 1980. *Chicago mastery learning reading program.* Chicago: Author.

Chipman, S. F., and J. W. Segal. 1985. Higher cognitive goals for education: An introduction. In *Thinking and learning skills.* Vol. 1, *Relating instruction to research*, edited by J. W. Segal, S. F. Chipman, and R. Glaser, 1–19. Hillsdale, N.J.: Lawrence Erlbaum Associates.

Chipman, S. F., J. W. Segal, and R. Glaser. 1985. *Thinking and learning skills.* Vol. 2, *Research and open questions.* Hillsdale, N.J.: Lawrence Erlbaum Associates.

Covington, M. V. 1985. Strategic thinking and the fear of failure. In *Thinking and learning skills.* Vol. 1, *Relating instruction to research*, edited by J. W. Segal, S. F. Chipman, and R. Glaser, 389–416. Hillsdale, N.J.: Lawrence Erlbaum Associates.

Covington, M. V., R. S. Crutchfield, L. B. Davies, and R. M. Olton. 1974. *The productive Thinking Program: A course in learning to think.* Columbus, Ohio: Charles E. Merrill.

deBono, E. 1969. *The mechanism of mind.* New York: Simon & Schuster.

deBono, E. 1970. *Lateral thinking.* New York: Harper & Row.

deBono, E. 1976. *Teaching thinking.* London: Temple Smith.

deBono, E. 1985. The CoRT Thinking Program. In *Thinking and learning skills.* Vol. 1, *Relating instruction to research*, edited by J. W. Segal, S. F. Chipman, and R. Glaser, 363–88. Hillsdale, N.J.: Lawrence Erlbaum Associates.

Dick, W., and L. Carey. 1978. *The systematic design of instruction.* Glenview, Ill.: Scott, Foresman.

Feuerstein, R. 1980. *Instrumental enrichment, an intervention program for structural cognitive modifiability.* Baltimore: University Park Press.

Feuerstein, R., M. B. Hoffman, R. J. Mogens, and Y. Rand, 1985. Instrumental enrichment, an intervention program for structural cognitive modifiability: Theory and practice. In *Thinking and learning skills.* Vol. 1, *Relating instruction to research*, edited by J. W. Segal, S. F. Chipman, and R. Glaser, 43–82. Hillsdale, N.J.: Lawrence Erlbaum Associates.

Glaser, R. 1977. *Adaptive education: Individual diversity and learning.* New York: Holt, Rinehart, & Winston.

———. 1983. *Education and thinking: The role of knowledge.* Pittsburgh: Learning Research and Development Center, Univ. of Pittsburgh.

———. 1985. Learning and instruction: A letter for a time capsule. In *Thinking and learning skills.* Vol. 2, *Research and open questions*, edited by S. F. Chipman, J. W. Segal, and R. Glaser, 609–618. Hillsdale, N.J.: Lawrence Erlbaum Associates.

Gordon, E. W., L. DeStefano, and S. Shipman. 1985. Characteristics of learning persons and the adaptation of learning environments. In *Adapting instruction to individual differences*, edited by M. C. Wang and H. J. Walberg, 55–59. Berkeley, Calif.: McCutchan.

Grinder, R. E., and E. A. Nelsen. 1985. Individualized instruction in American pedagogy: The saga of an educational ideology and a practice in the making. In *Adapting instruction to individual differences*, edited by M. C. Wang and H. J. Walberg, 24–43. Berkeley, Calif.: McCutchan.

Herber, H. L. 1978. *Teaching reading in the content area.* Englewood Cliffs, N.J.: Prentice-Hall.

Herber, H. L. 1985. Developing reading and thinking skills in content areas. In *Thinking and learning skills.* Vol. 1, *Relating instruction to research*, edited by J. W. Segal, S. F. Chipman, and R. Glaser, 297–316. Hillsdale, N.J.: Lawrence Erlbaum Associates.

Jensen, A. R. 1980. *Bias in mental testing.* New York: Free Press.

Jones, B. F., M. Amiran, and M. Katims. 1985. Teaching cognitive strategies within language arts programs. In *Thinking and learning skills.* Vol. 1, *Relating instruction to research*, edited by J. W. Segal, S. F. Chipman, and R. Glaser, 259–95. Hillsdale, N.J.: Lawrence Erlbaum Associates.

Lipman, M. 1985. Thinking skills fostered by philosophy for children. In *Thinking and learning skills.* Vol. 1, *Relating instruction to research*, edited by J. W. Segal, S. F. Chipman, and R. Glaser, 83–108. Hillsdale, N.J.: Lawrence Erlbaum Associates.

Mercer, J. R. 1973. *Labeling the mentally retarded: Clinical and social system perspectives on mental retardation.* Berkeley, Calif.: Univ. of California Press.

Reisman, F. 1971. Children's errors in telling time and a recommended teaching sequence. *The Arithmetic Teacher* 18: 152–55.

Reisman, F. 1981. *Teaching mathematics: Methods and content.* 2d ed. Boston: Houghton Mifflin.

Reisman, F. 1982. *A guide to the diagnostic teaching of arithmetic.* 3d ed. Columbus, Ohio: Charles E. Merrill.

Reisman, F., and S. H. Kauffman. 1980. *Teaching mathematics to children with special needs.* Columbus, Ohio: Charles E. Merrill.

Segal, J. W., S. F. Chipman, and R. Glaser, eds. 1985. *Thinking and learning skills.* Vol. 1, *Relating instruction to research.* Hillsdale, N.J.: Lawrence Erlbaum Associates.

Sternberg, R. J., and R. K. Wagner, eds. 1986. *Practical intelligence: Nature and origins of competence in the everyday world*. Cambridge: Cambridge Univ.

Walberg, H. J. 1985. Instructional theories and research evidence. In *Adapting instruction to individual differences*, edited by M. C. Wang and H. J. Walberg, 3–23. Berkeley, Calif.: McCutchan.

Wang, M. C., and M. C. Lindvall. 1984. Individual differences and school learning environments: Theory, research, and design. In *Review of research in education*, vol. 2, edited by E. W. Gordon. Washington, D.C.: American Educational Research Association.

Wilson, J. W. 1982. Foreword. *A guide to the diagnostic teaching of arithmetic*. 3d ed. Columbus, Ohio: Charles E. Merrill.

Wolf, R. 1966. The measurement of environments. In *Testing problems in perspective*, edited by A. Anastasi. Washington, D.C.: American Council on Education.

7 *Integrating computing into elementary school instruction*

Teacher programs that purport to facilitate integration of computing into elementary school instruction often inhibit this effort. Courses and workshops in computer education or computer literacy often focus on the wrong thing, teaching about the computer itself rather than how to use it as a tool in a learning situation.

The computer should be an invisible instructional tool, so integrated into the task for which it is being used that it is hardly noticeable. One uses a pencil without much thought of holding it or of moving it. A food processor or blender is invisible in the same sense as a pencil. A hairbrush is a useful tool that does not require analysis of its parts or how to pick it up to use it. How many people that you know have had courses in Pencil Education or Blender Education or Hairbrush Literacy?

Blocks to Integrating Computing into Education

Problems in introducing teachers to computing occur at both the **preservice** and **inservice** levels. Giannelli (1985) has specific sugges-

Teachers in computer lab help each other.

tions for making the introduction. These suggestions can serve as guidelines for what both preservice and inservice teachers should expect from courses or workshops on introductory computing in instruction. Giannelli's suggestions are as follows:

Much of teacher reluctance to get involved with computers can be traced to two factors: ignorance and fear. The fear of making a fool of oneself is a major obstacle in accepting computers into the classroom. . . . Instructors spent a lot of time on *programming* and no time explaining the concept of software. The following do's and don'ts may help . . . to convince the uninitiated to give the micros a chance.

What to Do

For most teachers, extensive computer use in the classroom will involve *using software*, not programming. . . . Discuss how teachers can find out about software that is geared toward their specific needs. Keep in mind that the average classroom teacher doesn't have the time . . . to keep abreast of developments in the field.

Bring in actual software and demonstrate it. Good software will sell itself.

Get everyone to take a turn at using the software that is being demonstrated. The teacher who actually loads the software and plays with the keyboard will feel that much more comfortable using the micro and that much more willing to try the micro in the classroom.

Find out what software and peripherals would appeal to which teachers. The art teacher may not be terribly impressed with the physics program that figures out projectile angles, but a demonstration of the graphics possibilities for a drawing class would be sure to win another convert.

Circulate reviews and lists of software available for your school's machines. Keep staff members up to date on programs and possibilities for the school's micros.

What Not to Do

Do not spend inservice time on programming. Most teachers will never have to program the machine, and programming "mumbo jumbo" will only scare off the technophobes who are convinced that all this "computer stuff" is too hard and too technical.

Do not discuss machines that the school doesn't own. Let the staff get comfortable using the equipment at hand. Once they get past their fear of the unknown, you can hold workshops on the possibilities additional hardware would provide.*

Bork (1984) discusses the following problems inhibiting a more rapid infusion of computing into education:

We are at a critical moment in human history. We are beginning a fundamental change in the way people learn; one of the few such changes that has occurred in all of recorded history. This change is based on modern computer technology. The change is likely to occupy primarily the next quarter century. At that point we will have a very different educational system than we have at the present time.

While the computer itself has the potential for improving education, in many ways its use is already proving to be poor, even a diaster. The critical aspect is not the computer itself, but how we choose to use the computer in education in our society during the next quarter century.†

Bork points out that rapidly developing technology has brought rapid but shallow commercial involvement. He predicts "near-zero cost hardware" and projects that now-inadequate capabilities, such as graphics, will also improve greatly. Bork notes that we now have a wide range of companies selling computer materials, including books, computer

---

*From Gary Giannelli, "Prompting Computer Use in the Classroom," *Educational Technology* (April 1985): 30–31. Reprinted by permission of the publisher.
†This and the three following extracts are from Alfred Bork, "The Computer in Education in the United States," *Computer Education* 8(4) (1984): 335–41. Reprinted by permission.

tools, and computer-based learning programs. However, he questions the quality of the material being marketed:

> ... the quality of the material that we are getting from the commercial sources is, as a whole, appalling. While some decent products have been published, the standards for commercially available computer modules are extremely low. Companies that would never dream of publishing material of this quality in textbooks, are gleefully doing it with computers.... Reviews are of little help, because of the quality of the reviews; few reviewers have adequate standards.

Bork calls for a more comprehensive curriculum effort to develop better software for schools. He points out the paucity of first rate computer-related curriculum material with the following example:

> Word processing has the capability to improve the way students write, starting from the earliest childhood and going the entire educational system. Yet the average teacher, given computers and word processing software, is not likely to make very effective use of the computer in education as an aid in improving writing. This teacher needs a whole set of curriculum material, *e.g.*, auxiliary material ... for pre-writing and post-writing activities. We *know* something about how to teach writing without computers, thanks to the success of the Bay Area Writing Project and other similar projects. We could use these same capabilities even more effectively on the computer and make them much more widely available. But no such curriculum effort has been made.

Lack of Teacher Knowledge about Computers

One major problem in integrating computing into schools is the lack of computer training in the teacher preparation programs of those teachers now in the workforce. Another is the discrepancy between current programming instruction and former instruction using BASIC. Bork (1984) discusses these issues as follows:

> Almost every teacher currently teaching in the United States was trained before computers were widely used in the classroom. Even today, *very* few schools of education have adequate programs in this direction.
> ... Furthermore, a growing discrepancy exists in how programming is taught in first rate computer science departments and how programming is taught in high schools. The distinction is a critical one. Many high schools are teaching programming tactics which are now regarded professionally as highly inadequate. Unfortunately, it is very difficult to get rid of these tactics because, as the student's first language, they become fundamental habits, difficult to change. The major culprit, but not the only one, is BASIC. We should immediately discourage the teaching of BASIC to any student at any particular level. Arguments for BASIC, fundamentally "junk food" arguments, suggest one should start babies on junk food because there is a lot of it around, and besides if you pick it carefully, it might turn out to be nutritional. Although this may be a parody, it is close to what is being argued for BASIC.

Research on Integrating Computers into Schools

Beall and Harty (1984) have investigated teachers' reactions to implementing microcomputers in elementary science and mathematics classes. They compared teachers participating in computing workshops to others not engaged in professional development activities who were not at the time concerned about microcomputer use. To gather their information, Beall and Harty developed a study-specific instrument, the "Inservice Teacher Microcomputer Implementation Proneness Scale," to tap the following nine dimensions:

1. disposition toward ideas/programs concerning microcomputers use,
2. willingness to try microcomputers knowing the extra work involved,
3. willingness to try microcomputers knowing the additional costs,
4. consideration of specific student microcomputer needs,
5. willingness to assist in developing a microcomputer implementation plan of action,
6. perceived sufficient freedom and professional respect to fulfill leadership roles for microcomputer implementation efforts,
7. persistence and diplomacy in sticking with new ideas,
8. keeping abreast of latest changes in computer assisted instruction and potential impact of microcomputers, and
9. interest in instructional experimentation with microcomputers.*

They conclude that much work remains in designing teacher education to bring about implementation of computing in elementary school classrooms. They also summarize conclusions from other relevant studies:

Cohen (1979) noted that inservice elementary teachers possessed fears about microcomputers and other current instructional technology systems, and recommended that inservice training and educational experiences with microcomputers begin with their points of view as starting points for professional development. Cohen also reported that teachers may not greet classroom computers with open arms. Many inservice teachers' conceptions of electronic technology are based on myths which have to be understood, clarified and changed. Cohen further reported that subtle feelings of intimidation and "math anxiety" by the computer literacy and programming processes can curb enthusiasm and interest in a microcomputer implementation effort. A degree of maturity and confidence is needed to be a facilitative teacher who does not have all of the answers, background, experiences or skills, but rather encourages student interest and special abilities and engages in the process with students.

The results of Cohen's study indicate that growing perceptions of competence among teachers have an influence on their microcomputer implementation prone-

---

*This and the following extract are from Dwight Beall and Harold Harty, "Inservice Teacher Reactions to Implementing Microcomputers in Elementary Science and Mathematics Classes," *Journal of Computers in Mathematics and Science Teaching* (Summer 1984), 34-38. Reprinted by permission of the Association of Computers in Math and Science Learning.

ness in a positive direction as well as increasing their interest in and enthusiasm for improving mathematics and science instruction through the use of microcomputers. High estimates of potential effectiveness with microcomputer-generated instruction by teachers may depend upon more than increased perceptions of competence. In fact, stability of enthusiasm and interest in delivering mathematics and science instruction by way of microcomputers can waver even while perceived competence levels steadily increase. Immersion in "real" science and mathematics classroom experiences with elementary school youngsters appears to be the teaching ground for enduring enthusiasm, interest and implementation proneness.

Carlstrom (1980) found that the key to accepting microcomputers in the elementary school was teacher and pupil enthusiasm where youngsters appeared to be learning more and enjoyed what they were learning.

Saunders (1978) asserted that the key to getting microcomputers into the classroom is generating interest among inservice teachers: once excited about the potentials of the approach, teachers will become innovative and will be willing to work a little more and prepare themselves by way of their own initiatives and professional development activities.

The results of these studies provide suggestions for those leading the effort to implement microcomputers in mathematics and science classrooms. The studies indicate that at least a segment of the elementary school teacher population supports widespread use of microcomputers. Questions still to be addressed are listed by Beall and Harty (1984) as follows:

1. What are the day-to-day concerns of elementary teachers who are implementing microcomputers into their math and science instruction?
2. What factors influence the infusion of microcomputers into the ongoing science and math programs?
3. Do concerns vary among teachers with different amounts and types of experiences with microcomputer classroom use?
4. How do teachers serve as effective role models for students who are using microcomputers?

Research on Expectations about Computers in Education

In many instances computers are being introduced into schools before their most effective uses have been determined. Little up-to-date information is available about how schools are employing computers or what uses educators and community members favor. Research into these questions was conducted by the Center for the Study of Computers in Education at the Cleveland State University, College of Education (Schuttenberg, McArdle, and Kaczala 1985). The study compared the expectations of parents, business leaders, and educators about computer use in the schools with their conceptions of what is actually being done. The educators surveyed were teachers, administrators, and nonteaching staff of sixteen school districts in the greater Cleveland area. The schools participating were of varying sizes, economic strata, and grade levels.

Parent surveys were distributed through PTA councils in the school districts. The business community was represented by executives from 80 of the 200 largest corporations in the greater Cleveland area.

Six major uses of computers in schools and thirteen computer skills for students to master were identified. Results were described as follows:

Ways of Using Computers. In general, educators, parents, and business people agreed on how they expected the computer to be used. The use most widely accepted was as an aid to administrators for keeping student records. Almost as frequently, computers were expected to be used as an aid for drilling students in subject matter and as an aid to teachers for keeping student records. The next level of acceptance was given to use of computers for administrative word processing and as an aid to teaching new material. The last use, as an aid to teachers in determining instructional needs of students (instructional management), was identified by considerably fewer respondents.

For all items, perceptions of how computers are actually being used in the schools differed markedly from how people thought they should be used. Part of this difference may be accounted for by the large number of respondents who indicated that they did not have enough information to respond.

What Students Should Know. There was a spread among responses when the three levels of schools are considered separately. For example, the survey indicated that parents generally held higher expectations of what should be happening in *elementary* schools than did either teachers or business leaders, especially in skill areas. Most parents thought that elementary children should be able to understand basic computer terms and to use a computer keyboard, whereas only about half of the teachers and business leaders felt that this was important for elementary students. Fifty-five percent of the parents, as opposed to only 25 percent of the educators and 33 percent of the business leaders, felt that elementary students should be able to create a simple computer program.

This study's findings show that respondents believed it is essential that students learn to use computers. Respondents thought more should be done in the schools in computing applications than they believed was actually being done.

Computer-based Instructional Technology: Why Is Integration So Slow?

Given the advantages of computer-based instructional technology, why is this technology not widely adopted? Are there rational reasons for resisting the integration of computing into education?

Hurly and Hlynka (1984) address these questions in outlining some limitations of instructional technologies and the organizational implications of change:

over reliance on operant [e.g., Skinner reinforcement theory] as opposed to cognitive learning strategies [e.g., Piagetian theory];

teacher-centered instruction [instead of student-centered];

inappropriate and poor instructional design resulting in learner boredom and frustration;

creation of a technocratic, information-rich elite;

advancement of a purely scientific model of education at the expense of aesthetic, self-actualization and discovery models;

insufficient and poor quality courseware;

inadequate integration of CAI [computer-assisted instruction] into existing curriculum.

Hurly and Hlynka point out that "these and other considerations will have to be addressed if the voices of the pessimists are to be silenced." They ask further whether computer-based instruction can accomplish what sixty years of educational technology and audio-visual instruction have not, "a qualitative improvement and a transformation" of the instruction process.

House (1974, 251) regards educational technologies as "achieving the traditional goals of education more efficiently in educating more people at less cost." Davies (1981) distinguishes between *efficiency* and *effectiveness*. Efficiency is doing things right; effectiveness is doing the right things. Educational technology, he concludes, too often ignores the far more significant question of effectiveness.

Cost Issues

The attempt to achieve cost effectiveness through instructional technology imposes unrealistic limitations that undermine the change process (More and Hunt 1980). Teachers are led to believe that high quality courseware can be produced by individual teachers. In fact, according to industry experience, interdisciplinary specialist teams might need to invest three-hundred person-hours per hour of actual instruction.

A review of Scarborough College's experiment with televised lectures (Lee 1971, 1975) shows that cost effectiveness rather than a desire to improve instruction was the driving force.

A study by the Lincoln County School Board of Ontario (1973) suggests that innovation in an economy of scarcity is next to impossible. Adequate incentives for teachers must be available, including:

- opportunities for advancement
- increased authority
- special assignments
- release time and study leaves, as well as more conventional remuneration

Administrators are often unwilling to provide additional resources and incentives if the original rationale for introducing an instructional technology is to save money.

Publishers' Fears   Instructional technology that is expensive (e.g., television or computers) requires uniformity and stability of curriculum in order to be economical. Rapid changes in knowledge or curriculum reforms threaten this stability. As a result, prospective producers of quality courseware are slow to enter the market for fear of losing on their investment.

Although the design of microcomputer hardware has improved significantly, educational software has been low in quality. The preoccupation with media hardware and with the technology itself is partly responsible. However, the tendency of administrators to cut media before cutting faculty and staff during austerity periods (the University of Toronto eliminated its TV production unit in May 1983), and to allocate insufficient funds for software, has made education an unreliable market. Without a firm market, software publishers and talented authors often concentrate on more cost effective efforts.

Software Quality   Since the application of computing to classroom use is still emerging, software developers may show great interest and knowledge about computers, the hardware, and programming. However, few demonstrate indepth knowledge of learning theory or experience in instructional design. Hurly and Hlynka (1984) compare results for CAI to date with those for programmed instruction (PI) in the fifties. They report that as the quantity of PI packages increased, the quality rapidly decreased. Bombarded with unreliable products, educators ceased to use PI materials in their classrooms. Teachers told their administrators not to make further purchases. Does computer-based education face this same danger?

School Organization Issues   House (1974) points out difficulties of educational innovation in classrooms:

> Efforts to modernize education have also been frustrated by the "traditional" structure of the institution. Despite the large educational bureaucracy the teacher is relatively autonomous, there is little true quality control, and skills are learned largely through imitation. This is particularly the case in higher education. Without adequate role models to emulate, often with a peer group unsupportive of innovation and jealous of individual excellence, coupled with the individual burden to implement innovation, there is little support for the individual instructor to innovate.

House describes the model of innovation in schools as a top-down process which he terms "structural imperialism." But he cites an extensive study conducted in Wisconsin (Barrows, Klenke, and Heffernan 1979) that shows the actual power of the teacher in the change process:

> Principals generally make the decisions regarding innovation in the school, after such decisions are passed down to them. The Wisconsin study, among others, concluded that teachers ultimately hold the final say over the implementation

of an innovation because of their ability to subvert it in the classroom. Thus, while teachers may appear to acquiesce to the principal, when decisions are made they possess the real power.

Benefits of Educational Computing

The potential benefits of computer-based education and learning can be summarized as follows:

- equal opportunity of access to education for everyone
- an open, deschooled education environment
- flexibility of time and place of study
- access to vast amounts of information for everyone
- ability to locate and access desired information quickly
- ability to use the technology to process information
- ability for everyone to add to the information
- individualized pace and content of instruction
- lifelong learning will be promoted and assisted

These are admirable aims; it remains to be seen whether CAI can bring them about.

Becoming an Instructional Designer

Despite concerns about cost, software quality, and school organization, Chan and Korostoff (1984) note that teachers are becoming more and more involved in designing their own instructional materials, including computer software. Skills used in designing instruction include:

- planning and making choices
- selecting and sequencing components of a topic
- translating instructional objectives into teaching activities
- evaluating the effects of your instruction
- using corrective feedback for improving the instruction

(See chap. 6 for more on becoming an instructional designer.)

Team Designing of Instructional Software

Chan and Korostoff (1984, 10) suggest that teachers can most easily design software as part of a team:

As an experienced teacher, you are a curriculum specialist in the subject area(s) you teach. Thus, you are in the best position to also design educational courseware since you know how students learn—as well as what they need to learn. For these reasons, you should become involved in designing educational courseware even if you don't know how to write computer programs. You can always team up with a professional programmer once the design is in place. The design of a program is critical to its effectiveness for students and its usefulness to teachers.

These days students often know as much as or more than their teachers about computing. Therefore, it is becoming realistic for teachers to team with students who know the subject area and who can help to design appealing programs.

Identifying and sequencing instructional goals and objectives is crucial to designing software. Capstone or major objectives indicate instructional milestones in the sequence of a topic. Task analysis of a capstone objective allows you to identify gaps between major instructional objectives.

Components of Software Design

Chan and Korostoff (1984, 14–15) identify the following components of a software program:

Identification Data

1. your name
2. the starting date
3. the completion date
4. the approximate number of hours it took you to complete the project

Content

Subject and content area. Decide on the subject or content area.

A group of students works with a teacher in a computer environment.

Topic or skill. Within each subject, specific topics and/or skills need to be mastered. Courseware that teaches a transferable skill and fits in with most academic subjects will be very popular.

Instructional objective. The objective of your program should be clearly stated at the beginning of any collateral material, such as a study guide or teacher's manual, for the convenience of potential users (e.g., teachers and parents). The objective should also be stated in the courseware program itself to tell students what they are learning, why they are learning it, and how it will be useful to them. If the objective for a program cannot be expressed in one or two sentences, then it may not have been clearly thought through by the courseware designer and should be rewritten.

The Student Population

Grade level(s). The grade level should be clearly identified in the written literature and on the disk label.

Ability levels. The ability level should also be specified because one group of third grade students identified as gifted would have very different needs from another group of third graders requiring remedial work. Ability level must always be kept in mind when designing and selecting courseware.

Learning styles. Learners can interact with the computer through several sensory channels: visual, auditory, and kinesthetic. Thus children with different learning styles can find computers equally beneficial.

Comparison of Films and Software as Instructional Tools

Chan and Korostoff (1984, 11) compare films and software in instruction. They suggest that computer courseware should be used much as educational films are used in the classroom. For example, before a film is shown to students, teachers usually do the following:

1. preview the film
2. plan for its purposeful use to supplement, augment, or enrich their teaching
3. make sure it promotes the instructional objective(s)
4. provide students with a purpose for viewing the film by giving them points to look for
5. follow up the viewing with a discussion or other meaningful activity to get the most value from the time spent viewing the film.

The same steps should be followed for educational software programs. With the proper teacher support, good software can be useful educational tools. Software that successfully addresses teachers' instructional goals is still sadly lacking, however, and may not come into being unless teachers and computer programmers join in cooperative instructional design.

Thought Activity

1. The following ideas are from an editorial entitled "Computers in Education: Where Do We Go From Here?" published in *Educational Technology* (1985), a journal of technology in education. Discuss these statements with your peers in order to think about integrating computers as learning tools into your own teaching.
   a. Schools, by and large, have not purchased computers to teach students subject matter. The schools are treating computers as a social artifact.
   b. The innate conservatism of educators means that it will be exceedingly difficult to convince teachers to turn over some part of their role to computers.
   c. We have a grand opportunity to begin the truly hard work of building a firm foundation for computer usage in the schools. Now that there is less need to rush out and buy, buy, the schools can begin to digest what they have consumed so greedily.
2. The notion that media do not affect learning seems unbelievable when one considers the impact that moveable type and the printed page have had on education. Generally, however, the "no significant difference" findings prevail (Alderman 1978; McLennan and Reid 1964). In your opinion, why then are we continually confronted with proposals for large scale implementation of instructional technologies?
3. Rakow (1980) identifies four "audiovisual myths":
   a. that traditional methods of instruction are inherently bad;
   b. that instructional media are the remedy;
   c. that content conveyed using instructional media is of the greatest value to students;
   d. that traditional methods and instructional technology methods are mutually exclusive.

   Tell whether you agree and why in light of Rakow's argument:

   In the past 40 years countless instructional technologies have come and gone, and they continue to be implemented, despite the apparent myths and the "no significant difference" findings. Most of the earlier instructional technologies are either now forgotten (e.g., teaching machines) or are greatly diminished (e.g., programmed instruction, 16mm film, instructional TV). We are left wondering whether the volumes of educational research on media effectiveness have been studying the wrong things for the wrong reasons. Their lack of impact would indeed seem to suggest that the crucial issues regarding the use of instructional technology are independent of learning methods and content. These studies may be more instrumental in distracting the attention of teachers and instructors to classroom issues and thus away from the underlying political efficiency rationale motivating the automation of education.

4. Based on your experience, write a critique of the following statement (Cory 1980, 245):

> The history of educational technology is littered with the failure to integrate educational media into the traditional teaching environment of the classroom. Hundreds of research studies concerning the impact of instructional technology on the learning process have, at best, produced "no significant differences." The educational institution is depicted as a "traditional" organization which is extremely conservative and which divests large amounts of autonomy in the individual. In universities this status quo is maintained by the oldest guild system still in existence. These organizational characteristics, coupled with numerous other factors, have acted as a resilient barrier to educational reform, despite the attempts of innovators and government bureaucrats to increase the efficiency and the productivity of education.

5. Implementing computer-based instruction will require care, imagination, expertise, and perseverance. Comment on how you as a teacher can make a difference in light of the following statement (Cory 1980, 245):

> The newer technologies are failing to penetrate the American educational system. But the cries of frustration which echo with monotonous regularity around media convention halls seldom lead to any real diagnosis of failure.

6. Write about a personal experience with computers in an educational setting—high school, college, etc.

References

Alderman, D.L. 1978. *Evaluation of the TICCIT computer-assisted instruction system in the community college*. Princeton, N.J.: Educational Testing Center.

Barrows, L.K., W.H. Klenke, and J.J. Heffernan. 1979. The adoption of innovation in schools. Technical Report No. 529. Madison, Wis.; Wisconsin Research and Development Center for Individualized Schooling, Univ. of Wisconsin.

Beall, D., and H. Harty. 1984. Inservice teacher reactions to implementing microcomputers in elementary science and mathematics classes. *The Journal of Computers in Mathematics and Science Teaching* (Summer): 34–36.

Bork, A. 1984. The computer in education in the United States: The perspective from the educational technology center. *Computer Education* 8 (4): 335–41.

Carlstrom, G. 1980. Operating a microcomputer convinced me—and my second graders—to use it again . . . and again. *Teacher* 97: 54–55.

Chan, J.M.T., and M. Korostoff. *Teachers' guide to designing classroom software*. Beverly Hills: Sage Publications.

Cohen, M.R. 1979. Improving teachers' conceptions of computer-assisted instruction. *Educational Technology* 19: 32–33.

Cory, G.H. 1980. Television experience in other nations. In *Providing continuing education by media and technology*, edited by M.N. Chamberlain. San Francisco: Jossey-Bass.

Davies, I. 1981. *Instructional technique.* New York: McGraw-Hill.

Editorial. 1985. Computers in education: Where do we go from here? *Educational Technology* (Jan.): 6.

Giannelli, G. 1985. Prompting computer use in the classroom: The teacher is always the last to know. *Educational Technology* (April): 30–31.

Hewes, J.J. 1985. The writer's tool chest. *Macworld* (July): 46–50.

House, E.R. 1974. The politics of educational innovation. Berkeley, Calif.: McCutchan.

Hurly, P., and D. Hlynka. 1984. Prisoners of the cave: Can instructional technology improve education? *Computer Education* 8(4): 427–34.

Lee, J.A. 1971. *Test pattern: Instructional television at Scarborough College.* Toronto: Univ. of Toronto Press.

Lee, J.A. 1975. Mentors and monitors: Mass media in the Canadian classroom. In *Communication in Canadian society*, edited by B.J. Singer. Toronto: Copp Clark.

Lincoln County School Board. 1973. *Innovation and the classroom teacher.* St. Charles, Ont.: Lincoln County School Board.

McLennan, D.W., and J.C. Reid. 1964. *Abstracts of research on instructional television and film: An annotated bibliography.* Stanford: Institute for Communication Research, Univ. of Stanford.

More, D.M., and T.C. Hunt. 1980. The nature of resistance to the use of instructional media. *British Journal of Educational Technology*: 141–147.

Rakow, J. 1980. The audiovisual myth in America: Filling the cracks of educational technology. *Journal of Education* 162: 34–54.

Saunders, J. 1978. What are the real problems involved in getting computers in high schools? *Mathematics Teacher* 71: 443–47.

Schuttenberg, E.M., R.J. McArdle, and C.M. Kaczala. 1985. Computer uses in schools: Research on what is and what should be. *Educational Technology* (April): 19–22.

8 *Questions and classroom communication*

There is little doubt that questions play an important, even vital role in teaching. Mishler (1975), a sociolinguist, formulated an "exponential law of successive questioning" which reveals that the chances are two to one that at any given point during the day a teacher will ask a question. However, frequency is not enough: the questions must be good questions.

Effective questioning can accomplish several functions. For example, a teacher can identify students' strengths and weaknesses by probing for more detailed answers. The teacher may also serve as a model for students to develop their own questioning skills. Questioning is part of the problem solving process, especially when it helps one to avoid premature closure and to look at all angles of a situation. This chapter will focus on spoken questions in a variety of instructional settings, including regular classroom teaching, conferences, and interviews. Written textbook and examination questions are covered in chapter 11.

The importance of teacher questioning has long been recognized. Research on classroom questions, however, indicates that most teachers do not use effective questioning techniques, although they ask a tremendous number of questions. The following studies support these conclusions.

Frequency of Questions

1. A sample of elementary teachers was found to ask an average of 180 questions in a single science lesson (Moyer 1966).
2. A sample of primary grade teachers asked an average of 348 questions in a single day (Floyd 1960).
3. A sample of fifth grade teachers asked an average of 64 questions per thirty-minute social studies lesson (Schreiber 1967).
4. Four-fifths of school time is taken up with the teacher asking, answering, or reacting to questions (Stevens 1912).
5. A sample of elementary and secondary social studies teachers posed knowledge questions most often, at a rate of 1.5 per minute (Daines 1982).

Quality of Questions

1. Most teacher questions go unanswered or are answered by the teacher (Corey 1940).
2. Teachers' questions are often confusing, poorly worded, and poorly timed. In addition, teachers fail to call on slower students and nonvolunteers, fail to reword or redirect questions, waste time on unimportant details, and fail to probe incomplete responses (Morgan and Schreiber 1969).
3. Teachers too frequently repeat their questions or students' answers and often fail to give enough wait-time before requesting an answer (Borg et al. 1970).
4. Teachers show little tolerance in waiting for pupil replies. Typically, only one second passes between the end of a question posed by the teacher and the next verbal interaction (Rowe 1974).
5. While teachers do ask many questions during a typical day, an inordinate number, approximately 70 to 75 percent, of those questions require only simple recall of information and rote memorization (Ashner 1961; Bellock et al. 1966; Davis and Tinsley 1967; Floyd 1960; Gallagher 1965; Hoetker, 1968).
6. Teacher questions can bring a positive change in academic achievement (Boone 1971; Buggey 1972; Hunkins 1968; Kleinman 1964; Ladd and Anderson 1970; Wright and Nuthall 1970; Yost 1970).
7. When teachers ask analysis, synthesis, or evaluation questions, the chances are only about 50–50 that they will receive answers reflecting these levels of thinking (Mills et al. 1980).
8. Teacher-question student-recitation periods seldom lead to meaningful classroom discussion (Dillon 1982).

Classification of Questions

The pedagogical literature includes a variety of classification schemes and observation devices for questions. These classification systems can include convergent or divergent, concrete or abstract, real or self-created, computer-listed or computer-generated, interest-free or interest-loaded questions. They provide a conceptual framework, an objective way of looking at questions, and better balance the types of questions asked during lessons. Gall (1970), in a review of dozens of studies of classroom lessons, concludes that up to 80 percent of all questions asked by teachers stress facts and knowledge. Memorizing of information is sometimes desirable and useful, but questions requiring higher levels of cognitive processing are also desirable because they allow students to think more deeply, critically, and creatively. Too often the accumulation of information becomes the end product of education; teachers should balance questions that help pupils acquire information with questions asked to help them use the information.

Levels of Questions

In an effort to simplify and reduce repetitiveness, we have selected only two classification systems for discussion. One such system is Bloom's *Taxonomy* (1956). Chapter 4 discussed in detail the use of the Taxonomy for classifying educational objectives. Just as objectives can be classified according to the Taxonomy, so can questions. The second system to be discussed will allow us to classify questions according to direction—divergent or convergent.

Bloom's Taxonomy is a classification scheme that allows teachers to formulate classroom questions for each of the six levels in the cognitive domain. Developing questions at each level will ensure that teachers ask pupils for more than simple recall of facts, the purpose being to activate higher-order thought processes in children. Hunkins et al. (1982,

A broad range of questions improves instruction

256–260), in *Social Studies in the Elementary School*, provide many examples of questions in the various taxonomy levels:

Knowledge

What is the oldest democracy in the world?

How many years may an American President serve?

Comprehension

What is the meaning of the concept "cultural interpretation of resources"?

What can you infer from the data presented in the chart?

Application

Study the map that shows the topographic features of this region. Assume you are a demographer. Where would you expect the next major population growth to occur?

How would you resolve the conflict between pro-nuclear and anti-nuclear forces?

Analysis

From our discussion of prejudice, what are two basic feelings we get about people?

How does the information we have prove that waste is the main reason for shortage of resources?

Synthesis

What do you think about the need for alternative forms of energy?

Can you think of a plan for getting the community to become conservation-minded?

Evaluation

Which of the following statements are examples of facts and which are examples of opinions?

According to the arguments we've talked about here, what is the best thing a person could do in this case?

While there are advantages in classifying objectives into these six categories, in reality most teachers ask questions only at the lowest level of the Taxonomy. It might be useful, therefore, to reduce the six levels to only two, the lowest level and all those higher than the lowest. Lower-level questions correspond to the first level of Bloom's Taxonomy, knowledge, and require memorization and recall of factual information. The pupil is not asked to manipulate the information (i.e., rephrase, apply, analyze, synthesize, or evaluate), but merely to remember it just as it was learned.

Examples of Lower-Level Questions:

Who was the first President of the United States?

What is the name of this number?

What did the boy eat in the story we just read?

Where is the capital of our state?

When is your birthday?

Higher-level questions may be said to correspond to the remaining five levels of Bloom's Taxonomy: to comprehend, apply, analyze, synthesize, or evaluate information. Higher-level questions go beyond simple recall of previously learned information.

Examples of Higher-Level Questions:

How do dogs differ from horses? (comprehension)

Which of the following shows the commutative law? (application)
$$5 + 0 = 5 \quad 3 + 4 = 4 + 3 \quad (2 \times 3) \times 1 = 2 \times (3 \times 1)$$

What do you think the writer's purpose was in this paragraph? (analysis)

What do you get when you mix flour and water? (synthesis)

What are your solutions, using all the things we've studied? (evaluation)

This two-category scheme is useful in judging the appropriateness of questions and enables teachers to determine what percentage of their questions are at the higher levels of the Taxonomy.

Convergent versus Divergent Questions

Another popular classification system to aid in formulating questions distinguishes between questions that allow for many answers and those with just one correct answer or end result (Jacobsen et al. 1985).

Convergent questions ask pupils to move toward closure, to draw conclusions, or to recall facts. They always have a correct answer. Convergent questions are usually low-level, requiring recall or recognition of factual information. However, questions that require pupils to apply previously learned information and/or analyze a problem for the correct answer may also be considered convergent. An example of such a convergent question might be: "Could you please summarize the main idea of the paragraph?"

Divergent questions allow pupils to arrive at unique responses, with no single correct response required. Divergent questions generally require a higher-level response, allow for more creative and critical answers, and ask for new thinking. These questions encourage elaboration of previous ideas, drawing of implications, generation of new data and ideas, as well as spontaneity, originality, flexibility, and initiative (Aschner 1961). An example of a divergent question is, "How might the course of history been changed if Columbus had landed on the west coast rather than on the east coast?"

Following are some questions for you to classify as high- or low-level and divergent or convergent.

1. What year did the Civil War begin?
2. Which child is taller?
3. Can you think of a title for this story?
4. One of these pictures shows what happens when something is heated or becomes warm. Point to that picture.

5. Why is this poem better than the other one?
6. What were some factors that might have contributed to the war between the states?
7. What do you think Martin Luther King, Jr., meant by "we shall overcome?"
8. What is the area of a square whose sides measure 4 inches?
9. What is the main idea of this poem?
10. We have learned the definition of *adjective*. What are four examples of adjectives?
11. What might your life be like if you were born during the age of the dinosaur?
12. Who is your favorite President and why?
13. Where does the sun rise and set?
14. Does oil float on water?

Check your responses to questions 1 through 14:

1. Low-level/convergent.	This involves simple recall of previously learned information with one right answer.
2. High-level/convergent.	This is an application question; a single response is correct.
3. High-level/divergent.	The teacher has asked a synthesis question to which an infinite number of answers is possible.
4. High-level/convergent.	This is a high-level question for a pupil being asked this question for the first time; it has one right answer.
5. High-level/divergent.	The teacher asks the student for a personal evaluation; answers will vary.
6. High-level/divergent.	This is a comprehension question; there is more than one factor.
7. High-level/divergent.	This is a comprehension question with many possible answers.
8. High-level/convergent.	The teacher has asked an application question with only one correct answer.
9. High-level/convergent.	This involves more than memory, but there is only one right answer.
10. High-level convergent.	This is a comprehension question; examples would vary, but any answer is clearly identifiable as either right or wrong.
11. High-level/divergent.	This is a synthesis question with many possible answers.
12. High-level/divergent.	This is a high-level question with many possible answers.

13. Low-level/convergent.   This is a memorization recall task with only one correct answer.
14. Low-level/convergent.   This too requires recall of a single correct answer.

Suggestions for Improving Classroom Communication Wait-Time

Wait-time is the time that elapses between the end of a question and the ensuing response, whether from the teacher or the pupil. We have mentioned that teachers ask many questions but show little patience in waiting for pupils to respond to them. Rowe (1973) conducted extensive studies on the questioning behavior of teachers and pupils. She discovered that teachers waited an average of only one second for an answer before repeating or rephrasing the question, calling on another pupil, or asking another question. The effect of this "bombing rate" of questions is that pupils have very little time to think or to formulate their answers. To make matters worse, if a pupil manages to get a response in, the teacher reacts or asks another question in less than one second. Rowe also discusses a second wait-time, the amount of time that is potentially available after a student starts a response or after a response is concluded.

Rowe (1973, 281–283) found that when teachers learned to increase their wait-time from one second to three or more seconds after asking a question, the following occurred:

Effects on Pupils
1. The length of pupils' responses increased. Explanatory statements increased by 400 to 800 percent.
2. The number of unsolicited but appropriate responses by pupils increased.
3. Failures to respond decreased.
4. Confidence, as indicated by fewer reflected responses, increased, i.e., fewer responses had the tone of "Is that what you want?"
5. The incidence of speculative thinking increased.
6. Teacher-centered teaching decreased, and pupil-centered interaction increased.
7. The number of questions asked by pupils increased.
8. Pupils whom teachers rate as relatively slow learners offered more questions and more responses, from 1.5 percent to 37 percent.
9. The variety of responses increased. There was more reacting to each other, structuring of procedures, and soliciting. The increase was 700 percent.
10. Discipline problems decreased.

Rowe also found that once teachers changed their wait-time and their behavior stabilized over a period of time, their classroom behavior changed:

Effects on Teachers
1. Teachers became more flexible in their responses.
2. The number and kind of teacher questions changed. Teacher questions decreased because pupils' responses were longer and unsolicited, but appropriate responses increased.
3. Teachers increased the variety of their questions.
4. Teachers improved their expectations of performance for "slow" pupils.

Reinforcement

One common way of disrupting wait-time is through repetitive and indiscriminate use of reinforcement. Verbal and nonverbal reinforcement can be vital teaching tools for recognizing the achievement of pupils during individualized work or basic skills activities. However, some research results call into question the use of reinforcement for facilitating class discussions (Rowe 1974). In fact, rewarding pupils may produce less pupil participation.

Many teachers, in an effort to reduce their anxiety or gain time to formulate their next statement, immediately respond to a pupil's answer with, "good," "okay," or "that's right." This interference by the teacher does several things to inhibit classroom discussions. First, it stops other pupils from continuing with their thinking and their ideas. Second, pupils can become more extrinsically motivated, more interested in pleasing the teacher than in developing their own thinking. Third, the same two or three phrases used again and again to reinforce pupils eventually become meaningless and lose their reinforcing properties. Fourth, reinforcement administered too quickly and too often interferes with complete development of pupil ideas and interaction. Fifth, it increases teacher-to-student interactions and correspondingly decreases student-to-student interactions. Last, teacher reinforcement regardless of the appropriateness of the pupils' responses results in a sacrifice of critical thinking and accuracy.

We have noticed that preservice teachers often reward or ignore incorrect answers for fear of discouraging or alienating pupils. Teachers need to evaluate the work of pupils, and incorrect responses should not be ignored or reinforced. At the same time, teachers should not feel it necessary to comment each time a pupil chimes in or answers a question. A better practice would be to reinforce the pupil's participation and still indicate that her response was incorrect. Rather than immediately follow a pupil's response with "that's correct" or "okay," a teacher might show acceptance of the child and his ideas with a noncommittal statement, such as "That is one idea" or "That is interesting," or with a nonverbal indicator such as a smile or a nod of the head. A teacher then might continue to obtain other responses from pupils, and use their responses to refocus attention on the correct answer. Another way to respond to incorrect answers is by prompting or coaching; this technique will be discussed later in the chapter.

In summary, reinforcement for the purposes of increasing and improving classroom communication should be used cautiously. Reinforcement

Questions and Classroom Communication 133

Wait-time is important.

can decrease pupil interaction, interfere with pupil thinking, and become ineffectual.

Calling on Pupils If you have spent any time in the classroom you have probably discovered that teachers do not distribute their questions evenly among pupils. They ask many questions of a few students, no questions of some, and more to one race or sex than another. Teachers tend to direct most of their questions at their better pupils, and should guard against the habit of calling primarily on pupils they expect to give good answers. Rosenthal and Jacobson (1968) summarize the findings of teacher expectation research and conclude that teachers:

1. Call on brighter pupils more.
2. Ask harder questions of brighter pupils.
3. Give brighter pupils more time to respond.
4. Help brighter students formulate answers more.

Pupils are sensitive to teacher behavior and are certainly aware of and affected by a teacher's attitudes toward them. Self-awareness may be the crucial factor distinguishing a fair teacher from a biased one. Thus it is important that prospective teachers become aware of their attitudes, preferences, and biases early. Teachers should strive for balanced classroom interaction, giving each pupil a similar amount of attention.

A related issue is the teacher's choice of who will respond. Kounin (1970) has found that when a teacher calls a student's name and then asks a question, the rest of the class is likely to "tune out" the teacher-student interaction and shift its attention to other things. The same may happen if the teacher calls on pupils in alphabetical order or by the seating pattern of the classroom. The teacher should, therefore, make a practice of asking a question first and then naming a pupil to answer, and should switch at random from one side of the room to another.

There is some disagreement about the relative merits of voluntary and required responding. The practice of calling on "nonvolunteers" certainly requires pupils to pay attention or pay the price of being caught daydreaming. However, we probably all can recall the terror we felt when we did not know the answer to a question, had not raised our hand, and were called on anyway. Obviously, this practice does not go far to establish a relaxed atmosphere conducive to free expression. To encourage pupil participation, then, we recommend that teachers call only on pupils who indicate that they wish to respond.

Prompting

What happens when a teacher's question draws no answer or an incorrect one? Teachers often move on to another pupil, ask another question, provide the answer, or sometimes even reinforce an incorrect answer. Rather than respond in one of these inappropriate ways, the teacher should provide hints or clues that will guide the pupil to the correct answer. Do not simply repeat or rephrase the question, but provide additional bits of information to help the pupil find the correct answer. The following example illustrates a simple and concrete use of **prompting**:

Teacher: How do you spell *president*, David?
David: (pause) I don't know.
Teacher: Let's pronounce the word *president* together. (prompt)
David (in unison with the teacher): "Pres-i-dent."
Teacher: O.K. Now spell the first syllable, *pres*. (prompt)
David: "p-r-e-s."
Teacher: O.K. Now spell the second syllable, *i*. (prompt)
David: "i."
Teacher: O.K. Now spell the last syllable, *dent*. (prompt)
David: "d-e-n-t."
Teacher: Good. Now put all the syllables together and spell *President*.
David: "P-r-e-s-i-d-e-n-t."
Teacher: That's great, David.

Notice in our example that the teacher gives David small hints that point him in the right direction and allow him to answer the question.

Probing or Coaching

What should teachers do when pupils respond to questions with correct but insufficient answers? Teachers often receive partial answers, lacking sufficient depth to assure them that the pupil thoroughly understands the answer. By **probing,** teachers can encourage pupils to add to and improve their responses. The teacher presents no new information or ideas, but simply tries to help pupils justify or further explain their answers. The quality and depth of the discussion is thereby enhanced. The following teacher-pupil dialogue demonstrates probing:

Teacher: How was the Grand Canyon formed, Marge?
Marge: There is a river at the bottom of it?
Teacher: Can you be more specific? (probe)
Marge: Millions of years ago the river cut through the rock and made the Grand Canyon.
Teacher: Very good, Marge.

The probing technique allows the pupil to classify or elaborate upon a statement already made. The teacher in the example does not accept Marge's initial response but probes for more information about what the river had to do with the Grand Canyon. Probing questions require pupils to provide more justification, clarification, originality, and specificity in their responses.

The other extreme of **coaching** is exemplified by a computer program, ELIZA (1981). The ELIZA program simulates a psychotherapist, "mirroring" a client's conversation. For example, if a patient says, "I don't like baseball," the psychiatrist might respond, "I hear that you do not like baseball," or "Why do you feel that you do not like baseball?" and thus the probes begin. Turkle (1984, 16, 19) states that

computers are affecting how today's children think, influencing how they construct such concepts as animate and inanimate, conscious and not conscious.

A computer program is a reflection of its programmer's mind. If you're the one who wrote it, then working with it can mean getting to know yourself differently.

The purpose of questions, probes, prompts, and coaching is to understand what is going on inside the child's head and heart. Turning a naive learner into a clear communicator is a very complicated task, and few teachers are born with this skill. But it is a skill that can be learned, and the computer will be a catalyst, both as a tool for questioning and as a model for probing.

Redirection

Redirection is a questioning technique that increases pupil participation and thus improves student interaction. Redirection can take many forms. If the purpose is to increase the amount of pupil participation in a discussion, then the teacher simply directs a question that has many possible answers to several pupils in turn. The teacher need only ask the question once and then call on pupils one at a time for their responses. Redirecting the original question to several pupils eliminates domination of the discussion by one pupil, bringing in as many others as the teacher chooses. Redirecting a question changes a two-way interaction between the teacher and one pupil into a conversation among several pupils and the teacher. The result is more student participation and less teacher talk. The following is an example of redirection:

Teacher: Give me the name of a President, Pam?
Pam: Abraham Lincoln.
Teacher: And another, Hugh? (redirection)
Hugh: John Kennedy.
Teacher: Malinda? (redirection)
Malinda: Ronald Reagan.
Teacher: (Nods her head at Tom.) (redirection)
Tom: Dwight Eisenhower.

It important to note that in redirection the teacher (1) asks a question for which there are a variety of answers, and (2) redirects the original question by simply stating a pupil's name or looking or gesturing at a child. Student participation is thus increased and teacher talk decreased.

How to Increase Classroom Interaction

Belch (1975, 48–49) lists ten suggestions for improving the verbal questioning of all classroom teachers:*

1. Ask questions which require more than a "yes" or "no" response. While there are occasions when the classroom teacher can justify a question which calls for such a response, such questions fail to activate higher thought processes in children. Also, such questions encourage guessing and do little for developing expressive language in children.
2. Allow sufficient time for deliberating the question. Count to five by saying, "One thousand one, one thousand two," etc. This allows about one second for each numeral, so counting to five equals five seconds. The teacher who expects an immediate response to each question precludes the opportunity for thought and consideration on the part of the student. A period of thinking should occur with all questions whether they call for factual recall or involved situations.
3. Reword or restate questions when students fail to respond or respond incorrectly. Frequently, teachers view silence or incorrect responses as the

---

*From P. J. Belch, "The Question of Teachers' Questions," *Teaching Exceptional Children* 7 (1975): 46–50. Reprinted by permission.

fault of the students; they did not study or did not pay attention. Often, however, the problem may be the result of a poorly worded or poorly stated question.

4. Challenge student responses. Because a student gives the correct response does not mean you should acknowledge that response and proceed to the next question. Often children, especially those who are in special classes, are easily swayed and persuaded to change their response, even when it is correct. These "outer-directed" children should learn to realize that they can contribute correct responses and that they should have confidence in their responses.

5. Do not call the name of a student before you ask the question. When a certain child is designated for a specific question, other children may tune out, believing the question is not their responsibility. While there are times a teacher should direct a question to a certain child and call the name beforehand, the teacher might add something like, "Let's listen to Brenda and see if we agree with her answer."

6. Direct questions to all students, not just volunteers or the brighter ones. Selective questioning and directing of questions can help all pupils and will permit the less able pupils to contribute to the lessons or discussion.

7. Do not always accept the first response to the question, even if that response is correct. Always get mileage from your question. For example, a teacher asks for the capital of Pennsylvania and gets the response, "Harrisburg." Ask others if they agree with the response; involve students in evaluating the responses.

8. Try to sequence your questions. Be a benign interrogator. After asking for the capital of Pennsylvania (see #7 above), follow with questions such as, "Where is Harrisburg located on the map of Pennsylvania?" or "Why do you suppose Harrisburg was selected as the capital city?"

9. Avoid repeating your questions. Often pupils stall for more thinking time by asking the teacher to repeat the question. This willingness to repeat may encourage inattentiveness since these pupils will soon recognize that all they have to do is ask, and the teacher will repeat.

10. Avoid constant handwaving by the pupils. Often there are pupils who wave their hands furiously, whether they know the answer or not. Such behavior will often discourage the pupils who are not so quick in thought or recall. For example, suppose a teacher asks the pupils to compute a certain math problem and to signify their completion by handwaving. Once hands begin waving, slower pupils may become discouraged and discontinue working, thinking the teacher will, as often is the case, call upon the faster pupils. Allow adequate work time for all children and then select someone to give the answer.

Summary

Research on questioning provides evidence that higher-level questions do facilitate learning. In a statistical review of twenty studies on teachers' use of higher and lower cognitive questions, Redfield and Rousseau (1981) conclude that the use of higher cognitive questions enhances student achievement. In other words, a typical student in a class exposed to a lesson without higher-level questions could be expected to score at the 50th percentile. That same student could be expected to score at the 77th percentile if exposed to the same lesson with many higher-level questions added.

Nevertheless, lower-level questions are not all bad. In fact, factual questions are functional for lower-ability students (Rosenshine 1976; Brophy and Evertson 1976). They promote participation, provide experiences of success for students, and correlate positively with achievement.

The following six points will help you improve classroom communication through questioning.

1. Practice good wait-time after your questions and following the pupils' responses.
2. Don't interrupt; wait until pupils have completed their statement.
3. Give nonverbal signals, using eye contact, posture, and facial expression to show you are interested and listening.
4. Ask "What other ideas do you have?" so as to invite further response before you involve yourself in the discussion.
5. If pupils appear inattentive, redirect questions to them or ask them to respond to someone's statement.
6. Finally, formulate your questions in advance and write them down in plans. Preservice and novice teachers, especially, may find it difficult to formulate diverse kinds of questions while in the act of teaching.

Thought Activity

1. Using Bloom's cognitive domain taxonomy, formulate questions across the hierarchy for a lesson that you teach either in a classroom or to a peer in a simulation.
2. Tell the difference between convergent and divergent questions and give examples for each.
3. Discuss the importance of wait-time in instruction.
4. Discuss the importance of prompting as a questioning technique.
5. Differentiate among prompting, probing, coaching, and redirection.
6. Describe and give an example for each of Belch's ten suggestions for improving verbal questioning.
7. State the strengths and weaknesses of higher-level and lower-level questions and cite appropriate uses for each type.

References

Aschner, M. J. 1961. The language of teaching. In *Language concepts in education*, edited by B. O. Smith and R. H. Ennis. Chicago: Rand McNally.

Belch, P. J. 1974. An investigation of the effect of different questioning strategies on the reading comprehension scores of secondary level educable mentally retarded students. Unpublished doctoral dissertation, West Virginia Univ.

Belch, P. J. 1975. The question of teachers' questions. *Teaching Exceptional Children* 7: 46–50.

Bellock, A. A., H. M. Kliebard, R. T. Hyman, and F. L. Smith. 1966. *The language of the classroom*. New York: Teachers College Press, Columbia Univ.

Bloom, B. S., ed. 1956. *Taxonomy of educational objectives: The classification of educational goals, handbook I: Cognitive domain*. New York: David McKay.

Boone, S. M. 1971. An investigation of the effect of higher level questions on reading comprehension (doctoral dissertation, Univ. of Washington). Ann Arbor, Mich.: University Microfilms, No. 72-7322.

Borg, W. R., M. L. Kelley, P. Langer, and M. Gall. 1970. *The minicourse: A microteaching approach to teacher education*. Beverly Hills, Calif.: Macmillan Educational Services.

Brophy, J. E., and C. Evertson. 1976. *Learning from teaching: A developmental perspective*. Boston: Allyn & Bacon.

Brophy, J. E., and C. M. Evertson. 1979. *Process-product correlations in the Texas teacher effectiveness study*. Final Report No. 74-4. Austin: Research and Development Center for Teacher Education, Univ. of Texas.

Buggey, J. L. 1972. A study of the relationship of classroom questions and social studies achievement of second grade children. Paper presented at the meeting of the American Educational Research Association, Chicago, Ill. (ERIC Ed: 06 066-391).

Corey, S. M. 1940. The teachers out-talk the pupils. *The School Review* 48: 285-92.

Daines, D. 1982. Teachers' oral questions and subsequent verbal behavior of teachers and students. Provo, Utah: Brigham Young Univ. (EDRS/ERIC ED 225979).

Davis, O. L., and D. C. Tinsley. 1967. Cognitive objectives revealed by classroom questions asked by social studies student teachers. *Peabody Journal of Education* 45: 21-26.

Dillon, J. T. 1982. Do your questions promote or prevent thinking? *Learning* 11: 56-57, 59.

ELIZA (A Counseling Computer Program). 1981, March. Los Angeles, Calif.: Artificial Intelligence Research Group.

Floyd, W. D. 1960. An analysis of the oral questioning activity in selected primary classrooms (doctoral dissertation, Colorado State College). Ann Arbor, Mich.: University Microfilms, No. 60-6253.

Gall, M. D. 1970. The use of questions in maintaining attention to textual material. *Review of Educational Research* 40: 707-21.

Gallagher, J. J. 1965. Expressive thought by gifted children in the classroom. *Elementary English* 42: 559-68.

Hoetker, W. J. 1968. Analysis of the subject matter related verbal behavior of nine junior high English classes (doctoral dissertation, Washington Univ.) *Dissertation Abstracts International* XXVIII-A: 4000.

Hunkins, F. P. 1968. The influence of analysis and evaluation questions on achievement in sixth grade social studies. *Educational Leadership* 1: 326-32.

Hunkins, F. P., J. Jeter, and P. F. Maxley. 1982. *Social studies in the elementary school*. Columbus, Ohio: Charles E. Merrill.

Jacobsen, D., P. Eggen, D. Kauchak, and C. Dulaney. 1985. *Methods for teaching: A skills approach*. 2d ed. Columbus, Ohio: Charles E. Merrill.

Kleinman, G. 1964. General science teachers' questions, pupil and teacher behaviors, and pupils' understanding of science (doctoral dissertation, Univ. of Virginia). *Dissertation Abstracts International* XXV-A: 5753.

Kounin, J. 1970. *Discipline and group management in classrooms.* New York: Holt, Rinehart, & Winston.

Ladd, G. T., and H. O. Anderson. 1970. Determining the level of inquiry in teachers' questions. *Journal of Research in Science Teaching* 7: 395–400.

Mills, S.R., C.T. Rice, D.C. Berliner, and E.W. Rousseau. 1980. The correspondence between teacher questions and student answers in classroom discourse. *Journal of Experimental Education* 48: 194–209.

Mishler, E.G. 1975. Studies in dialogue and discourse: 1. An exponential law of successive questioning. *Language in Society* 4 (1): 31–51.

Morgan, J.C., and J.E. Schrieber. 1969. How to ask questions. *National Council for the Social Studies* (ERIC Ed: 033–887).

Moyer, J.R. 1966. An exploratory study of questioning in the instructional processes in selected elementary schools (doctoral dissertation, Columbia Univ.). Ann Arbor, Mich.: University Microfilms, No. 66-2661.

Redfield, D.L., and E.W. Rousseau. 1981. A meta-analysis of experimental research on teacher questioning behaviors. *Review of Educational Research* 51(2): 237–45.

Rosenshine, B. 1976. Classroom instruction. In *The Psychology of Teaching Methods*, edited by N. Gage. Seventy-fifth yearbook, National Society for the Study of Education.

Rosenthal, R., and L. Jacobson. 1968. *Pygmalion in the classroom.* New York: Holt, Rinehart & Winston.

Rowe, M.B. 1973. *Teaching science as continuous inquiry.* New York: McGraw-Hill.

Rowe, M.B. 1974. Wait time and rewards as instructional variables. Part one: wait time. *Journal of Research in Science Teaching* 11: 81–84.

Schreiber, J.E. 1967. Teachers' question asking techniques in social studies (doctoral dissertation, Univ. of Iowa). *Dissertation Abstracts International* XXVIII-A: 0523.

Stevens, R. 1912. *The question as a measure of efficiency in instruction: A critical study of classroom practice.* New York: Teachers College Contributions to Education.

Turkle, S. 1984. *The computer culture.* New York: Simon & Schuster.

Wright, C.J., and G. Nuthall. Relationships between teacher behaviors in three experimental elementary science lessons. *American Educational Research Journal* 7: 477–91.

Yost, M. 1970. *The effect on learning of post-instructional verbal responses to questions of different degrees of complexity.* Fort Lauderdale, Fla.: Nova Univ. (ERIC Ed: 045–39).

Part 2   *Assessment of Student Progress*

9 *Educational measurement, evaluation, and testing*

Test data can help us to improve both teaching and learning. The intelligent, thoughtful, and careful use of measurement and evaluation procedures is one of the most important things a teacher can do in the classroom. Information from students about their achievement can profoundly influence their instruction and learning.

Defining Terms

Common words often take on new and sometimes difficult meanings when used by specialists. Such is the case with the terms *test, measurement,* and *evaluation.* As commonly used, they are interchangeable. In an educational assessment situation, however, this can lead to confusion.

Under the umbrella category "assessment," **evaluation** is the most inclusive term. It describes a general process of making judgments and decisions. The data used in evaluation may be quantitative or qualitative.

A teacher may draw upon classroom exams, anecdotal materials, scores from standardized tests, and informal observations in deciding whether to promote a pupil.

Measurement, on the other hand, requires systematic collection, quantification (i.e., the assignment of numerals to represent things), and ordering of information. It implies both the process of quantification and the result. Measurement may take many forms, ranging from the application of elaborate and complex electronic devices to paper-and-pencil exams, rating scales, or checklists.

A **test** is a form of measurement. In current usage, it is a formal standardized procedure in which students know that they are being tested for a particular purpose at a specified time. A test might be defined as a systematic method of gathering data in order to make intra- or inter-individual comparisons. It is a sample of behavior.

Tests might further be categorized in various ways. **Mastery** tests are designed to assess basic knowledge and skills. Other kinds of tests include (1) **informal** (teacher-made) and **standardized** (specialist-made); (2) **oral** and **written**; (3) **survey** (of general achievement) and **diagnostic** (of specific categories or content; (4) **speed** (using items of approximately equal difficulty) and **power** (using items of increasing difficulty, with speed de-emphasized); and (5) **verbal** and **nonverbal** or **performance** (requiring manipulation of objects). Other classifications are possible, depending on the needs or philosophy of the developer

Instruction and evaluation may involve the same activity.

or user. Since mastery, survey, and diagnostic tests that are written have come to predominate, we will emphasize paper-and-pencil tests in this chapter.

The Importance of Measurement and Evaluation

Measurement and evaluation are integral to the instructional process. Progress toward instructional goals must be periodically evaluated if teaching and learning are to be effective. Educational objectives, learning experiences, and measurement or evaluation are intimately related. It is the interaction of these three elements in a well-planned program of education that promotes the desired changes in pupil behavior. The intimate relationship of instruction and assessment is outlined by Dressel (1954, 23–24); table 9.1 shows his listing of common objectives and parallel elements in teaching and evaluation.

Instruction and evaluation may be thought of as two sides of the same coin. In chapter 4, we discussed writing instructional objectives to guide instruction. A good look at an instructional objective reveals a clue for evaluation embedded in it. For example, in the following objectives for teaching geometric shapes, the evaluation can be deduced for three levels—manipulative, picture, and word, both oral and written.

Manipulative

Objective: To hand the teacher a given geometric shape.
Evaluation: Given four blocks—a cube, a triangle, a rectangle, and a sphere—ask the student to hand you the triangle.

Table 9.1
Dressel's Comparison of Teaching and Evaluation

1. Instruction is effective to the degree that it leads to desired changes in students.	1. Evaluation is effective to the degree that it provides evidence of the extent of changes in students.
2. New behavior patterns are best learned by students when the inadequacy of present behavior is understood and the new behavior patterns thereby made clear.	2. Evaluation is most conducive to learning when it provides for and encourages self-evaluation.
3. New behavior patterns can be more efficiently promoted by teachers who recognize the existing behavior patterns of individual students and the reasons for them.	3. Evaluation is conducive to good instruction when it reveals major types of inadequate behavior and the contributory causes.
4. Learning is encouraged by problems and activities that require thought and/or action by each individual student.	4. Evaluation is most significant in learning when it permits and encourages the exercise of individual initiative.
5. Activities that provide the basis for the teaching and learning of specified behavior are also the most suitable for evoking and evaluating the adequacy of that behavior.	5. Activities or exercises developed for the purpose of evaluating specified behavior are also useful in the teaching and learning of that behavior.

Picture

Objective: To point to a picture of a given shape.

Evaluation: Given a page with pictures of various shapes, ask the child to point to a triangle.

Written Word

Objective: To underline the name of a shape.

Evaluation: Given the words "square," "circle," "rectangle," and "triangle," ask the student to underline the word that names a pictured shape.

Oral Word

Objective: To state the names of given shapes.

Evaluation: Given a page of pictured shapes, ask the student to name each of the shapes.

Uses of Measurement and Evaluation Data

The results of measurement can help teachers (1) select and refine instructional objectives, (2) describe and report pupil achievement, and (3) design effective learning experiences.

1. *Selecting, Appraising, and Clarifying Instructional Objectives.* Achievement in school means movement toward a specified set of objectives. In developing an instrument to collect data for evaluating this progress, teachers must by the very nature of the task define and review their instruction. Ideally, objectives are specified before instruction begins and continue to develop as the curriculum is modified to meet individual student needs. You may even want to administer an achievement test to reveal strengths and deficiencies at the beginning of a course of study. The original objectives can then be modified, enlarged upon, or discarded, as the data suggest.

2. *Determining and Reporting Pupil Achievement of Educational Objectives.* Educational measurement is most often used to assess pupil achievement in school subjects. Measurement yields more objective data on achievement than does subjective appraisal. Such information is obviously of critical importance to students, giving them some perspective on their position relative to acceptable educational standards. These standards may be those of society, the school, the teacher, or students themselves.

Others besides the teacher and student are interested in individual pupil performance. School administrators are obviously concerned. College admissions personnel find high-school grades useful in making decisions. Despite the proliferation of national admissions and scholarship testing programs, previous academic performance remains the single best predictor of future performance.

3. *Planning, Directing, and Improving Learning Experiences.* The diagnostic use of measurement data can be extremely helpful. Tests can identify strengths and weaknesses in the achievement of individual pupils of whole classes. If the teacher and student can identify the areas in which achievement is less than adequate, individual learning efforts and, for that matter, teaching can become more efficient.

For the improvement and facilitation of learning, data on the sequence, continuity, and integration of learning experiences can be of great value. For example, prerequisite skills and knowledge for certain courses or units can be identified, or the effectiveness of selected instructional practices can be evaluated. This process involves using tests for research. A teacher might compare the results under a new device or program to previous educational outcomes with the same class, outcomes obtained in control groups, or results commonly obtained by similar classes. This use of measurement is becoming more important each year with the appearance of new curricula, particularly in science, mathematics, and social studies.

If the information from successful measurement and evaluation instruments can accomplish these three goals, how do we judge if we have a good instrument?

Characteristics of a Quality Instrument

How can I judge the quality of a classroom test? This question frequently goes unanswered due to (1) lack of knowledge about standards and criteria for testing, or (2) lack of effort. Under either of these conditions, evaluation cannot be meaningful for students or teacher, both of whom need to profit from the experience. The students will profit if in preparing for the test they review and consolidate the material. We might call this learning experience a pretest or motivational effect. Following the test, provided students find out the results soon afterward, a posttest or learning effect should also occur. The teacher should profit from information derived about student learning.

In constructing tests, teachers must summarize salient elements of instruction—content, student behavior, and classroom activity—and translate these elements into questions to ask students. When the results are in, think through your instruction, looking for possible beneficial ways to reorganize the material. This sequence usually benefits both teachers and students.

Ebel (1965, 281–307) summarizes ten qualities of a good test:

1. *Relevance.* Relevance is the correspondence between the behavior required to respond correctly to a test item and the purpose or objective in writing the item. The test item should be directly related to the course objectives and actual information. In educational measurement, relevance must be considered the major contributor to validity.

2. *Balance.* Balance in a test is the degree to which the proportion of items testing particular outcomes corresponds to the "ideal" test. The framework of the test is outlined by a table of specifications.
3. *Efficiency.* Efficiency is defined in terms of the number of responses per unit of time. Some compromise must be made among available time for testing, scoring, and relevance.
4. *Objectivity.* For a test question to be considered objective, experts must agree on the "right" or "best" answer. Objectivity, then, is a characteristic of the scoring of the test, not of the form of the questions (e.g., multiple choice, true-false).
5. *Specificity.* If subject-matter experts should receive perfect scores, test-wise but course-naive students should receive near-chance scores, indicating that course-specific learnings are being measured.
6. *Difficulty.* The test items should be appropriate in difficulty level to the group being tested. In general, a maximally reliable test is one in which each item is passed by half of the students.
7. *Discrimination.* The ability of an item to discriminate is generally indexed by the difference between the proportion of good (or more knowledgeable) and poor (or less able) students who respond correctly.
8. *Reliability.* Reliability is a complex characteristic, but generally involves consistency of measurement. Consistency of measurement might be judged in terms of time, items, scores, examinees, or examiners.
9. *Fairness.* To insure fairness, a teacher should construct and administer the test in a manner that allows each student an equal chance to demonstrate knowledge.
10. *Speed.* To what degree are scores made on the test influenced by speed of response? For achievement tests, speed should generally *not* be allowed to play a significant role in determining a score, and sufficient time should generally be allowed for all or most examinees to finish the test.

Teachers may evaluate their tests in light of the foregoing ten factors by carefully examining the test and/or the data it yields. Obviously, teachers should consider these factors before, during, and after test development and administration. The reinforcement of a test is a continuous and ongoing process.

Difficulty and discrimination are the most relevant characteristics if one wishes to maximize the differences in individual performance. If the purpose of the instrument is to assess progress toward a specified set of objectives, those two are less applicable.

Wall and Summerlin (1972) used Ebel's list of the characteristics of a good measuring instrument to compare teacher-made and standardized tests. Table 9.2 summarizes their analyses.

Table 9.2
Relative Merits of Teacher-Made and Standardized Tests

Characteristic	Teacher-made	Standardized
Relevance	Measures objective for the class	Measures achievement for typical class
Balance	Measures objectives in same proportion as time spent on instruction	Measures a large variety of objectives
Difficulty	Is geared to the group being tested	May vary; usually averages around 50 percent passing for all items
Reliability	Usually not calculated; normally very low but can be as high as standardized tests if carefully planned	Usually high; normally 85 and above
Speed	Sufficient time is usually given for completion of test	Strict time limits are typical
Discrimination	Each question helps to differentiate between high- and low-scoring students if differentiation is goal; if testing for mastery this characteristic is meaningless	Attempts to find individual differences between students, with each question contributing to differentiation of those scoring high and low
Specificity	Measures specific learnings	Attempts to measure specific learning
Objectivity	There is agreement among experts on answers to items chosen	Answers have usually been checked by subject-matter experts

Source: J. Wall and L. Summerlin, "Choosing the Right Test," *The Science Teacher* 1972 (Nov.): 32–36. Reprinted by permission from *The Science Teacher*, a publication of the National Science Teachers Association, © 1972.

Formative and Summative Evaluation

Formative evaluation provides ongoing feedback throughout a lesson or a unit of instruction. It serves as a basis for revising instruction for an individual or a class, so that problems may be quickly identified and corrected. It "forms" the instructional program. Examples of formative evaluation are pop quizzes, the Wednesday trial spelling tests, and teacher-made informal tests at the end of a lesson.

Summative evaluation is done at the end of an instruction sequence, with no emphasis on revising instruction. The purpose of summative evaluation is to assess what has been learned. Examples of summative evaluation are end-of-chapter tests, unit tests, and end-of-year achievement tests.

Summary

If teachers are to use tests, they must know about basic test theory and its use in everyday evaluation. Differentiating between tests, measurement, and evaluation is often difficult. The three concepts are related, yet markedly different.

Formative evaluation may involve the same activity.

Tests are instruments used to obtain systematic samples of behavior presumed to reflect the trait you wish to measure. Measurement is the process of obtaining a numeric description of the degree to which a student possesses a particular attribute or characteristic. Measurement describes quantitatively; its results are always expressed in numerals: "Jim correctly solved 45 out of 50 science questions." Evaluation is a systematic process of making a value judgment or decision after collecting, analyzing, and interpreting information.

School and pupil evaluation is currently a major concern of state legislatures, state and local school boards, local schools, and teachers. Evaluation can contribute directly to the teaching-learning process, in particular to decisions about educational objectives, learning experiences, and pupil achievement.

Thought Activity

1. Differentiate among the terms tests, measurement, and evaluation.
2. The following grid portrays three levels of objectives and evaluation: manipulative, picture, and word (oral and written). Write an objective and its related evaluation as shown by the cells with a ◇ within the grid.

		OBJECTIVE		
		Manipulative	Picture	Word
EVALUATION	Manipulative	◇		
	Picture		◇	
	Word			◇

3. Match the terms in column A, all characteristics of a quality instrument, with the most closely related definitions in column B.

A	B
1. relevance	1. consistency
2. balance	2. experts receive perfect scores
3. efficiency	3. function of time
4. objectivity	4. validity
5. specificity	5. ideal test reproportion of items
6. difficulty	6. responses per unit of time
7. discrimination	7. allows each testee equal chance
8. reliability	8. characteristic of the scoring
9. fairness	9. difference in proportion of able and less able who get item right
10. speed	10. each item passed by 50 percent of students

4. State the difference between formative and summative evaluation.

References

Dressel, P. L. 1954. Evaluation as instruction. In *Proceedings of the 1953 Invitational Conference on Testing Problems.* Princeton, N. J.: Educational Testing Service.

Ebel, R. L. 1965. *Measuring educational achievement.* Englewood Cliffs, N.J.: Prentice-Hall.

Wall, J., and L. Summerlin. 1972. Choosing the right test. *The Science Teacher* 39: 32–36.

10 *Methods for assessing student achievement*

There are many ways for a teacher to assess pupil performance. As we said in chapter 9, the objective being evaluated determines what kind of assessment is appropriate. The objective "to group objects by a given attribute" requires assessment at the concrete manipulative level. On the other hand, the objective "to classify words in a sentence by writing them under the headings 'verb,' 'noun,' 'pronoun,' 'adjective,' or 'adverb' " requires a paper-pencil assessment. Assessment procedures may be classified as **informal** and **formal.**

Test Procedures

Informal Test Procedures

In many learning situations, informal techniques are the only feasible sources of needed information. Behavioral changes in social-emotional development and manipulative and psychomotor skill area learning outcomes are particularly difficult to evaluate through formal testing. But how do we assess them? Because general impressions are often unreliable, a systematic procedure is called for.

Informal test procedures differ from formal ones in that (1) the student is unaware that data are being gathered, and (2) the student is not involved in recording responses.

It is not our intent to consider informal test procedures in detail. We will, however, mention some of the techniques available and illustrate situations in which they might be applied.

Rating Scales. Rating scales can be used to assess either cognitive or affective outcomes of instruction. They are frequently used to record the results of observations and evaluate the degree to which certain situations or characteristics are present. For example, a rating scale might be developed to describe how well a student uses the library, gives an oral book report, or relates to other children. Because they are subjective, rating scales are usually used as supplementary evaluations or in areas where more objective instruments are not available.

The teacher lists characteristics or behaviors to be judged on a scale from present to absent. Observing the pre-specified behaviors in the student being rated, she circles a number or places a check on a line to indicate the degree to which the behavior is present.

Rating scales, like objective tests, permit a common evaluation for each child's performance. They have the advantages of being easily constructed and simple to use. They are flexible and adaptable, since responses may be recorded by a teacher or an observer. Rating scales are typically of two types: graphic or numerical. Tables 10.1 and 10.2 are representative examples of each.

Table 10.1
Rating Scale—
Graphic

Directions: Indicate the degree to which the student can use the library by placing an x at any point along the horizontal line.
1. To what extent does the student use the card catalog when in the library?

never occasionally always

2. To what extent does the student locate books independently?

never occasionally always

Table 10.2
Rating Scale—
Numerical

Directions: Indicate the degree to which the student can use the library by circling the appropriate number:
5 = always
4 = frequently
3 = occasionally
2 = seldom
1 = never

1. To what extent does the student use the card catalog when in the library?

 1 2 3 4 5

2. To what extent does the student locate books independently?

 1 2 3 4 5

Table 10.3
Checklist for Telling Time

Directions: Circle YES or NO to indicate whether the skill has been demonstrated.

YES or NO   1. Can say the names of the numerals 1 to 12.
YES or NO   2. Identifies numerals 1 to 12.
YES or NO   3. Counts to 60 by ones using a number line.

Checklists. Another popular method of recording observations is the checklist. It differs from the rating scale in requiring no qualitative judgment. The behavior or characteristic is either present or not present. It is imperative, however, that the categories be as clear and precise as possible. Checklists may be used to assess:

1. Which instructional objectives or skills have been met or mentioned.
2. Student interests, hobbies, problems, preferred reading matter, preferred radio or television programs, and the like.
3. Student behavior in a variety of settings.
4. Conformity to prescribed sequences of steps in task performances.
5. Student products.

Checklists are especially useful at the elementary school level where much of the student evaluation depends on observation rather than testing. Checklists may be used to assess both cognitive and affective outcomes. The one in table 10.3 is a partial list of skills necessary for learning to tell time.

Anecdotal Records. An anecdotal record is a short, objective description of behavior in an incident. It describes concretely the situation in which the action or comment occurs, and what others present do or say.

The anecdotal record is used mainly to record social and emotional facets of a pupil's growth and adjustment. It can also record other relevant classroom or extraclassroom behavior, including all types of learning difficulties, social and academic. In general, the anecdotal record contributes to your understanding of individual students. Collected over time, anecdotal material can provide a longitudinal view of a student's growth and patterns of change.

Table 10.4 (p. 155) is a sample anecdotal record. The kinds of information summarized in the anecdotal record could probably not be gathered in any other way.

Barker and Wright (1954) and Gronlund (1985) make several suggestions for developing and improving anecdotal records:

1. Determine in advance what is to be observed and be alert to unusual behavior.
2. Report only the "what" and "how" of the subject's actions and interactions with others.

A teacher makes notes for a student's anecdotal record.

3. Describe in detail the scene at the beginning of each period of observation.
4. Report in sequence each step in the course of every action by the subject.
5. Allow no overlap between factual description and interpretation of the incident(s).
6. Observe and record sufficient material to make the report meaningful and reliable.
7. Record the incident during or as soon after the observation as possible.
8. Restrict a given record to a single incident.

Table 10.4 Anecdotal Record	**Date:** 9/17/84　　**Student's Name:** LaWayne **Observer:** Wilma (Student teacher) **Description of Student:** 　　The fifth grade class was working on a social studies display which involved constructing models of many different kinds of homes common to different nationalities and countries. LaWayne was asked to work with Stella, a black girl, to build, study, and report to the class on a typical South American home. At first LaWayne was upset about the assignment and asked to be allowed to work with one of her friends, another white girl. When the teacher insisted that she carry out the first assignment she began her project quite reluctantly. As her work progressed, her interest in South America and working with Stella became overtly enthusiastic. **Comment:** 　　It appears that LaWayne has gained more than a knowledge of other lands and customs from the project. LaWayne has begun to work through some of her feelings regarding other races, and apparently is becoming more accepting and less fearful as a result of her experience.

9. Record both positive and negative incidents.
10. Collect a number of anecdotes on a given student before attempting to make inferences.
11. Gain practice in writing anecdotal records.
12. Establish a plan for obtaining periodic systematic anecdotal samples.

Observations. The chief drawback of observational techniques is their susceptibility to distortion arising from the idiosyncrasies of the observer. In order to insure objectivity and attempt to control distortion, first describe the situation and then evaluate it in a separate paragraph (see chap. 2 on observing and analyzing child behavior).

Sociometric Methods. Occasionally a teacher, particularly in the elementary grades, is interested in describing the personal-social adjustment of students. The teacher might ask each student to identify three peers he likes to sit by or work with on projects. By summarizing the choices in the form of a **sociogram** (a chart relating names by connected lines), the teacher can identify clique(s) and isolate(s). Such information is useful in describing interpersonal relationships and may identify individuals whose behavior in or outside the classroom might profitably be observed further.

Formal Test Procedures

The four most frequently used formal test procedures for measuring educational achievement are oral exams, essay tests, teacher-made objective tests, and standardized tests.

Oral Exams. The oral exam is commonly used with (1) elementary-school children, (2) graduate students, and (3) students physically unable to take written tests. Although not used systematically in American education, the oral exam is potentially useful; certain measurement purposes can be better served with this technique than any other.

The value of oral exams is readily apparent. While written exams assume that the student understands the questions, oral exams allow the teacher to see if questions are understood. Further, the teacher can probe the depth of a student's knowledge of a topic; such probing also gives some sense of the student's thought processes (see chap. 6 on diagnostic teaching). Not to be overlooked is the advantage of flexibility—a variety of behaviors can be sampled, and the oral exam can be tape recorded for later analysis. Oral examination allows for testing both generalization and specific fact. In addition, the teacher can observe a wide range of reactions to different stimulus questions, such as hesitation in responding, fumbling for appropriate words, and signs of stress. These reactions provide important information in the affective and psychomotor domains and should be taken into account when appraising students' level of competence.

Despite these potential advantages, several weaknesses of oral exams inhibit their widespread use. Probably the most thoroughly documented weakness of the oral exam is its reliability—the difficulty of maintaining comparable standards of judgment, the selectivity of perception, and the necessarily limited sampling of the breadth of the student's knowledge. Such factors as failure to preplan the questions (avoidable) and the time-consuming nature of the exam (unavoidable) also detract from its usefulness. Some factors to consider in planning and using oral exams are summarized in table 10.5.

Essay Tests. Essay items and tests are particularly valuable for appraising certain kinds of behavioral changes. Essay items give students latitude to express themselves in divergent or open-ended ways. They allow students to find their own way of organizing the material and to present it in their own words. They allow teachers to assess objectives for expression (spelling, grammar, and punctuation) as well as for mastery of subject matter. Essay items are good for assessing higher-order mental abilities, particularly levels 5 (Synthesis) and 6 (Evaluation) of the cognitive domain taxonomy.

Gronlund (1985) identifies twelve complex learning outcomes that can be measured effectively with essay items:

1. Explaining cause-effect relationships.
2. Describing applications of principles.
3. Presenting relevant arguments.
4. Formulating tenable hypotheses.
5. Formulating valid conclusions.
6. Stating necessary assumptions.
7. Describing the limitations of data.
8. Explaining methods and procedures.

Table 10.5
Principles of Oral Examinations

1. Use oral examinations only for the purposes for which they are best suited, i.e., to obtain information as to the depth of students' knowledge, where oral presentation is clearly a purpose of the course or program, or where other means are simply inappropriate.
2. Prepare in advance a detailed outline of materials to be sampled in the examination even to the extent of writing questions which will be asked.
3. Determine in advance how records of student performance will be kept and what weights will be assigned various factors.
4. Keep the questioning relevant to the purposes of the course or program.
5. Word questions in such a way that the students can see the point of the questions with minimum difficulty.
6. Where several examiners are involved, make each one responsible for questions on a specified part of the full examination.
7. Judge students on the basis of their performance precisely defined—not in terms of generalized impressions of their total appearance.
8. Pose questions which students with the training which has preceded a particular examination can reasonably be expected to know. An examination is not the place for teachers to demonstrate their own erudition.
9. Use both general and specific questions but do so in some logical order.
10. Do not spend a disproportionate time probing for the answer to one question. If the first several questions do not elicit the desired response, move to some other matter.
11. Develop some facility with several basic techniques for successful oral examining, such as (a) creating a friendly atmosphere, (b) asking questions and (c) recording responses.
12. Make a written record of the student's performance at the time it is given. However, do so without disturbing the student or disrupting the flow of the examination.
13. In most situations allow students ample time to think through and make responses to questions.
14. Avoid arguing with the student. It is his or her show—let him or her make the most of it.

Note: Adapted with permission from *Testing Bulletin No. 7*. East Lansing: Office of Evaluation Services, Michigan State University, 1967.

9. Producing, organizing, and expressing ideas.
10. Integrating learnings in different areas.
11. Creating original forms (e.g., designing an experiment).
12. Evaluating the worth of ideas.

This list is not exhaustive but should highlight some potential learning outcomes that can be assessed using essay items and tests. Some advocates of the essay item also claim that it can be used to elicit creative behavior.

A primary weakness of essay items is their susceptibility to unreliable scoring. A teacher may very well judge a paper as failing one day and passing on the next. She may judge the first paper in a set more or less rigorously than the last, or may be influenced by such irrelevant factors as handwriting, prior work by the student, or length of response. Essay items can be scored quite objectively (see chap. 12 for a detailed discussion of essay items), but the task is time-consuming and requires considerable planning and effort.

Essay tests frequently require extended responses to a few questions. This procedure, by limiting the samples of behavior, may result in low instrument reliability.

A student concentrates on an essay test.

Teacher-Made Objective Tests. Objective (or short-answer) teacher-made tests were first used in an attempt to overcome the weaknesses of other forms of testing, particularly oral and essay exams. Oral and essay tests tend to yield unreliable measurements because of the influence of such factors as the mental set of the teacher, past student performance, and limited sampling of course material. Questions to be answered by a choice among specified alternatives provide more consistent and comparable responses, which allow more reliable measurement.

There are two kinds of **objective items, supply** and **choice** (or selection). In supply items, students respond to a simple direct question, e.g., "What are the two main gases found in air?" or to an incomplete statement, e.g., "The two main gases found in air are _____ ." They are required to construct or supply their own brief answer. These items measure recall of knowledge well, although they are sometimes scored less objectively than are selection or choice items.

Three kinds of choice questions have been found useful in achievement testing: true-false, multiple response, and matching. Of the three, the multiple response or multiple choice item is most commonly used. It is probably the most adaptable kind of objective item, allowing testing for command of factual information or of more complicated thought processes. Students are given a question or statement followed by four or five options, one of which is correct; the others are distractors or foils. If a relatively large number of possible responses is given for each item, the effect of chance selection of correct answers is reduced. Research, however, indicates that, at least from the standpoint of information theory, only three alternatives may be necessary (Tversky 1964).

The key-list or matching item has been found useful in making a quick survey of knowledge. Students are given two lists of objects and are asked to match them on the basis of some indicated relationship. Examples are matching inventions with their inventors or battles with dates. See chapter 12 for specific suggestions useful in constructing teacher-made objective tests.

Standardized Tests. A standardized test is an instrument that (1) contains a specified set of items, (2) gives explicit and standardized directions for administration and scoring, and (3) has usually been administered to a representative population of individuals to secure normative data. The availability of normative data useful in interpreting individual scores is considered by some to distinguish standardized tests from other instruments. Other important characteristics of standardized tests are the high quality of items and high reliability. The key factor, however, is uniformity of administration and scoring. Standardized achievement tests may be published as a **battery,** which contains a series of individual tests standardized on the same population, or as individual subject-matter tests.

Criterion-referenced and Norm-referenced Measures

One recent trend in educational assessment is the rekindling of interest in criterion-referenced measures. Although the idea of basing a series of test items on specific performance criteria has existed since the turn of the century, not until the advent of mastery learning and individualized curricula was proper attention paid to this use of test scores. A criterion-referenced measure is one used to compare a student's performance with an established standard (Popham and Husek 1969). The standard of performance is usually a highly refined behavioral objective describing expected pupil changes and the conditions under which these changes are to be exhibited. For a norm-referenced measure, by contrast, a student's performance is compared to those of other individuals being tested. A criterion-referenced measure cannot be distinguished from a norm-referenced measure merely by looking at it. The difference lies in the interpretation of scores: relative for norm-referenced and absolute for criterion-referenced. It is quite possible for a criterion-referenced measure to be used in a norm-referenced way, but the converse is less likely.

Developing Criterion-referenced Measures

Mayo (1970) notes that the development of criterion-referenced measures closely parallels that of a traditional achievement test. The development of the usual classroom test—or standardized test, for that matter—follows four general steps:

1. Specification of expected student performance outcomes.
2. Construction, identification, collection, or adaptation of measuring methods appropriate to each outcome.
3. After a tryout, selection of items that yield maximum discrimination against an internal criterion and are answered correctly by an average of 50–60 percent of the students.
4. Establishment of guidelines for interpreting the scores against normative standards.

The first two steps apply to the development of criterion-referenced measures. The final two steps require adjustments. Inasmuch as criterion-referenced measures focus on an individual's performance on a set of tasks, discrimination—defined as the capacity of an item to distinguish between groups of more and less knowledgeable individuals—is not an applicable concept. Cox (1971) has suggested that an index of discrimination based on the relative proportions of students passing an item before and after a unit or course is the best indication of the effectiveness of instruction. One might expect an item on a mastery test to have a difficulty level as high as 85 percent at the conclusion of instruction, whether self-administered or teacher-directed instruction. In other words, 85 percent of the total number of students who take the test should answer the test item correctly (see chap. 13 for a more thorough discussion of discrimination and difficulty level).

The meaning of a student's score on a criterion-referenced test is derived from comparing the displayed skills or knowledge to the level that is aimed for. What is proposed is a kind of diagnostic interpretation. Assuming no deficiencies in the items, a criterion-referenced measure is a valid sample of student behavior.

Differences between Measures

Several differences between criterion-referenced and norm-referenced measures are briefly summarized in table 10.6. The differences are in most cases matters of degree rather than kind.

Standardized Achievement Tests

Standardized achievement tests are useful for such purposes of testing as planning, assessing, and reporting the results of educational experiences. They are successful to the extent that the items measure the specific objectives of instruction. In general, they attempt to measure outcomes and content common to educational programs in the United

Table 10.6 Comparison of Criterion- and Norm-referenced Tests

	Dimension	Criterion-referenced Measures	Norm-referenced Measures
1.	Intent	Information on degree to which absolute external performance standards have been met	Information for relative internal comparisons
		Description of maximum performance by individuals, groups, and treatment	Comparisons of individuals, particularly when high degree of selectivity is required
2.	Directness of measurement	Great emphasis	Less emphasis
3.	Variability among scores	Relatively low	Relatively high
4.	Difficulty of items	Items tend to be easy, but with some range	Item difficulty localized around percent
5.	Item type	Great variety, but less reliance on selection items	Variety, but emphasis on selection items
6.	Discrimination of items	Not emphasized	Greatly emphasized
7.	Methods of establishing validity	Reliance on content validity	Emphasis on criterion-related validity
8.	Emphasis on reliability	Focus on reliability of domain sampling; therefore internal consistency of some interest	Greater concern with parallel form and test-retest estimates of performance stability
9.	Influence of guessing	Can be of consequence	Generally not a problem
10.	Importance of which items are missed	High	Emphasis on number of missed items
11.	Necessity for maintaining security of test items	Relatively low	Relatively high
12.	Area of education best served	Instruction	Guidance, selection, grading

States. They are less well suited to measuring learning outcomes unique to a particular class or school. Relevance, then, is a crucial question when selecting a standardized achievement test; the items should measure the same behavior and content dimensions as would a teacher-made test.

A Comparison of Instructor-made and Standardized Tests

Ideally, one would not expect teacher-made and standardized achievement tests to differ significantly in quality. In practice, however, they do. Because of time pressures and limited resources, a classroom teacher cannot consistently produce the kind of measuring instruments that might be preferred. The major differences between the two types of tests, as summarized by Gronlund (1985), are presented in table 10.7. The most noticeable differences involve the availability of normative data useful in interpreting scores and the specificity of the learning outcomes measured. The standardized test is likely to cover a broad spectrum of content taught over a fairly long instructional period. Based on the pooled judgments of leading subject-matter experts, it represents a collection of implied educational objectives and provides an informative picture of overall educational progress across schools and classes.

Table 10.7 Comparative Advantages of Standardized and Teacher-made Classroom Tests of Achievement

	Standardized	Teacher-made
Learning Outcomes and Content Measured	Measures outcomes and content common to majority of United States schools. Tests of basic skills and complex outcomes adaptable to many local situations; content-oriented tests seldom reflect emphasis or timeliness of local curriculum.	Well adapted to outcomes and content of local curriculum. Flexibility affords continuous adaptation of measurement to new materials and changes in procedure. Adaptable to various size work units. Tend to neglect complex learning outcomes.
Quality of Test Items	General quality of items high. Written by specialists, pretested and selected on basis of effectiveness.	Quality of items unknown unless test item file is used. Quality typically lower than standardized because of limited time and skill of teacher.
Reliability	Reliability high; commonly between .80 and .95, frequently above .90.	Reliability usually unknown; can be high if carefully constructed.
Administration and Scoring	Procedures *standardized*; specific instructions provided.	Uniform procedures possible but usually flexible.
Interpretation	Scores can be compared to norm groups. Test manual and other guides aid interpretation and use.	Score comparisons and interpretations limited to local school situation.

Note: Reprinted with permission of Macmillan Publishing Company from *Measurement and Evaluation in Teaching*, 5th ed., by Norman E. Gronlund. Copyright © 1985 by Norman E. Gronlund.

Types of Standardized Achievement Tests

There are two general types of standardized achievement tests. The first is the **survey battery,** which consists of a group of individual subject-matter tests designated for use at particular levels. The second category is the **diagnostic test,** usually administered when a survey battery of specific subject tests indicates a substandard performance. Its purpose is to diagnose the area or areas of weakness so that remedial instruction may be instituted. Brief discussions of these two categories of standardized achievement tests follow, accompanied by descriptions of representative tests of each type.

Survey Batteries. Comprehensive survey achievement batteries are the mainstay of school testing programs, providing valuable information about the effectiveness of various instructional programs. The last two or three decades have seen a sigificant improvement in the quality of achievement batteries, particularly in the learning outcomes measured and the quality of normative data available.

A distinct advantage of the survey battery over a series of individual subject-matter tests from different publishers is its simultaneous standardization of all subtests. Scores on individual subtests can thus be considered comparable, since the normative data were derived from the same population.

Diagnostic Tests. Diagnostic tests are usually administered after a period of instruction, sometimes to a group but usually individually, to identify learning strengths and weaknesses in a detailed and analytical way so as to improve instruction. We recommend using an achievement battery to identify students who demonstrate inadequate learning. A standardized diagnostic test can then be used to (1) identify for the student and teacher the types of errors being made, (2) make the teacher aware of the important elements, difficulties, and subject and skill sequences in the learning process, and (3) suggest instructional strategies. Diagnostic testing to obtain even more detailed information about pupil difficulties often uses informal teacher-made devices and direct observation of behavior.

In addition to exhibiting the usual characteristics required of a test (e.g., reliability, validity, and objectivity), diagnostic tests should (1) be tied to specific curricular objectives and expected learning outcomes; (2) include items that directly measure and analyze specific functions or emphasize selected mechanical aspects of learning; (3) suggest specific remedial procedures for the errors indicated by responses to specific items; and (4) cover reasonably broad integrated learning sequences. Hayward (1968) suggests three questions that need to be asked when selecting a diagnostic reading test and that can be generalized to any diagnostic test:

1. Does the test measure the necessary component skills, and do the subscores represent meaningful areas for providing remedial instruction?
2. Are the subscore reliabilities sufficiently high (above .90) for individual application?
3. Are the intercorrelations among the subscores sufficiently low (below .65) to warrant differential diagnosis?

Unfortunately, most available diagnostic tests do not meet even minimal criteria. We lack efficient high-quality instruments that can be used diagnostically in program planning. Many achievement batteries attempt to serve as both survey instruments and diagnostic tests by providing between five and ten subject scores and an item-by-item breakdown of each. But such a breakdown is too general and based on too few lines to be considered reliable; although of some value as an initial screening, it should not form the basis for instruction. It might be fairer to say that diagnostic tests differ from specific subject-matter tests in the degree of refinement with which they measure achievement than to say they measure different kinds of achievement.

Outline for Critical Analysis of a Standardized Test

In selecting a standardized test many factors need to be considered. Use the following outline to gather information about standardized tests for decision-making purposes.

1. **Title** — Note complete and exact title of test.
2. **Author** — A brief summary of professional affiliations and credentials would be informative.
3. **Publisher** — Some publishers are more reputable than others. Check with testing experts.
4. **Copyright date** — Note dates of first publication and each revision.
5. **Level or group for whom test is intended** — Such factors as age, grade, and ability level need to be considered. What background does the author presuppose for examinees? Is the test available at different levels? If so, which ones?
6. **Forms of the test** — What forms of the test are available? If the forms are not essentially the same, major differences should be mentioned and evaluated. What evidence is presented on equivalence of forms?
7. **Purpose and recommended use** — Summarize the use of the test recommended by the author.
8. **Dimensions or areas that the test purports to measure** — Give a brief definition or description of the variables involved. If the test has a great number of scales it may be necessary simply to mention the subscores and highlight only the group or distinctive scores.

9.	Administration	Describe briefly. The median time requried to complete the test should be indicated. If parts of the tests are timed separately, note how many "starting points" are necessary. Are the directions easy for the test administrator to follow and the test-takers to comprehend? Is special training required for valid administration? Is the test largely self-administering? Are there objectionable features?
10.	Scoring	Scoring procedures should be described very briefly. Is the test planned and organized so that machine-scored answer sheets can or must be used? Is a correction for guessing justified and/or applied?
11.	Source of items	Where did the author get the items? What criteria did he use in item selection? Are some items taken from other tests? If so, which ones?
12.	Decription of items (format and content)	Briefly describe the types of items used. Attention should be given to *item form* (e.g., multiple-choice, analogy, forced-choice) and *item content* (e.g., culture-free symbols, nonsense syllables, food preferences, occupational titles). How many response categories are there? Note a typical example of each major type of items used. It is imperative that the actual items be evaluated in light of the questions a teacher would ask of the data.
13.	Statistical item analysis	Was an item analysis made to determine item discrimination and difficulty? What were the results? What criteria were used to select items for the final form(s) of the instrument? What analytic techniques were used?
14.	Method and results of validation reported by publisher and author	For most tests this topic is related to categories 11, 12, and 13. One must ask, "What was done to make the test valid and useful?" Some tests are validated by expert judgment, some by an external criterion, and so on. What has the author done to demonstrate the validity of the test? What correlations with other tests does she present? Has she used an external criterion to evaluate the usefulness of the scores? This section should deal with data other than those obtained in the construction of the test. What specific "predictions" could one make from an individual's test score on the basis of the validity data presented?
15.	Validity as determined by others	This is in many respects the crucial evaluative criterion. The recent literature should be consulted and studies briefly summarized.
16.	Reliability	State briefly how reliability was determined. Report interesting or unusual data on reliability. Was reliabili-

		ty computed separately for each subgroup or part of the test?
17.	Norm group(s)	How many were involved? How were they selected? Are separate norms available for each group with which one might wish to compare an individual's score, i.e., for each sex, age level, curriculum major, occupation?
18.	Interpretation of scores	How are scores expressed? (Percentile ranks, standard scores, grade scores?) What is considered a "high" score? A "low" score? How are these scores interpreted? What significance do they have in view of the answers to category 10?
19.	Major evaluations by experts	What assumptions about the test are examined, and what questions are raised in Buros' *Mental Measurements Yearbooks?* What do measurement textbooks say about the test?
20.	Cost factors	The initial cost of booklets and answer sheets could be considered, as well as such factors as cost of scoring, reusability of booklets, and availability of summary and research services.
21.	Distinguishing characteristics	What are the outstanding features of this test, its construction, and its use? Note both desirable and undesirable features.
22.	Overall evaluation	How well do such factors as validity, reliability, standardization, and item content coincide with the intended use of the test?

How should the information in these twenty-two categories be weighted? No general answer can be given, since the selection of a particular test or battery will depend on the individual needs of specific teachers or schools. The purpose of testing must be foremost in the teacher's mind. Such questions as "What specific information is needed?" and "How will the test data be interpreted and used?" are highly significant. Questions of validity, reliability, and the composition of normative data should be critically reviewed and heavily weighted in the final decisions if the test is to be used in a norm-referenced way.

Evaluating a standardized achievement test is a time-consuming and involved process. But considering the kinds of decisions that will be made about students and programs as a result of such tests, the expenditure of effort is more than justified.

Locating Information about Tests

It would be impossible to list, let alone critically evaluate, all tests that might be of interest to a particular teacher or administrator. A potential user needs information such as: (1) What types of tests are available that will yield the kind of information I need? (2) What do the "experts" say about the tests I am interested in? (3) What research has been undertaken on this test? (4) What statistical data about validity and reliability are available for examination? and (5) With what groups may I legitimately use this test? Answers to these and other relevant questions may be found in one or more of the following sources:

1. Buros' *Mental Measurements Yearbooks.*
2. Test reviews in professional journals.
3. Test manuals and specimen tests.
4. Text and reference books on testing.
5. Bibliographies of tests and testing literature.
6. Educational and psychological abstract indexes.
7. Publishers' test catalogues.
8. UCLA Center for the Study of Evaluating Elementary and Preschool/Kindergarten Test Evaluations.
9. *Test Collection Bulletin* published quarterly by Educational Testing Service, Princeton, N.J.
10. *Tests in Print.*

Thought Activity

1. State the characteristics of the following: rating scales, checklists, anecdotal records, observations, and sociometric methods.
2. State the advantages and disadvantages of oral examinations.
3. Write a sample essay question for each of Gronlund's complex learning outcomes (see p. 157). Ask a colleague to evaluate your responses.
4. Differentiate between supply and choice items.
5. Name the three different kinds of choice items discussed in the chapter and give an example of each.
6. State the characteristics of standardized tests.
7. Name the main difference between criterion-referenced and norm-referenced tests.
8. Tell why discrimination is a concept not applicable to criterion-referenced tests.
9. State the characteristics of survey and diagnostic tests.
10. Locate a copy of a standardized test. Based on the stated purpose of the test, apply the outline for evaluating a standardized test and write an evaluation based on the criteria.

References

Barker, R. G., and H. F. Wright. 1954. *Midwest and its children: The psychological ecology of an American town.* New York: Harper & Row.

Cox, R. C. 1971. Evaluative aspects of criterion-referenced measures. In *Criterion-referenced measurement: An introduction,* edited by W. J. Popham. Englewood Cliffs, N.J.: Educational Technology Publications.

Gronlund, N. E. 1985. *Measurement and evaluation in teaching.* 5th ed. New York: Macmillan.

Hayward, P. 1968. Evaluating diagnostic reading tests. *The Reading Teacher* 21(6): 353–71.

Haywood, P. 1972. Twelve sound ways to announce test results. *Nation's Schools* 89(4): 45–52.

Mayo, S. T. 1970. Mastery learning and mastery testing. *Measurement in Education* 1(3): 1–4.

Popham, W. J., and T. R. Husek. 1969. Implications of criterion-referenced measurement. *Journal of Educational Measurement* 6: 1–9.

Tversky, A. 1964. On the optimal number of alternatives at a choice point. *Journal of Mathematical Psychology* 1: 386–91.

11 *Getting ready to build your test*

Effective educational assessment will result from careful planning, imaginative and skillful question writing, careful formulation of questions into a total test, and fair and proper administration and scoring. Effectiveness also depends on the quality of instruction before testing and on intelligent interpretation and use of test scores. Test planning includes deciding what learning outcomes should be measured, in what contexts they are most likely to be demonstrated, and what kinds of questions are likely to elicit the outcomes.

Item writing follows next in this test develpment sequence. Writing test questions, items, or exercises means finding the most suitable way to pose problems to students, whether the problems require recall of learned information or the use of higher-order mental abilities. Item writing is discussed fully in chapter 12.

Planning the Test

To insure the best possible test, you must plan for it. Appropriate planning considers a large number of factors, including (1) type of measurement procedure to be used, (2) length of the test, (3) range and difficulty level of the items, (4) arrangement of items, (5) time limits, (6) scoring system, (7) manner of reporting results, (8) method of recording responses, and, most important of all, (9) the subject matter, mental operation, or behavior to be sampled. This chapter will discuss several of the more important decision points in test planning.

Developing a Table of Specifications

Matching tests to instructional objectives is the basis of classroom evaluation. Ordinarily the first step teachers take in developing a measuring instrument is to review the objectives of their instructional program, both those originally proposed and those actually attended to.

A convenient way to conduct this review is using a table of specifica-

Teachers plan the test.

tions, a two-way grid that relates to two major components of an educational objective: the content element and the behavioral element. First list the important topics or objectives covered in the instructional unit along the left margin of the table. This ensures that no topic will be totally neglected in the evaluation process. Then insert appropriate headings from the taxonomy of objectives for the cognitive domain, or for the affective or psychomotor domain, if appropriate (see chap. 4), across the top of the table. This prevents you from neglecting any important learning outcomes. The digits in the grid spaces indicate the number of test items used to evaluate each content-objective pairing. Seeing the distribution will help you discover if you are overloading or neglecting some categories of the taxonomy. For example, in the fourth grade weather unit in table 11.1 two test items are used to evaluate knowledge level skills on the topic of condensation, one item is used for the comprehension level, and one item for the application level. The row and column totals include both numbers and percentages of items for each category. In the right column, for example, 16.5 percent of the items (5 items) are to cover evaporation, 13.5 percent (4 items) for condensation, and so on down the column. In the bottom row, 40 percent (12 items) are

Table 11.1
Table of Specifications for a Unit on Weather for Fourth Grade Students

Topics	Behavior			Total # of Items / % of Test
	Knowledge	Comprehension	Application	
1. Evaporation	3		2	5 / 16.5
2. Condensation	2	1	1	4 / 13.5
3. Wind	2	1	1	4 / 13.5
4. Temperature	3	3	3	9 / 30
5. Clouds	2	3	3	8 / 26.5
Total # of Items / % of Test	12 / 40	8 / 26.5	10 / 33.5	30 / 100

devoted to knowledge level learning, 26.5 percent (8 items) to comprehension, and 33.5 percent (10 items) to application skills. The teacher can weight the importance of each objective or topic in the instructional situation and consider the amount of instructional time devoted to it.

In practice the content categories would probably be more detailed than those in table 11.1. The greater the detail in the test blueprint or table of specifications, the easier will be the construction task. Some compromise between the extremes of objectives—highly specific and highly general—will result in a reasonably balanced test.

Having developed a table of specifications, it is now time to write items corresponding to each cell in the table. From table 11.1 under the topic of clouds, you would construct two knowledge, three comprehension, and three application questions. The following are sample objectives and corresponding test items for the topic *clouds*.

Topic: Clouds
Behavior: Knowledge
Objective: The student will list three major types of clouds.
Test Item: Name the three major types of clouds. _____ , _____ , _____ .

Topic: Clouds
Behavior: Knowledge
Objective: The student will define *clouds*.
Test Item: What is the name of water vapor that collects in the cool air of the sky?
a. dew
b. clouds
c. rain

Topic: Clouds
Behavior: Comprehension
Objective: The student will identify acceptable inferences for predicting weather from observed conditions.
Test Item: *Directions:* In column A are types of weather. In column B are weather conditions. Predict the weather from the observed weather condition by drawing a line from the word in column A to the matching word in column B. One term in column B is not used.

A	B
warm front	funnel-shaped clouds
cold front	cirrus clouds
tornado	cumulus clouds
thunderstorm	cumulonimbus clouds
	fog

Many elementary school teachers prefer short worksheets and exercises to long tests. In such cases, several worksheets or exercises covering a single instructional unit can be formulated from a table of specifications.

If the teacher is using essay items, the percentages might be used to determine the amount of time and scoring weight given to individual items. In this way the teacher ensures proportionality or what we referred to in chapter 8 as "balance" in the test. Balance is interpreted relative to the amount of time spent on certain topics and skills in class, which in turn reflects the importance the teacher assigns to each.

In summary, the use of a table of specifications to develop tests will ensure that (1) only those objectives actually pursued in instruction will be measured, (2) each objective will receive the appropriate emphasis in the test, and (3) by using subdivisions based on content and behavior, no important objectives will be overlooked.

Developing Test Directions

Traxler (1951) presents seven criteria to keep in mind when developing directions for a test:

1. Assume that the examinees and examiner know nothing at all about objective tests.
2. In writing the directions, use a clear, succinct style. Be as explicit as possible, but avoid long drawn-out explanations.
3. Emphasize the more important directions and key activities through use of underlining, italics or different type size or style.
4. Give the examiner and each proctor full instructions on what is to be done before, during, and after the administration.
5. Try out, if possible, the directions with a sample of both examinees and examiners to identify possible misunderstandings and inconsistencies and gather suggestions for improvement.
6. Keep the directions for different forms, subsections, or booklets as uniform as possible.
7. Where necessary or helpful, give practice items (or, if possible, tests) before each regular section. This is particularly important when testing the young or those unfamiliar with objective tests or separate answer sheets—e.g., the educationally or culturally disadvantaged, foreign students, or special education students.

Any important test should be announced well in advance; do not dangle the threat of a surprise test over students' heads. An "announced test" procedure is more likely to result in effective study.

If possible, give practice in taking tests. This is very important if unusual items or ways of asking questions (e.g., analogy items) are to be used. Again, younger students probably benefit most from this practice.

Unless a teacher considers time a major factor in learning, achievement tests should be administered in a way that allows all students, or nearly all, enough time to finish. In general, speed of response is not a relevant variable; allowing sufficient time for the test tends to reduce guessing and results in a more reliable measure, particularly if one is concerned with relative achievement. In some situations, of course, speed alone or a combination of speed and level of performance is significant, as in tests of motor skills.

It is probably a sound idea to arrange items on the basis of increasing difficulty or complexity. Placing easy items at the beginning of the test encourages students with initial successes. It is also best to group together items requiring similar responses. Such a grouping allows students to develop a pattern or routine for answering each kind of question.

Test Administration

After obtaining or developing a measurement instrument, the teacher must decide on administration procedures to follow. If the teacher has selected a standardized test, many of the decisions have already been made (See chaps. 9 and 10). The test manual will contain detailed directions which must be followed precisely. If the test scores of this group are to be legitimately compared with those of the standardization group, the standardized testing conditions must be duplicated as closely as possible.

Rigidly controlled administration is just as important to a teacher-made test as to a standardized test. If test scores are to have any meaning, they must be gathered under uniform and optimal conditions, particularly if you intend to make comparisons between individuals or against an absolute scoring standard. Administering any group or individual test, particularly a standardized test, is a complex task. To facilitate the process of test administration, Prescott (1957) has prepared a set of guidelines for administrative activity before, during, and after the test. Prescott's suggestion that the examiner take the test is a very good one. The guidelines, which can be used as a checklist by the teacher, are as follows:

Before the Testing Date

1. Understand nature and purposes of the testing.
   a. Tests to be given.
   b. Reasons for giving tests.
2. Decide on number to be tested at one time.
3. Decide on seating arrangements.
4. Decide on exact time of testing.
   a. Avoid day before holiday.
   b. Avoid conflicts with recess of other groups.
   c. Make sure there is ample time.

Getting Ready to Build Your Test 175

5. Procure or duplicate and check test materials:
   a. Directions for administering.
   b. Directions for scoring.
   c. Test booklets: one for each pupil and teacher.
   d. Answer sheet (if used).
   e. Pencils (regular or special).
   f. Stopwatch or other suitable timepiece.
   g. Scoring keys.
   h. "Testing—Do Not Disturb" sign.
   i. Other supplies (scatch paper, etc.).
6. Study test and directions carefully.
   a. Familiarize yourself with:
   (1) General makeup of test.
   (2) Time limits.
   (3) Directions.
   (4) Method of indicating answers.
   b. Take the test yourself.
7. Arrange materials for distribution; count number needed.
8. Decide on order in which materials are to be distributed and collected.
9. Decide what pupils who finish early are to do.

Just Before Testing
1. Make sure central loudspeaker is disconnected.
2. Put up "Testing—Do Not Disturb" sign.
3. See that desks are cleared.
4. See that pupils have sharpened pencils.
5. Attend to toilet needs of pupils.
6. Check lighting.
7. Check ventilation.
8. Make seating arrangements.

During Testing
1. Distribute materials according to a predetermined order.
2. Caution pupils not to begin until you tell them to do so.
3. Make sure that all identifying information is written on booklet or answer sheet.
4. Read directions exactly as given.
5. Give signal to start.
6. Write starting and finishing times on the chalkboard.
7. Move quietly about the room to:
   a. Make sure pupils are marking answers in the correct place.
   b. Make sure pupils are continuing to the next page after finishing the previous page.
   c. Make sure pupils stop at the end of the test.
   d. Replace broken pencils.
   e. Encourage pupils to keep working until time is called.
   f. Make sure there is no copying.
   g. Attend to pupils finishing early.

Testing environments should be pleasant.

8. Permit no outside interruptions.
9. Stop at proper time.

Just After Testing

1. Collect materials according to predetermined order.
2. Count booklets and answer sheets.
3. Make a record of any incidents observed that may tend to invalidate scores made by pupils.

Directions for Students

The directions for taking the test should be as complete, clear, and concise as possible. Students must be told what is expected of them. The method of responding should be kept as simple as possible, especially for younger students. Instead of using one of the many convenient IBM or other preprinted answer sheets, students (up to grade four) should be allowed to respond on the test booklet. They should be made aware of time limits, how to select and record answers, instructions on guessing, and how the test will be scored.

To help prepare elementary school children to respond correctly to directions and formats of standardized tests, teachers may want to have them practice with sample tests. In addition, the Educational Testing Service rents and sells movies that explain how to take a standardized test.

Test Scoring

Common sense probably yields more helpful suggestions for test scoring than does prolonged discussion. Obviously, responses need to be recorded in a convenient form so that scoring can proceed efficiently. If scoring is to be done by hand, it should be checked. Various devices using mechanical, electrical, or optical mark-sensing methods are available to assist in test scoring. Their cost, however, is still beyond the budgets of most schools. Answer keys and scoring rules should of course be prepared before actual scoring. This is very important if supply questions, particularly essay questions, are used. In addition, it is an excellent idea to have a colleague check the content, phrasing, and keying of the items. Cross-checking answers with a colleague can be a real eye opener.

Developing Hand Scoring Answer Keys

If standard commercial or separate preprinted answer sheets are to be used, a punch-out overlay scoring template can be applied. These templates are available from most commercial test and answer sheet producers and service organizations. However, most teachers must develop their own answer sheets. Three major types of hand scoring keys—fan (or accordion), strip, and cut-out keys—can be developed by teachers.

Fan Key. This key consists of a series of columns, extending from the top to the bottom of the page, on which are recorded acceptable answers or directions scored for the individual items. The key and answer sheet are the same size and identically spaced. Usually each column corresponds to a page of the test or a column of the answer sheet to which it refers. The key is folded along vertical lines between columns, giving it the appearance of a fan. It is then superimposed on the appropriate page of the test or next to the appropriate column of the answer sheet and matched to the corresponding responses. Figure 11.1 presents a sample fan or accordion key for scoring responses recorded on the test sheet. When a separate answer sheet is provided, equal spacing of lines can be used, as shown in figure 11.2.

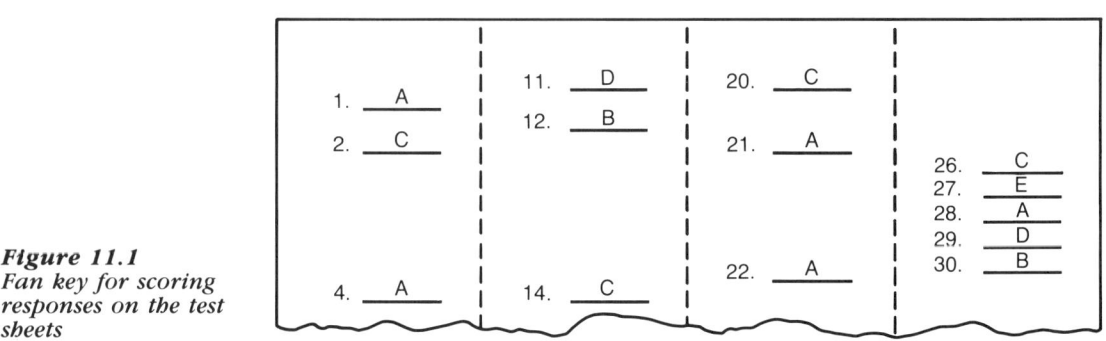

Figure 11.1
Fan key for scoring responses on the test sheets

Figure 11.2
Fan key for scoring responses recorded on separate answer sheet

Strip Key. Similar to the fan key, this method uses separate columns, cut along the vertical lines. Strip keys are easier to use if made of cardboard or stiff paper. A strip key is illustrated in figure 11.3.

Cut-out Key. This key is also a sheet of paper the same size as the test or answer sheet. Windows are cut or punched out to reveal letters, numbers, words, or phrases on the answer sheet. The key is superimposed on a page of the test or answer sheet, and holes where nothing appears are marked in red. This provides the teacher with the number of items missed and marks the correct answers for the student. A cut-out key is shown in figure 11.4.

Figure 11.3 Strip key

1. B	16. B	31. D
2. B	17. C	32. D
3. B	18. C	33. B
4. C	19. A	34. A
5. A	20. D	35. D
6. B	21. A	36. C
7. A	22. B	37. B
8. D	23. C	38. B
9. D	24. C	39. A
10. B	25. D	40. C

Figure 11.4 Cut-out key

Summary

Too often teachers throw together a test at the last minute without carefully considering even its purpose. The test development process is a complex one, consisting of a variety of tasks and activities. First, prepare a table of specifications for the content areas to be covered by the test and then determine the levels of learning to be assessed within each area. Next, construct test items corresponding to each cell in the table. This procedure ensures that you build test items for each topic in the unit and assess instructional outcomes beyond the knowledge level. A table of specifications offers a convenient and concise overview of the instructional unit.

The same care that goes into constructing the test should also go into the final stages of test development and use. The procedures for administering the test should give all students a fair chance to demonstrate knowledge of the subject. The form in which the test is presented, the students' preparation, and the actual conditions of testing all need to be considered. How students are to record their answers is another detail that cannot be ignored in giving directions.

Teachers usually develop their own answer sheets. A test can be scored using fan, strip, or cut-out keys.

Thought Activity

1. State considerations important in planning a test.
2. Develop tables of specifications for a first and a fifth grade mathematics unit.
3. Discuss reasons for adhering to directions when administering a test.
4. List important data to be given students who are about to take a test. Tell why these explanations are important.
5. Describe the following three types of handscoring keys: fan, strip, and cut-out.

References

Prescott, D. A. 1957. *The child in the educative process.* New York: McGraw-Hill.

Traxler, A. 1951. Administering and scoring the objective test. In *Educational measurement,* edited by E. F. Lindquist, 329–416 Washington: American Council on Education.

12 *Constructing test items*

Five principles need to be considered as you prepare to construct items:

1. Adequate provision should be made for measuring all important outcomes of instruction.
2. The test and its items should reflect the approximate emphases given various objectives in the course.
3. The test and its items must take into account the nature of the group to be examined.
4. The test and its items must be appropriate to the conditions under which the test is to be administered.
5. The test and its items must be suited to the purpose it is to serve.

These principles imply several prerequisites for sound item construction. The first is competence in the subject matter to be examined. Teachers should be scholars in the broadest and finest sense of the word. The basic principles and knowledge, as well as the common fallacies, should be at their command.

Command of the subject matter is a necessary but not sufficient condition for writing effective items. Teachers must also be skilled in item writing. They must be aware of the various ways in which questions can be asked and the kinds of objectives for which each method is best suited. Some of this knowledge can be acquired in test construction courses or from the references listed at the end of this chapter. The best approach, of course, combines formal study and experience. You must actually write many items of all types and try them out with students in order to develop skill and perspective on the advantages and disadvantages of the various question forms.

Item-writing skill is based on mastery of verbal communication. The teacher must be able to apply the rules of grammar and rhetoric. Test items are probably read more closely than any other type of nonlegal written communication. Skill in conducting item analyses and in estimating reliability and validity is also desirable.

If item construction and test development do not proceed from a rational and well-developed philosophy of education, the items written are likely to treat only superficial aspects of instruction. The resulting test will be of variable quality. Specifying defensible instructional objectives is of paramount importance in test construction.

Teachers must be educational and developmental psychologists—they must know how students learn and develop. Understanding individual

The nature of the test must consider the purpose it is to serve.

differences will allow them to create test questions suitable for their students. We do not, for example, use analogy items with first grade students, because the mechanically contrived question form does not match the usual instructional style at this level and would be unfamiliar to students. The mechanics of a test question should not interfere with measurement.

We will now provide guidelines for writing various sorts of items. Many of the suggestions in the remainder of this chapter will be considered simple common sense. Unfortunately, however, common-sense principles are often not applied in test development. If, in the following five sections, we can make clear the importance of common sense in item writing, we will have made a worthwhile contribution.

General Guidelines for Item Writing

Before considering specific item types, we will present some general principles for item writing. Remmers, Gage, and Rummel (1965) list six principles applicable to all short-answer items:

1. *Avoid using items which, in terms of either content or structure, could be considered obvious, trivial, meaningless, or ambiguous.* If a test developer does not rely heavily on a table of specifications to guide item and test development, such unsatisfactory items may result.
2. *Follow the rules of punctuation, grammar, and rhetoric.* Again, the command of language and expressive skills in item development is crucial.
3. *Use items that have a "right" or "definitely correct" answer, or at least an answer upon which experts agree.* These item characteristics were described in chapter 9 as "objectivity."
4. *Avoid items that rely on obscure or esoteric language.* Unless your intent is to test vocabulary, it is not desirable to elicit responses whose correctness depends on size of vocabulary or reading ability. If key words are obscure, even the better students will fail to give them sufficient attention, and the items may become "trick" or "catch" questions.
5. *Avoid interrelated items.* These occur when the content of one item (e.g., the stem or alternatives in a multiple-choice item) furnishes the answer to other items. As we frequently test the same content area a number of times, it is difficult to avoid interrelated items, and only careful inspection of the test will reveal them.
6. *Avoid items containing "irrelevant cues."* Irrelevant cues probably constitute the chief fault of most classroom tests. Irrelevant cues are a class of defect that leads a student to the correct answer independent of knowledge or skill. Grammatical clues, word associations or definitions, a systematic difference in the correct answer, or stereo-

typed language are only a few examples. The type of cue varies with the type of item. A test that contains a large number of items with irrelevant cues is probably measuring nothing more than test wiseness, or shrewd test-taking.

Writing Supply Items

Supply items are generally either simple direct questions (e.g., Who was the first American astronaut to fly in space?) or completion items (e.g., The name of the first American astronaut to fly in space is _____). The chief advantage of supply items is that it minimizes the effect of guessing. Because students construct their own responses, supply items are one of the best ways of measuring objectives at the first level (knowledge) of the cognitive domain taxonomy. An emphasis on memory, in moderation, is probably not unreasonable. Students must know a certain amount of factual information before they can do anything else. Thus a teacher's decision to check on specific facts requisite to further work is entirely justified in many instances.

Another advantage of supply items, particularly for those teaching and testing in the elementary grades, is that they are "natural." Elementary teaching frequently employs the so-called Socratic question-and-answer format. In testing, the use of simple direct questions follows logically from this method of instruction. Supply items are also efficient from the teacher's standpoint; they allow students to summarize long and often complex problem solving processes in a single brief statement, thereby facilitating scoring.

The chief disadvantage of supply items is that scoring is not always completely objective. It is surprising how often students come up with correct but unanticipated answers. Unless the scoring key is revised in light of alternative correct answers, serious injustices may be perpetrated on students. Lack of objectivity can frequently be traced to the use of ambiguous words in the item. Also, because they are easily prepared, supply items too often become only a matter of identification or naming. A test composed primarily of supply items is unlikely to reflect all relevant instructional objectives.

The following guidelines are not strict rules, but ways of asking questions that have been found useful. Question style will depend much on the personal preferences of the teacher.

1. *Require short, definite, clearcut, and explicit answers.* An indefinite statement is likely to lead to scoring problems for instructors and response problems for students.

    Poor: Ronald Reagan is a _____ .
    Improved: The political party to which Ronald Reagan belongs is the _____ party.

2. *Avoid multi-mutilated statements.* Introducing blanks too liberally into a statement, from a text for example, can only lead to ambigu-

ity. Popham (1981) calls this a "Swiss cheese item." The instructor is not always sure which portion of the statement the student is responding to and therefore which objective is being measured. One can end up with a nonsensical sequence of blanks.

Poor: The _____ of _____ was signed in the year _____ .
Improved: The Declaration of Independence was signed in the year _____ .

3. *If several correct answers (e.g., synonyms) are possible, equal credit should be given to each one.*
4. *Specify and announce in advance whether scoring will take spelling into account.*
5. *In testing for comprehension of terms and knowledge of definitions, it is often better to supply the term and require a definition than to provide a definition and require the term.* Students are less likely to benefit from verbal association cues if this procedure is followed. Asking students to supply the definition is a better measure of their knowledge.

Poor: What is the name given to the interrelationship of organisms among themselves and with their environment?
Improved: Define *ecology*.

6. *It is generally recommended that in completion items the blanks come at the end of the statement.* Beginning an item with a blank is awkward for students and may interfere with comprehension of the question. In general, the best approach is a simple and direct one.

Poor: _____ is the device used to measure temperature.
Improved: The device used to measure temperature is called a(n) _____ .

7. *Minimize the use of textbook expressions and stereotyped language.* When statements are taken out of context, they tend to become ambiguous. The use of paraphrased statements will reduce the incidence of correct responses that represent meaningless verbal associations. In addition, it should reduce the temptation to memorize the exact wording of the text or lecture material.
8. *Specify the terms in which the response is to be given.* It should be clear to the student that the required answer is, for example, a date, place, event, or person's name.

Poor: Where is the Statue of Liberty located?
Improved: In what city of the United States is the Statue of Liberty located?

Precision is particularly important in mathematics questions stated in free-response form. Otherwise, the student may be faced with the problem of trying to guess the degree of error to be tolerated. Is one decimal place sufficient? Two? Different students may come to different conclusions.

Poor: If a circle has a 4-inch diameter, its area is _____ .
Improved: A circle has a 4-inch diameter. Its area, correct to two decimal places, is _____ square inches.

9. *In general, direct questions are preferable to incomplete declarative sentences.*

Poor: Columbus discovered America in the year _____ .
Improved: In what year did Columbus discover America?

10. *Avoid extraneous clues to the correct answer.* The grammatical structure of an item may lead a student to the correct answer, independent of his knowledge, particularly if the number of alternative answers is small.

Poor: A fraction whose denominator is greater than its numerator is a _____ .
Improved: Fractions whose denominators are greater than their numerators are called _____ fractions.

In the faulty item above, the article *a* is an irrelevant clue, since "proper fraction" could come after it and "improper fraction" could not. Similarly, blanks should be of uniform length so as not to suggest the length of the expected response.

Writing Constant-Alternative Selection Items

In a constant-alternative selection item, the examinee chooses one of two or more alternatives that remain the same throughout a series of items. The alternative answers are usually *true* and *false*. Other forms, however, may be used: *yes-no, right-wrong, true-false-depends, correct-incorrect, same-opposite, true-false and converse true or converse false, true-false with correct variety,* and *true-false-qualification.* Because it is the most common constant-alternative type, the true-false item will be used as an example in this section.

Despite difficulties in constructing them, true-false questions are potentially valuable for gathering data. Most prominent among their advantages is efficiency. Teachers can present many such items per unit of testing time. This allows them to survey large content areas to estimate students' knowledge. Scoring of true-false items is, of course, rapid and easy. If great care is exercised in their construction, such items can be used to test understanding of principles and generalizations. In addition, they can profitably be used to assess persistence of popular misconceptions, fallacies, and superstitions (e.g., "Swallowing watermelon seeds will result in appendicitis"). It should be pointed out that students have not been shown to learn significant amounts of misinformation from true-false items. What little mislearning does take place can be "washed out" if the test is reviewed by students and teacher. This is, of course, a recommended class activity no matter what type of item is used. Finally, true-false items are useful for questions in which only two responses are possible (e.g., "School emergency exits should open inward").

The disadvantages and limitations of true-false items may outweigh their merits unless you use judgment and intelligence. Some experts say that, although seemingly easy to construct, meaningful and error-free constant-alternative items are the most difficult of all "objective" questions to write. Quality and precision of language are crucial to these items. Ambiguous terminology on the one hand and careless reading on the other probably have the strongest effect for true-false items, since a student must respond, in most instances, to a single unqualified statement. Obviously, the smaller the stimulus the greater the chance for misinterpretation. Guessing can also have a significant effect. Using a fairly large number of items reduces the overall effect of guessing and increases the reliability of the test.*

Despite their clear limitations, true-false items can prove useful in classroom tests if used in moderation with upper elementary students. We do not recommend tests composed entirely of constant-alternative items. Suggestions for improving true-false items follow:

1. *Avoid the use of "specific determiners."* Specific determiners are a class of words that function as irrelevant cues. For example, it has been found that, on most classroom tests, items that include the words "only," "all," "no," "none," "always," "never," etc., are generally false. On the other hand, items containing words like "could," "might," "can," "may," and "generally" will usually be true, because they imply a reasonable qualification.

   Poor: The President of the United States is always elected to that office.

   The statement is generally true but must be marked false because there are exceptions. For example, if the President dies the Vice-President is sworn into that office without an election.

   Improved: The electoral college is designed to elect the President and Vice-President of the United States.

   If the number of true and false specific determiners is evenly balanced, their influence is reduced. There are, of course, situations in which

---

*On a 50-item true-false test, "blind guessing" is likely to result in a score of 25. The result is to reduce the usable range of scores from 50 (0 to 50) to 25 (25 to 50). It would, however, be a rare event for a student to respond blindly. Almost all students will have some information about an item. In addition, although the odds of a chance score of 25 on a 50-item test are 1 in 2, those of a chance score of 35 are 1 in 350. Once the indifference point (50–50) is passed, chance responses through guessing will work against the student.

a teacher may successfully use specific determiners in true-false items whose answers are the opposite of those suggested by the words in question (e.g., "All planets revolve around the sun of our solar system").

2. *Base true-false items on statements that are absolutely true or false, without qualifications or exceptions.* This is a difficult requirement in some subject-matter areas (e.g., history, literature) where trends, generalizations, concepts, and principles are hard to demonstrate empirically. Statements that are not absolutely true or false are likely to confuse examinees, particularly the more knowledgeable. Examinees may read different assumptions into the statements, and you will no longer be sure what the item is measuring.

Poor: There are 24 hours in a day.

This appears to be a good item, but appearances can be deceiving. Responses to the item will depend upon one's definition of a day. Strictly speaking, a day has twelve hours. However, many individuals commonly think of the total day as a combination of the daylight and nighttime hours.

Improved: A total of 24 hours would pass between the hours of 8:00 A.M. Monday and 8:00 A.M. Tuesday.

3. *Avoid negatively stated items when possible and eliminate all double negatives.* Such phrasing may cause students to miss an item because they do not comprehend the question. Double negatives are frequently interpreted as emphatically negative. Such items might be used to measure translating ability in an English course, but their general usefulness is negligible; they should be avoided. Where a negative word must be used, it should be underlined so that students will notice it.

Poor: None of the rules of the game was necessary.
Improved: All of the rules of the game were necessary.

4. *Use quantitative and precise rather than qualitative language where possible.* Again, the specificity of word meanings comes into play in judging the effectiveness of an item. Such words as 'few," "many," "young," "long," "short," "large," "small," and "important," unless accompanied by a standard of comparison, are open to interpretation and thus ambiguous.

Poor: Many people voted for Ronald Reagan in the 1984 Presidential election.
Improved: Ronald Reagan received more than 60 percent of the votes cast in the Presidential election of 1984.

5. *Avoid stereotypic and textbook statements.* Such statements, when taken out of context, are ambiguous and frequently meaningless and trivial (e.g., "From time to time efforts have been made to explode the notion that there may be a cause-and-effect relationship between arboreal life and a primate anatomy"). A related problem arises when text material is quoted verbatim and turned into a true-false statement by inserting *no* or *not.* Such statements may appear ambiguous and place too great a premium on rote memorization.

6. *The crucial elements of an item should be placed at the end of the statement.* The function of the first part of a two-part statement is to "set the problem." To focus on the effect in a cause-and-effect relationship, for example, state the true cause in the first portion of the statement and a false effect at the end. Conversely, to focus on the cause, state the true effect first and a false cause at the end. This procedure is suggested because students are likely to focus on the last portion of a statement they read. Thus the teacher's objective and the student's attention will be synchronized. The following item is intended to focus on the effect.

Poor: Oxygen reduction occurs more readily because carbon monoxide combines with hemoglobin faster than oxygen does.

Improved: Carbon monoxide poisoning occurs because carbon monoxide dissolves delicate lung tissue.

7. *The numbers of true items and false items should be approximately equal.* Some students who are in doubt of the correct answer tend to guess *true* more often than *false* or *false* more often than *true.* We call this a **response set.** So that students are not unduly penalized, neither response set should be favored by overloading the test with items of one type.

Writing Changing-Alternative Selection Items

Changing-alternative items require the examinee to select an answer from among several alternatives, which change with each item. Such items are usually referred to as multiple choice questions. The selection may be made on any number of bases, e.g., *correct* or *best and most inclusive, cause* or *effect, most similar* or *dissimilar,* and so on.

Each item is composed of a stem or lead, which sets the problem, and the alternative responses. The stem may be an incomplete statement (to be completed by the alternatives) or a direct question. Only one response is correct, and the others should be plausible but incorrect. For this reason the incorrect alternatives are sometimes referred to as **foils** or **distractors**—they distract the less knowledgeable or skillful student away from the correct answer.

Probably the most flexible of all item types, the multiple choice item can be used to assess knowledge as well as such higher mental processes as application and analysis. Since alternative answers provide a standard of comparison, these items are relatively free from ambiguity—one of their advantages over true-false items.

Multiple choice items are most useful when the correct answer is long or can be expressed in a variety of ways. Plausible incorrect alternatives can then be used to test fine discriminations and allow the teacher easily to control the difficulty level of the items by varying the homogeneity of responses. Multiple choice items can provide more valuable diagnostic information than true-false items if the alternatives are carefully constructed and represent different degrees of "correctness."*

The primary limitation of multiple choice items is that they are difficult to construct well. Plausible distractors are often hard to find or construct (particularly if four or five are needed). One excellent source of alternatives is the pool of incorrect answers supplied when the stem of the mutiple choice item is administered as a free-response item.

Multiple choice items are subject to almost as many irrelevant cues as is any other type of short-answer question. The greater written length contributes to this situation, and also, by increasing reading time, reduces the number of items (as compared with supply and true-false methods) that can be presented per unit of time. Greater flexibility and reliability, however, more than compensate for this lessened efficiency. Some suggestions for writing multiple choice items follow:

1. *We recommend that the stem be a direct question.* Although no research evidence supports the advantages of the direct question lead over the incomplete statement, it has been found in practice that the novice item writer will produce fewer weak and ambiguous items if the direct question lead is used.
2. *The stem should pose a clear, definite, explicit, and singular problem.* This suggestion follows from the preceding one. The major potential weakness of incomplete statement leads is that they are frequently incomplete; in many instances the student must read the alternatives to determine what the question is. The direct question stem is more likely to make explicit the basis on which the correct response is to be chosen. An item writer can generally express complex ideas more easily with the direct question format. If an incomplete statement lead is used, it should be meaningful in itself and imply a direct question rather than leading into a collection of unrelated true-false statements.

---

*The effect of guessing is markedly reduced, though not eliminated. In a 10-item four-alternative multiple choice test, the probability of obtaining a score of 7 by chance alone is 1 in 1000. Freedom from guessing comparable to that of a four-alternative 25-item multiple choice test would require a true-false test of 200 items. The effectiveness of multiple choice items is obvious.

Poor: America
a. was named after Vespucci.
b. contains 52 states.
c. is the world's oldest civilization.
d. is the world's largest country.

Improved: After whom was America named?
a. Columbus
b. Magellan
c. Ponce de León
d. Vespucci

3. *Include in the stem any words that might otherwise be repeated in each response.* Streamlining an item in this way reduces reading time and makes for a more efficient question.

Poor: Water can be turned into ice when it reaches
a. a temperature of 0 °C.
b. a temperature of 50 °C.
c. a temperature of 75 °C.
d. a temperature of 100 °C.

Improved: Water can be turned into ice when it reaches a temperature of
a. 0 °C
b. 50 °C
c. 75 °C
d. 100 °C

4. *Items should be stated simply and understandably, excluding all nonfunctional words from the stem and alternatives.* The inclusion of extraneous words increases reading time and thereby reduces item efficiency. In addition, the central problem may become obscured, which leads to ambiguity.

Poor: Magellan was the first person to
a. circumnavigate the globe.
b. discover the Pacific Ocean.
c. discover the Fountain of Youth.
d. discover Mexico.

Improved: Magellan was the first person to
a. go around the world.
b. discover the Pacific Ocean.
c. discover the Fountain of Youth.
d. discover Mexico.

5. *Avoid interrelated items.* Teachers occasionally and unintentionally write items that overlap. That is, the stem or alternatives to one

item give away the answer to other items. This is more likely to happen when the test is long. It may be necessary in some cases to index key words or concepts to check on overlap. Casual perusal is rarely sufficient.

6. *Avoid negatively stated items.* Keep the use of such items to a minimum, as they are frequently awkward and difficult to comprehend. If "not," "no," "never," "none," "except," or a similar term is to be used, it should be highlighted for the student by underlining or capitalizing it. You are often better off rewriting the item in positive terms.

    Poor: None of the following cities is a state capital except
                    a. Bangor
                    b. Denver
                    c. Los Angeles
                    d. New Haven

    Improved: Which of the following cities is a state capital?
                    a. Bangor
                    b. Denver
                    c. Los Angeles
                    d. New Haven

7. *Avoid making the correct alternative systematically different from other options.* The usual example of a "systematically different correct alternative" is a correct answer that is obviously longer and more precisely stated than the distractors. There is an unconscious tendency to include all relevant information so that the correct alternative will be unequivocally correct. A related error is the attempt to make the correct alternatives more technical than the foils.

8. *If possible, the alternatives should be presented in some logical, numerical, or systematic order.* Again, structure the question so that responding to it will be facilitated. Alphabetizing single-word, concept, or phrase alternatives has not been shown to bias responses.

    Poor: Which of the following states is *not* located on the Mississippi River?
                    a. Louisiana
                    b. Arkansas
                    c. Tennessee
                    d. Ohio

    Improved: Which of the following states is *not* located on the Mississippi River?
                    a. Arkansas
                    b. Louisiana
                    c. Ohio
                    d. Tennessee

Poor: In what year was the Declaration of Independence signed?
a. 1746
b. 1796
c. 1776
d. 1786

Improved: In what year was the Declaration of Independence signed?
a. 1746
b. 1776
c. 1786
d. 1796

9. *Response alternatives should be mutually exclusive.* Overlapping or synonymous responses should be eliminated because they reduce the discrimination value of an item and either confuse examinees, if more than one answer is correct, or allow them to eliminate two or more alternatives for the price of one.

Poor: Who wrote *Tom Sawyer?*
a. Lewis Carroll
b. Samuel Clemens
c. Booth Tarkington
d. Mark Twain

Improved: Who wrote *Tom Sawyer?*
a. Lewis Carroll
b. Bret Harte
c. Booth Tarkington
d. Mark Twain

Poor: What is the population of Atlanta, Georgia?
a. Over 100,000
b. Over 250,000
c. Over 500,000
d. Over 1,000,000

The answer is *d*, over 1,000,000, but because of the way the alternatives are phrased a student is likely to be unsure how to respond. Alternatives *a, b,* and *c* overlap *d* and must also be considered correct.

Improved: What is the population of Atlanta, Georgia?
a. 100,000
b. 250,000
c. 500,000
d. more than 1,000,000

10. *Make all responses plausible and attractive to the less knowledgeable or skillful student.* The options to a multiple choice item should include distractors that will attract unprepared students. Foils should include the common misconceptions and/or errors. They should be familiar, natural, and reasonable.

Poor: Which of the following men was at one time Vice-President of the United States?
a. John Glenn
b. Richard Nixon
c. Marco Polo
d. Franklin Roosevelt

Improved: Which of the following men was at one time Vice-President of the United States?
a. John Kennedy
b. Richard Nixon
c. Ronald Reagan
d. Franklin Roosevelt

In the first version if students do not know the answer a few miscellaneous pieces of information can help them find it. Responses *a* and *c* are unlikely possibilities; John Glenn will be remembered as an astronaut and Marco Polo as a discoverer. The second version includes only names of men who have served as President of the United States. This homogeneity makes each alternative much more plausible.

When the distractors are constructed so they contain common mistakes that students make, the test can provide useful diagnostic information for the teacher. Note how the incorrect choices in the following item are based on typical student errors.

$1/2 \div 3/4 =$ _____ .
a. 3/8
b. 1 1/2
c. 2/3
d. None of the above

Choice *a*, 3/8, is the answer if the student multiplies rather than divides. Alternative *b*, 1 1/2, is the answer if the student inverts the wrong number. The correct response is *c*, 2/3. Choice *d* covers all other errors the student may make.

11. *The response alternative "None of the above" should be used with caution, if at all.* Although some testing experts recommend the use of this alternative, particularly with mathematics items, we do not. When "None of the above" is the correct answer, there is no assurance that the examinee does, in fact, know the answer. Consider the following elementary example:

Poor: What is the area of a rectangle whose sides measure 4 inches and 3 inches?
  a. 7 sq. inches
  b. 15 sq. inches
  c. 25 sq. inches
  d. None of the above

The answer is 12 square inches, and the knowledgeable student would select alternative *d*. But a student who solved the problem incorrectly (e.g., solving for the perimeter, which is 14), and came up with an incorrect answer not found among the alternatives, might select the correct *d*. The response "None of the above" may function well as an alternative if the correct answer is included among the preceding alternatives. In such a situation, it functions as an all-inclusive incorrect alternative covering a multitude of sins.

Improved: What is the area of a rectangle whose sides measure 4 inches and 3 inches?
  a. 7 sq. inches
  b. 12 sq. inches
  c. 25 sq. inches
  d. None of the above

12. *Make options grammatically parallel to each other and consistent with the stem.* Lack of parallelism makes for an awkward item and may cause the examinee difficulty in grasping the meaning of the question or the relationships among the alternative answers. Lack of parallelism between stem and alternatives may also lead to a "grammatical clue" to the correct answer.

Poor: A large body of water is an
  a. creek
  b. ocean
  c. river
  d. stream

The article *an* leads the student to the correct answer.

Improved: What is the name used to refer to a large body of water?
  a. creek
  b. ocean
  c. river
  d. stream

13. *Avoid such irrelevant cues as "common elements" and "pat verbal associations."* Because multiple choice items require association between several options and a lead statement, any similarities between key words in the stem and those in the alternatives may function as irrelevant cues. In fact, common elements in the stem and correct alternatives are the most obvious type of irrelevant cue.

14. *In testing for understanding of a term or concept, present the term in the stem and alternative definitions in the options.* The examinee is less likely to benefit from pat verbal associations, particularly if the correct answer is a paraphrase rather than a verbatim extract from the text.

Poor: What is the name of the branch of science that studies the location, movement, and nature of planets, stars, and other celestial bodies?
a. astrology
b. astronomy
c. geology

Improved: Astronomy can be defined as the science that studies the
a. location, movement, and nature of planets, stars, and other celestial bodies.
b. effect of celestial bodies on humans.
c. location, movement, and consistency of the earth's surface.

15. *Use "objective" items.* In other words, use items on whose correct answers virtually all experts would agree. It is an interesting, humbling, and informative experience to have a colleague key one's tests. But it is perhaps more important to go over each test with students, who are probably the best "test critics."

Writing Matching Exercises

The matching exercise is a variant of the multiple choice question. While the multiple choice question usually presents a single problem and several solutions, the matching exercise presents several problems and several solutions. The list of alternative solutions is constant for each new problem or stimulus. It is because of this constancy of alternatives that the quality and homogeneity of options so significantly influence the effectiveness of the exercise. Matching exercises may concentrate on form or on content (see chap. 4). Pictorial material can be used with success. Exercises might cover events, inventions, results, definitions, quotations, dates, or locations. At a more sophisticated level, students might be asked to match (1) causes to effects, (2) theoretical statements to experimental bases, or (3) a phenomenon to its explanation in terms of principles, generalizations, or theories.

Most matching exercises contain two columns, the left column containing the stimuli or premises, the right containing responses. Compound matching exercises (e.g., state to major industry to city or authors to novels to nationalities) are, of course, possible, but are used infrequently.

The matching exercise's chief advantage is efficient use of time and space. A single set of response alternatives serves a whole group of items. The matching exercise is a compact and efficient method of surveying knowledge of the who, what, and where variety.

Using a computer for testing facilitates use of matching items.

The matching exercise is not well suited to measuring higher-order abilities. It is particularly susceptible to irrelevant cues, implausible alternatives, and awkward arrangement of stimuli or responses; thus, it must be developed with care. Several suggestions for constructing or revising matching exercises follow:

1. *Matching exercises should be complete on a single page.* Splitting the exercise is confusing, distracting, and time-consuming for the student. Random errors may be made as a result of turning the page back and forth.
2. *Use responses that are homogeneous but mutually exclusive.* If this suggestion is not followed, ambiguous items or items requiring multikeying will result. Responses should be drawn from the same domain (e.g., do not mix dates and names of inventors in the same response list) but should not overlap. The degree of similarity among stimuli and/or responses will, of course, dictate the difficulty of the exercise.
3. *Have more responses than stimuli.* This practice will limit the effect of guessing. If you provide four more responses than stimuli, students have only a one in five chance of guessing correctly on the last stimulus.
4. *Arrange stimuli and responses in some logical order, i.e., alphabetically or chronologically.* This suggestion is intended to facilitate response to the exercise. The responses should be so stated and arranged that the student can scan them quickly.

5. *Limit the number of items in each set.* Use no more than five or six items per set for elementary students. If a matching exercise is too long, the task becomes tedious and the discrimination too fine. A six-item list of stimuli will probably have about ten possible responses. To avoid the likelihood that a student will benefit from guessing or the process of elimination, the response "None of the above" may be used cautiously. You might also state in the test directions that the responses may be used more than once.
6. *The directions should clearly specify the basis for matching stimuli and responses.* Although the basis for matching is usually obvious, sound testing practice dictates that the directions spell out the nature of the task. The student should not have to read through the stimulus and response lists in order to discern the intended basis for matching.

   Poor: *Directions*: Match List A with List B.

	A	*B*
___ a.	invented cotton gin	a. Alexander Graham Bell
___ b.	invented telephone	b. George Washington
___ c.	first President of U.S.	c. Ferdinand Magellan
___ d.	first U.S. astronaut to walk on the moon	d. Eli Whitney
___ e.	discovered America	e. None of these

The primary shortcomings of this matching exercise are:

1. The directions fail to specify the basis for matching or mechanics for responding.
2. The two lists are enumerated identically.
3. Both lists lack homogeneity.
4. The responses are not listed logically—in this case, alphabetically.
5. There are equal numbers of elements in both lists.
6. The use of "None of these" is questionable in this exercise, serving as a giveaway to List A items *d* and *e*. If a student uses it to answer these items, it is not clear that she knows what U.S. astronaut first walked on the moon and who in fact discovered America.

   Improved: *Directions*: Famous inventions are listed below in the left-hand column, and inventors in the right-hand column. Place the letter corresponding to the inventor in the space next to the invention for which he is famous. "None of these" may be the correct answer. Inventors may be used more than once.

	Inventions	*Inventors*
___ 1.	steamboat	a. Alexander Graham Bell
___ 2.	cotton gin	
___ 3.	sewing machine	b. Robert Fulton
___ 4.	reaper	c. Elias Howe

_____ 5. telephone

    d. Cyrus McCormick
    e. Benjamin Franklin
    f. Eli Whitney
    g. Orville Wright
    h. Henry Ford
    i. None of these

Writing Test Items for Elementary Students

Developing test items for young students is a difficult task.* This is particularly true if the teacher has decided to use so-called "objective" or short-answer questions. Writing items for the young requires development of (1) comprehensible and appropriate stimulus materials, and (2) a scheme for recording student responses efficiently.

At the kindergarten level, the best way to record answers may be to have the youngsters draw an X on a picture. A series of pictures can be accompanied by a series of questions, as shown below:

1. Put an X on the pictures of things that are alive.
2. Put a Y on the picture of each thing that is an animal.
3. Put a Z on the picture of each thing that is a mammal.

---

*The material in this section is based on Dr. Clarence Nelson's monograph, *Improving Objective Tests in Science* (1967), pp. 18–21. Sample items reproduced by permission of the National Science Teachers Association, 1742 Connecticut Ave., N.W., Washington, D.C. 20009.

4. One of the following pictures is a kitty. Put an X on that picture.

5. One of these pictures shows what happens when something is heated or becomes warm. Put an X on that picture.

To test for understanding of concepts, use a picture card illustrating objects similar but not identical to those discussed in class. If identical objects are used, you may be measuring recall rather than understanding. A similar method of recording responses can be used at the first grade level. Using pictorial material, the teacher reads the questions to the students, who again mark the correct picture with an X. Two examples follow:

6. (The teacher demonstrates boiling, filtering, and straining of water and then reads the test question.) Pure water can be taken out of salt water by

7. Salt has been mixed with chopped ice. If some of this chopped ice is packed around a container full of water, what will probably happen to the water in the container?

Second and third graders can probably use a special answer sheet containing lettered or numbered squares like the following:

8. a □ b □ c □   10. a □ b □ c □
9. a □ b □ c □   11. a □ b □ c □

An alternative is to have the students circle the letters on an answer sheet. The questions could be handed out in duplicated form, and after the method for recording the answers is explained, the questions and answers could be read slowly to the students:

8. When a watch is laid flat on a table, if 12 on the dial represents north, then 9 on the dial represents
   a. south.
   b. east.
   c. west.
9. If 12 on your watch dial represents north, what represents southeast?
   a. 4:30
   b. 7:30
   c. 12:30
10. A person standing at the seashore looking at a ship several miles from the shore can see the
    a. entire ship.
    b. upper part of the ship only.
    c. lower part of the ship only.
11. The horizon would be farthest away
    a. if you were standing on the seashore and looking out over the ocean.
    b. if you were on top of the Empire State Building or the Washington Monument and looking straight ahead.
    c. if you were looking out of an airplane while flying four miles above the earth.

Essay Items

Essay tests should allow students to solve problems, analyze, synthesize, and evaluate. Because students must organize their answers and express them in their own words and handwriting, essay tests are not very effective in the lower and intermediate primary grades. As children move into the upper elementary grades, these tests increase in value.

Essay items take less time to construct than do objective items and, according to some educators, encourage more appropriate study habits. Essay items may measure content, expression, or both and may require extended or restricted responses (Gronlund 1981; Popham 1981).

Content vs. Expression

It is frequently claimed that essay items or tests allow students to present their knowledge and understanding and also to organize the material in a unique form and style. More often than not, such factors as expression, grammar, and spelling are evaluated in conjunction with content. If the teacher has attempted to develop students' expressive skills, and if this learning outcome is included in the table of specifications for the test, then evaluating such skills is legitimate. If expressive skills are not part of the instructional program, it is not ethical to evaluate them.

If the score of each essay item includes an evaluation of its mechanics of expression, this should be brought to the attention of the student. If possible, compute separate scores for content and expression.

The decision to include either or both of these elements in a score, and the weight given to each, should be based on the table of specifications.

Extended vs. Restricted Response

Essay items differ in the extensiveness of the desired response. Freedom of response has obvious practical implications for both teacher and student. From the teacher's standpoint, extensive responses to a few broadly based questions allow an indepth sampling of a student's knowledge, thinking processes, and problem solving methods for a particular topic. The open-ended task posed by a question like "What does pollution mean to you?" challenges a student. To respond correctly, the student must recall specific information, organize, evaluate, and write an intelligible composition. On the other hand, such free-response essay items tend to yield responses that vary widely both in content and in organization, making reliable grading difficult. The potential ambiguity of essay items is probably the singlemost important contributor to their unreliability. In addition, the more extensive the responses called for, the fewer questions time permits—which, in turn, may lower the content validity of the test.

Therefore, a restricted-response essay item and/or test is generally preferable. Consider this instruction: "Explain why we need unpolluted fresh water. Include in your answer three causes of freshwater pollution and three suggestions for ways of eliminating such pollution." This instruction presents a well-defined task that lends itself to reliable scoring and yet allows students to organize their thoughts creatively.

Instructional Objectives and Essay Items

Essay items may be used to measure very specific or very general outcomes of teaching. In practice, many teachers use essay items to measure factual knowledge, although objective tests are more effective for this purpose. For example, here is a knowledge level essay item:

Poor: List three causes of the Civil War.

In this essay item students have very little freedom to structure their responses. All they need to provide is a list, a simple recall or memorization task. In fact, the main distinction between this essay item and an objective (multiple choice) item is that they depend respectively on recall and recognition.

Types of Essay Questions

Chapter 4 showed how objectives can be stated behaviorally to make them precise. This same procedure can be used in writing essay items.

The following set of sample item stems can help you frame questions to elicit particular behaviors and levels of response:*

1. Comparing
    Describe the similarities and differences between . . .
    Compare the following two methods for . . .
2. Relating cause and effect
    What are major causes of . . . ?
    What would be the most likely effect of . . . ?
3. Justifying
    Which of the following alternatives would you favor and why?
    Explain why you agree or disagree with the following statement.
4. Summarizing
    State the main points included in . . .
    Briefly summarize the contents of . . .
5. Generalizing
    Formulate several valid generalizations from the following data.
    State a set of principles that can explain the following events.
6. Inferring
    In light of the facts presented, what is most likely to happen, when . . . ?
    How would [Senator X] be likely to react to the following issue?
7. Classifying
    Group the following items according to . . .
    What do the following items have in common?
8. Creating
    List as many ways as you can think of for . . .
    Make up a story describing what would happen if . . .
    Write a list of questions that should be answered before . . .
9. Applying
    Using the principle of . . . as a guide, describe how you would solve the following problem situation.
    Describe a situation that illustrates the principle of . . .
10. Analyzing
    Describe the reasoning errors in the following paragraph.
    List and describe the main characteristics of . . .
    Describe the relationship between the following parts of . . .
11. Synthesizing
    Describe a plan for proving that . . .
    Write a well-organized report that shows . . .
    Write a set of specifications for building a . . .
12. Evaluating
    Criticize or defend each of the following statements.
    Describe the strengths and weaknesses of the following . . .
    Using the criteria developed in class, write a critical evaluation of . . .

---

*Reprinted with permission of Macmillan Publishing Company from *Measurement and Evaluation in Teaching*, 3d ed., by Norman E. Gronlund. Copyright © 1976 by Norman E. Gronlund.

Essay tests, despite their limitations, are held in high esteem by many teachers from elementary through graduate school. If we are to use essay tests, we must construct them carefully. The following suggestions should be helpful in writing essay items:

1. *Use essay items only for those processes to which they are most applicable.* When a learning outcome can be satisfactorily measured by more objective means there is very little justification for using essay questions. The problems of scoring and limited sampling of content covered suggest we should not use essays simply to measure lower level learning. However, outcomes at higher cognitive levels are better assessed using restricted response essay items.

2. *Essay items should elicit the behavior specified in the instructional objectives.* Broadly stated questions such as "What were some causes of the Civil War?" do not clearly indicate to the student what the teacher is looking for. They evoke guesses as to what the teacher wants, i.e., how many causes are enough and how much weight each will receive in scoring. We could aim at a much more specific objective if we asked the question, "Compare and contrast the role of slavery in the North and in the South at the outset of the Civil War."

3. *For a test composed solely of essay items, shorten each item and increase the number of questions.* Essay items are usually broad in scope and take a long time to answer. Consequently, students can respond to only a few essay items during a typical testing period. This limited sampling of the content can be improved by constructing a larger number of restricted-response items rather than few extended-response items.

4. *Indicate an approximate amount of time to spend on each question and the number of points each question is worth.* Students, particularly young ones, need guidelines on how to budget the time required to answer the essay questions. Remember, you are not measuring how fast students can organize their thoughts or write. Carefully estimate how long each question will take to answer, and provide this information to the students either orally or in writing. Most of us have experienced the panicky feeling that comes when time runs out and we still have one more question to go!

   Telling students the point value of each question will also help them to budget their time. Time restrictions and point allotments can be written in next to each question:

   1. (10 minutes, 5 points) Explain the . . .

5. *Require all students to respond to the same questions.* Teachers often provide students with more essay questions than they will have to answer. For example, a teacher may provide six essay questions and allow the student to choose any four to answer. There are a number

of problems with this practice. First, items differ in complexity and difficulty. Second, when students answer different questions they are essentially taking different tests, and the teacher will not have a common basis to compare and evaluate their achievement. If students are allowed to choose the questions to respond to, choice of topic rather than amount of knowledge could account for differences in achievement. Third, if students know they will be given optional questions they can be selective in what they prepare and study for.

Scoring Essay Tests

Scoring essay items and tests is time-consuming and may be frustrating. Teachers are frequently unwilling to set aside the large chunks of time necessary to score a stack of essays carefully and reliably.

Before we turn to specific methods of scoring, some general comments are in order. First, the teacher should prepare in advance a detailed "ideal" answer. This answer will serve as the criterion by which each student's answer will be judged. If this is not done, the results could be disastrous. Second, student papers should be scored anonymously. This reduces bias or the halo effect, the tendency to allow general impressions of students to influence your evaluation of their performance. Third, all the answers to a given item should be scored at one time, rather than grading each student's test in turn. That is, start with the first question on the first paper and grade it, then proceed to the next paper and grade only the first question. After going through all the papers, move on to the second question. Even following this procedure, a teacher may be influenced by the quality of the essays already graded. Hales and Tokar (1975) found that essays of average quality were rated more highly when preceded by five poor-quality essays than when preceded by five good-quality essays.

The mechanics of scoring generally take one of two forms, the rating method and the analytic method.

Rating Method. The rating method involves evaluating a number of categories, generally fewer than ten, and making qualitative judgments in each. This method considers the response as a whole and is used when the teacher is focusing on expression as well as content. Rating methods are efficient, but their reliability is tied to the number of categories and subdivisions within categories. The categories will usually be chosen based on the "ideal" answer the teacher has constructed. A standard set of categories can also be useful, particularly if you are evaluating primarily the essays' composition. Table 12.1 presents a rating method used by Paul Diederich, in his research on writing ability, and by many classroom teachers. This scale counts organization 50 percent, style 30 percent, and mechanics 20 percent. With appropriate, if arbitrary, multiplications, the 40-point scale translates into a 100-point scale. Such a translation is useful for reporting percentage grades.

Table 12.1
Diederich's Scale for Grading English Composition

	1 = Poor 2 = Weak 3 = Average 4 = Good 5 = Excellent		
	Quality and development of ideas	1 2 3 4 5	
	Organization, relevance, movement	1 2 3 4 5	___ × 5 = ___ Subtotal
	Style, flavor, individuality	1 2 3 4 5	
	Wording and phrasing	1 2 3 4 5	___ × 3 = ___ Subtotal
	Grammar, sentence structure	1 2 3 4 5	
	Punctuation	1 2 3 4 5	
	Spelling	1 2 3 4 5	
	Manuscript form, legibility	1 2 3 4 5	___ × 1 = ___ Subtotal
			Total grade ___ %

Note: Adapted from A. Jewett and C. Buster, eds., *Improving English Composition*. Washington: National Education Association, 1965. Used with permission of the National Education Association.

Analytic Method. The analytic or checklist-point-score method partitions the "ideal" response into a series of points or features, each specifically defined. The technique is particularly useful if content is to be emphasized over expression. Each element in the model answer is identified and given a credit value. If possible, the teacher's table of specifications should be used as a guide for determining credits.

As an illustration, consider the following restricted-response question: "Why might the earth be the only planet of the solar system suited for life as we know it?" The teacher's ideal answer might be: "Atmospheric density and temperature are two major factors that permit life as we know it on Earth. The planets in our solar system have atmospheres ranging from none to dense. The temperatures range from very hot to very cold. Earth is the only planet with a medium amount of atmosphere and a warm temperature. These conditions permit life on Earth as we know it."

Essential elements in this ideal answer are identified and quantitative weights assigned to each. The checklist-point-score sheet might look like this:

Element of Answer	*Possible Points*
1. temperature and atmospheric density	2
2. planets have density extremes	1
3. planets have temperature extremes	1
4. Earth's temperature warm	1
5. Earth's atmosphere medium	1

This approach to scoring has several advantages. An analysis of the teacher's ideal response often reveals that the original question needs to be recast to elicit the desired response. The time limit may also need readjustment. Another advantage of the checklist-point-score method is its reliability. If used conscientiously, the analytic method can yield consistent scores on restricted-response essay items for different graders.

Table 12.2
Suggestions for Constructing, Evaluating, and Using Essay Exams

1. Limit the problem that the question poses so it will have an unequivocal meaning to most students.
2. Use words which will convey clear meanings to the student.
3. Prepare enough questions to sample the material of the course broadly, within a reasonable time limit.
4. Use essay questions for the purposes they best serve, i.e., organization, handling complicated ideas, and writing.
5. Prepare questions which require considerable thought but can be answered in relatively few words.
6. Determine in advance how much weight to accord each of the various elements expected in a complete answer.
7. Without knowledge of students' names, score each question for all students. Use several scores and scorers if possible.
8. Require all students to answer all questions on the test.
9. Write questions about materials germane to the course.
10. Study past questions to determine how students performed.
11. Make gross judgments of the quality of answers as a first step in grading.
12. Word a question as simply as possible in order to make the task clear.
13. Do not judge papers on the basis of external factors unless they have been clearly stipulated.
14. Do not make a generalized estimate of an entire paper's worth.
15. Do not construct a test consisting of only one question.

Note: Adapted with permission from Testing Bulletin No. 1, *Essay Tests: General Considerations.* East Lansing: Office of Evaluation Services, Michigan State University, 1971.

Suggestions for Using Essay Tests

Many of the suggestions we have made for using essay items, as well as other recommendations by measurement authorities, are summarized in table 12.2. All are self-explanatory with the exception of #8. Testing experts generally recommend against optional questions. Their use results in essay tests that measure what students know, rather than what they don't know. To gain useful information about what has been learned, you need negative as well as positive evidence. We are emphasizing here the diagnostic use of essay tests. In some other situations, it may be legitimate to let students select the questions they will answer. In a statewide testing program with little control of the curriculum, a choice of questions might be a fairer testing practice. But in a classroom test, a choice of questions is generally not recommended.

Summary

Careful planning, imaginative and skillful question writing, careful formulation of questions into a total test, and fair and proper administration and scoring will result in effective educational assessment. However, effectiveness also depends on the quality of the instruction preceding testing.

The writing of test questions involves finding the most suitable way to pose problems to students, whether such problems require recall of learned information or the use of higher-order mental abilities. This chapter has presented guidelines and suggestions for constructing, administering, and scoring supply, true-false, multiple choice, matching, and essay items.

Item construction, if approached seriously, requires considerable expenditure of time and effort.

Thought Activity

1. State the major principles that underlie item construction.
2. List the advantages and disadvantages of supply items.
3. List the advantages and disadvantages of constant-alternative selection items.
4. Evaluate some true-false tests according to the suggestions on pages 187–189 for writing true-false items.
5. State the difference between constant-alternative selection and changing-alternative selection items.
6. Evaluate some multiple choice tests according to the suggestions on pages 190–196.
7. Evaluate some matching tests according to the suggestions listed on pages 197–199. Rewrite the poor example on page 198 to incorporate the suggestions for writing matching tests.
8. Discuss the differences between content and expressive essay questions.
9. State the differences between extended and restricted responses.
10. Write an essay item for each of the types of essay questions listed on page 203.
11. Evaluate essay items you have taken or that are published in tests according to the suggestions for writing essay items on pages 204–205.
12. List the three suggestions for scoring essay exams presented on page 205.
13. Compare the rating and analytic methods for scoring essay exams.

References

Diederich, P. B. 1964. *Short-cut statistics for teacher-made tests.* 2d ed. Evaluation and Advisory Service Series, pamphlet no. 5. Princeton, N.J.: Educational Testing Service.

Gronlund, N. E. 1981. *Measurement and evaluation in teaching.* 4th ed. New York: Macmillan.

Hales, L. W., and E. Tokar. 1975. The effect of the quality of preceding responses on the grades assigned to subsequent responses on an essay exam. *Journal of Educational Measurement* 12: 115–117.

Nelson, C. 1967. *Improving objective tests in science.* Washington, D.C.: National Science Teachers Association.

Popham, W. J. 1981. *Modern educational measurement.* Englewood Cliffs, N.J.: Prentice-Hall.

Remmers, H. H., N. L. Gage, and J. F. Rummel. 1965. *A practical introduction to measurement and evaluation.* 2d ed. New York: Harper & Row.

13 Summarizing, analyzing, and reporting student achievement data

After you have worked hard to build your evaluation instruments and in fact have administered them, a lot of work remains to be done. Next you must put the student data into a form which will aid you in making decisions. Grading and evaluation rest on answers to questions like the following:

How can I organize test data efficiently?
How valid a test do I have?
How reliable a test do I have?
Which were the bad items on my test?
What is the best way to report student performance?

Such questions seem fearsome when added to an already overwhelmed schedule. But these final quantitative evaluation tasks are extremely important, helping us judge the quality of the data we will use to make decisions about students and about our own effectiveness as educators. Taking time to do a good job will improve not only the effectiveness of instruction but also its efficiency.

Summarizing

After collecting information about students, we need to summarize it in a meaningful form so that we can interpret it to individuals and classes. The data can be used to help make instructional decisions as well as report pupil progress.

Neither time nor space permits an in-depth treatment of statistical methods. Those who wish to increase their statistical skills and knowledge are referred to Elzey (1985) or Inman and Conover (1983).

Organizing Data

The most efficient way to summarize data is to use a frequency distribution. List the scores from high to low and tally the frequency with which each score occurs. A sample frequency distribution for 24 third grade student scores on an animal identification test appears in table 13.1. The scores show a relatively balanced distribution, with 11 of the 24 scores falling between 18 and 16. The scores do tail off to the low end of the score scale. That low score of 4 might be an error, an incomplete paper, or somebody who really doesn't know the animals—or at least can't associate a name and picture. The scores are quite spread out, ranging from the low score of 4 to a high of 23. And 23 out of 25 correct is quite a good score (92 percent).

Averageness

Often a number is needed to represent the average score of the class. This average can take one of two forms. In the first the simple arithmetic

Table 13.1 *Summary of Twenty-four scores on a Twenty-five Item Third Grade Animal Identification Test*

Raw Scores				
23	21	21	20	20
18	18	18	18	17
17	16	16	16	16
16	15	15	14	12
13	12	9	4	

Scores	Tally	Frequency	Cumulative Frequency	Percentile Rank
23	I	1	24	100
21	II	2	23	96
20	II	2	21	88
18	IIII	4	19	79
17	II	2	15	63
16	IIII	5	13	54
15	II	2	8	33
14	I	1	6	25
13	I	1	5	21
12	II	2	4	17
9	I	1	2	8
4	I	1	1	4

Table 13.2
Calculations of Mean, Standard Deviation, and Percentile Rank (using data of table 13.1)

Mean

$$M = \frac{\Sigma \text{ (sum of) } X \text{ (scores)}}{N \text{ (sum of frequencies)}} = \frac{386}{24} = 16.08$$

Standard Deviation (estimated)

$$SD = \frac{\Sigma U\frac{1}{6} \text{ (sum of score in upper } \frac{1}{6}\text{) minus } \Sigma L\frac{1}{6} \text{ (sum of score in lower } \frac{1}{6}\text{)}}{N/2}$$

$$SD = \frac{85 - 37}{12} = \frac{48}{12} = 4.00$$

Percentile Rank (for score of 14)

$$PR_{14} = \frac{\Sigma cf \text{ (sum of frequencies at and below 14)}}{N} \times 100 = \frac{6}{24} = 25$$

average or mean is calculated by adding up all the scores and dividing by the total number of scores. Table 13.2 illustrates this calculation using the data from table 13.1. A second average, less affected by extreme scores, is the median—the point that has half the scores above it and half the scores below it. For the data on table 13.1 we can estimate the median to be about 16, as about half the scores are larger and half are smaller than this value.

Variability

The spread or dispersion in a set of scores is a very important characteristic. It is a clue to the performance of the class as well as to the reliability of the test. Generally the larger the variability the greater the range of individual differences in the class and also the higher the reliability of the test. The usual method of describing variability is to calculate a standard deviation. Substracting all the scores from the mean, square each of those deviations, add them all up, divide by the total number of scores, and then take the square root of that result. A simpler shortcut procedure allows estimations of the standard deviation within 5 percent accuracy. First add the scores for the highest scoring one-sixth of the class. From this sum subtract the total of the lowest scoring one-sixth of the class. Divide the difference by one-half the total number of scores. The method is illustrated in table 13.2 using our animal identification data. Since we have 24 scores, one-sixth is 4. Add 4, 9, and two 12's to get the "lower one-sixth" total; to get the "upper one-sixth," add 23, 21, 21, and 20. The estimated standard deviation comes out to be 4.00. This is a reasonable amount of variability given the number of test items and the number of students. Fifteen to 20 percent of the number of possible points is an appropriate standard of comparison for deciding how large a standard deviation is. Note that if we calculate the standard deviation the longer, more complex way, it comes out to be 4.07. Our estimate of 4.00 was not far off.

Relative Position

Often we need to describe how individual students have performed on a test. One readily understood index of performance is the percentile

The individual is more important than test scores.

rank. For our purposes a percentile rank (PR) will be defined as a number representing the percentage of scores at and below a given score. Lets look at our animal identification test again (table 13.1). If Chelsea has a raw score of 14, what is her percentile rank? There were 6 people with scores of 14 or less. Dividing 6 by 24 and multiplying by 100 gives us a percentile rank of 25. Chelsea did as well as or better than 25 percent of the people who took the test. Accumulating large amounts of test data and expressing the results as percentile ranks is one method of establishing norms for tests.

Among other methods of expressing test scores are standard scores, normalized scores, and grade equivalents, the last probably the most popular. A grade equivalent is the mean raw score for a given grade/month placement. If a raw score of 83 on a nationally standardized test of word usage translates to a grade equivalent of 5.7, then 83 was the average score for students in the seventh month of the fifth grade. Be careful in interpreting grade equivalents, as students learn at different rates and the tests themselves are subject to all kinds of curriculum influences.

Analyzing Test Items

Item-analysis techniques are among the most valuable tools classroom teachers can apply in attempting to improve their achievement tests. The use of even the most elementary item-analysis procedures can bring about a remarkable improvement in classroom instruments. The methods discussed in this chapter will be aimed primarily at improving norm-referenced measures.

Item analyses have four general purposes: (1) to select the best available items for the final form of a test; (2) to identify structural or content defects in the items; (3) to detect learning difficulties of the class as a whole, identifying content areas or skills that need to be reviewed by the teacher; and (4) to identify areas of weakness for individual students.

An item analysis has three main elements. One is examining the difficulty level of the items, i.e., the percentage of students responding correctly to each item in the test. Another is determining the discriminating power of each item. Item discrimination in its simplest form usually, but not always, relates performance on each item to performance on the total test. For a classroom test, item discrimination is generally indexed by comparing the number of high-scoring individuals (based on total score) responding correctly to the number of low-scoring individuals responding correctly.

A third part of item analysis, if multiple choice or matching items are used in the test, is examining the effectiveness of the distractors (foils, or alternative answers). Again, data derived from the high and low scores are used. Now, however, the response patterns for every alternative in each item are studied, rather than just the correct answer.

Preparing Data for Item Analysis

Preparing data for the item analysis of a classroom test involves counting the number of individuals in high- and low-scoring groups who answer each item correctly. Make this count by a show of hands in class or by examining the answer sheets. An efficient show of hands approach, outlined by Diederich (1964), is recommended if the class is relatively small and sufficient time is available. In general, use the following steps to gather and record data for an item analysis:

1. *Arrange the answer sheets in order from high to low.* This ranking is usually based on the individual's total score on the test. An item analysis of data derived from high and low total scores is known as an internal item analysis. If an external criterion is used (e.g., another test that is supposed to measure the same thing as the one under analysis), the item analysis is known as an external item analysis. Total score on the test is the most satisfactory criterion on which to base a ranking of individuals for an analysis of a classroom test.

2. *Identify high- and low-scoring groups.* For purposes of item analysis, these two sets of papers are called criterion groups. Each subgroup will contain from 25 to 50 percent of the total number of people who took the test. The goal is to include enough people in the criterion groups to justify confidence in the results, and yet keep the criterion groups distinct enough to ensure that they represent different levels of ability. In an item analysis of a classroom test, between 25 and 33 percent would be a reasonable size for the criterion groups. The high and low groups must contain the same number of individuals.

3. *Record separately the number of times each alternative was selected by individuals in the high and low groups.*
4. *Add together the number of correct answers to each item made by the combined high and low groups.*
5. *Divide the total number of correct responses by the maximum possible, i.e., the total number of students in the combined high and low groups, and multiply the result by 100.* This percentage is called the difficulty index. Some test constructors allow items to be omitted, and students may inadvertently omit items. If not all individuals attempted all items, calculate item difficulty indices by dividing the total number of correct responses by the number of individuals who attempted the item. On speeded tests, omitted items in the middle of the test should probably be considered wrong, but those at the end should not be considered.
6. *Subtract the number of correct answers made by the low group (L) from the number of correct answers by the high group (H).*
7. *Divide this number (the difference, H − L) by the number of individuals contained in the high (or low) group.* The decimal result is the discrimination index.

Sample item data and the indices derived using the procedures described above are presented in table 13.3. These data refer to four hypothetical multiple choice items answered by different classes (thus producing fluctuating numbers of cases in high and low groups). The procedure for deriving indices of difficulty and discrimination can, of course, be used profitably with two-choice (e.g., true-false), matching,

Table 13.3
Sample Item-Analysis Data Derived from Four Hypothetical Multiple Choice Items

Item	Group	Group Size	Response Alternatives*					Total No. Correct (H + L)	Difficulty Index	Difference (H − L)	Discrimination Index
			1	2	3	4	5				
Item 1	High	12	0	<u>11</u>	0	1	0	20	83%	2	+.17
	Low	12	2	<u>9</u>	1	0	0				
Item 2	High	25	2	2	<u>20</u>	1	0	26	52%	14	+.56
	Low	25	5	8	<u>6</u>	2	4				
Item 3	High	16	2	2	8	2	<u>2</u>	6	19%	−2	−.13
	Low	16	4	3	4	1	<u>4</u>				
Item 4	High	30	<u>20</u>	3	2	1	4	28	47%	12	+.40
	Low	30	<u>8</u>	1	8	9	2				

*Underlined numbers indicate correct answers.

or any type of multiple choice objective item. Further, the concepts of difficulty and discrimination may be applied in evaluating more subjective item types, e.g., completion and, with some difficulty, essay items.

Using Information from Item Analyses

Item Difficulty. An item's difficulty level is an index for the teacher of students' comprehension of, or performance on, material or tasks contained in the item. Looking at item 1 in table 13.3, you can see that the item is easy (estimated difficulty index = 83 percent). Note here that the higher the difficulty index the easier the item. This apparent paradox is comprehensible when we recall that the difficulty index represents the percentage of respondents answering the item correctly. In other words, there is an inverse relationship between the magnitude of the index and what it purports to represent. In any event, a teacher might conclude that for item 1, nearly everyone had command of the material. Sometimes, however, an extremely high difficulty index indicates a structural defect in the item. The data for item 1 might have been obtained from the following item:

Item 1: A large body of water is an

1. stream
2. ocean (*keyed as correct*)
3. creek
4. river

Obviously a grammatical clue exists. The stem calls for a response beginning with a vowel, and the only such response is #2, which is the correct answer. A student who noticed this clue could respond correctly to the item without knowing the answer. This irrelevant cue could alone account for the high difficulty index, particularly in the low group. The lesson here is obvious. In selecting items for a test, consideration of content alone or item-analysis data alone can be very misleading. Both factors need to be considered in accepting items for the final form of the test.

A test composed entirely of items at the 50 percent difficulty level is maximally reliable, or more precisely, shows maximum internal consistency. In other words, items at the 50 percent level allow item-discrimination indices to reach their maximum possible value: unity. Mathematically, median difficulty is a necessary though not sufficient condition for acceptable discrimination. In practice, however, you will probably wish to include in the test items that are fairly easy (placed at the beginning for psychological reasons) or fairly difficult (to measure highly complex learning outcomes).

A useful application of item analysis is to develop a chart showing student performance on each item (correct = +, incorrect = 0) and the content of the item. This sample chart for five students and four items shows that the concept of weather could be profitably reviewed:

Item Content	Student				
	S1	S2	S3	S4	S5
Identify terms related to weather	+	+	0	0	+
Draw inferences about weather	+	+	0	0	+
Interpret thermometer readings	+	0	+	0	0
Follow steps in experiment	+	+	0	+	+

In addition, areas in need of review for individual students are highlighted when you can see the responses of each examinee to each item. If the class and number of items are large, recording responses can be quite laborious. The benefits for both students and teachers can, however, be substantial. In such cases, items similar in content could be grouped together. Another interesting variation is to refer to the original table of specifications, particularly if the cognitive domain taxonomy was used to develop it, and use its behavior categories instead of content categories.

Item Discrimination. Item discrimination has been defined as the degree to which an item differentiates the high achievers from the low achievers. A perfect positively discriminating item would be answered correctly by all of the high group and none of the low group; the discrimination index would then be +1.00. If all of the low group and none of the high group responded correctly, the index would be −1.00. In a sense, we might interpret the discrimination index as the correlation of the item with the total test score. In practice, discrimination values in the middle positive range are usually found on classroom tests.

The data reported in table 13.3 for item 2 were obtained from the following item:

Item 2: A teacher proposes the following objective for a unit in Fine Arts: "The pupils should be able to understand and appreciate good music." The principal drawback to this objective, from a measurement standpoint, is that it is a

1. general objective.
2. student objective.
3. nonbehavioral objective. (*keyed as correct*)
4. teacher objective.
5. compound objective.

This item is sound from a number of standpoints. The "middle difficulty level" criterion has been met, with an index of 52 percent. Discrimination between the high and low groups is indicated by the index of +.56. The item is structurally sound and measures a desirable outcome, the ability to apply knowledge about objectives in a new situation. One possible explanation for the good discrimination is that the alternatives contain plausible but incorrect answers.

In general, all items in a test for relative achievement should discriminate positively. We are striving for an additive scale, in which item scores are summed, and we want each item to make a positive contribution. We are also developing a test of relative achievement, as opposed to a mastery test, in which items do not necessarily need to meet an internal discrimination criterion.

A teacher will occasionally find a negatively discriminating item such as the following (refer to table 13.3 for appropriate item-anlysis data):

Item 3. Which of the following alternatives best summarizes the limitations of the *Taxonomy of Educational Objectives*?
1. For the most part it is written in nonbehavioral terms.
2. It deals with "inferred" rather than "real" behavior.
3. It may restrict our thinking only to the categories of the *Taxonomy*.
4. The categories of the *Taxonomy* are not mutually exclusive.
5. All of the above are limitations of the *Taxonomy*. (*keyed as correct*)

This item, answered correctly by more of the low group than the high group, is apparently ambiguous. One possible source of ambiguity is the nature of the task. In essence, the student is required to make a value judgment, and most students apparently do not possess enough information to make it appropriately. The use of "all of the above," though correct in the teacher's eyes, may have contributed to the difficulty of the task (difficulty index = 19 percent) and made responding to the item easier for the low than for the high group. Students in the low group may have been able to identify correctly two of the "limitations" and therefore been drawn to answer 5. It is difficult to speculate about the line of thinking followed by the high group. The item obviously does not work well and should be rewritten or discarded.

Another point is raised by the data on item 3. Discrimination for this item was low (−.13), as was the difficulty index. In general, extremely difficult or extremely easy items will show poor discrimination.

Teachers should select for future forms of their tests those items that have the highest discrimination indices and measure the desired outcomes of instruction. Ebel (1965) suggests that items with discrimination indices below +.40 could benefit from rewriting and that those below +.20 should be improved or discarded.

An ideal item, from a statistical item-analysis standpoint, is one that all students in the high group answer correctly and all students in the low group miss. In addition, the responses of the low group should be evenly distributed among the incorrect alternatives.

Incidentally, there is nothing sacred about the practice of providing four or five alternatives for all multiple choice items. Tversky (1964) has shown mathematically that the use of three alternatives for each question will maximize the discriminability, power, and information yielded per unit of time. This makes intuitive sense; we all know how hard it is to invent consistently good fourth and fifth distractors. They frequently turn out to be merely space fillers.

Developing an Item Data File

Teachers are encouraged to develop a file of test items. Recording items on three-by-five- or five-by-eight-inch cards and reporting their difficulty and discrimination data over several administrations allows you to refine and improve your classroom tests. Such a file has the advantages of

1. Encouraging the teacher to make an item analysis as often as is practical.
2. Storing accumulated data that make item analyses more reliable.
3. Providing for a wider choice of item format and objectives—in other words, greater flexibility in test construction.
4. Facilitating revision of items and suggesting ideas for new items.
5. Facilitating the relation of the test item and its objective to the table of specifications.
6. Facilitating the physical construction and reproduction of the test, because each item is on a separate card.
7. Helping you accumulate a large enough pool of items that some items can be shared with students for study purposes.

A test item file has the disadvantages of

1. Requiring a great deal of clerical time.
2. Discouraging the teacher from creative test construction efforts by providing ready-made items.
3. Providing the opportunity for the file of items to dictate the content of instruction.

These negative factors can influence a teacher's measurement practices, but the overall advantages of an item file certainly compensate.

Table 13.4 shows a sample item-analysis data card suitable for objective items from classroom tests.

Assessing the Reliability and Validity of Your Tests

A test you use to make decisions about students and their behavior must be **reliable** and **valid**—that is, it must measure accurately and consistently. These topics can only be touched on lightly here, but you are urged to consult extended discussions in Bloom, Hastings, and Madaus (1971),

Table 13.4
Sample Item-Analysis Data Card

(FRONT)

Item: 37 Topic: Trade barriers Level: Comprehension Cell: 14 Objective: 14	Reference: Farquhar's *Introduction to Economics*, rev. ed., 1984, pp. 201–214.

Item 37. A tariff may be defined as a tax on
  *1. imported goods.
  2. money brought into the country.
  3. exported goods.
  4. imported cats and dogs

(BACK)

Item: 37   Test: Two

Options	Upper Third	Lower Third	Upper Third	Lower Third	Upper Third	Lower Third
*1 2 3 4 5	15 0 3 2	8 3 3 1				
Omits	0	0				
Difficulty Discrimination	58% .35					
Date	2/14/85					
Class Size						
Comments						

Gronlund (1985), Kubiszyn and Borich (1984), Mehrens and Lehmann (1984), and Payne (1974).

Defining and Estimating Validity

The concept of constant error, as it relates to test validity, implies that standards exist for evaluating the presence or absence of such errors. Criteria of validity must be identified, constructed, and collected by the test developer, or sometimes by the user. The nature of the criteria used will depend on the purposes of the test. Three broad aims or purposes of testing are identified below (American Psychological Association 1966):

1. *"The test user wishes to determine how an individual performs at present in a universe of situations the test situation is claimed to represent.* For example, most achievement tests used in schools measure the student's performance on a sample of questions intended to represent a certain phase of educational achievement or certain educational objectives." The type of validity described here is referred to as **content validity.**

2. *"The test user wishes to forecast an individual's future standing or to estimate an individual's present standing on some variable of particular significance that is different from the test.* For example, an academic aptitude test may forecast grades, or a brief adjustment inventory may estimate what the outcome would be of a careful psychological examination." Validity defined in this way is called **criterion-related validity.**

Let's illustrate criterion-related validity by showing how the animal identification test data introduced earlier in this chapter (table 13.1) relate to a relevant criterion. The teacher assumes that students who scored well on the test will also do well on the general science portion of the nationally standardized Wide World Achievement test administered two weeks after the animal identification test. Neither a perfect relationship between these two measures nor the absence of a relationship is to be expected. To describe the degree of relationship, calculate a Spearman rank-order correlation coefficient. The process, illustrated in table 13.5, involves assigning ranks to the two sets of scores, obtaining a difference-between-ranks score for each subject, squaring that number, and adding the squared differences. If two or more students have the same score, assign them the average of the ranks for which they are tied. On the animal identification test, students F and K both scored 21. Each receives a rank of 2.5, as they are tied for the ranks of 2 and 3. As shown in table 13.5, the correlation comes out to be .83. Since the coefficient ranges from -1.00 to $+1.00$, we would interpret our obtained correlation as indicating a moderately strong positive relationship between the animal identification test and the Wide World Achievement Test. If we accept the nationally standardized test as a kind of standard, we have evidence of substantial criterion-related validity.

3. *"The test user wishes to infer the degree to which the individual possesses some hypothetical trait or quality (construct) presumed to be reflected in the test performance.* For example, he wants to know whether the individual stands high on some proposed abstract trait such as 'intelligence' or 'creativity' that cannot be observed directly. This may be done to learn something about the individual, or it may be done to study the test itself, to study its relationship to other tests,

Table 13.5
Calculation of Rank Order Correlation

Formula

$$r_s = 1 - \left(\frac{6(\Sigma D^2)}{N(N^2 - 1)}\right)$$

where
  ΣD^2 = the sum of the squared difference in ranks (the number 6 is a constant value)
  N = the number of ranked pairs of scores

Example

Student	Animal Identification Score	Achievement Test Score	Animal Rank	Test Rank	D	D²
A	23	51	1	1	0	0
B	18	50	7.5	2	5.5	30.25
C	17	47	10.5	4	5.5	30.25
D	16	37	14	14.5	−.5	.25
E	13	28	20.5	22.5	−2.	4
F	21	48	2.5	4	−1.5	2.25
G	18	45	7.5	7	.5	.25
H	16	39	14	11	3	9
I	15	32	17.5	20	−2.5	6.25
J	12	28	22	22.5	−.5	.25
K	21	36	2.5	17	−14.5	210.25
L	18	40	7.5	10	−2.5	6.25
M	16	38	14	12.5	1.5	2.25
N	15	37	17.5	14.5	3	9
O	9	31	23	21	2	4
P	20	46	4.5	6	−1.5	2.25
Q	18	38	7.5	12.5	−5	25
R	16	36	14	17	−3	9
S	14	36	19	17	2	4
T	4	20	24	24	0	0
U	20	49	4.5	3	1.5	2.25
V	17	44	10.5	8	2.5	6.25
W	16	43	14	9	5	25
X	13	35	20.5	19	1.5	2.25

$\Sigma D^2 = 390.5$ 390.5

$N = 24$

$$r_s = 1 - \left(\frac{6(390.5)}{N(N^2 - 1)}\right) = 1 - \frac{2343}{13800} = 1 - .17 = .83$$

or to develop psychological theory." We are here concerned with the **construct validity** of a test.

The type of validity you calculate will, of course, depend on the use to be made of the test results. From the broad test-use categories above, we have defined three types of validity. However, the method employed to determine validity could form the basis for an alternative classification. Thorndike and Hagen (1961) have proposed such a classification, distinguishing between types of validity that primarily depend on a rational analysis of items and those that rely on empirical and statistical evidence.

The real demands and limitations of a classroom situation do not allow the luxury of exploring all these types of validity. Probably the best that classroom teachers can do is to examine their teaching situation and instruction and decide which outcomes need to be assessed. All instructional programs involve three things: objectives, a curriculum, and an instructional process. When assessment time comes, the teacher must consider the relation each of these three elements bears to the measure of student progress being used. The following diagram represents the three elements in the instructional process and a summative achievement test.

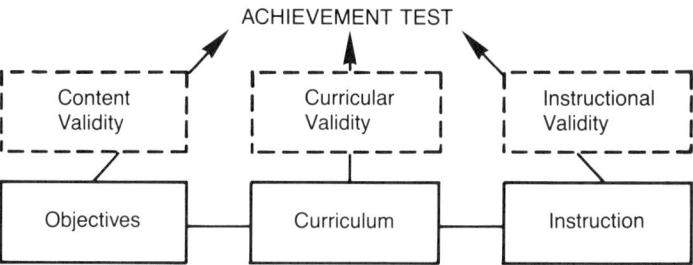

Content Validity. In general, content validity is evaluated on the basis of a rational analysis of the item content. Take, for example, an educational achievement test. Validity should be assessed by a teacher in light of the instructional objectives of the class or school. The instructor should ask: How adequately do the items of this test measure the objectives, both for subject matter and for cognitive skills, that I want them to measure? Determining content validity requires specifying the universe of behaviors the test will sample. For a standardized achievement test, this specification might take the form of a statement in the test manual summarizing the textbooks or subject-matter experts consulted or the course syllabi reviewed. For an informal classroom test, the universe might be defined in a table of specifications developed by the teacher. In either case, content validity is the match between a test item and the objective it is supposed to measure—also sometimes referred to as relevance.

Curricular Validity. As stated above, the validity of a test or item depends on its matching the objective. Objectives are operationalized in many different ways. In other words, a variety of instructional materials could be used to address a particular objective. To tell if a test or item matches the curriculum materials, you should map the relations of these two elements. For example, use a table of specifications (a two-way grid with content along one dimension and expected behavior along the other) to cross-reference the test and materials (Schmidt 1983).

Instructional Validity. The ultimate test of a test or item is whether or not it represents a reasonable sample of what actually went on in the classroom. Theoretically, objectives, curriculum, and instruction correspond almost perfectly. But many factors can disturb this perfection. Students don't always behave in predicted ways and therefore we must sometimes adjust or modify our instruction. For the test to be valid, the student should have had a reasonable opportunity, based on actual classroom instruction, to learn the material or develop the skill necessary to perform successfully on each item. Ideally this evaluation should come from an independent observer. Usually instructional validity rests on a subjective judgment of the teacher.

Defining and Estimating Reliability

Reliability is the consistency of measurement. This consistency might be examined over different (a) forms of the test, (b) examiners, (c) scorers, (d) administration times (test-retest), or (e) samples of items. The first four methods are correlation methods—we obtain pairs of scores and determine their relationship using a Pearson product-moment or Spearman rank-difference formula. Most teachers don't have the time to gather these data. A shortcut method can be used on classroom tests whose items are all scored right or wrong, are not influenced by speed, and measure a common factor. This type of reliability, called internal consistency, is calculated using the following formula (Cureton et al. 1973):

$$r = 1 - .043\, k \left(\frac{N}{\Sigma X_U \frac{1}{6} - \Sigma X_L \frac{1}{6}} \right)$$

Where
k = total number of dichotomously scored items on test
N = total number of subjects about whom we have data
$\Sigma X_U \frac{1}{6}$ = the sum of the total scores for individuals in the upper one-sixth of the distribution
$\Sigma X_L \frac{1}{6}$ = the sum of the total scores for individuals in the lower one-sixth of the distribution

Let's try out the formula with some real data. Below is the distribution of scores on a ten-item test for 25 students:

Score	Frequency
10	1
9	2
8	1
7	4

6	3
5	5
4	3
3	1
2	2
1	2
0	1
	$N = 25$

One-sixth of 25 is 4.17, but to make it easy we will round down to 4. The sum of the scores in the upper one-sixth is then 36 (10 + 9 + 9 + 8) and for the lower one-sixth is 4 (0 + 1 + 1 + 2). Our reliability is therefore estimated as follows:

$$\text{Reliability} = 1 - .043 \, (10) \times \frac{25}{36 - 4} = .74$$

This coefficient should be interpreted in light of the usable range of 0 to +1.00. An estimate of .74 is quite acceptable for a classroom test.

Do not use unreliable tests (or invalid ones) for making decisions about students or programs. These are important decisions that affect the lives of people for whom you have educational responsibility.

Reporting and Marking

Purposes of Marking and Reporting

Students and teachers, and to some extent parents, become noticeably tense as marking time approaches. This tension is especially characteristic of beginning teachers and can generally be attributed to their lack of experience in assigning marks and reporting student progress. Summing up complex human behavior into a single letter or number mark may well seem presumptuous. If, in addition, marks are not based on a rational philosophy of education and a set of operational definitions of expected learning outcomes, their meaning will be obscure and ambiguous and their purposes will be subverted.

Four broad purposes of marking and reporting can be identified:

1. *Communicating to students and parents.* Marks provide a useful and efficient way to communicate data to students and their parents. Marking and reporting are essentially information-processing activities and might be likened to elements in a communications network. Marks are merely the simplest means by which teachers communicate their evaluations of the progress each student has made toward specified educational goals. As in any communications system, the message, i.e., information about achievement, may be incorrectly transmitted to the receiver because of faulty encoding or decoding or because

Communication is crucial to the evaluation process.

of "noise" or "static" in the network.

Students have a right and a need to learn about their progress. In addition to achievement data like class rank, grade equivalents, standard scores, and percentile ranks, students seem to desire more subjective and criterion-referenced evaluations of their performance. They want to know if their work is outstanding, good, acceptable, or unacceptable. The teachers are probably in a better position than anyone else to integrate the many factors in learning and achievement and communicate their summary to the student.

Parents, too, have a right and need to learn of the educational progress of their progeny. Marks are sensible summarizing appraisals that parents can use to counsel their children about their schoolwork and future educational and vocational plans.

2. *Communicating to present and future school personnel.* Just as the results of standardized achievement tests can be used to evaluate the overall progress of particular instructional programs and schools, so can distributions of marks help indicate progress. Such data are useful in making decisions about promotion, graduation, transfer, and future education.

Indices of past achievement are the best indicators of future achievement so far devised. College admissions personnel, therefore, view marks as indicating the level of performance likely by individual students admitted to their institution. Marks become academic currency in the college marketplace, although their exchange and conversion properties are limited.

Promotional decisions should, of course, never be made on the basis of marks alone. In fact, research has shown that requiring a student to repeat a grade results in very little improvement in achievement.

3. *Motivating student learning.* Marks may function either to reinforce or to inhibit learning. Although we would ideally like learning to result from intrinsic motivation, the extrinsic force exerted by marks must be acknowledged.

To benefit most from the motivational function of marks, define the basis on which you assign them. If a mark simply indicates status at a particular point in time, most students will probably not feel challenged to work for higher marks. If, however, marks reflect improvement or achievement relative to ability, students may be spurred to greater efforts.

4. *Guiding future instruction.* We have noted that past achievement is the best prognosticator of future achievement. Information on skills and knowledge already acquired and developed, then, is immensely helpful in designing future educational programs for individual students, groups, or classes. Data on important affective educational outcomes can also serve as a basis for planning meaningful student experiences. Data from criterion-referenced assessment and "goals cards," to be discussed later in the chapter, can be extremely helpful if carefully examined.

A few schools prefer informal letters or parent-teacher conferences to report cards. These two techniques can provide more detailed descriptions of a child's progress but demand considerably more teacher time.

Similar innovations are shown in the sample kindergarten, grades 1–3, and grades 4–6 elementary report cards in figures 13.1, 13.2, and 13.3.

Summarizing, Analyzing, and Reporting Student Achievement Data 227

CLARKE COUNTY SCHOOL DISTRICT
ATHENS, GEORGIA

Kindergarten Report Card
19___ to 19___

Student: Jeffrey Dean　　　　　Teacher: Karen Payne
School: Wilton Manors　　　　　Principal: Dr. James Creighton

E = Has Developed Skill　　G = Is Developing Skill　　S = Developing Skill With Difficulty　　N = Needs Time to Grow

Marking System: If an item is not marked, it is not applicable at this time.

LANGUAGE ARTS	Q1	Q2	Q3	Q4
Recognizes Printed Name	G	G	G	G
Prints Name Using Capital & Lower Case Letters	G	G	G	G
Recognizes, Names & Writes Capital Lower Case Letters	S	S	G	E
Reads Simple Sentences	N	N	S	S
Identifies Beginning Letter Sounds	G	G	G	G
Recognizes Rhyming Words	G	G	G	G
Recalls Events in Sequence	S	S	S	S
Demonstrates Spatial Awareness (over, under, top, middle, bottom, etc.)	E	E	E	E
Demonstrates Left/Right Progression	S	S	S	G
Expresses Self Clearly	N	N	S	S
Recognizes Likenesses and Differences	S	S	S	G
Understands Concepts of Opposite	N	S	G	G
Listens Attentively to Stories	E	E	E	E
Has Sight Vocabulary ___ Words	G	G	G	G

MATHEMATICS	Q1	Q2	Q3	Q4
Identifies Basic Shapes	S	G	G	E
Matches Objects of Sets One-to-One	N	N	S	S
Adds Using Concrete Objects	N	S	S	S
Orders Objects by Characteristics	N	S	S	S
Matches a Set of Objects to a Numeral	N	S	S	S
Subtracts Using Concrete Objects	N	N	S	S
Recognizes Numerals to 10	S	S	G	G
Orders Numerals to 10	S	G	G	G
Writes Numerals to 10	S	G	G	G
Completes a pattern	S	E	G	G
Understands Number Concepts	N	N	S	G
Classifies Objects by Characteristics	N	N	S	G

MUSIC	Q1	Q2	Q3	Q4
Participates in Singing Activities	✓	✓	✓	✓
Participates in Rhythmic Activities	✓	✓	✓	✓

ART	Q1	Q2	Q3	Q4
Demonstrates Ability to Color & Draw	E	E	E	E
Uses a Variety of Art Media	G	G	E	E
Demonstrates Ability to Cut, Paste and Model	S	S	G	G

SOCIAL DEVELOPMENT/WORK HABITS	Q1	Q2	Q3	Q4
Practices Self-Control	G	G	G	G
Follows School/Class Rules	G	G	G	G
Plays/Works with Others	G	G	G	G
Shows Self Esteem (Confidence)	G	G	G	G
Follows Directions	S	S	G	G
Makes Good Use of Time	S	G	G	E
Listens Attentively	S	G	G	G
Completes Work	N	S	S	S
Takes Care of Materials	G	E	E	E

SCIENCE	Q1	Q2	Q3	Q4
Participates in Current Science Activities	✓	✓	✓	✓

Units by Quarters:
1. The Senses
2. Zoo Animals
3. Nutrition
4. Simple Machines

SOCIAL STUDIES	Q1	Q2	Q3	Q4
Participates in Current Social Studies Activities	✓	✓	✓	✓

Units by Quarters:
1. Community Helpers
2. All About Me
3. Listening & Following Directions
4. Visiting a Pet

PHYSICAL DEVELOPMENT	Q1	Q2	Q3	Q4
Demonstrates Large Motor Skills	G	G	E	E
Demonstrates Small Motor Skills	S	S	G	G

ATTENDANCE	Q1	Q2	Q3	Q4
Days Present	39	40	42	44
Days Absent	5	5	3	1
Days Tardy	2	2	0	3

COMMENTS

1. Jeffrey is doing well with his work. However, he is experiencing some difficulty with numbers. I would like to request a conference.
2. Jeffrey is such an asset to our class. He works well with the children, accepts responsibility and helps other children.

ASSIGNED TO 1st **GRADE NEXT YEAR**

3. Jeffrey's hard work both at home and school has helped him to improve and become more confident in math.
4. Jeffrey has come a long way and has mastered the skills necessary for him to be promoted to the first grade.

DETACH AND RETURN TO SCHOOL WITH STUDENT

Student _____ School _____ Date _____
Comments:

Conference Requested
☐ YES　☐ NO

Signature of parent or guardian

FOURTH GRADING PERIOD

Figure 13.1
Sample Progress Report, Kindergarten

Note: Reproduced by permission of Clarke County School District, Athens, Georgia.

Figure 13.2
Sample Progress Report, Grades 1–3

Note: Reproduced by permission of Clarke County School District, Athens, Georgia.

Summarizing, Analyzing, and Reporting Student Achievement Data

CLARKE COUNTY SCHOOL DISTRICT
ATHENS, GEORGIA
Progress Report to Parents Grades 4-5
19 **86** to 19 **87**

Student: **Jonathan Chaplin** Teacher: **Mrs. Malinda Durham**
School: **Sunrise Elementary** Principal: **Dr. David Allen**

A = Excellent (90-100)	B = Above Average (80-89)	C = Average (70-79)	D = Below Average (60-69)	F = Unsatisfactory (59 & Below)

S = Satisfactory   N = Needs Improvement

	QUARTER					QUARTER			
	1	2	3	4		1	2	3	4
BEHAVIOR	B	B	A	A	**MATHEMATICS**	B	B	A	A
Controls excessive talking	B	B	A	A	Grade Level	4	4	5	5
Is courteous to adults and other students	B	B	A	A	Basic number facts:				
Is willing to take turns	B	B	A	A	A. Addition	B	A	A	A
Respects rules of school and class	A	A	A	A	B. Subtraction	B	A	A	A
					C. Multiplication	B	A	A	A
Accepts responsibility	B	B	A	A	D. Division	B	B	A	A
Demonstrates good attitude toward all learning activities	B	B	A	A	Works Accurately	B	B	B	A
					Reasons well in problem solving	B	B	A	A
					Works with reasonable speed	A	A	A	A
Makes wise use of time	C	B	B	A					
					SOCIAL STUDIES				
LANGUAGE ARTS					Self-Concept	A			
READING	C	C	B	B	Cultural Diversity		B		
Grade Level	3	4	4	4	Economics			B	
Reads with understanding	C	C	B	B	Rules and Laws				A
Decodes new words	C	C	B	B	**SCIENCE**				
Reads well orally	D	C	B	B	Plant Life	A			
Has an adequate and growing vocabulary	B	B	A	A	Animal Life		A		
					Ecology			B	
SPELLING	C	C	C	C	The Human Body				A
Spells assigned words correctly	C	C	C	B	**ART**				
Spells correctly in written work	C	C	C	C	Participates in art	S	S	S	S
					MUSIC				
					Participates in music	S	S	S	S
WRITING AND SPEAKING	B	B	C	B	**PHYSICAL EDUCATION**				
Uses correct punctuation	B	B	C	B	Participates in physical education	S	S	S	S
Uses correct grammar in speaking	B	B	C	B	Practices good sportsmanship	S	S	S	S
Uses correct grammar in writing	B	B	B	B	**SUPPLEMENTAL INSTRUCTION**				
Uses rules of capitalization	B	B	C	B					
PENMANSHIP	C	C	C	C	**ATTENDANCE**				
Other areas of Language Arts					Days present	45	40	41	45
					Days absent	0	5	4	0
					Days tardy	2	0	3	0

COMMENTS ASSIGNED TO **5th** GRADE NEXT YEAR

1. Jonathan is a very good student. He follows school rules, gets along well with others, and puts forth a great deal of effort. He does need to work more with his reading.

2. Jonathan's hard work and change of reading groups has helped him to improve and become a more confident and fluent reader.

3. Jonathan's reading continues to improve. He seems to really enjoy math and has performed exceptionally well this quarter.

4. I have thoroughly enjoyed having Jonathan in my class this year.

DETACH AND RETURN TO SCHOOL WITH STUDENT

Student_____ School_____ Date_____

Comments:

Conference requested
☐ YES ☐ NO

Signature of parent or guardian

FIRST GRADE PERIOD

Figure 13.3
Sample Progress Report, Grades 4–5

Note: Reproduced by permission of Clarke County School District, Athens, Georgia.

Note in particular the kinds of activities being evaluated at different grade levels. The forms are flexible, allowing for traditional grades or marks as well as specification of factors contributing to those grades. In addition to cognitive outcomes, some attention is given to students' affective development.

Winnetka Public Schools
MATHEMATICS GOAL RECORD CARD 1

Pupil _____ Teacher _____ Year _____

	Check
Can count 10 objects	
Can read and write numerals to 10	
Recognizes number groups up to 5	
Recognizes patterns of objects to 10	
Can read and write numerals to 20	
Can count objects to 100	
Recognizes numbers to 100	
Can read and write numerals to 50	
Recognizes addition and subtraction symbols	
*Understands meaning of the inequality signs	
Can count objects:	
by 2's to 20	
by 5's to 100	
by 10's to 100	
Recognizes geometric figures:	
triangle	
circle	
quadrilaterial	
Recognizes coins (1¢, 5¢, 10¢, 25¢)	
Knows addition combinations 10 and under using objects	
Knows subtraction combinations 10 and under using objects	
Recognizes addition and subtraction vertically and horizontally	
*Can construct simple plane figures with straight edge and compass	
Shows understanding of numbers and number combinations (check one)	
1. Using concrete objects	
2. Beginning to visualize and abstract	
3. Makes automatic responses without concrete objects	
Can tell time	
1. Hour	
2. Half hour	
*(Goals starred are not essential for all students)	
Comments:	

Figure 13.4
Sample Grade 1 Mathematics Goal Card

Note: From R. F. Bauernfeind, "Goal Cards and Future Developments in Achievement Testing," *Proceedings of the 1965 Invitational Conference on Testing Problems*, 76–77. Reprinted by permission of the Educational Testing Service.

Goal Cards

Bauernfeind (1967) describes a reporting procedure in keeping with the behavioral objectives movement. A teacher's instructional objectives are stated on a "goal card" in clear and appropriate language. Both teacher and student have copies of the goal card, which ordinarily lists the minimal objectives to be attained and can be used to monitor progress

---

Winnetka Public Schools
MATHEMATICS GOAL RECORD CARD 2

Pupil _____ Teacher _____ Year _____

	Check
Addition combinations 10 and under (automatic response)	
Subtraction combinations 10 and under (automatic response).	
Can count to 200.	
Can understand zero as a number.	
Can understand place value to tens	
Can read and write numerals to 200	
Can read and write numeral words to 10	
Can read and write number words to 20	
Use facts in 2-digit column addition (no carrying).	
Roman numerals to XII	
Can tell time:	
Half hour.	
Quarter hour.	
Calendar (months, days of week, dates)	
Coins and their equivalent value to 25¢	
Recognition of 50¢ coin and $1.00	
Recognize and use ½, ¼, ⅓ of a whole	
Addition facts to 18 (aim for mastery)	
Subtraction facts to 18 (aim for mastery)	
*Can identify simple plane figures:	
Quadrilateral.	
Pentagon.	
Hexagon	
Octagon	
*Can use compass to bisect line segment, construct triangles, and construct perpendiculars	
Word problems: (check one)	
1. Can set the problem up	
2. Can understand process involved	
3. Can notate word problems	
*(Goals starred are not essential for all students)	
Comments:	

Figure 13.5
Sample Grade 2 Mathematics Goal Card

Note: From R. F. Bauernfeind, "Goal Cards and Future Developments in Achievement Testing," *Proceedings of the 1965 Invitational Conference on Testing Problems*, 76–77. Reprinted by permission of the Educational Testing Service.

and report to parents. Sample goal cards are shown in figures 13.4 and 13.5. Figure 13.4 lists basic goals for grade 1 mathematics, and figure 13.5 presents goals for grade 2. These cards, described by Bauernfeind (1967), have been used in the Winnetka, Illinois, Public Schools. A given student may progress quickly through one set of objectives and into another, and goals can be tailored to a student's ability and progress. Bauernfeind (1967) notes six advantages of using goal cards:

1. Goal cards help students "see" progress as they acquire information and develop skills.
2. Goal cards help the teacher specify objectives and arrange them in a logical way.
3. Goal cards are an effective way to communicate with parents and the general public. They serve as an excellent basis for a parent-teacher conference.
4. Goal cards can contribute to planning for instruction, particularly if individualized programs are desired.
5. Goal cards facilitate communication among educators, e.g., the grade 1 arithmetic teacher with grade 2 teachers, or the regular teacher with a substitute teacher.
6. Because they emphasize important objectives, preferably specified in behavioral terms, goal cards can serve as a sound basis for classroom assessment.

Marking Models

Before discussing the assignment of marks, several words of caution are in order. First, the use of quantitative procedures does not eliminate the human factor from marking. Marking decisions are still basically philosophical. Second, the meaning ascribed to marks, be they letters or numbers, really rests on arbitrary conventions. The measures we use to assign marks must reflect behavioral changes in students if the resulting marks are to have any meaning.

The Inspection Model

A method of assigning grades that is widely used but rarely acknowledged is the inspection method. The teacher examines the distribution of composite scores in hopes of finding "natural breaks" or "cutoff points" and assigns marks on a relative curve. The distribution of scores, then, in a sense determines the numbers of each mark to be assigned. Some experts have argued that these "natural breaks" in distribution are unreliable. This is to some extent true, but if the marks are based on reliable data, confidence can be placed in the results.

To avoid a completely arbitrary distribution of marks you need some reference point. We have suggested that you use the objectives of the course and summary tables of specification to determine a minimal level of performance. Such a procedure, used in conjunction with "inspection," allows for either a high or a low percentage of high marks. The conclusions will have some basis in reality, since any given class during any given grading period may display relatively high or low performance. Other methods may also be used to determine minimal standards. A teacher may determine what chance performance would have been on all exams, relate this to the distribution composite scores, and use it as a starting point to evaluate the overall performance of the group. Some teachers like to use first quartile level and third quartile level performance on all measures as reference points to gauge the performance of the group. Ideally, one would like to have normative data from past groups to use in assessing present class performance.

The "Normal Curve" Method

The so-called normal curve model for assigning marks rests on several assumptions of varying degrees of credibility. First, the curve assumes that achievement is normally distributed and that if the resulting distribution is abnormal, it is a result of sampling error. Second, it is assumed that the sample means and standard deviations are the best estimates of the means and standard deviations of the population of which this particular class represents a sample. These assumptions involve about as much subjective judgment as any teacher must make in order to mark.

Figure 13.6 shows a typical "normal curve" distribution of marks. This curve may be used to assign marks in at least two ways. First, the teacher may mark off appropriate standard deviation units along the score scale and assign the appropriate marks to them. Second, the percentage of marks dictated by the normal curve may be assigned the class. Will either procedure ensure that the normal curve assumptions have been met? Yes, if and only if the underlying class distribution is normal. Despite this restriction, the actual and theoretical percentages of marks come fairly close together.

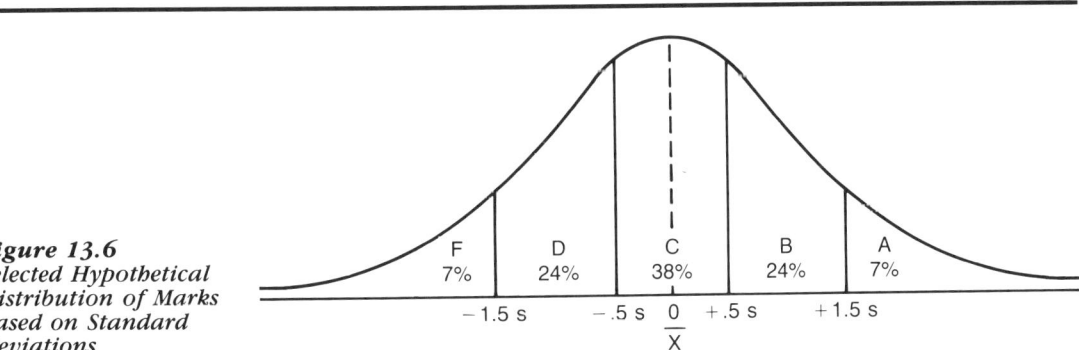

Figure 13.6
Selected Hypothetical Distribution of Marks Based on Standard Deviations

The "Absolute Model"

In the "absolute model" a percentage of correct answers or of the total number of points to be earned is specified for a particular grade. A teacher may specify that you must get 70 percent correct to get a *C* or that of the 160 points in the class you must earn 140 to get an *A*. These are very difficult judgments and it is probably best if a group of teachers in a particular grade level or class collectively arrives at the standard. Setting such standards of course allows the possibility for the extreme case of all *A*s or *F*s.

You must also decide whether to use an alphabetic or numeric system. At the very early grades, *Satisfactory* or *Needs Improvement* is probably sufficient. Later, the number of possible grade categories may be increased. Numeric systems are not recommended, as they imply greater precision than is possible with the kinds of data we have.

Dishonest Ways of Marking

We cannot leave the topic of marking without pointing out some of the pitfalls that await the unwary, unthinking, or unmotivated grader. Palmer (1962) lists seven danger signs that need to be heeded if we are to grade successfully. Do not fall victim to grading by

1. *Abdication*, i.e., don't, because of overwork or lack of effort, tailor courses to tests or rely on tests developed by other teachers or textbook publishers.
2. *Employing the carrots and clubbing system*, i.e., don't add bonus credit for good behavior or avoidance of the prejudices of the teacher.
3. *Default*, ie., don't because of a deep-seated hatred of grading and testing, base a final grade on a single exam in which a misstep could spell disaster.
4. *Becoming a zealot*, i.e., do not set the student racing with a vengeance and make the course an ordeal, endurance contest, or problem in survival in which you measure everything short of classroom posture.
5. *Changing rules in midgame,* i.e., don't strew the line of march with booby traps and obstacles aimed at tightening up the standards after the game has started.
6. *Becoming a psychic grader*, i.e., don't believe you have powers inaccessible to ordinary man, allowing only you to "see" how much a student has learned without any measurements.
7. *Anchoring everyone in a system of impossible perfection*, i.e., don't overlook the fallibility of man-as-student or set yourself up as guardian of standards.

In short, don't fall victim, as the Dean did in the following limerick, to basing marks on irrelevancies:

There was a young girl at McMaster
Whose head was alfalfa and plaster

But she looked like a queen
And she smiled at the dean
So he graded the paper—and passed her.

On the Philosophy of Marking

It is incumbent on every teacher, at every level of instruction, to spell out for students the basis on which marks will be assigned. The practice of marking, despite the problems of accuracy and realiability, will no doubt continue for many years to come. Despite a particular teacher's disagreement with the whole notion of marking, he has an obligation to assign the most valid and most reliable marks possible. The many and important decisions made about students every day, throughout their educational and occupational careers, dictate such care. Teachers who pursue a "no-grade" philosophy abrogate their responsibility as educators to communicate with the students about their progress.

There is no solution to the marking problem that would satisfy all concerned. Suffice it to say that the assignment of marks creates a powerful system of reward and punishment that can be used to bring about highly desirable behavioral changes. Such a point of view implies the expenditure of a significant amount of time and effort in arriving at student marks. But preoccupation with marks, on the part of either teacher or student, must be considered unhealthy. Keeping in mind their limitations, the basis of their assignment, and the fact that many significant outcomes of education are neither marked nor markable (e.g., attitudes, values, interests) should lead to a proper perspective. Marks represent an integral, fallible, potentially meaningful though perhaps irritating element in the educational process.

Thought Activity

1. Construct a hypothetical frequency table and tell what the data mean.
2. Tell the difference between the mean and the median of a group of scores.
3. Define variability of a set of scores and its importance.
4. The three main elements in item analysis are item difficulty, discriminating power, and effectiveness of distractors. Tell how these factors affect the teacher's interpretation of test data.
5. State advantages and disadvantages of a test item file.
6. Define test validity and reliability.
7. Define criterion-related validity.
8. Define construct validity.
9. Define content validity.
10. Define curricular validity.
11. Define instructional validity.
12. Define test reliability.
13. Discuss the four main purposes of marking and reporting discussed in the chapter.

References

American Psychological Association. 1966. *Standards for educational and psychological tests and manuals.* Washington, D.C.: Author.

American Educational Research Association et al. 1985. Standards for educational and psychological testing. Washington, D.C.: American Psychological Association.

Bauernfeind, R. F. 1967. Goal cards and future developments in achievement testing. In *Proceedings of the 1965 Invitational Conference on Testing Problems.* Princeton, N. J.: Educational Testing Service.

Bloom, B., J. T. Hastings, and G. Madaus. 1971. *Handbook on formative and summative evaluation of student learning.* New York: McGraw-Hill.

Diederich, P. 1964. *Short-cut statistics for teacher-made tests.* 2d ed. Evaluation and Advisory Service Series, pamphlet no. 5, Princeton, N. J.: Educational Testing Service.

Ebel, R. 1965. *Measuring educational achievement.* Englewood Cliffs, N. J.: Prentice-Hall.

Elzey, F. F. 1985. *Introduction to statistics: A mocrocomputer approach.* Monterey: Brooks/Cole.

Gronlund, N. E. 1985. *Measurement and evaluation in teaching.* 5th ed. New York: Macmillan.

Inman, R. L., and W. J. Conover. 1983. *A modern approach to statistics.* New York: Wiley.

Kubiszyn, T., and G. Borich. 1984. *Educational testing and measurement.* Glenview, Ill.: Scott, Foresman.

Mehrens, W. A., and I. J. Lehmann. 1984. *Measurement and evaluation in education and psychology.* New York: Holt, Rinehart & Winston.

Palmer, O. 1962. Seven classic ways of grading dishonestly. *The English Journal* 51: 464–67.

Payne, D. A. 1974. *The assessment of learning: Cognitive and affective.* Lexington, Mass: D. C. Heath.

Schmidt, W. H. 1983. Content bases in achievement tests. *Journal of Educational Measurement* 20 (2): 165–78.

Thorndike, R. L., and E. Hagen. 1961. *Measurement and evaluation in psychology and education.* 2d ed. New York: Wiley.

Tversky, A. 1964. In the optimal number of alternatives at a choice point. *Journal of Mathematical Psychology 1: 386–91.*

Part 3   Pulling It All Together

14 *Classroom management and discipline*

Ask a new teacher what part of the job is most challenging and the answer is often—discipline. A National Education Association survey by Bartholomew (1980) presents data indicating that 42 percent of schools surveyed have discipline problems. Gallup polls in the seventies reported that discipline was a major public school problem. Elementary school teachers report on the average three behavior disordered students in their classroom each year. Discipline is a problem.

Definition Traditional definitions of discipline suggest obedience to external control. Recent interpretations speak of inner control as well as adherence to external restrictions; the nurturing of self-control has become an instructional goal.

Discipline is also viewed as classroom management. Doyle (1980) and Weiner (1972) suggest that a well-developed lesson plan is the best deterrent to a noisy and disruptive classroom. Although research does not support the idea that a quiet and orderly classroom is necessary for learning, classroom management is a major concern of teachers, parents, and supervisory personnel. Even if not essential to learning, it may be necessary to the survival of teachers.

Designing Discipline Strategies

Discipline in the classroom has included a variety of approaches. Taylor and Usher (1982) summarize current common discipline strategies:*

1. *Self-concept.* This strategy emphasizes that an individual's concept of self is the most important determinant of behavior. School conduct and achievement are best improved by the student who, in the process of developing a more healthy and positive self-concept, is learning self-discipline. Growth in self-concept occurs in an accepting, warm, empathetic, open, and nonjudgmental environment, which allows students the freedom to explore their thoughts and feelings in order to solve their own problems. (For further information on this strategy see Purkey 1978 and Canfield and Wells 1976.)
2. *Communication skills.* Ginott (1972) calls for a firm setting of limits on behavior but never on feelings. All feelings are to be accepted, no matter how destructive or outrageous. But limits are to be placed on actions that might result from such feelings. Ginott's approach suggests the following steps: (1) reflecting the feelings of the "misbehaver" to demonstrate understanding; (2) setting limits on the behavior; (3) providing a symbolic outlet for feelings; and (4) acknowledging that the symbolic outlet is not as good as the "real" thing.
3. *Natural and logical consequences.* Misbehavior occurs because children have developed faulty beliefs about themselves. These faulty beliefs lead to personal goals that may result in misbehavior. The goals for misbehavior are attention-seeking, power, revenge, and display of inadequacy. Two suggestions for dealing with misbehavior are (1) to pinpoint the goal of the behavior and thereby understand how to help the behaver work through the faulty belief, and (2) to use natural or logical consequences for misbehavior. (For further study see Driekurs, Grunweld, and Pepper 1971 and Dinkmeyer and Dinkmeyer 1976.)
4. *Values clarification.* According to this view, discipline problems are caused by two factors: (1) students with unclear values who experience inner turmoil that may result in troublesome behavior, and (2) conflicting and colliding value positions held by the student, on the one hand, and the school, principal, or teacher, on the other. This strategy is designed to help individuals answer some of their

---

*Adapted from "Discipline," by John G. Taylor and Richard H. Usher. Excerpted with permission of Macmillan Publishing Company from ENCYCLOPEDIA OF EDUCATIONAL RESEARCH, Fifth Edition, Harold E. Mitzel, Editor in Chief. Vol. 1, pp. 448–449. Copyright © 1982 by American Educational Research Association.

questions about values and build their own value systems. (Also see Simon, Howe, and Kirschenbaum 1972.)

5. *Teacher effectiveness training.* The aim of this approach is to replace "repressive and power-based methods" (punishment, blaming, shaming, or threatening) with a model of communication based upon: (1) active listening—responding in a reflective manner to the feelings of the behavior; (2) I-message—responding in a nonblaming, descriptive manner to misbehavior that creates a serious problem for the teacher; (3) problem ownership—understanding the differences between situations in which the learner has a problem and those in which the learner has no real problem but is behaving in a manner that is giving the teacher a problem; and (4) negotiation and problem solving—use of a collaborative, "no-lose" approach to resolve classroom conflict and establish classroom rules and policies. (See Gordon 1974.)

6. *Transactional analysis.* Discipline problems are viewed in terms of the communications transactions between people and may be either avoided or confronted through an understanding of the ways in which a teacher gets "hooked" into playing a game with a disruptive student. Communication is strengthened by an understanding of the ego states of both teacher and student at the moment. Transactional analysis principles suggest that teachers should learn to stay in the "adult ego state," particularly when they face students who have problems with authority. The "adult ego state" is the rational, thinking "computer-like" mental state that involves reflection upon information from both the "parent-ego state" and the "child-ego state"; it is thus more likely to be able to deal with the daily turmoil of most classrooms. (See Ernst 1972.)

7. *Reality therapy.* Disruptive events take place in the classroom when students lack involvement with the school, when they feel like failures, and when they do not take responsibility for their own actions. The school should attempt to eliminate failure and to increase involvement, relevance, and thinking. Responsibility is learned through a strong, positive, emotional involvement with a responsibile person. Teachers need to be positive and responsible persons who are trained to implement Glasser's (1965, 1969) ten disciplinary steps and to conduct classroom meetings that lead to improved student involvement.

8. *The LEAST approach to classroom discipline.* This method (Darkhuff and Griffin 1978) provides teachers with five main tools to improve classroom discipline. LEAST is an acronym based upon the following steps for good discipline: (*L*)Leave it alone; many actions may simply be left alone. (*E*)End the action; many times teachers can simply end the misbehavior without undue emotion. (*A*)Attend more fully; if a teacher must take further steps beyond merely ending the disruption at the moment, then it is time to get to the root of the problem. (*S*)Spell out directions; if the procedures listed thus far do

not work, it is time to clearly tell the student what to do. (*T*)Track the student's progress by keeping a simple, written private record of disciplinary encounters.

9. *Project TEACH.* This program combines ideas from many different approaches and philosophies. The training includes skills development, in both verbal and nonverbal communication (see 2, 5, and 6 above), positive reinforcement and related behavior modification principles (see 10 and 11 below), changing the environment, natural and logical consequences (see 3 above), and assertiveness (see 10 below).

10. *Assertive discipline.* This plan emphasizes the teacher's full control of the classroom to establish and preserve order. Systematic behavior modification principles are implemented in each classroom, including use of the chalkboard for recording the names of disruptive students and placement of a visible glass jar of marbles in the classroom for use in reinforcing positive behavior. (See Canter 1976.)

11. *Behavior modification.* According to Skinner (1968), misbehavior occurs because it is reinforced by the environment. As a remedy, the child's behavior is changed by changing the environment, and thereby reinforcing appropriate behavior. This shaping process occurs through rewarding successive approximations of the target behavior. Other techniques include reinforcement of behavior that is incompatible with a student's misbehavior; use of extinction procedures to remove reinforcement from an undesirable behavior; scheduling of reinforcement of desired behaviors for maximum effectiveness; and the use of praise.

12. *Dare to discipline.* The teacher is expected to be businesslike, highly organized, and in firm control. This approach assumes that children will test limits on the first day of school and that the teacher needs to let them know at the start who is in charge. (See Dobson 1971.)

These strategies have been around for a long time and there is still no consensus as to which is the best for a teacher—let alone a beginning teacher. The answer seems to be that you do what works for you in a particular situation. Just as we differentiate instruction for different objectives, we must also differentiate discipline strategies for different circumstances. Teachers need to be aware of internal and external pressures on themselves as well as on the students.

If a learning problem stems from an underlying or primary anxiety, then a more general kind of help is needed—perhaps psychotherapy. On the other hand, according to Reisman and Kauffman (1980, 36–37), a teacher can help a child whose anxiety is secondary—symptomatic of immediate problems, perhaps learning problems:

Symptoms may take the forms of hyperactivity, withdrawal, aggression, physical maladies, bed wetting, and so on. This level of anxiety may be exemplified as follows: A child has a perceptual, spatial, temporal, or motor problem, or a combination of these. He or she wants to learn, but cannot produce. The child tries, but the results are inadequate. The child becomes anxious. In this case, the teacher should try to determine what is going wrong at the learning level. Is the work too difficult? Are there gaps in the . . . curriculum? Does the child need more work at the concete level? Does a perceptual disability need to be circumvented? Once an instructional problem is diagnosed and corrected, the teacher may be instrumental in decreasing the child's anxiety by providing success situations.

Social and emotional factors that influence learning, discussed in chapter 2, underlie the following instructional strategies designed for mathematics instruction by Reisman and Kauffman (1960, 197–200):

Instructional Strategy	*Procedures*
Use behavior modification techniques.	Reward the child's desirable behavior and follow undesirable behavior with either no consequences or punishing consequences. This may involve shifting teacher attention from inappropriate to appropriate behavior. More complicated techniques involve token reinforcement or earning points for desirable behavior. These tokens or points may be exchanged for reinforcers such as school supplies, free time, or for whatever the child agrees would be worth changing his behavior for.
Provide a structured environment.	A highly structured classroom has the following characteristics.* • A minimum of distracting stimuli • Clear expectations are developed with regard to children's movements about, and classroom routine is predictable • Consistent consequences are applied to hyperactive and nonhyperactive behavior • The teacher is highly directive, making most decisions until the child can manage himself • For students who do not exert self-control, manipulative materials should be used in a one-to-one or peer-team situation lest they end up being thrown around the room, having tempted the child into trouble. The purpose of materials and rules for their use should be made clear to the child.
Use self-instruction.	Children can learn to control their excessive motor behavior by giving themselves instructions.† The student who is easily distracted can be instructed to talk himself through a task.

---

*See Cruickshank, Bentzen, Ratzeburg, and Tannhauser 1961; Haring and Phillips 1962; Haring and Whelan 1965; Hewett 1968; and Kauffman 1977.
†See Goodwin and Mehoney 1975; Hallahan and Kauffman 1976; and Luria 1973.

	Those who have difficulty staying on task can be prevented from sidetracking by self-monitoring.
Eliminate irrelevant or potentially distracting stimuli from instructional materials.	Eliminate distracting colorful pictures or diagrams in textbooks by cutting out what is salient and pasting it on a plain sheet of paper. Present arithmetic computations one at a time. Use cues such as color or texture to highlight relevant and salient parts of a problem —for example, for the child who needs help noticing the difference between $+$, X, or $-$. Eliminate hard-to-ignore stimuli.
Use modeling.	Children learn by imitating adults or peers in their environment. Undesirable behavior—hitting, kicking, poking—can be reduced in elementary school children by inducing attention to, and reinforcing, desirable behavior.*
Select successful tasks to obtain high success rates.	The student who has episodes of aggression also has quiet times and is willing to engage in success yielding activities.
Arrange appropriate environmental conditions.	Provide equipment or toys conducive to social play, and bring the isolate in proximity to peers who have good social interaction skills. A store in the room can help a withdrawn child develop socialization skills while role playing.
Teach recognition of important social cues.	Showing the child videotaped replays of his own behavior and then role playing and modeling appropriate behavior help teach the child such cues as when to be quiet, when to listen, when to take one's turn, when to cooperate. Children may role-play buying clothes in a store and discuss budgeting, saving, banking, buying on credit, etc.
Insure success in tasks.	Disturbed children refuse to even try—they are defeated in their own minds before they give themselves a chance.† The use of task analysis of goals enables the teacher to identify components of a task. Then the teacher can present a step leading to a goal that the child already has in his or her repertoire, insuring that the child will be successful. This shaping of the self-concept encourages the child to try, to interact.

There is evidence that children are more likely to accept responsibility for their successes or failures if they have helped set the objectives (Arlin

---

*See Csapo 1972; Cullinan, Kauffman, and LaFleur 1975; Goodwin and Mahoney 1975.
†See Kauffman 1977, 239.

and Whitley 1978). Cooperative goal setting appears to encourage positive self-concept, self-control, and acceptance of failures without the sense of personal inadequacy often found in classes where a strong sense of competition prevails (Ames, Ames, and Felker 1977).

Why Is Discipline Such a Problem?

Causes of discipline problems are not always apparent. Sometimes there is a cultural difference between the child and the teacher as to what behavior is expected from both child and adult. Parents' values concerning school and learning may be very different from those of the teacher. What is important to the teacher may not be important to either the student or her family. Always consider the relation between discipline and motivation as you design instruction. Sometimes you have to address misbehavior by changing your own teaching methods.

Teachers cannot assume students agree that certain disciplinary measures are fair, effective, or reasonable. This is another good reason to involve students in setting rules for classroom living. Sometimes it is very difficult for a teacher to maintain consistent behavior in a classroom situation. Inconsistent behavior by the teacher sends mixed signals to students. For example, if you preach acceptance of others, you had better demonstrate accepting behavior yourself—and be aware when you have slipped.

Possible Causes of Discipline Problems

Elementary school children are affected mainly by self, peers, family, teachers, school situations, and out-of-school situations. These categories are all possible sources of discipline problems. They can be clustered into three groups: Me, Places, and Others. A list of possible causes of discipline problems of each kind follows.

Me-caused Problems

Discuss what is expected so that limits for behavior in your classroom are clear. Students are often aware of why they are causing discipline problems:

I want attention so I push it too far.
I don't often feel well.

Place-related Problems

Place-related problems are reflected in the following statements:

How can I get my homework done—I don't have any place that's my own at home.
I stay up and watch cable until I fall asleep—and that's real late.
How can I do the homework when I can't read it—and neither can anyone else at home—and they're doing all right.
Why can't I be roaming with my brothers? Why do I have to be here?
The teacher's rules are different from my folks'—whom do I follow?

Others–caused Problems

Some of the "others" are teachers who cause problems by:

Showing impatience
Being insensitive to students' needs
Using sarcasm
Being impolite or inconsiderate
Intimidating students
Ignoring the physical needs of students (e.g., classroom too hot or too cold, in disarray)
Showing favoritism
Teaching only at the symbols level—seldom at the concrete
Showing lack of trust in students
Being disorganized
Preparing inadequately for lessons
Keeping instruction moving at too slow a pace—or so fast that students give up
Giving vague assignments
Handing out blanket punishments for total class
Using punishment more than reward
Losing temper and yelling at class

Family members can also cause discipline problems in school by:

Applying too much pressure for high grades, leading a child to cheat on examinations
Never being satisfied with a child's level of performance
Comparing children to others
Demanding too much in general
Undermining the teacher's authority
Feeling threatened by the teacher and showing this to the child
Showing disrespect for the teacher
Complaining to the principal a lot

Guidelines for Handling Class Disturbances

Hoover and Hollingsworth (1982, 91–93) list general guidelines that teachers have found effective in keeping classroom discipline:*

Disturbing Conversation. Sometimes such a disturbance can be ignored. If it threatens to spread, the teacher can move to the area of the disturbance. One may offer to help the pupils get started on an assignment. If the teacher is talking to the entire group, a pause or a question to one of the disturbing pupils can effectively solve the problem. Although some teachers are quick to separate

---

*From Kenneth H. Hoover and Paul M. Hollingsworth, A HANDBOOK FOR ELEMENTARY SCHOOL TEACHERS, Third Edition. Copyright © 1982 by Allyn and Bacon, Inc. Reprinted with permission.

pupils who disturb, this is often an inadvisable procedure. The practice may create resentment and serve to spread the problem.

Passing Notes. Such activities are symptomatic of a boring experience or lack of appropriate challenge. Frequently a change of pace takes care of the situation. It is not appropriate to read notes aloud to the class.

Overdependence of One Child on Another. This is a problem that usually will work itself out. Such pupils sometimes need each other until wider social acceptance is encouraged through emphasis on group work in which pupils are grouped sociometrically.

Hostility between Individuals and/or Groups. Talk with each of the participants individually. Try to find the cause prior to any drastic attempts at reformation.

Cheating. Cheating may occur as a result of overemphasis on grades or the establishment of unrealistic standards. It is important to make assignments and tests that are commensurate with pupils' abilities. If the task is too hard, pupils may be forced to cheat in order to meet the requirement.

Tattletales. Children should be taught the difference between tattletales and reporting. A tattletale is one who tells *personal* things, whereas a child who *reports* about another child has been given the responsibility to do so because the child being reported is breaking a school or classroom rule. Children need to learn and be helped to distinguish between tattling as a busybody operation and reporting as an essential group function. Tattling deals with the insignificant; reporting deals with consequential information regarding the health, safety, and welfare of the children in the class and with a particular classroom routine or regulation essential to effective classroom operation. Teachers need to treat tattling and reporting with consistency. Young children need many opportunities to consider the subtle differences between these two behaviors.

Temper Tantrum. When a child in the classroom has a temper tantrum everyone in the classroom should avoid giving the child an audience. The teacher should move the child to one's desk or table, or the teacher may need to remove the child from the classroom altogether so other children will not give him or her an audience. The teacher may find out what caused the child to have a temper tantrum and then try to help the child see the behavior in a different way. This may prevent it from happening again.

Refusal to Comply with a Teacher Request. Sometimes a teacher makes a simple request, only to discover that the child refuses to obey. What should be done under the circumstances? The action to be taken will, of course, depend upon the nature of the request. Refusal to comply with simple requests usually is associated with high emotional tension. Don't argue with the child, continued argumentative dialogue makes things worse. Don't make statements or threats that cannot be enforced or that give the teacher or the child no alternative for subsequent behavior. Usually the teacher can take the child by the hand and direct him or her to that which was requested; however, it may be necessary to take the child from the room to discuss the problem. It is very important, however, that teacher requests be followed. Failure to comply should be subject to certain consequences. Unreasonable requests should be avoided. A reasonable request for one pupil may be unreasonable for another. Provide a cooling-off, reflective period to allow both child and teacher to reduce emotional levels and to become more objective; then the problem may be more easily handled by both teacher and pupil.

Isolation. Separating a child from peers tends to reinforce the craving that induced the behavior in the first place. It may be necessary to isolate a pupil *temporarily* as a stopgap measure, but continued use of this technique can only lead to greater frustration, and deeper feelings of guilt and resentment.

Removal from the Situation. While there will be times when a child must be removed from the classroom, it should be used only as a last resort. In such instances the teacher is admitting that one cannot handle the situation. When it becomes necessary the offender should be sent to a specific member of the teaching or administrative staff. In other words, the child should not be sent from the room without adequate provisions for supervision.

Classroom Management

Classroom management is a skill that creates a learning environment within a classroom or broader school setting. Classroom environment has the potential to enhance or inhibit learning. Maintaining discipline is but one aspect of classroom management. Other variables needing attention include physical comfort, seating arrangements, pupil movement in space within the classroom, rules and policies and their making, collection of milk or lunch money, taking attendance, handing out and controlling materials, accessibility or resource materials, and management outside of the classroom.

Physical Comfort

The physical environment can facilitate or inhibit learning. If individuals are unaware of their physical comfort, it usually means their needs are being met. However, if the room is too warm, too cold, or uncomfortable for some reason, then that discomfort is brought to the forefront of attention and must be satisfied before students can return to meeting the higher needs that prompt learning (Maslow 1954).

Comfortable classroom temperatures range between sixty-five and sixty-eight degrees. Ventilation must be effective so that fresh air is available. Sufficient lighting in all appropriate areas is necessary. Design seating arrangements so as to avoid glare from light on chalkboards that interferes with vision. Students should not be seated facing windows and shades should be properly adjusted to avoid glare from sunlight.

Seating Arrangments

Desks, tables, chairs, and other hardware including computers can affect students' behavior and willingness to learn. Furniture arrangement is very important to elementary school children. Who they sit by, where they sit, and where their friends are seated are of concern. Discuss and design seating arrangements together with the children. Possible arrangements should be brainstormed, criteria for selection of alternatives de-

The physical environment can facilitate or inhibit learning.

cided upon, and the decision should result from group problem solving (see chap. 15).

Seating students in clusters of four with two desks side by side and two desks facing each other creates a feeling of more space in a crowded room. If clusters are parallel to the window, glare from the outside is avoided. This arrangement, illustrated below, is appropriate for grades three through six.

Before grade three, desks should be arranged so that children do not view each other's written work upside down. It is important to facilitate development of right-left orientation and of spatial relations. Seeing written words and numbers upside down may interfere with development

```
                         Bulletin board
        Teacher's desk/work table


                     XX          XX         XX
                     XX          XX         XX
   Window                                              Chalkboard/
   side of                                             film
   room                                                screen
                   XXX          XX         XX      XX
                   XXX          XX         XX      XX


                 Library table            Computer
                 Bookshelves               center

                         Bulletin board
```

of orientation in space. A similar spatial problem may occur in tasks of copying from the board. Going from a vertical plane (the chalkboard) to a horizontal plane (the written work on the desk) confuses some youngsters, especially in grade one. Thus, assignments requiring students to copy computation problems or spelling words from the chalkboard should be replaced with tasks that directly address the instructional objective. For example, if the objective is "To add one-digit numbers," then provide a worksheet. Often students in early grades do poorly on such objectives because of copying errors rather than errors in computation. If a copying problem is compounded by a seating arrangement that makes seeing the chalkboard difficult, the task is not meeting the instructional objective and the resulting behavior is not clear.

From grades two or three on, the cluster seating arrangement allows children to engage in quiet conversation and see each others' faces instead of the backs of heads. The cluster seating arrangement can be tied to classroom discipline. If a group misbehaves, they lose their cluster privilege and are placed in a row until they decide they can return to the cluster organization.

Pupil Movement in the Classroom

The extent of pupils' freedom to move in space depends on the philosophical premises of the classroom. Some teachers are comfortable with a minimum of rules for pupil movement within the classroom. Others strictly regulate where students may be and when. For example, in some classrooms students may not leave their seats for any reason without permission. In others they may sharpen pencils, go to the wastebasket, go to learning centers, get a drink, and go to the bathroom

The extent of pupil freedom is related to classroom philosophy.

without permission—so long as this freedom is not abused. The more emphasis is placed on developing self-control and self-discipline, the more freedom of movement will be allowed.

Discipline problems that may emerge in free environments can often be headed off if the teacher is aware of what is going on. Glancing around the classroom every few minutes allows the teacher to spot approaching problems and eliminate the potential before the crisis occurs.

Freedom to move around the classroom has important implications for the physical and psychological development of elementary grade children. Lining children up as a class to march to the drinking fountain or to the bathroom is an unnecessary interference with physical well-being. Teachers can keep track of where students are by having them sign their name or initials in the lower corner of the chalkboard when they go to the bathroom. They erase their name or initials when they return, and that signals that another child may go. The form below allows for both a boy and a girl to be out of the room at the same time.

Boy	Girl

Usually, in controlled environments, if children are thirsty or need to go to the bathroom at times other than the "march" they are told to wait until the next "march." This goes against important psychological tasks such as developing control of one's body, ability to make decisions, self-control, and self-concept.

Rules and Policies Classroom rules and policies and how they are made also reflect the teacher's philosophy of what learning environments should be. Are rules set down by the teacher for students to follow, or are they developed in cooperation with the children? Hoover and Hollingsworth (1982, 80) point out that "when the children are involved and have a voice in making the rules, there seem to be less dissenters."

Rule-setting is a developmental phenomenon. Kohlberg (1969) presents a stage theory of moral development based on the developmental theory of Jean Piaget:

Preconventional morality Where children's behavior is controlled by external forces that involve obtaining material rewards and fear of punishment. Later during this stage children become less concerned with physical rewards and punishments and become more concerned with pleasing significant others (parents, teachers, authority figures). Concepts of reciprocity and sharing emerge and children begin to consider reactions of others to their own actions.

Conventional morality Involves self-control and conscious need for acceptance and social approval. Later in this stage morality takes on a legal aspect—a law and order morality.

Postconventional morality Involves making independent moral judgments.

Biehler (1974, 395) compares Kohlberg's stages of moral development to Piagetian stages:

> Just as Piaget argues that the child advances through stages of intellectual development in sequence, Kohlberg maintains that children must pass through lower stages of moral development in order to become capable of postconventional thinking. . . . The Kohlberg stages are not clearly related to specific age levels, particularly since many individuals never progress beyond the conventional level. However, the switch from preconventional to conventional thought typically takes place around the end of the elementary grades.

Thus, teachers need to be aware of the expected ability of children to engage in rule making and policy setting. Rules to be developed should be important to the daily lives of the children. In addition to getting a drink and going to the bathroom, the array of classroom jobs necessary to a well-organized tidy environment may be identified and delegated according to group consensus. The discussion of creative problem solving in chapter 15 offers suggestions for setting rules and policies.

Finally, the new teacher must quickly get to know school rules and policies. Classroom rules cannot go against school rules; thus, school policy should be discussed during your interview. Unless you can live with policies at the school level—or above—you will have difficulty developing classroom rules and policy that will not get the children and you into trouble within the school context.

Collection and Attendance

Taking attendance and collecting money for various purposes are important tasks. Attendance records are legal documents and may be subpoenaed by the court in custody suits, delinquency or child abuse cases and others, as well as documenting attendance for financial aid for the school district. Many schools now provide secretarial and computer support in completing quarterly attendance reports. At one time, teachers were required to carry the attendance book out of the building during fire drills, in addition to seeing that windows were shut, lights out, children quiet, orderly, and out, and the classroom door closed. The legal record of school attendance had to be saved from burning.

Once a routine is established for start-of-the-day housekeeping chores, little class time is needed to complete them. These tasks can be used as learning experiences. Student monitors may be elected to help take attendance. These monitors could report absences either orally or in writing. A seating chart can be used to check attendance quickly as well as to summarize which children will be buying lunch. One child within a cluster, row, or table may be in charge of collecting money, getting the lunch count, or collecting the milk or lunch tickets.

To make the morning routine quick and efficient, children should work with the teacher to develop ground rules for entering the class and for behavior at the start of the day. For example, instead of running into the classroom laughing loudly, pushing, knocking each other around in play, or flopping on the floor, children should enter calmly, and quietly engage in a task of choice such as reading for pleasure, completing homework with the help of a classmate, working on an ongoing project, or other quiet, independent activities that the class has agreed on.

Handing Out and Collecting Materials

Distributing and collecting materials can be chaotic for new teachers. These seem like simple tasks. They can be, with a bit of organization, but they can also cause havoc. Managing materials involves three phases: preparation, distribution, and collection. Materials should be prepared for distribution ahead of time to avoid behavior problems that could result from too long a wait. Children may become impatient and even lose interest in the task if the materials are not ready. Extra materials should be available if a child makes a mistake and needs to begin again.

Books and supplies should be distributed in a preplanned businesslike manner. Student monitors can be assigned distribution and collection tasks. If supplies and teaching materials are kept in a particular place, then anyone in the classroom family can help distribute, collect, and return instructional equipment and/or supplies. Students should also keep desks orderly and neat. Once a week, time should be set aside for cleaning out desks.

Management Outside the Classroom

Children may cooperate within the classroom and yet constantly get into trouble outside it. This problem could be caused by inconsistencies in classroom and school policies, differences in rules among teachers, or lack of self-control in less structured environments like the school playground, cafeteria, hallways, bathrooms, drinking fountains, school auditorium, school library, bus, or on field trips. Children may get along with the classroom teacher but not with other supervising adults such as reading teachers, physical education instructors, or the librarian.

Sometimes students get into trouble for vandalism or stealing in neighborhood stores. Good citizenship outside the classroom is not a given. Transfer of self-control to situations external to the classroom must be encouraged directly. Classroom role play depicting an actual life problem may aid analysis and study and facilitate the transfer of self-control. A widely used role-playing technique is role reversal. For example, a child who defies the reading teacher might portray himself in a situation likely to occur during instruction in the reading resource room. Then the roles are reversed and he plays the part of the reading teacher. Such activity often prompts understanding of each other's goals so that cooperative solutions can emerge. Role play should not be confused with play therapy or psychodrama. Role play is a tool for developing understanding. Therapy delves into subconscious feelings and motives, and should be left to trained clinicians.

Self-Control and Special Needs Students

Children who are impaired or talented often display behavior that interferes with developing self-control; these youngsters may become discipline problems in the classroom. The teacher who knows what warning signs to look for is better able to prevent flare-ups. Behaviors displayed by special needs students may include the following:

- Some children may be unable to inhibit their reactions to classroom situations. They may speak out at inappropriate times, not wait their turn, or engage in other disruptive acts. Disruptiveness may be episodic or they may be generally uncooperative. They may be aware that their behavior is unsuitable, but incapable of altering it.
- Some youngsters are easily distracted; they rarely listen and their attention frequently wanders.
- Some students have difficulty planning, they cannot organize tasks sequentially and often need suggestions as to the next step.
- Some children do not tolerate change. They may overreact when under stress or fatigued.
- Some lack ability to relate well to others—especially other children.
- Some youngsters have difficulty assuming responsibility and following through on assigned tasks.
- Some children are plain rude. They often lack sensitivity to the wishes of others. They are not aware of the meaning of social cues and of how their actions affect others.

The instructional strategies presented earlier in this chapter have been found helpful with students who display these behaviors.

Thought Activity

1. List generic influences on learning that would most likely be involved in discipline problems.
2. Describe how you can apply these generic factors to avoid causing behavior problems in your students.
3. List additional social and emotional influences that in your experience cause discipline problems in various settings such as the following:
    a. classroom
    b. cafeteria
    c. playground
    d. resource room
    e. school library
    f. the home
    g. religious setting
    h. youth group activity
4. List me-caused discipline problems that you personally are aware of creating in one of your field placements or in some activity with children.

5. Outline the rules and policies that you will guide your class to develop.
6. Describe the physical arrangement of your dream classroom including furniture arrangement and paths for pupil movement.
7. Develop a role play situation for an out-of-class objective such as "To cooperate with other teachers." Show your draft to a colleague and ask what she thinks the objective is. Use this feedback to refine the design of your role play scenario.

References

Ames, C., R. Ames, and D. W. Felker. 1977. Effects of competitive reward structure and valence of outcome on children's achievement attribution. *Journal of Educational Psychology* 69:1–8.

Arlin, M. and T. W. Whitley. 1978. Perceptions of self-managed learning opportunities and academic locus of control: A causal interpretation. *Journal of Educational Psychology* 70:988–92.

Bartholomew, B. R. (Project Director). 1980. Nationwide teacher opinion poll, 1980. In *National Education Association Research Memo*. Washington, D.C.: National Education Association.

Biehler, R. F. 1974. *Psychology applied to teaching*. 2d ed. Boston: Houghton-Mifflin.

Canfield, J. D., and H. C. Wells. 1976. *One hundred ways to enhance self-concept in the classroom*. (ERIC Document Reproduction Service No. ED 117 031). Englewood Clifs, N.J.: Prentice-Hall.

Canter, L. 1976. *Assertive discipline*. Los Angeles: Lee Canter & Associates.

Carkhuff, R. R., and A. H. Griffin. 1978. *The LEAST approach to classroom discipline*. (ERIC Document Reproduction Service No. ED 166 143). Washington, D.C.: National Educaiton Association.

Cruickshank, W. M., F. Bentzen, F. Ratzenberg, and M. A. Tannhauser. 1961. *A teaching method for brain-injured and hyperactive children*. Syracuse, N.Y.: Syracuse Univ. Press.

Csapo, M. 1972. Peer models reverse the "One bad apple spoils the barrel" theory. *Teaching Exceptional Children* 5(1):20–24.

Cullinan, D. A., J. M. Kauffman, and N. K. LaFleur. 1975. Modeling: Research with implications for special education. *Journal of Special Education* 9:209–21.

Dinkmeyer, D., and D. Dinkmeyer, Jr. 1976. Logical consequences: A key to the reduction of disciplinary problems. *Phi Delta Kappan* 57:664–66.

Dobson, J. 1971. *Dare to discipline*. Wheaton, Ill.: Tyndale House.

Doyle, W. 1980. *Classroom management* (ERIC Document Reproduction Service No. ED 198 075). West Lafayette, Ind.: Kappa Delta Pi.

Driekurs, R., B. B. Grunwald, and F. C. Pepper. 1971. *Maintaining sanity in the classroom*. New York: Harper & Row.

Ernst, K. 1972. *Games students play and what to do about them*. Milbras, Calif.: Celestial Arts.

Ginott, H. 1972. *Teacher and child*. New York: Macmillan.

Glasser, W. 1965. *Reality therapy*. New York: Harper & Row.

Glasser, W. 1969. *Schools without failure*. New York: Harper & Row.

Goodwin, S. E., and M. J. Mahoney. 1975. Modification of aggression through modeling: An experimental probe. *Journal of Behavior Therapy and Experimental Psychiatry* 6:200–202.

Gordon, T. 1974. *Teacher effectiveness training.* New York: Wyden.

Hallahan, D. P., and J. M. Kauffman. 1975. Research on the education of distractible and hyperactive children. In *Perceptual and learning disabilities in children.* Vol. 2: *Research and theory,* edited by W. M. Cruickshank and D. P. Hallahan. Syracuse, N.Y.: Syracuse Univ. Press.

Haring, N. G., and E. L. Phillips. 1962. *Educating emotionally disturbed children.* New York: McGraw-Hill.

Haring, N. G., and R. J. Whelan. 1965. Experimental methods in education and management. In *Conflicts in the classroom,* edited by N. J. Long, W. C. Morse, and R. G. Newman. Belmont, Calif.: Wadsworth.

Hewett, F. M. 1968. *The emotionally disturbed child in the classroom.* Boston: Allyn & Bacon.

Hoover, K. H., and P. M. Hollingsworth. 1982. *A handbook for elementary school teachers.* Boston: Allyn & Bacon.

Kauffman, J. M. 1977. *Characteristics of children's behavior disorders.* Columbus, Ohio: Charles E. Merrill.

Kohlberg, L. 1969. Stage and sequence. The cognitive-development approach to socialization In *Handbook for socialization theory and research,* edited by D. Goslin. Chicago: Rand McNally.

Luria, A. R. 1973. *The working brain: An introduction to neurophyschology.* New York: Basic Books.

Maslow, A. H. 1954. *Motivation and personality.* New York: Harper.

Project TEACH. 1977. (ERIC Document Reproduction Service No. ED 167 527). Westwood, N.J.: Performance Learning Systems.

Purkey, W. W. 1978. *Inviting school success: A self-concept approach to teaching and learning.* Belmont, Calif.: Wadsworth.

Reisman, F. K., and S. H. Kauffman. 1980. *Teaching mathematics to children with special needs.* Columbus, Ohio: Charles E. Merrill.

Simons, S. B., L. W. Howe and H. Kirschenbaum. 1972. *Values clarification.* (ERIC Document Reproduction Service No. Ed 069 585). New York: Hart.

Skinner, B. F. 1958. *The technology of teaching.* New York: Appleton-Century-Crofts.

Taylor, J. G., and R. H. Usher. 1982. Discipline. In *Encylopedia of educational research.* 5th ed. (Harold E. Mitzel, Editor in Chief), 447–50. New York: Macmillan.

Weiner, D. H. 1972. *Classroom management and discipline.* Itasca, Ill.: F. E. Peacock.

15 *Applying what I've learned*

This chapter is designed to help you synthesize what you have learned so far in your path toward becoming a designer of learning and instructional environments. Topics at first may appear unrelated, but as you engage in cognitive monitoring to synthesize what you as a developing instructional designer are learning, relationships should begin to emerge.

The first part of this chapter summarizes diagnostic teaching (see chap. 6) and describes a diagnostic mathematics assessment. The next part describes the most recent data about writing as an important process for stimulating thinking and also as a tool for reading instruction. We will then discuss creativity, guidelines for creative problem solving, and personal application of adaptive education. A discussion of basal texts completes the chapter.

Becoming a Diagnostic Instructional Designer
Atkins (1985) summarizes Reisman's model of diagnostic teaching as well as the Sequential Assessment in Mathematics Inventories (SAMI) (Reisman

and Hutchinson 1985), a diagnostic mathematics test for kindergarten through eighth grade. Reisman's model of diagnostic teaching aims to help prevent learning problems and not merely to focus on remediation or prescribe a treatment after problems occur.

To prevent learning problems, it is necessary to assess the child's cognitive performance. Then the task to be learned must be analyzed to determine what aspects of it the child already knows. This analysis of the interaction of the child and the curriculum helps the teacher to understand how generic factors that influence learning (see chap. 2) are affecting the child's acquisition of knowledge. The next step is to design instruction that facilitates development of pupil learning strengths and circumvents learning problems—the most critical step in diagnostic teaching. Since diagnostic teaching is adoptive in nature, this approach may be used with slow, average, and gifted students.

Children have difficulty learning mathematics for a number of reasons. Problems may arise from gaps in a student's mathematical foundation, lack of readiness, emotional problems, deprived environment, poor teaching, and/or learning disability. If students have gaps in basic mathematical concepts, it is inevitable that they will run into difficulty when encountering new mathematics material that depends on previous understanding. Emotional problems can be brought on by failure in mathematics, since it is such a high-status subject; and emotional problems may cause learning difficulties in mathematics. A child may take on a parent's negative feelings about the subject or may even fail intentionally in response to the parents' demand for high grades.

A model for diagnostic teaching, the Diagnostic Teaching Cycle, defines five processes (Reisman 1982, 22):

1. Identifying the child's strengths and weaknesses in arithmetic performance,
2. Hypothesizing possible reasons for these strengths and weaknesses,
3. Formulating instructional objectives to serve as a structure for the enrichment of strengths or the remediation of weaknesses,
4. Creating and trying corrective procedures, and
5. Ongoing evaluation of all phases of the diagnostic cycle to see if progress is being made in either alleviating trouble areas or in enriching strong areas.

Atkins (1985) further describes Reisman's diagnostic teaching model by noting that when attempting to diagnose learning difficulties the teacher should obtain as much evidence as possible. Concrete activities such as Piagetian tasks (e.g., one-to-one correspondence, conservation of number, and serial correspondence) help to determine a child's readiness for work with numbers. Children should be able to perform these Piagetian tasks by grades two or three.

Teachers need to be able to identify the kind of learning required for a particular task so that they can select an appropriate method of instruction. Brownell and Hendrickson (1950) identify four types of learning:

arbitrary associations (facts), concepts, generalizations or principles, and problem solving. Gagne's (1965) expanded hierarchy of eight types of learning includes *signal learning* (Pavlov's conditioned response), *stimulus-response learning* (emphasizes a single connection between some stimulus situation and some response), *chaining* (involves motor behavior—e.g., cutting with scissors), *verbal association* (naming or labeling), *multiple discrimination learning* (discriminating shape, color, texture, words, numerals), *concept learning* (involves abstracting similarities among objects in a group), *principle learning* (forming a relational combination of two or more concepts—e.g., round things roll, 2 + 4), and *problem solving* (**heuristics**). The following cross reference of elementary school content, learning types, and instructional strategies is provided as a model for synthesizing and using these ideas about instruction.

Elementary School Content	*Learning Types*	*Instructional Strategies*
emotional aversion to learning mathematics	signal learning	tacit learning
learns names of digits 0–9	stimulus-response, arbitrary association	didactic teaching
cuts with scissors	chaining	didactic teaching
learns alphabet, says digits 0–9 in order	verbal association	didactic teaching
distinguishes shape, color, texture, size	multiple discrimination	didactic and discovery
classification	concept learning	discovery
generalizations	principle learning	discovery and tacit
heuristics	problem solving	discovery

Another tool used in diagnostic teaching is the *Taxonomy of Educational Objectives: Cognitive Domain* (see chap. 4). The Taxonomy categories are useful in designing evaluative tools for elementary mathematics students.

Reisman also incorporates Carl Rogers' comparison of the client-centered psychotherapeutic situation to the teacher-student relation into the diagnostic teaching model. To Rogers (1959), the role of the teacher is to create a classroom environment that facilitates learning. Teachers need to develop personal relationships with their students. The affective domain taxonomy (see chap. 4) helps teachers define goals and objectives that emphasize Rogers' ideas about teaching.

Diagnostic Assessment—A Tool for the Diagnostic Teacher

Atkins (1985) describes a diagnostic mathematics testing tool, the Sequential Assessment Mathematics Inventories (SAMI)—Standardized Inventory (Reisman and Hutchinson 1985). Teachers may use norm-referenced or standardized tests to carry out the identification component of the Diagnostic Teaching Cycle. Standardized tests are of several types: aptitude or intelligence, achievement, assessment, and diagnostic. A diagnostic test is usually called for when a student's below-grade-level performance is not consistent with aptitude. For a more complete picture, the teacher may use a formula to compute the student's expected grade equivalent based on intellectual capacity (Reisman 1982, 46–52). Since standardized tests reveal only part of a student's mathematics profile, many teachers develop their own diagnostic tests that allow for a more refined look at a student's abilities.

The SAMI provides a model for teacher-made diagnostic tools. Two instruments make up the SAMI: (1) the SAMI Standardized Inventory, designed for use by school psychologists or special education personnel (Reisman 1986); and (2) the SAMI Informal Inventory, designed for classroom use and still under development. The two instruments may be used independently or in combination to yield an overall profile of a student's performance in mathematics, highlighting specific strengths and weaknesses.

The SAMI Standardized Inventory is a standardized test for students in a K–8 mathematics curriculum. The test has eight subtests or curriculum strands. Two strands, Mathematical Language and Ordinality, contain items that test students' knowledge and understanding of basic mathematical relationships and concepts. These two subtests act as good screening devices, or they may serve as "warm-up" tests for an anxious child. The eight strands and related grade levels are as follows:

Strand	*Grade Levels*
Mathematical Language	K, 1
Ordinality	K–3
Number and Notation	K–8
Computation	K–8
Measurement	K–8
Geometric Concepts	K–8
Mathcmatical Applications	4–8
Word Problems	1–8

The test is administered to students individually and takes twenty to sixty minutes, depending on age and performance of the pupil. As we mentioned, the SAMI Standardized Inventory is intended for use by school personnel who assess or instruct students with problems in learning mathematics (i.e., school psychologists, special education teachers, learning therapists, etc.)

Atkins (1985) explains that the SAMI has two primary purposes: (1) to differentiate among students in their overall mathematics performance, and (2) to measure an individual student's strengths and weaknesses in mastering the mathematics curriculum. Diagnostic assessment includes both differentiation (ordering of students within a specified group) and measurement (evaluating knowledge of content). The SAMI addresses both of these issues, comparing students both within and across grades.

Raw scores for individual subtests and for the total test can be converted to several types of normative scores. The SAMI is a tool for comparing observed student performance with the range of performances observed in a representative national sample of students. Content specifications for the SAMI allow for comparisons and interpretations. The student's performance in mathematics may be compared with norming samples to determine where the student falls in relation to grade level.

The content of the SAMI represents the mathematics curriculum which students must master. Subtests correlate with the major categories or strands of the curriculum. In the development of the SAMI, attention was given to two important aspects of mathematics learning. First, one needs to understand the mathematical relationships underlying the curriculum. The process of learning mathematics is a spiral or hierarchy. Second, the psychological nature of the curriculum demands developmental readiness for constructing relations, concepts, and generalizations.

The SAMI is cross-referenced with an up-to-date analysis of mathematics curricula on a national scale. SAMI item objectives are correlated with grade level goals in seven of the leading basal mathematics textbook series.

There is no one simple explanation as to why a student succeeds or fails in learning mathematics. Generic influences affecting the learner were presented in chapter 2 of this book. Teachers' awareness of these influences may provide insights to guide instruction. Mathematics is a symbolic relational system—much like general language, which is discussed next.

Writing as Inquiry

Can writing be taught? This question is analogous to the question: Can concepts be taught—or are they constructed by the learner? Recent research into writing instruction emphasizes writing as a cognitive process rather than as a product. Emig (1982, 2023) compares traditional methods of teaching writing to the newer focus:*

---

*From "Writing, Composition, and Rhetoric" by Janet Emig. Excerpted with permission of Macmillan Publishing Company from ENCYCLOPEDIA OF EDUCATIONAL RESEARCH Fifth Edition, Harold E. Mitzel, Editor in chief. Volume 4, pages 2021–2023. Copyright © 1982 by American Educational Research Association.

Applying What I've Learned

Students learn to use a word processor.

Traditional	Newer
Writing is a product to be evaluated.	Writing is a process to be experienced.
Writing is predominately taught rather than learned.	Writing is predominantly learned rather than taught.
Students must be taught from parts to whole. Children must be taught to write words before they write sentences before they can be allowed to write paragraphs before they can be permitted to attempt whole pieces of discourse.	Writers of all ages as frequently work from wholes to parts as from parts to wholes. In writing, there is a complex interplay between focal and global concerns: from an interest in what word comes next to a concern with the shape of the total piece.
There is essentially one process of writing that serves all writers for all aims, modes, intents, and audiences.	There is no monolithic process of writing. There are processes of writing that differ because of differing aims, intents, modes, and audiences. Although there are shared features in the ways

Traditional	Newer
	we write, there are also individual, even idiosyncratic, features.
The process is linear: all planning precedes all writing, as all writing precedes all revising.	The processes of writing do not proceed in a linear sequence; rather, they are recursive. We not only plan, then write, then revise, but we also revise, then plan, then write.
That process is almost exclusively conscious: as evidence, a full plan or outline can be drawn up and adhered to for any piece of writing in any mode. The requirement to produce an outline also assumes that writing is transcribing; since it can be so totally prefigured, thought must exist fully formed prior to any linguistic formulation.	Writing is as often an unconscious or a preconscious roaming as it is a planned and conscious rendering of information and events.
Perhaps because writing is conscious, it can be done swiftly and in order.	The rhythms of writing are uneven, indeed erratic. The pace of writing can be very slow, particularly if the writing represents significant learning. Writing is also slow since it involves what Vygotsky (1962) calls "elaborating the web of meaning," supplying the explicit links to transform lexical, syntactic, and rhetorical pieces into organic wholes.
There is no community or collaboration in writing: it is exclusively a silent and solitary activity.	The processes of writing can be enhanced by working in, and with, a group of other writers, perhaps especially a teacher, who gives vital response, including advice.

This shift in emphasis from product to process represents a significant change in research on design of instruction for writing. Characterizations of the writer have become as important as characterizations of the process of writing. Focus is now on the interrelationships among process, product, and writer. Writing is now viewed as one manifestation of general cognitive development. Investigations have occurred with learners from ages four through college age. One study (Graves 1975) has reported that seven-year-olds who were allowed to select their own topics, rather than having them assigned, wrote four times as much and with good quality.

Writing, Listening, Talking, and Reading. These four verbal processes are intertwined, and all four must be accounted for simultaneously during design of instruction. These four verbal processes have been differentiated by researchers, especially in special education, as follows:

Listening and Reading	*Talking and Writing*
Receptive language	Productive language
Decoding	Encoding
Passive processes	Active processes

It appears, then, that writing is a learning process, since the act requires analysis and synthesis—higher-order intellectual functions. In fact, in a study with college students Weiss and Walters (1980) found that students clarified concepts in content subject matter better through writing activities than without writing assignments.

Creativity

There are two approaches to studying creativity. The first approach is measurement using normed tests of divergent thinking. The Torrance Tests of Creative Thinking (Torrance 1966), Thinking Creatively with Sounds and Words (Torrance, Khatena, and Cunnington 1973), and The Purdue Creative Thinking Program (Feldhusen, Speedie, and Treffinger 1971) are creativity measures. The second approach to studying creativity is an attempt to measure real-life creativity directly by observing creative works like poems, symphonies, books, inventions, and scientific theories. This focus seems more appropriate for adults.

Wallas (1926) listed four steps in creative thinking:

1. *preparation,* during which one becomes aware of and defines the problem, gathers information, and initiates an unconscious phase that is essential to the next two steps,
2. *incubation,* the problem is put into the unconscious where ideas are generated, many of which are later discarded,
3. *illumination,* selected ideas reach consciousness again, among which is the solution to the problem (insight),
4. *verification,* validates the selected solution based on preset criteria.

Theories of Creativity

Psychoanalytic theories (Kris 1952; Kubie 1958) emphasize the preconscious. Preconscious activity is believed to occur when conscious rational thought is temporarily supplanted by daydreaming and fantasy. Ideas produced during this process can later be evaluated as in Wallas's step four, verification.

Associationist theories (Gruber 1974; Hadamard 1945; Haslerud 1972; Koestler 1978; Mednick 1962) focus on the production of novel or unusual connections among ideas. Originality of thought resulting from a synthesis of ideas, i.e., combining elements to form a new whole, is the essence of creative thinking from this point of view.

Gestalt theories (Kohler 1969; Wertheimer 1959) describe a continuous restructuring of problems until a solution appears. The gestalt, or whole, emerges with an unusual aspect that had not previously been seen.

Edwards (1979, 40) lists the following traits, ascribed to the two cerebral hemispheres, that the creative person can access equally well:

Left	*Right*
verbal	nonverbal
analytic	synthetic
symbolic	concrete
abstract	analogic
temporal	nontemporal
rational	nonrational
digital	spatial
logical	intuitive
linear	holistic

Parke (1985, 386) suggests that instructional activities may be designed to activate one hemisphere over the other. Edwards has argued that people can be trained to use right brain thinking. Although these hypotheses are interesting, evidence is still unclear as to the effectiveness of teaching to the right or left brain processes.

Guilford's Structure of the Intellect (SOI) Model (1967), which defines creativity as an intellectual function rather than as a separate ability, is a classical interpretation of creativity. Major elements of Guilford's SOI are abilities (operations), classes of information (contents), and organization (products). Frierson (1969) points out that the operations component underlies much of the present-day research in creativity. The three major components of Guilford's model are further broken down as follows:

Operations	*Contents*	*Products*
Evaluation	Figural	Units
Convergent production	Symbolic	Classes
Divergent production	Semantic	Relations
Memory	Behavioral	Systems
Cognition		Transformations
		Implications

Applying What I've Learned

Computer graphics intrigue students.

Meeker (1969, 20) states that besides divergent thinking, creativity also involves

- Sensitivity to problems (associated with the evaluation operation)
- Fluency of thinking (ability to generate many ideas)
- Flexibility of thinking (ability to change categories of ideas)
- Originality (ability to produce the unusual)
- Redefinition (using the familiar in a different way)
- Elaboration (ability to embellish on an idea or object to make it more complex)

Can You Teach Creativity?

Mansfield and Busse (1982) describe three programs for creativity training. A summary of their description follows:

- The Productive Thinking Program (Covington et al. 1974) is a self-instructional program for fifth and sixth graders, consisting of fifteen booklets depicting detective stories in cartoon format. The program includes divergent and convergent thinking.
- The Purdue Creative Thinking Program (Feldhusen, Speedie, and Treffinger 1971) consists of twenty-eight audio tapes aimed at fostering divergent-thinking abilities in children at about a fourth grade level.
- Guide to Creative Action (Parnes 1967; Parnes, Noller, and Biondi 1977), a program for college students, highlights brainstorming.

Keating (1980) points out that in addition to divergent-thinking abilities, education must foster content knowledge, critical analysis, and communication skills. Content knowledge is specific information in a field or fields. Critical analysis involves selecting promising paths of inquiry in order to maximize the probability of creative discovery. Communication skills are necessary for translating the creative idea into a creative product.

Hudgins (1977, 289–90) points out that "creativity demands continuous emphasis upon divergent thinking, coupled with discipline. . . . The intention of programs is not to build creative people, but to nurture the creativity in each person." This is not accomplished in a forty-minute lesson on creativity, but by designing instruction so as to nurture creative problem solving. Torrance (1977, 24) lists the following guidelines for fostering creativity:

1. Provide opportunity for creative expression
2. Develop skills for creative learning
3. Reward creative achievement
4. Establish creative relationships with children

Krippner (1967) lists beliefs that are blocks to creativity and must be avoided:

- Everything you do must be useful.
- Everything you do must be successful.
- Everything you do must be perfect.
- Everyone you know must like you.
- You must not prefer solitude to togetherness.
- Remember concentrated attention and keep it holy.
- You must not diverge from culturally-imposed sex norms.
- You must not express excessive emotional feeling.
- You must not be ambiguous.
- You must not rock the cultural boat.

Brainstorming

Brainstorming (Osborn 1963) is a group process designed to elicit many ideas without restrictions or evaluation. Ideas should be relevant and unusual. Four basic rules underlie brainstorming:

1. *No criticism.* Evaluation of ideas generated must be held until later.
2. *Freewheeling is encouraged.* The sky's the limit on ideas.
3. *Quantity is important.* The greater the number of ideas, the greater the probability of success.
4. *Generate ideas cooperatively.* Combine two or more ideas to obtain an improved version.

Brainstorming is most effective in groups of five to ten students, although it also can be an individual activity. It has been used successfully at all levels from elementary school through corporate training sessions in situations where a flow of ideas is the goal.

Synectics

Gordon (1971) has proposed synectics as a problem solving strategy. The strategy aims to make the strange familiar through understanding and to make the familiar strange by changing viewpoint. Gordon suggests four metaphors as tools for making the familiar strange: *personal analogy* (taking the role of an element of the problem to see the problem from a new perspective), *direct analogy* (making comparisons among different classes of objects, e.g., car keys and an amoeba or a sunset), *symbolic analogy* (describing the problem in words), and *fantasy analogy* (linking the rational and the irrational mind). Synectics involves the following three premises (Gordon 1971, 17–18):

1. Creativity can be increased through understanding one's psychological processes.
2. In creativity, emotion is more important than reason, the irrational more important than the rational.
3. Understanding the emotional and the irrational increases the probability of success in problem solving.

Creative Problem Solving

Torrance and Meyers (1970, 83) list skills necessary for creative problem solving:

... making accurate observation, becoming sensitively aware of surroundings, fully utilizing all senses, shifting points of view, questioning, making both deliberate and random association, making predictions, organizing and reorganizing patterns, taking careful inventories, manipulating ideas, and making use of analogy.

Creative problem solving is a disciplined and systematic movement through the problem solving process using creative thinking techniques. The creative problem solving (CPS) process begins with a person's awareness that something is incomplete, wrong, missing, needs fixing, or is somehow a problem. This awareness is often accompanied by emotional concomitants. The person may feel anxious, uneasy, or restless while trying to identify what is out of synch. Parnes (1972) refers to this energizing phase of CPS as the "fuzzy mess." Clearly a problem exists, but its exact nature remains unclear.

Creative problem solving involves five steps:

1. *Fact-finding* involves organizing the knowns into some sort of order; determining what is already known about the fuzzy mess; deciding what else needs to be known or done to bring clarity to the problem.
2. *Recognizing the real problem* involves identifying a number of problems, some related, some not; studying the mess from all angles (see synectics, above). Torrance (1970, 80) notes that at this step it is important to "maintain openness and maintain the deferred judgment necessary for a thorough job of fact finding and problem definition."

3. *Producing alternative solutions* involves brainstorming once a problem has been decided on.
4. *Evaluating solutions* involves establishing criteria by which to judge ideas generated during step three. Criteria are selected in relation to the characteristics of the problem. Students brainstorm possible criteria for evaluating solutions and select those most appropriate to the problem.
5. *Selecting and implementing a solution* "involves creating many alternatives or strategies, and then weaving the best of them into a plan of action after considering variables such as where support will come from, where the opposition will be, what steps must be taken, and who needs to be involved to ensure success" (Treffinger and Parnes 1980, 31).

Since creativity is an ongoing process, Treffinger and Parnes suggest that CPS incorporate consideration of new problems that may arise from solving the old.

Creative Problem Solving Grid

One tool for creative problem solving is the evaluation grid, illustrated in table 15.1 for a first or second grade social studies lesson in preventing accidents on the playground. How can we set and follow safety rules to solve the problem of playground accidents? First, let the children brainstorm possible solutions. Then agree on those ideas you want to keep on the table (e.g., styrofoam or rubber-protected playground equipment, protective clothing, outdoor carpeting to cover cement playground areas, more supervision with directed play). Next brainstorm possible criteria for judging the alternative solutions (cost in time to accomplish goals, cost in money, feasibility of plan, availability of human resources, effect on enjoyment of the play period, parental approval, principal's approval). Then select the criteria you will use. Use a rating scale of least desirable (1) to most desirable (4) and add the ratings across the grid. Use the number of possible solutions as the range of your rating scale. That is, if you have three alternatives, use 1–3; if five, use 1–5. You can

Table 15.1 Evaluation Grid: Preventing Playground Accidents

Alternatives	Evaluation Criteria				
	Cost: Time	Cost: Money	Feasible	Enjoyable	Total
1. Safer equipment	1	2	1	4	8
2. Protective clothing	3	4	4	2	13
3. Carpeting	2	1	2	3	8
4. Supervision	4	3	3	1	11

either have the children rate the possible solutions independently and then average their responses, or evaluate the alternatives as a group and vote or reach consensus. The alternative with the highest score is the solution to try. In the example, since additional supervision was a close second, the children might decide to consider that solution—especially if summer is near and protective clothing would be too warm and uncomfortable.

Basal Textbook

Textbooks provide 80 to 90 percent of instructional materials (Solomon 1978; English 1980). A *basal text* is a grade level text in a series published by a textbook publishing company such as Charles E. Merrill, Ginn, or Addison Wesley. Usually a separate basal text is published for each of the grades kindergarten through eight by subject, e.g., mathematics, science, social studies, language arts, reading. Basal texts for pupils are accompanied by a teacher's manual, usually laden with helpful background information and suggestions for instruction.

Selection and Adaptation Procedures

Although classroom teachers make the most use of basal texts, they usually have the least to say about selection. For example, 45 percent of teachers surveyed by Solomon (1978) were not involved in any part of the selection process even though they were required to use the books selected. Bowler (1978) points out that the need for curricular uniformity and quality control as mandated by school boards affects adoption procedures. However, the final decision as to how to use the textbook as an instructional tool resides with the classroom teacher.

Research on effective use of basal texts is sparse. However, in science instruction, helping students analyze a text and understand the authors' intent appears to aid their understanding of the text's contents (Walker 1981; Armbruster and Anderson 1981; Deese 1981).

Future of the Textbook Industry

Will the electronic age result in the demise of the printed text? Warming (1982, 1936) believes "its future as the predominant classroom resource seems secure because it is easily accessible and can be used outside the classroom." Benthul (1978, 90) states that government "funding is provided more consistently for textbooks than for other instructional materials." Kuykendall (1978) points out that decreased federal spending on development of instructional materials (2 percent in the 1960s to 0.7 percent in 1978) curtailed development of nonbasal materials. However, in the late 1980s and in the 1990s this trend may change as the cost of computers decreases and as software for elementary schools moves on from mindless drill and practice to more learnable forms of instructional design.

Elements to Look for in a Basal Text Teacher's Manual

Some teacher's manuals serve as tools for organizing instruction and provide valuable information for the teacher. A helpful teacher's manual includes a variety of elements that support instruction. The teacher's manual in the *Merrill Mathematics Series* (Buffington et al. 1985) provides such helpful information:

Learning Objectives identify the learning goals of the chapter. These objectives are the basis of the instruction and evaluation of each chapter. The lessons that correspond to each objective are listed in parentheses.

Mathematics of the Chapter summarizes topics covered in the chapter and explains the methodology used to present these topics.

Teaching the Chapter gives suggestions and hints for teaching the entire chapter and for teaching individual lessons.

Introductory Activities can be used as lead-ins to teaching the lesson.

Teaching the Lesson gives suggestions for teaching each page of the lesson.

The *Vocabulary* list contains all new terms presented in the chapter and notes the page on which each is introduced.

Chalkboard Examples sections provide extra examples in red.

An *Error Analysis* is provided when applicable.

A *Mixed Review* containing exercises from previous lessons is given. Answers are printed in red.

An *Assignment Guide* suggests three coverage levels for individualized instruction (remedial, average, enriched).

The *Follow-up Notes* for the lesson list the worksheets available and give activities for additional work at three levels (remedial, average, enriched).

A *Calculator* symbol is placed next to exercises that lend themselves to calculator-assisted solutions.

Challenge Exercises are indicated with a red asterisk. Answers to exercises are printed in red on the students' pages shown in the teacher's manual.

Drill is provided in a systematic manner to help students memorize basic facts.

A *Bibliography* of suggested reference materials provides an opportunity for further extension of the chapter.

Symbols introduced in the chapter are listed.

Materials suggested in the teacher's notes are keyed to the lesson or page with which they can be used.

The *Chapter Inventory and Lesson Plan* shows all materials in the program that are appropriate for use with the chapter. Each lesson, feature, and optional worksheet is correlated to one of the learning objectives.

The plan suggests pages in the student's text for each day and offers review and testing schedules.

A *Bulletin Board Suggestion* enhances the content of each chapter. These suggestions may be modified to accommodate various teaching styles and classroom situations. Bulletin board suggestions include three sections: *Purpose, How to construct it,* and *How to use it.*

In addition to the Teacher's Manual, a Teacher's Resource Book includes the following instructional aids:

Family Math Notes in the Teacher's Resource Book give students an opportunity to share with their families the material they have learned in the chapter. Activities are also provided for the family to work on together at home.

Cumulative Review. The cumulative review worksheets in the Teacher's Resource Book parallel the cumulative reviews given in the student text. These worksheets provide students with a chance to review previously learned skills.

Quizzes. These quizzes may be used for quick checkups.

Chapter Tests. These tests may be used for review, as class tests, or for individualized instruction.

Cumulative Tests. These tests parallel the skills tests in the student text. An answer sheet is provided in the Teacher's Resource Book.

Book Test. Two forms of a five-page book test are provided in the Teacher's Resource Book. Each item on the test corresponds to a learning objective and tests for mastery of that objective.

Blackline Masters include worksheets entitled *Remediation, Enrichment, Readiness, Change of Pace, Extra Practice, Reinforcement and Practice,* and *Problem Solving.*

Additional components of the Merrill Series include the following:

The *Computer Management System* for levels 1 through 8 offers help in diagnosing and assessing mathematical skills. The Computer Management System Test Booklet contains a test and two quizzes for each chapter. The tests are keyed to the learning objectives. The averages of the class or of an individual can be computed and printed out for evaluation.

The *Problem Solving Resource Book* provides problem solving activities correlated to each chapter.

Three separate *Manipulative Kits,* designed for levels K, 1, and 2, and one kit for levels 3–8 help make the connection from the concrete to the abstract. Suggestions for the use of the manipulatives are included in the Teacher's Editions.

The *Poster Package* includes a set of six posters for each level and a teacher's guide.

The *Math Pal Stickers* for levels K–6 are designed to encourage and reward students' work. These stickers feature the Math Pals (e.g., for level 6, an eagle with a mortarboard) that are used throughout the student text to focus attention on new concepts, to point out areas of difficulty, and to encourage students.

A *3-Ring Binder* is designed to store the Answer Key, the Problem Solving Resource Book, the Manipulative Kit Instructions, the Teacher's Poster Guide, and the Blackline Masters.

As you get to know the various features of a particular teacher's manual you will find it more and more useful. If it lacks aids you need, write to the publishers and perhaps they will incorporate those features in their next edition.

Many aids to planning and designing instruction are available in a well-written teacher's guide. However, just as computers are tools, and diagnostic tests are tools for the diagnostic teacher, so textbooks are tools. Textbooks have a place in instruction but should be used only when appropriate to the lesson objectives. Children cannot learn just by reading symbols; they need pictures and hands-on experience as well.

Thought Activity

1. Compare the steps in the Diagnostic Teaching Cycle (p. 257) and the creative problem solving technique (pp. 267–268).
2. Write an instructional objective appropriate to an elementary school grade level for each of Gagne's (1965) learning types.
3. State the differences between a diagnostic test, an IQ test, and an achievement test.
4. Explain the following statement: "Reading impinges on writing, which in turn is transformed by listening and talking."
5. Discuss the relationships among personality, cognitive preference, generic influences on learning, and writing as learning.
6. Write what the following statement means to you and then discuss your answer with a colleague: "Through writing, as through other activities with symbols, like mathematics, brain becomes mind."
7. Write a one-page analysis of the implications of each of the following statements, summarized from Miller (1984), for design of instruction:*
    a. When we think about literacy, we usually think about it with regard to print and the verbal aspects of language. Verbal literacy is not only an indicator of an individual's education and poten-

---

*Summarized from Laverne Miller, "The Media and Visual Literacy," *Educational Media International* 4:25–28. Used with permission.

tial effectiveness in the culture, but nations are spoken of and respected in terms of the literacy of their populations.

b. In addition to verbal literacy, there is another literacy which is as old as time but now, through sophisticated electronic media, demands our attention. This is visual literacy. Reading is a form of visual literacy, but a much wider range of visual information is electronically produced and controlled. Visual literacy is the ability to interpret and draw on and make inferences based on reading non-verbal visual and auditory messages.

c. Students outside the school environment constantly learn a whole range of concepts from visual/auditory media like film, television, or video. More seriously, they are exposed to a set of values designed to make them want to do something with their ideas, money, and time and quite unrelated to their academic environment.

d. In the U.S., the average television is on six hours a day, though this does not necessarily mean the people in the household are actively watching or listening to that set. It is no longer enough to be verbally literate; one must be visually literate as well. In the bitter cold of the arctic night, workers in the underground mines could, during their leisure hours, watch the latest films on a video deck. This concern has commanded the attention of a growing number of people who form the International Visual Literacy Association and whose purpose is to bring together researchers as well as practitioners in the field and from all walks of life. Marshall McLuhan's term, "the global village," describes where we sit today—around a campfire of screens reflecting untold bits and bytes of information, but also sending us the stimulus of picture and sound that brings a wide range of cultures and cultural manifestations to our living rooms.

e. To meet the educational needs generated by fast-paced electronic stimuli, the educator must teach students to analyze what they see on the screens they watch, to sharpen their critical thinking about what they see, to get the medium into a perspective which will not make it the center of their extra-school life and values. Students must be made conscious of their ability to observe not only whole messages but the details of the message.

f. Students can be taught, regardless of the medium, to ask questions like,

What is the message of the visual? (Often it is "buy this" or "vote for me.")

What is the intention of its creator?

Is the maker trying to get me to think something? Do something? Experience something?

What inferences can be drawn from the visual?

How do the details contribute to the effect the creator wants the visual to have?

Who are the people or what are the things the visual talks about? Are they like me? Is what they are doing or what they have attainable? At what cost? How will it affect me? My health? My standards and values?

Can the maker be believed? Do I/can I believe her? What will be the consequences of what I believe? How will my actions be affected? My relationship to others? How will the aims of the visual affect my decisions, and thus my life?

g. The cameraman's eye and its resulting images control information—the automobile looks long and sleek because it is photographed to look that way; the less popular person in the news may be photographed from a less flattering angle; the product advertised will not make you as beautiful as the person in the advertisement who appears to be using that product; the beer you see in the advertisement will not give you the status the picture suggests; the interviewer will ask questions which will solicit the answers he wants the audience to hear; the world of television or video is a world of hype and getting on the bandwagon is a favorite technique of its advertising. One role of education is to teach students to be visually literate about what they see and to be aurally literate and discriminating about what they hear.

8. State the two basic approaches to measuring creativity.
9. State Wallas's four steps in creative thinking.
10. Tell which of the characteristics of creativity suggested by Meeker (p. 265) you display.
11. Design a lesson for an elementary school age child that will foster creative problem solving.
12. List the similarities and differences between brainstorming and synectics.
13. Develop a problem solving grid that incorporates evaluation criteria and possible solutions for selecting an appropriate instructional design for the following objective designed for fifth grade: "To make creative book reports."
14. Evaluate elementary school teachers' manuals in different subject areas as compared to the Merrill Mathematics series components as described on pages 270–272.

References

Armbruster, B., and T. Anderson. 1981. *Analysis of science textbooks: Implications for authors.* In *Research in science education: New questions, new directions,* edited by J. Robinson, 21–52. Louisville, Ky.: Center for Educational Research and Evaluation.

Atkins, J. 1985. Summary of *A guide to the diagnostic teaching of arithmetic* and the SAMI. Unpublished manuscript.

Axelrod, R. 1984. *The evaluation of cooperation.* New York: Basic Books.

Benthul, H. F. 1978. Trends in education: The textbook past and future. *Curriculum Review* 17(2): 89–91.

Bowler, M. 1978. The making of a textbook. *Learning* 6(7): 38–42.

Brownell, W. H., and G. Hendrickson. 1950. How children learn information, concepts, and generalizations. *The forty-ninth yearbook of the National Society for the Study of Education, Part I.* Chicago: Univ. of Chicago Press.

Buffington, A. V., A. R. Garr, J. Graening, P. P. Halloran, M. Mahaffey, and M. O'Neal. 1985. *Merrill Mathematics, Grades K–8.* Teacher's Edition. Columbus, Ohio: Charles E. Merrill.

Covington, M. V., R. S. Crutchfield, L. Davies, and R. M. Olton. 1974. *The Productive Thinking Program: A course in learning to think.* Columbus, Ohio: Charles E. Merrill.

Deese, J. 1981. Text structure, strategies, and comprehension in learning from science books. In *Research in science education: New questions, new directions,* edited by J. Robinson, 53–68. Louisville, Ky.: Center for Educational Research and Evaluation.

Edwards, B. 1979. *Drawing on the right side of the brain.* Los Angeles: J. P. Tarcher.

Emig, J. 1982. Writing composition, and rhetoric. In *Encyclopedia of educational research.* 5th ed. (Harold E. Mitzel, Editor in Chief), 2021–31. New York: Macmillan.

English, R. 1980. The politics of textbook adoption. *Phi Delta Kappan* 62(4): 275–78.

Feldhusen, J. F., S. M. Speedie, and D. J. Treffinger. 1971. The Purdue Creative Thinking Program: Research and evaluation. *National Society for Performance and Instruction Journal* 10(3): 5–9.

Fierson, E. C. 1969. The gifted. *Review of Educational Research* 39: 25–37.

Gagne, R. M. 1965. *The conditions of learning.* New York: Holt, Rinehart & Winston.

Gordon, W. 1971. Synectics. In *Training creative thinking,* edited by G. Davis and J. Scott. New York: Holt, Rinehart & Winston.

Graves, D. 1975. An examination of the writing process of seven-year old children. *Research in Teaching of English* 9: 227–241.

Gruber, H. E. 1974. *Darwin on man: A psychological study of scientific creativity, together with Darwin's early and unpublished notebooks transcribed and annotated by P. H. Barrett.* New York: Dutton.

Guilford, J. P. 1967. *The nature of human intelligence.* New York: McGraw-Hill.

Hadamard, J. 1945. *The psychology of invention in the mathematical field.* Princeton, N.J.: Princeton Univ. Press.

Haslerud, J. 1972. *Transfer, memory, and creativity.* Minneapolis: Univ. of Minnesota Press.

Hudgins, B. 1977. *Learning and thinking: A primer for teachers.* Itasca, Ill.: F. E. Peacock.

Keating, D. P. 1980. Four faces of creativity: The continuing flight of the intellectually underserved. *Gifted Child Quarterly* 24: 61–65.

Koestler, A. 1978. *Janus: A summing up.* New York: Random House.

Kohler, W. 1969. *The task of Gestalt psychology.* Princeton, N.J.: Princeton Univ. Press.

Krippner, S. 1967. The ten commandments that block creativity. *Gifted Child Quarterly* 11: 144–51.

Kris, E. 1952. *Psychoanalytic explorations in art.* New York: International Universities Press.

Kubie, L. S. 1958. *Neurotic distortion of the creative process.* New York: Noonday.

Kuykendall, C. 1978. A view from the crossroads. *English Journal* 67(1): 13–14.

Mansfield, R. S., and T. Busse. 1982. Creativity. In *Encyclopedia of educational research.* 5th ed. (Harold E. Mitzel, Editor in Chief), 385–94. New York: Macmillan.

Mednick, S. 1962. The associative basis of the creative process. *Psychological Review* 69: 220–32.

Meeker, M. 1969. *The structure of the intellect: Its interpretation and uses.* Columbus, Ohio: Charles E. Merrill.

Miller, L. W. 1984. The media and visual literacy. *Educational Media International* 4: 25–26.

Molnar, A. 1985. Introduction. *Current thought on curriculum: 1985 ASCD yearbook.* Alexandria, Va.: Association for Supervision and Curriculum Development.

Osborn, A. 1963. *Applied imagination.* 3rd ed. New York: Scribner.

Parke, B. N. 1985. Methods of developing creativity. In *Teaching gifted children and adolescents,* edited by R. H. Swassing, 377–401. Columbus, Ohio: Charles E. Merrill.

Parnes, S. J. 1967. *Creative behavior guidebook.* New York: Scribner.

Parnes, S. J. 1972. *Creativity: Unlocking human potential.* Buffalo, N.Y.: D.O.K. Publishers.

Parnes, S. J., R. B. Noller, and A. M. Biondi. 1977. *Guide to creative action: Revised edition of Creative behavior guidebook.* New York: Scribner.

Reisman. F. K. 1982. *A guide to the diagnostic teaching of arithmetic.* 3d ed. Columbus, Ohio: Charles E. Merrill.

Reisman, F. K. 1986. *Sequential Assessment in Mathematics Inventory.* San Antonio, Tex.: Psychological Corp.

Reisman, F. K., and T. Hutchinson. 1985. *Manual for SAMI.* Columbus, Ohio: Charles E. Merrill.

Rogers, C. R. 1959. A theory of therapy, personality, and interpersonal relationships. In *Psychology: A study of science.* Vol. 3, edited by S. Koch. New York: McGraw-Hill.

Romberg, T. A., 1985. *Toward effective schooling: The IGE experience.* Lanham, Md.: Univ. Press of America.

Solomon, M. 1978. Textbook selection committees: What teachers can do. *Learning* 6(7): 43.

Torrance, E. P. 1966. *Torrance Tests of Creative Thinking: Norms technical manual.* Princeton, N.J.: Personnel Press.

Torrance, E. P. 1977. *Creativity in the classroom.* Washington, D.C.: National Education Association.

Torrance, E. P., J. Khatena, and B. F. Cunnington. 1973. *Thinking creatively with sounds and words.* Lexington, Mass.: Ginn.

Torrance, E. P., and R. E. Meyers. 1970. *Creative learning and teaching.* New York: Dodd, Mead.

Treffinger, D., and S. Parnes. 1980. Creative problem solving for gifted and talented students. *Roeper Review* 2: 31–32.

Vygotsky, L. S. 1962. *Thought and language.* Cambridge, Mass.: MIT Press.

Wallas, G. 1926. *The art of thought.* New York: Harcourt.

Walker, D. 1981. Towards a balanced assessment of textbooks in science. In *Research in science education: New questions, new directions,* edited by J. Robinson, 5–20. Louisville, Ky.: Center for Educational Research and Evaluation.

Warming, E. 1982. Textbooks. In *Encyclopedia of educational research.* 5th ed. (Harold E. Mitzel, Editor in Chief), 1933–37. New York: Macmillan.

Weiss, R. H. and S. A. Walters. 1980, April. *Writing to learn.* Paper presented at the annual meeting of the American Educational Research Association, Boston.

Wertheimer, M. 1959. *Productive thinking.* Enlarged ed. New York: Harper.

16 *How do I cope?*

You have now come to the end of a book on teaching from kindergarten through grade eight. Some of the material has been traditional because its basic information is still useful. Chapters on assessment or student progress were particularly traditional; thus far, this material has not been significantly improved on. In fact, techniques like specifying instructional objectives and testing at all levels of the cognitive domain taxonomy are being reemphasized in the design of computing programs.

On the other hand, many issues discussed reflect new emphases in teacher preparation and teacher performance, including recent research on teacher effectiveness, the teaching-learning relationship, technology in education, and the need for common sense in teaching.

In this chapter we will discuss various issues not usually addressed in basic teacher preparation texts. Economics and the role of teacher's unions are significant and often pressing issues for today's teachers. Moreover, teacher education textbooks usually focus on what you will be teaching—but your own education should be of particular concern to you as you prepare to direct another's. A look into yourself is encouraged. Other topics discussed include teaching as a profession and the role of computers in instruction.

Economics

Teachers' economic concerns are both general and personal. Broad economic conditions and events drive educational decisions that rely on funding. These conditions include

- classroom circumstances, including condition of the school plant;
- teacher-student ratio;
- quality of instructional materials;
- degree of support for special programs, such as foreign language instruction in the elementary school, art, music, physical education, field trips;
- caliber of instructors as a function of salary and instructional support;
- access to computers and effective software for the computing environment.

The role of technology in economics and the workforce also affects decisions about education. Predictions of the effect of technology on support for education in the next twenty-five years take the following three directions (Culliton 1985):

1. fewer jobs for the unskilled worker with an increased demand for workers with mathematics or science competence.
2. a workforce comprised of a small core of well-educated, highly skilled adults supported by a mass of unskilled minimum salaried workers.
3. a small portion of the population working because machines will perform most of the work.

How our leaders react to these three predictions will determine the economic support education will receive. If the first prediction is accepted by those with decision-making power, then the current support for education, particularly science and mathematics education, will come to fruition.

If leaders believe the second position, that desirable employment will be available for only a small number of educated adults, then funding based on economic patterns will not be forthcoming. If education has a chance for economic support, the case will have to be made on social rather than economic grounds.

The third prediction, that machines will perform most of the work, opens up a Pandora's box of human issues. What would people be like in such a society?

Teachers' primary personal economic concern is of course the ratio of their salaries to those in other occupations. Beginning teacher salaries are not now high enough to attract the top talent if money is the major concern. The most talented students who do come into teaching are committed to rewards other than monetary.

Funding for teachers' salaries compounds the issue because the source of funds is usually tied to property taxes. Thus, citizens may agree that teachers should make more money, but if it means their having to pay more taxes, the support fades. Teacher dissatisfaction often leads to unionization as a means for individual voices to band together into a chorus so as to be heard.

Economic issues are often decided by supply and demand. With a large number of teachers approaching retirement age, with the current shortage of mathematics and science teachers, with the approaching increase in school population as a result of a moderate baby boom, and with increasing pressure as business and industry siphon off prospective talent including potential mathematics and science teachers, the eonomic issues will have to be addressed if schooling itself is to continue.

Organization Membership

As of the 1980 Department of Education data, the majority of the approximately 3 million Americans employed in lower and higher education belonged to one or more organizations. Guthrie (1982, 1458) notes that organizations serve four major functions:

1. to enhance the flow of information among members,
2. to represent the interest of members with other organizations, particularly governmental organizations,
3. to engage in political activity, and
4. to engage in unionized activities on teacher-welfare issues.

Political activities include endorsing and providing financial aid for candidates for public office and taking part in political conventions and election procedures. For example, a group of members of one teacher organization, the National Education Association (NEA), was the largest bloc of delegates to a national presidential nominating convention in 1980.

Organizations of particular interest to K–6 teachers include general groups such as the NEA, American Federation of Teachers (AFT), National Catholic Education Association (NCEA), and the Association for Supervision and Curriculum Development (ASCD). Subject matter oganizations include the National Association for Education of Young Children (NAYC), Association for Childhood Education International (ACEI), Association for the Devleopment of Computer-based Instructional Systems (ADCIS), National Council of Teachers of Mathematics (NCTM), National Council for Exceptional Children (CEC), International Reading Association (IRA), National Council for the Social Studies (NCSS), National Council of Teachers of English (NCTE), and School Science and Mathematics.

The journals of the various professional organizations include articles by experts in the particular disciplines. The cost of membership in a professional organization includes at least one of the publications.

Teacher Unions

Finn (1985, 99) discusses teacher unions and school quality and asks whether the two are potential allies or inevitable foes:

Teacher unions are here to stay. That much is clear. But it remains to be seen whether they will turn out to be beneficial, or irrelevant to the quality of education in the nation's public schools in an era when quality matters more to more Americans than at any other time in modern history.

Almost 90 percent of the 2.1 million public school teachers belong to either the NEA or the AFT. Three motives are generally given for joining a teachers' union (Finn 1985, 101):

1. desire to improve one's own material well-being, job security, and working conditions;
2. desire to associate with one's peers for companionship, shared knowledge, and vocational betterment; and
3. desire to strengthen the enterprise of public education itself, both for reasons of self-interest and for the benefit of the children one teaches and the society one inhabits.

In fact, the NEA's federal charter states that "the purpose and objects of the said corporation shall be to evaluate the character and advance the interest of the profession of teaching and to promote the cause of education in the United States."

The NEA and the AFT have various basic philosophical differences:

NEA	AFT
Opposes standardized testing of children	Endorses testing as a means of monitoring pupil performance
Opposes any kind of testing of teachers	Insists that new teachers not be hired unles they can pass appropriate tests of intelligence and knowledge
Calls for special (and usually separate) treatments of various groups	Skeptical of policies (e.g., bilingual education) that segregate pupils
Debates back-to-basics	Endorses back-to-basics
Opposes career ladder model*	Supports career ladder model

It should be noted that collective bargaining has potential for good and for ill (Finn 1985, 102):

If a union is—or is thought to be—oblivious to student learning and educational quality, interested only in short-run material gains for its members, and willing to use high-pressure tactics (including strikes) to secure those gains, then the immediate contractual "pay-off" for teachers may be considerable, but the long-term public reaction is liable to be detrimental to their interests. This is no trivial

---

*Career ladders allow teachers to "climb" up over many years to attain added status, salary, and responsibility at every level. Another name is "master teacher plan."

matter: in the fall of 1983, there were seventy-one teacher union strikes, affecting ten states and 1.3 million schoolchildren and involving 67,000 teachers. If, on the other hand, the union uses the bargaining process to bring about changes in the schools themselves that the public regards as desirable, benefits may accrue to students as well as to teachers.

Abruscato (1985) argues that increased teacher salaries and improved working conditions would change the effect of teacher organizations because teachers would feel less need for "collective representation." However, since these improvements are unlikely to occur spontaneously, teacher organizations probably will become more powerful and more of a force to be dealt with.

Your Own Education

Obviously, your own education is of concern to you. Many states have initiated statewide teacher testing as a requirement for certification in addition to satisfactory completion of an approved program of study. An induction year on the job is required by some states before initial certification is granted. A few states consider the job evaluation in the certification process; this is called *performance-based certification.*

Teacher education programs based in settings other than colleges of education* are springing up in response to the call for more rigor in teacher preparation. If education is to improve, teachers must be better educated.

Deans from several colleges of education† have formed the Holmes Group Consortium (named after Henry W. Holmes, Dean of Harvard Graduate School of Education from 1920 to 1940) to establish "new high standards of quality" in the preparation and continuing education of schoolteachers. Preservice teachers in particular should read the Holmes Group document entitled *Tomorrow's Teachers* (1986).

Glazer (1985, 216–17, 219) distinguishes between excellence and competence:

To speak of "excellence" in education is to speak . . . of peaks of achievement: Nobel Prize winners. The best school. The best secondary school. The best college. Inevitably, excellence implies distinction, the greatest distinction. . . . The use of *excellence* had the effect, even if not the intention, of eliciting exaggerated

---

*The Teacher-Scholar program at Drexel University in Philadelphia is a teacher preparation program in mathematics and science (grades K–6 and 7–12) that is based in a technological university. Also, see Eurich (1985) for a discussion of corporate classrooms.
†The 28 universities represented in the Holmes Group are California–Berkeley, California–Los Angeles, California–Santa Barbara, Chicago, Colorado, Columbia, Connecticut, Delaware, Harvard, Illinois–Chicago, Illinois–Urbana-Champaign, Indiana, Iowa, Michigan State, Minnesota, SUNY–Albany, North Carolina–Chapel Hill, North Carolina State, Ohio State, Oregon, Stanford, Syracuse, Texas, Utah, Vanderbilt, Virginia, University of Washington, and Wisconsin–Madison.

praise for modest achievements. The praiser understands, one likes to think, that the praised really has not done all that much, but hopes that his enthusiastic approval will spur the praised on to greater efforts. The praised, however, may misunderstand the praise as indicating really superior achievement—"excellent!"—but if young and in a continuous process of education will soon understand where he or she stands in relation to others. The danger is that in a situation in which almost everyone is engaged in giving praise, the student will never understand that even mere competence, let alone excellence, is a difficult achievement requiring substantial work.... It is revealing that the movement to raise levels of competence by testing teachers, by requiring exit examinations from high school, by raising requirements for college—and all through 1983 and the first months of 1984 one saw story after story from state after state on what we might call the competency movement—was inspired not by the search for "excellence" but by the fear of declining levels of competence.*

Competence and Professionalism

There is a gap between being competent and perceiving oneself as a professional—and the bridge is self-esteem. Competent teachers may be so affected by society's low image of teaching that they do not feel professional. Lasley and Galloway (1983, 6) discuss the effects of teachers' perceptions about themselves:

Unless the present corps of practicing classroom teachers begin to establish a new image of themselves as professionals, the best efforts of teacher educators will proceed unwanted and unrewarded. That is, new teachers will be unable to counteract the effects of the socialization process. Classroom teachers must reconceptualize definitions of their own professional practice. They must begin to assume new educational roles and adopt new ways of thinking.

However, progress toward respect for teaching as a profession also demands competence. Just as those in medicine, law, and the clergy enjoy professional status because we who receive their services know that competence had to be demonstrated through education and exams, teachers are now required to show the same competence through similar licensing procedures in many states.

Is Teaching a Profession or an Emerging Profession?

Howsam et al. (1976, 6–7) list twelve characteristics of a profession developed by the Commission on Education for the Profession of Teaching, American Association of Colleges for Teacher Education:[†]

---

*From Nathan Glazer, "The Problem with Competence," in *Challenge to American Schools*, edited by John H. Bunzel (New York: Oxford University Press, 1985). Reprinted by permission.

[†]From Robert B. Howsam et al., *Educating a Profession* (Washington, D.C.: American Association of Colleges for Teacher Education), p. 6–7. Reprinted by permission of the publisher.

1. Professions are occupationally related social institutions established and maintained as a means of providing essential services to the individual and society.
2. Each profession is concerned with an identified area of need or function.
3. The profession, collectively, and the profession, individually, possesses a body of knowledge and a repertoire of behaviors and skills needed in the practice of the profession; such knowledge, behavior, and skills normally are not possessed by the nonprofessional.
4. Members of the profession are involved in decision making in the service of the client, the decisions being made in accordance with the most valid knowledge available. . . .
5. The profession is based on one or more undergirding disciplines from which it builds its own applied knowledge and skills.
6. The profession is organized into one or more associations which, within broad limits of social accountability, are granted autonomy in control of the actual work of the profession and the conditions which surround it. . . .
7. The profession has agreed-upon performance standards for admission to the profession and for continuance within it.
8. Preparation for and induction into the profession is provided through a protracted preparation program, usually in a professional school on a college or university campus.
9. There is a high level of public trust and confidence in the profession and in individual practitioners, based upon the profession's demonstrated capacity to provide service markedly beyond that which would otherwise be available.
10. Individual practitioners are characterized by a strong service motivation and lifetime commitment to competence.
11. Authority to practice in any individual case derives from the client or the employing organization; accountability for the competence of professional practice within the particular case is to the profession itself.
12. There is a relative freedom from direct on-the-job supervision and from direct public evaluation of the individual practitioner.

Emerging professions meet some but not all of these twelve criteria, and teaching may be one example. Reports of studies and commissions* since 1982 on the current state of American education have received national attention and have moved the authority of "schooling" away from

---

*Those commanding the most attention include *A Nation at Risk: The Imperative for Educational Reform,* by the National Commission on Excellence in Education (1983); *Report of the Twentieth Century Fund Task Force on Federal Elementary and Secondary Education Policy* (1983); *Action for Excellence,* by the Education Commission of the States' Task Force on Education for Economic Growth (1983); *Academic Preparation for College* by the College Board (1983); *The Paideia Proposal,* by Mortimer Adler (1982); *America's Competitive Challenge,* by the Business-Higher Education Forum (1983); *Horace's Compromise: The Dilemma of the American High School,* by Theodore Sizer (1984); *Schools and Colleges: Partnerships in Education,* by Gene Maeroff, sponsored by the Carnegie Foundation for the Advancement of Teaching (1983); *National Conference on Studies of the American High School* (1982); *A Nation Prepared: Teachers for the 21st Century,* by the Carnegie Forum on Education and the Economies Task Force on Teaching as a Profession (1986).

the "professional" elementary and secondary school educator to university presidents, corporate executive officers, politicians, and citizens-at-large. For example, the National Commission on Excellence in Education, which published *A Nation at Risk,* was chaired by David P. Gardner, President of the University of Utah at the time; leaders of the Education Commission of the States, whose summary is entitled *Action for Excellence,* included in 1986 James B. Hunt, Jr., Governor of North Carolina, Pierre S. duPont IV, Governor of Delaware, and Frank T. Carey, Chairman of the Executive Committee, International Business Machines, Inc.

Increasing concern over the quality of education is seen in the following main themes from various studies (Bunzel 1985, 4):

Our schools are confused about their educational mission and have no shared sense of what their major goals should be or how they can achieve them.

The weakening of the high school curriculum (sometimes called the "permissive" or "soft" curriculum) has contributed to the decline in courses that are part of the traditional "core" curriculum—reading, writing, mathematics, science. . . . There should be considerable more homework, a longer school day, and an extended school year.

Teaching-training standards should be improved to reaffirm the nation's commitment to quality education. The recommendations include requiring teachers to demonstrate competence in the subject-matter area they will teach, improving the ways of recruiting and paying them, and reconsidering merit pay and master teacher proposals.

High school principals should be trained and chosen to provide educational vision and leadership rather than to administer and preside over the school bureaucracy.

The federal government's minimal obligation "to identify the national interest in education" must not be reduced, but the primary responsibility for our elementary and secondary schools remains with the state and local authorities.

Closer and more effective partnerships between individual schools and the larger community should be strengthened, particularly partnerships between businesses and our colleges and universities.

America's role as a world leader and its ability to maintain its international competitiveness can be assured only if more and higher-quality education is available to all students. Equality and quality are not in conflict with each other. They are mutually reinforcing goals in the quest for better schools and educational excellence for all of our young people.

In the words of one observer, "there is a spirit pervading the nation that, somehow, a promise has been broken, an ideal betrayed."*

One effort to nourish teaching as a profession is the Philadelphia Teachers in Industry Program, initiated during the summer of 1985. This program places secondary mathematics and science teachers in industry

---

*From *Challenge to American Schools,* edited by John H. Bunzel (New York: Oxford University Press, 1985), p. 4. Reprinted by permission.

jobs for the summer. The Teaching Fellows, as they are called, use their expertise to aid the business or industrial setting in a specific area of need. The Fellows design, develop and implement an application of their summer work experience for use with their own students. The Committee to Support the Philadelphia Schools sponsors the program, Temple University has responsibility for helping Fellows develop their projects, Drexel University aids in formative evaluation, and the Philadelphia Renaissance in Mathematics and Science (PRISM) is responsible for summative evaluation.

How Do I Cope with Computers?

Salomon (1984) notes that hardly a question raised in the past by philosophers, educators, social scientists, or natural scientists does not apply in one way or another to the computer. He argues that the most urgent questions concern the long-range cumulative effects of computer use. Visionaries, computer and artificial intelligence (AI) experts, and educators have suggested that work with the computer, particularly LOGO, may enable children to acquire the computer's "styles of thinking," which may result in new degrees of intellectual sophistication. According to Papert (1980), "The computer can make it easier to understand that there is such a thing as a *style of thinking*. And giving children the opportunity to choose one style or another provides an opportunity to develop the skill necessary to choose between styles."

Bolter (1984) points out that the computer, a one-in-several-centuries invention, is bound to enter and affect every phase of our lives, much as the industrial revolution did in the past; he argues that already the computer has remade and redefined our relationship to nature and to ourselves. Salomon and Gardner (1984, 8) are more skeptical:

We may have heard of such promises time and again with respect to other technologies and media, and hardly ever really observed them. Did television revolutionize thinking, as envisioned by McLuhan? The truth is that we really don't know. Although there is much speculation that television has had extremely profound effects on us, as did the shift from a culture of oral utterance to one of printed texts, the empirical evidence is poor.

The following statements can help you identify the salient questions for coping with a technological society:

- We already know that the ways girls approach computer activities differ from those of boys. Similarly, we already know that lower-class inner-city children are more often given computer drill and practice, while middle-class children are more often given open-ended opportunities for exploration. The results are unlikely to be the same.

Computers allow for individual learning styles.

- To study the cumulative effects of computers on cognition, emotion, and behavior is an urgent task, for it is projected that by 1990 there will be at least 38 million personal computers used in the U.S., a spread which is likely to be matched by some other countries as well, such as the U.K., Germany, and Israel. Few appropriate control groups will then be available.
- The development of television was left to the entertainment industry. The academic community never became involved in its design. The computer, on the other hand, being the brainchild of a number of

- academic disciplines, is not only their product but also their tool of development, attracting the best minds around.
- It is indeed very typical of research on a new device to ask *What does it do to us? To our children? To some others?* while disregarding the possibility that the subjects of such effects partly determine these effects.
- Television can be processed mindlessly, guided by stimulus demands, and still render satisfaction. Many computer-afforded activities can also be mastered to a low level of automaticity, and hence can be carried out mindlessly.
- An important lesson we have learned from television research in education is that no medium or technology, in and of itself, has much impact on learning and cognition. It is always something specific in them which may afford new activities, experiences, or aroused cognitions hitherto uneffected.
- Can we argue that the activities afforded by, say, computer simulation cultivate cognitive counterparts of mental operations (Salomon and Gardner 1984)? If so, what specific unique features of computers can have such effects? The identification, conceptualization, and careful study of such unique features can (a) save us the effort of studying anew each and every technological twist and activity only because it looks different from preceding ones; and (b) help us understand the promise that computer-related activities offer.
- Computers may promise much for education, but there is a long road from promise to realization. Not everything depends on the quality of software nor on the price of computers. To make full use of computers' potential, schools must be radically changed, and this they are unlikely to submit to. The past has shown us that schools are quick to adopt new technologies, often because of the public's pressure and because they need to maintain legitimacy. But once introduced, the schools do not much change; they assimilate the technologies, and thus render them harmless but also impact-less (Sarason 1982).

What Am I Going to Do About Integrating Computing into My Class?

Stevens (1980) reports that in 1979 a Computers in Education survey was given to 657 Nebraska K–12 teachers, 79 teachers' college faculty members, and 227 student teachers at the University of Nebraska–Lincoln (UNL). The survey was replicated in 1981 with 714 K–12 Nebraska teachers, 88 teacher educators, and 238 student teachers as subjects. The surveys were designed to ascertain the perceived training needs of educators and their views towards computers in education, and to assess educators' computer skills and knowledge about computers. In the spring of 1982 a third survey was given to a sample of 238 K–12 educators. This survey focused on educators' present perceptions and future expectations of the role of computers in education and on their knowledge about computers.

Educational programs integrate computing into instruction.

Stevens writes that although a large majority of participants in the 1981 and 1979 surveys believed students should be computer literate, fewer subjects rated themselves as qualified to teach computer literacy in 1981 than in 1979. Educators in the 1982 study forecasted that computers would have a strong influence on classroom instruction and on the curriculum. Educators in this study, however, anticipated that computers would cause very little change in their own classroom procedure and slightly less than moderate change in their instructional strategies or in the content taught to students.

Over three-quarters of the subjects surveyed either viewed their methodology as not conducive to microcomputers or were not sure whether microcomputers would blend with their instructional techniques. In other words, educators perceived that computers would strongly influence classroom instruction and the curriculum but *not in their classrooms*. There was general agreement that computer-assisted instruction was not for all students, disciplines, or teachers.

The following recommendations were made:

Teacher preparation should accept the challenge of preparing educators to teach using appropriate computer technology.

Barriers to training teacher education students to use computer technology exist, e.g., (1) the lack of adequate hardware and peripherals, (2) the lack of financial support, (3) the lack of knowledgeable teachers, and (4) the reluctance to change.

Resources and group effort can solve the hardware and the software issues. The lack of financial support is more difficult to solve. Dwindling resources may require teacher preparation institutions to reallocate funds. If sufficient funds are not allocated, then preparing teachers for schools using computers must not be important.

Reluctance to change is a natural barrier at all levels of education. Participants in this study expressed their reluctance by wondering if they would actually change classroom instructional procedures or change content taught to students. Many educators believe computers offer ways of changing the learning process itself. Computers could affect what students learn and how students learn. These changes will occur in what we teach and how it is taught. The inclusion of computer technology can best be fostered if teacher preparation programs create a positive climate.

Teacher preparation programs should not abdicate their responsibility of training teachers to use appropriate computer technology as an instructional strategy. If they do, then teachers will have to acquire these skills outside of teacher education institutions.

Inservice programs should provide educators with the opportunity to acquire computer technology skills commensurate with their needs.

Perhaps the most important is to provide inservice for teacher educators. The crucial question for teacher educators is how best to respond to the preservice and inservice needs of educators. Program quality will be determined by how effectively teacher education responds to the challenge of computer technology.*

Another major survey about use of computers in schools was that of Moskowitz and Birman (1985). Their findings highlight the kinds of problems you will encounter in schools as attempts are made to integrate computing.

The study was designed to examine the introduction of microcomputers in large city school districts over time. Eight large city school districts and two large heterogeneous suburban school districts were examined between November, 1982, and March, 1984. All school districts confronted the choice of which computers to purchase. Most were inclined to purchase Apple II's, especially for the elementary grades. Three ingredients appeared to be essential for schools and school districts to move ahead in their use of computers: trained teachers, some equipment, and some curriculum development. The following are generalizations from the survey:†

---

*Abstracted from D. J. Stevens, "Educators' Perceptions of Computing in the Classroom," *AEDS,* July 13, 1980, pp. 221–32. Used with permission.

†Abstracted from J. H. Moskowitz and B. F. Birman, "Computers in the Schools: Implications of Change," *Educational Technology* (Jan. 1985), pp. 7–14. Used with permission.

Problems During the First Year

The three most prevalent problems observed were:

1. Lack of clearly presented goals for computer activities. Whether a district will use computers to teach computer awareness, literacy, or programming, or will use the equipment for computer-assisted instruction is obviously a pivotal decision—yet in most districts, officials had not tackled it. Some did not even understand the importance of making the decision!
2. Lack of implementation plans for computer activities. Districts had little overall district focus even though they were purchasing equipment as fast as possible and had computer labs in each high school and PTA-purchased equipment in each elementary school. Having specific plans, however, did not ensure their implementation. For example one district had explicit objectives and plans for the introduction of a comprehensive computer-literacy program, but few microcomputers.

    Officials who were acquiring hardware at a rate that exceeded their acknowledged ability to train teachers or develop curriculum exuded confidence that everything will "work out." When asked about their lack of plans or inconsistencies in objectives, district officials gave the same response: they did not have the time to take a holistic approach because community pressures for immediate action were simply too great. In addition, many officials, particularly senior district administrators who were feeling the brunt of parental concern, expressed the conviction that they should give high school pupils a cram course before graduation. As a result, *ad hoc* approaches to meet immediate needs were part of many plans.
3. Advanced and gifted students with an inclination toward mathematics were most likely to have direct access to microcomputers. This pattern stemmed from two phenomena. First, many computer buffs are mathematics and science teachers, who tend to teach academically talented students. Second, many school administrators were allocating limited hardware on the basis of where the greatest pressure for equipment existed and where they were likely to get the most positive feedback.

Second-Year Results

District officials had made substantial progress toward articulating long-term instructional and policy goals, and were dealing with increasing demand and the complexities of implementation. There was no shortage of teachers interested in receiving training. In contrast to DeVault and Chapin's findings (1981), the findings in this survey were that elementary grade teachers were the most receptive to the use of microcomputers.

Federal, State, and Local Options

Officials in many of the sample districts did not contemplate the widespread use of educational technology until three or four years ago. They have made a promising beginning in responding to this unique challenge and, what is more, except for some limited financial support from the federal government, they have done it alone.

The states can break down barriers that may already have undermined student access. For example, states may wish to reconsider requirements that courses in programming or computer science be taught by teachers in mathematics. Mathematics is not necessarily any better preparation for the teaching of these courses than is English or psychology, and the requirement for certification in mathematics might discourage women from participation.

You are entering teacher preparation in a transition period that will tell whether or not technology will make a difference in education. You were too early for the integration of computer-based education, even though your schools may have had microcomputers. You may have learned to program in BASIC—or if you were lucky, perhaps LOGO or Pascal. You probably were in computer education or computer literacy courses, instead of using the computer as an invisible tool. But at least you may have been exposed to computing. Your strategy for integrating computing into your own instruction will depend on your college and inservice experiences in computing and on your access to computers and quality software that meet your students' needs. How will you cope?

Thought Activity

1. The best answer to the question of what organizations to join will depend on a variety of factors. The major influence will be your selection of a teaching position. Think about the following questions as you investigate job opportunities:
   a. Will you teach in an urban, suburban, or rural setting?
   b. Will you teach in a unionized or non-unionized district?
   c. Will you teach in the primary or upper elementary grades?
   d. Will you be a subject matter specialist?
2. Abruscato (1985, 334) asks if teacher power will cripple the schools. He suggests you ask yourself the following questions. Would you carry a sign and walk a picket line? Would you cross a picket line to teach? Write a one-page answer to these questions, reread your answer at a later date, and see if you have changed your mind.
3. Review the list of characteristics that define a profession on page 284. Compare the characteristics of a profession with what you have observed about teachers and teaching. Defend your conclusion as to whether teaching is a profession or an emerging profession.

References

Abruscato, 1985. *Introduction to teaching and the study of education.* Englewood Cliffs, N.J.: Prentice-Hall.

Bolter, J. D. 1984. *Turing's man: Western culture in the computer age.* Chapel Hill: Univ. of North Carolina Press.

Bunzel, J. H. (ed.) 1985. *Challenge to American schools.* New York: Oxford Univ. Press.

Culliton, B. J. 1985. Carnegie launches education forum. *Science* 227:925–26.

DeVault, V. M., and J. Chapin. 1981. The teacher factor in the supply and demand curve for technology in the schools. *Educational Technology* (Feb.).

Eurich, N. P. 1985. *Corporate classrooms: The learning process.* Princeton, N.J.: Carnegie Foundation for the Advancement of Teaching.

Finn, C. E. 1985. Teacher unions and school quality: Potential allies or inevitable foes? In *Challenge to American schools,* edited by J. H. Bunzel. New York: Oxford Univ. Press.

Glazer, N. 1985. The problem with competence. In *Challenge to American schools,* edited by J. H. Bunzel. New York: Oxford Univ. Press.

Guthrie, J. W. 1982. Professional organizations. *Encyclopedia of educational research.* 5th ed. (Harold E. Mitzel, Editor in Chief): 1458. New York: Macmillan.

Holmes Group, 1986. *Tomorrow's teachers: A report of the Holmes Group, 1986.* East Lansing, Mich.: Author.

Howsam, R. B., et al. 1976. *Educating a profession.* Washington, D.C.: American Association of Colleges for Teacher Education.

Lasley, T. J., and C. M. Galloway. 1983. Achieving professional status: A problem in what teachers believe. *The Clearing House* 57(1):6.

Moskowitz, J. H., and B. F. Birman. 1985. Computers in the schools: Implications of change. *Educational Technology* (Jan.): 7–14.

Papert, S. 1980. *Mindstorms.* New York: Basic Books.

Salomon, G. 1984. Computers in education: Setting a research agenda. *Educational Technology* (Oct.): 7–11.

Salomon, G., and H. Gardner. 1984. *The computer as educator: Lessons from television research.* Harvard Project Zero.

Sarason, S. B. 1982. *The culture of the school and the problem of change.* 2d ed. Boston: Allyn & Bacon.

Stevens, D. J. 1980. Educators' perceptions of computers in the classroom. *AEDS* (July 13): 221–32.

Stevens, D. J. 1982. Educators' perceptions of computers in education: 1979 and 1981. *AEDS* (July 16): 1–15.

Stevens, D. J. 1984. Microcomputers: An educational challenge. *Computer Education.* 8(2):263–67.

U.S. Department of Education, National Center for Educational Statistics. 1980. *The conditions of American education, 1980.* Washington, D.C.: GPO.

Appendix *Suggestions for bridging to secondary education*

Since much of the contents of this book is generic in nature, it can be used with little change by secondary as well as elementary education teachers. This appendix will expand some of the concepts to high school where appropriate and provide additional examples that apply to secondary students.

Introduction (Chapter 1)

An urban university has developed the following plan designed to address some of the challenges to secondary education put forth by the Carnegie Report entitled *A Nation Prepared: Teachers for the 21st Century* (1986).

Certification is offered at the secondary level in mathematics and science only—the university's strengths as a noted engineering school.

(There is also an elementary program, and this too emphasizes mathematics and science.) The curriculum and activities of the program address the concepts of the various commission reports that have emerged during the eighties (see footnote, p. 284). A major goal is to recruit minority students from the large local school district, who will "pay back" to their community by themselves becoming positive teacher role models for its students. The program has the following characteristics:

- Rigor and depth in content—requirements of up to ninety quarter credit hours in mathematics and science to satisfy the related undergraduate major (e.g., mathematics, biology, chemistry, physics, or the unified science major, used for general science and for earth/space science certification). Students will graduate after five years with a mathematics or science major and secondary school certification. Coursework taken to satisfy state certification requirements will be applicable toward a master's degree in the content area or toward a newly proposed Master of Science in Instructional Design degree.
- Mainstreaming students in certification programs into regular classes—not a separate track, e.g., "Mathematics for Secondary Teachers."
- Diagnostic teaching emphasis, as described in chapters 6 and 15.
- Use of technology—especially computing—as an instructional tool, as discussed in chapters 7 and 16.
- Emphasis on communication skills, including use of double-entry logs (discussed in chap. 1) and of writing as a learning strategy (presented in chap. 15).
- A combination of comprehensive field experiences in both educational and industrial settings, including early interaction with children and one or two paid six-month industry co-ops.
- Methods courses which are generic in nature.
- Focus on creative problem solving techniques, as presented in chapter 15.
- Collaboration with schools as regards pedagogy, i.e., appointment of adjunct "master educators" to model instructional strategies for certification students.
- Recruitment of minorities and women to teach mathematics and science, including involving high school students as well as fifth and sixth graders in early diagnostic teaching with first to third graders or peers, so that they begin "teaching" early on. The primary goal is to keep students in the pipeline for higher-level mathematics and science courses so that minority and female students stop blocking themselves from mathematically and scientifically oriented careers. Another goal is to awaken in students a commitment to becoming teachers. The young "diagnostic tutors" may look to the teacher education students as mentors. The diagnostic tutors and the college-level students would together comprise the staff for intervention programs in urban schools.

It is hypothesized that diagnostic tutors become more effective learners; their own learning is enhanced by their teaching.
- Recruitment of those with a baccalaureate degree in mathematics or science who are ready for a career change and who wish to obtain certification to teach, especially in grades 9–12. The Intern Certificate opens up the program to nontraditional students, including corporate and industrial retirees such as engineers, chemists, physicists, and biologists.

The following slogan for teacher education was suggested by Dr. Shirley Malcolm, one of the authors of the Carnegie Report, in a conversation with one of the authors of this book: *Invest today so we don't have to remediate tomorrow.* This goal is particularly appropriate to teacher education programs that incorporate diagnostic teaching.

Support Needed. If students are expected to undertake rigorous programs of this nature, they will need some incentive to work so much harder than those who can obtain the same certification in a much less rigorous program. We need to explore a range of ideas here: Salary supplements? Scholarships and stipends for advanced academic work that directly supports classroom activity? Government savings bonds? Free computers? Forgiveness of student loans? Pay for field experience, as in industry co-ops? Choice of school/grade placement? Option of job sharing with a counterpart in business or industry? More flexibility in hours? A chance to serve as mentors to preservice teachers who in turn assist with classroom duties?

Characteristics of Secondary Students (Chapters 2 and 3)

The age span from twelve to eighteen years is generally referred to as adolescence and bridges the gap from childhood to attainment of maturity. Children undergo rapid physiological and psychological changes, redefine their relationships to family, friends, and school, and shift attention to college or the workplace. The rapid bodily changes that occur often affect self-image. The acceptance of sex roles is a crucial component of identity development. The value of sex education has not as yet been adequately assessed, but the majority of adolescents favor sex education taught in a responsible way. The path toward maturity involves greater independence in the home, lifestyle, commitment to sexual orientation, selection of peer group, and self-discipline, although parents remain a major influence throughout this time.

As we noted in chapter 2, a teacher must be a detective—always sensitive to personal observations. This ability is very important with high school students, since nonverbal behavior may provide more important clues than what is said. Secondary students' peers probably learn more about their friends' true feelings and thoughts than do teachers. Observe some secondary students and apply what you have learned about generic influences on learning (chap. 2) to them. You will see that such influences affect learners in any age group. The psychomotor, social, and emotional influences are very helpful for interpreting secondary students' learning. Behavior that is developmentally appropriate in an elementary school student may well indicate a learning or behavior problem in high school.

Develop profiles similar to those presented in chapter 3 by applying generic influences that affect learning to secondary students. What similarities and differences do you notice that affect learning? The discussion of instructional design (see second bold heading below) presents cognitive style issues that affect learning.

Instructional Goals and Lesson Planning (Chapters 4 and 5)

Our discussions of instructional goals and lesson planning are generic and applicable from kindergarten through grade twelve. Teachers of elementary *and* high school students develop instructional objectives for the same purposes—to determine specifically what is expected of students and how it will be evaluated. The steps involved in the development of lesson plans are also identical for both groups of teachers. A sample lesson plan for a ninth grade descriptive writing lesson is shown in table A.1.

Additional activities:

1. Visit the secondary school classrooms of a first year teacher and of an experienced teacher. Talk with both teachers about how they plan for instruction. How do they differ? Why?
2. Develop a daily lesson plan in a secondary school curriculum area such as science, language arts, mathematics, social studies, art, or music.

Becoming an Instructional Designer (Chapter 6)

How would you describe a student's learning style, or cognitive response tendency, in the following dimensions? Answers can often be reached simply by asking the student what she notices about how she learns best.

- *Field independent/field dependent.* Field independent learners are not bound by background distractions such as noises, color, or design; the figure stands out. On the other hand, field dependent learners tend

Table A.1
Sample Ninth Grade Lesson Plan

	Unit Title:	Descriptive Writing
	Goal:	Students will gain an appreciation of how descriptive words add to the enjoyment of writing or speech.
	Objective(s):	Given a chart and a grape, the student will complete the chart by describing a grape in relation to each of the five senses.
	Procedures	
	Rationale:	*Teacher begins:* When writing to communicate an idea, we must not simply tell the reader what we want to say; we must *show* the reader. A picture should be created in the reader's mind.
	Materials:	Tape recorder, tape of commercial, chart for each student, grape for each student.
	Content:	Students listen to a commercial and answer questions. Discuss other commercials. Draw chart of apple, discuss sensory resonses to apple. Group students and give each student a grape and chart. Chart sensory responses to grape.
	Motivation:	To begin class, students will close eyes and listen to a tape recording of a commercial that appeals to the senses. After the commercial is completed, students will be asked: 1. How did it make you feel? 2. What did you see in your mind? 3. What could you see or smell? 4. What words were used to describe the product being advertised?
	Activities:	1. Ask if the students can think of commercials that have appealed to their senses. If students think of a food chain commercial (McDonald's, Burger King, etc.), ask if the commercial would have affected them differently had it merely said, "Stop by between the hours of 6:00 and 11:00 a.m. We will be glad to serve you breakfast or lunch or dinner." 2. "Today we will begin working on activities that will help us focus on writing more descriptively." Again, the teacher will review the purpose of the lesson. 3. Pass out Chart #1. The class will be told to think of an apple. 4. The chart will be completed on the board as students complete Chart #1 at their desks. Words that could be used to describe an apple in relation to each of the senses will be listed. (It may be necessary to discuss the difficulty of describing taste.) 5. Students will be placed in groups. Each student will be given a grape and another chart. Each student will see, smell, touch, hear, and taste the object for which they are listing sensory words. 6. Each student in the group will complete a chart. 7. Students return to seats and review the day's activities.
	Closure:	Gather up charts. Review some of the descriptions of the grape based on responses of the five senses.
	Evaluation:	Teacher assessment of the students' descriptions of the grape representing all five senses.
	Critique:	Was the lesson too long? Too short? Was the lesson too complicated or too easy for the ninth graders? What needs to be changed for this particular group of students? What parts of the lesson were particularly successful? Were the students able to describe a grape using words representing all five senses?

Source: This lesson plan was written by Shari Richardson, an undergraduate Middle School Education major at the University of Georgia.

to notice the context and do not immediately distinguish figure from ground. Field dependent students may have difficulty noticing salient aspects of situations.

- *Convergent/divergent thought.* Convergent thinkers like closure; they are task oriented and like learning to be structured with specified goals. Divergent thinkers tend to brainstorm, are flexible in their thinking, resist premature closure, and often go off on tangents. Although divergent thinking is the style usually considered characteristic of creative problem solving, both convergent and divergent thinking are in fact involved.

- *Right/left brain activity.* Right hemisphere activity is characterized by intuitive, holistic, simultaneous thinking. Left-brain activity is thought to be analytic and linear in nature. Often, lefthandedness or ambidextrousness accompany right hemisphere dominance. High school curricula tend to favor left-brain dominance. They encourage too little visual thinking, provide too few concrete experiences, and place too much emphasis on the analytical with insufficient opportunity for intuitive thought. The fact that computer-oriented activities require more simultaneity of thought while print-oriented activities emphasize the linear nature of thinking should encourage integration of computing into the instructional experience of right-brain/divergent thinkers in particular. Computer graphics packages especially help right dominant learners to organize and display data from science or social studies observations. (See pp. 300–301 for Norton's comparison of computer and print-oriented activities, and p. 264 for a discussion of hemispheric activity.)

- *Complex/simple preference.* Some people deal well with complexity, whether in looking at a textbook page, assessing a problem, engaging in social interactions, or sorting out the salient aspects of auditory and visual situations. Others need these same types of situations simplified, specified, structured, and organized. Considering that many secondary students have emotional overlays to their daily concerns, complex situations may become especially overwhelming during these years. Thus, the secondary teacher must be sensitive to changes in how students deal with complexity. Instructional materials must be able to accommodate students who have trouble with complexity. On the other hand, too simple a situation might turn off, bore, or even insult a student who thrives on complexity.

- *Reflective/impulsive.* The reflective learner thinks about things before answering. The impulsive learner thinks out loud and tends to generate many responses, some of which may be incorrect. Secondary teachers must provide "think time" for reflective students and guide impulsive students to engage in cognitive monitoring before blurting out answers.

- *Risk-taking/cautious.* Related to reflectivity or impulsivity is the willingness or unwillingness to take risks. This dichotomy is apparent in sports at the secondary level, as well as in such activities as chess or computer programming.

- *Sensory modality preference.* Although the issue of whether people learn better through visual, auditory, or tactile presentation is controversial, teachers often hear statements such as "I have to see it in order to understand what you are saying," or "Let me read it aloud so I can understand the text." It is important to design a variety of sensory inputs and to provide concrete experiences in the secondary classroom.

What instructional considerations would be most affected by these learning characteristics? What about large group lectures, where some students are easily distracted, or cannot pick out important information from background embellishment, or learn better with graphing and visual presentation, or need to pace their speed of information intake, or who need time to incubate new ideas? What about the visual presentation in traditional high school mathematics texts, which consists of pages of equations and line drawings, but few real world pictures? What reinforcements and motivational techniques are indicated at the secondary level?

When addressing reinforcement and motivation, consider *locus of control* (Rotter 1966). Some students are leaders and others are followers—within teenage gangs, fraternal organizations, clubs, academic situations, and social situations. Locus of control is external or internal. Control is external for a follower, someone who responds to outside pressures. Control is internal for the leader type, someone who is his own person. The locus of control is especially important when considering high school students, who by the very nature of their developmental level are becoming independent in some ways but still need the security of dependency. Grades are an important reinforcement to the externally controlled student, but the internally controlled student does not particularly value them. If a grade is considered unfair by such a student, then it will serve no reinforcing function.

Analyze a task that you might teach to a secondary student and see if the analysis helps you discover a better way of presenting the lesson. Also, given the organization of high school classes into scheduled slots, tell how **advance organizers** can help keep continuity for the learner as well as for the teacher. Refer to the Teaching/Testing Modes Grid on page 106 and list instructional goals for each cell that relates to your subject.

Integrating Computing into Instruction (Chapter 7)

In light of availability of calculators and computers, review high school curricula in your content area and list what topics need to be deleted, modified, resequenced, or added. The following comparison of print-oriented and computer-oriented problem solving activities, presented by Norton (1985, 39) may be helpful in carrying out this task.

Print-oriented Activities	*Computer-oriented Activities*
If-then reasoning	What-if reasoning
Deductive reasoning	Inductive reasoning
Pattern recognition	Pattern formation
Linear, sequential reasoning	Patterns and connections
Reasoning in a closed system	Reasoning in an open system
Single solutions	Probabilities

Cause-effect	Rules of interaction
Analytical reasoning	Synthetic reasoning
Logical reasoning	Intuitive reasoning
Active	Interactive
Rigid	Flexible

An urban university initiated a collaborative project entitled Computer Applications in Teaching Program (CAITP) with mathematics and science department heads in a local school district. The major goal was to integrate computing into instruction at the secondary level. Phase one of this endeavor focused on introducing Appleworks as an integrative software package—emphasizing how a word processing package, a spreadsheet, and a data base management program can be used together to form a document. For example, the word processing tool is the vehicle for writing an essay or a lab report, data can be compiled in the data base system, and selected data can be organized on the spreadsheet. Then, data from the spreadsheet can be inserted into the body of the report. Other useful applications include recording grades, keeping lab equipment inventories, and providing parents with updated summaries of their child's progress.

In phase two, high school department heads responded to a Request for Proposal (RFP) where they had to describe how they would involve high school teachers in using computers in instruction. The university received a $45,000 state grant, and a committee of university, corporate, and industrial persons provided $5,000 for each of ten proposals to be funded. Proposals from seven high schools, including eight department heads, were selected for funding by a panel of seven readers, composed of high school district, university, and corporate funding source personnel. The following are excerpts from the narrative summaries for four of the funded projects:

- [The school] is a vocational high school in which every student majors in some area of agriculture and thus gains a saleable skill. . . . Students have a wide range of abilities and perform on many levels in any given course. This grant will allow us to purchase two computers for the use of math teachers in their rooms which students can use for remediation, drill, practice, and enrichment while the teachers can use them for demonstrations as well as record keeping, test construction and other management functions.

- . . .we propose to train the science teachers to use Apple computers as laboratory instruments for demonstration and experimental purposes in their classrooms and laboratories. We will use the tutorial process developed by the American Association of Physics Teachers (AAPT) to initiate our program and will guide the science teachers through the tutorial package until all the teachers have completed it. When the initial tutorial is completed, we will demonstrate the practical applications of the tutorial to the experiments that the teachers are already performing (e.g., melting point curves) and suggest extended activities (e.g., melting point curves for different masses of substances). The teachers will then be encouraged to present computer-based experiments for their own design, in their own disciplines. These presentations will then be critiqued and, after appropriate modifications, be used in classroom situations.

- Every mathematics teacher must be prepared to teach a new course, Mathematics in Application. Presently, the majority of mathematics teachers have had very little exposure to computers. This project aims to:

    1. Give the mathematics teachers the time and opportunity to interact with the computer.
    2. Make a portable Apple II computer set-up available for use by the mathematics teachers in their classrooms to broaden their access to the computer.
    3. Get the teachers familiar with the Mathematics in Application course and its computer component.
    4. Develop a list of software and software related activities that the mathematics teachers recommend for use in teaching the Mathematics in Application course.
    5. Share this compilation of material with the rest of the senior high school teachers of mathematics in the school district.

    Goals of the project—Staff:
    1. To train six science teachers in the use of Cambridge Development Laboratory's "Experiment Interface" for use in biological and physical science laboratory instruction.
    2. To familiarize science teachers with the mathematical theory involved in sorting, tabulating, and displaying scientific data.

    Goals of the project—Students:
    1. To use the computer to collect, sort, tabulate, and display scientific data.
    2. To conduct an independent research investigation (a) using the housefly, *Musca domestica*, as an experimental organism, (b) using the computer to collect, sort, tabulate, and display data, and (c) using the library as a resource for gathering full text scientific information.

- The proposed program will consist of three parts:

    1. The use of computer-aided instruction in the teaching of genetics.
    2. The incorporation of computer technology in the laboratory programs of chemistry, physics, and physical science classes.
    3. The use of computer applications in record-keeping.

    The success of the project will be measured not only by how much the department increases the use of the computer, but, more importantly, how much better students learn and how much more efficiently paperwork can be managed.

An intensive seven-day summer institute was designed to kick off phase two of the project. Department heads were brought onto the instructional team. A telecommunication component was introduced, and all participants were provided a modem and an Apple IIe for home use during the entire summer. Department heads were given a stipend of $500, and teachers $300. Some asked for course credit, and this option was provided by the university (2 credits and $50 stipend).

The CAITP Director of Instruction and the Executive Director of the corporate funding organization attended the 1986 National Educational Computing Conference (NECC) in San Diego and arranged for representatives from software companies to demonstrate relevant software during the summer institute. Companies, all of which participated at their own expense, included Sunburst Communications, 39 Washington Avenue, Pleasantville, New York 10570–9971; HRM Software, 175 Thompkins Avenue, Pleasantville, New York 10570; and CBS Software, One Fawcett Place, Greenwich, Connecticut 06936.

Other presenters included the NASA Teacher in Space for the state and representatives from two of the local Tech Centers (state-funded centers housing technological instructional materials that may be borrowed by local education agencies). The CAITP project gave instructional materials, including software and print, to the participants. In addition to demonstrations and distribution of selected applications software packages, institute topics included telecommunications capabilities and applications to networking, whereby students can use school-based modems (e.g., the library) to search data bases for homework assignments as well as using student-owned home-based modems and computers to receive daily assignments when absent. Additional topics included software evaluation, project evaluation issues, instructional design issues (as discussed in chap. 6 of this book) organizational issues (as discussed in chap. 14), and creative problem solving (as discussed in chap. 15).

Questioning (Chapter 8)

Bloom's Taxonomy (1956) is a classification scheme that allows for the formulation of classroom questions at each of six levels of the cognitive domain. The following sample questions at the various taxonomy levels are appropriate in content for secondary school use:

Knowledge
Who discovered penicillin?
What color when added to yellow makes orange?
Comprehension
What is the main idea of this poem?
Compare capitalism and communism.
Application
Classify the animals according to the five categories discussed in class.
We have learned the rules for using commas. In this excerpt, where would you place the commas?
Analysis
Analyze the causes of World War I.
Why did Japan lose World War II?
Synthesis
What would happen if it did not rain in Georgia for three-hundred days?
Write a story describing your ideal day.

Evaluation
Is this book appropriate reading for high school students?
What is your opinion of rock music?

Methods for Assessing Student Achievement (Chapter 10)

Informal test procedures such as rating scales, checklists, anecdotal records, observations, and sociometric methods are appropriate means for collecting information about both elementary and secondary students.

Rating Scales. Rating scales may be developed to assess cognitive or affective outcomes of instruction. For example, a rating scale might be developed to describe how well a student can use a microscope or complete a dissection in zoology class. The teacher might use such a rating scale while observing a particular student or group of students.

The most frequently used rating technique by far is the numerical scale. For example, an art teacher might check on a nine-point scale the degree to which a student's painting represents a symmetrical relationship of central to peripheral elements. A series of scales like the following might be used to assess a variety of outcomes.

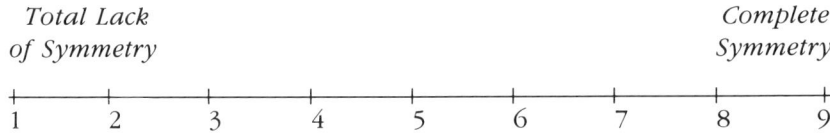

Checklists. Bonney and Hampleman (1962) cite the following example of a checklist used by an industrial arts teacher to identify the unsatisfactory items in a woodwork product before it goes to the finishing room.

Unsatisfactory Items in Woodwork Product

____	1.	Knots	____	11.	Dimensions
____	2.	Lack of Filling	____	12.	Operation Missing
____	3.	Core or Glue	____	13.	Veneer Discolored
____	4.	Joint Shrinkage	____	14.	Veneer Split
____	5.	Veneer Sand-through	____	15.	Rounded Edges
____	6.	Glaze or Burnish	____	16.	Exposed Glue
____	7.	Loose Veneer	____	17.	Coarse Sanding
____	8.	Tear-outs	____	18.	Grain and Color of Veneer
____	9.	Rough Machinery	____	19.	Damage
____	10.	Warpage	____	20.	Open Joints

A student's "score" on the checklist may simply be the number of items checked or not checked, or a standard for an acceptable product may be established.

Table A.2 *Sample Secondary School Anecdotal Record*	Date: 11/10/86	Student's Name: Jared
	Observer: Pam (Teacher)	
	Description of Student:	
	Jared is a student in my tenth grade World History class and has been performing below average all term. He does not usually pay attention and frequently puts his head on the desk and seems to sleep. He has never shown much inclination to do more than the minimum assignment and seldom participates in class discussions or projects. This week, however, we began a discussion on World War II and I found that Jared is a veritable storehouse of knowledge on the period. He answers questions posed to him, volunteers answers to many other questions with enthusiasm, and even offered to bring in related materials from home.	
	Comment:	
	It appears that I have misjudged Jared. He certainly has the ability to pay attention, contribute to the class, and retain factual information when he is interested in a topic. He is even willing and eager to participate. I am going to discuss the new discovery with Jared's other teachers.	

Some teachers tend to use too many or too few items in a checklist. This tendency can be combated by requiring a fixed number of checks. Whether or not to use this technique will, of course, depend upon the nature and intended use of the checklist.

Anecdotal Record. The anecdotal record (see table A.2) is as useful for secondary as for elementary students, especially given the need we have noted for close observation of adolescent students.

Constructing Test Items (Chapter 12)

Principles of sound test item construction apply to all levels of education. The following test items illustrate the application of these principles to secondary education. (See pp. 184–201 for more detailed discussion as well as for elementary examples.)

Writing Supply Items

1. *Require short, definite, clearcut, and explicit answers.*

    Poor: Ernest Hemingway wrote _____ .

    Improved: *The Old Man and the Sea* was written by _____ .

2. *Avoid multi-mutilated statements.*

    Poor: _____ pointed out in _____ that freedom of thought in America was seriously hampered by _____ _____ _____ _____ .

    Improved: That freedom of thought in America was seriously hampered by social pressures toward conformity was pointed out in 1830 by (De Tocqueville).

3. *If several correct answers (e.g., synonyms), are possible, equal credit should be given to each one.*

Poor: What is the general measurement term describing the consistency with which items in a test measure the same thing?

Improved: Define *internal consistency reliability*.

4. *It is generally recommended that in completion items the blank comes at the end of the statement.*

Poor: A(n) _____ is the index obtained by dividing a mental age score by chronological age and multiplying by 100.

Improved: The index obtained by dividing a mental age score by chronological age and multiplying by 100 is called a(n) _____ .

5. *Specify the terms in which the response will be given.*

Poor: When does the Security Council of the United Nations hold its meetings?

Improved: In what city of the United States does the Security Council of the United Nations hold its meeting?

6. *In general, direct questions are preferable to incomplete declarative sentences.*

Poor: Gold was discovered in California in the year _____ .

Improved: In what year was gold discovered in California? _____

Writing Constant Alternative Selection Items (True-False)

1. *Avoid the use of "specific determiners."*

Poor: No picture and no sound in a television set may indicate a bad 5U4G tube.

Improved: A bad 5U4G tube in a television set will result in no picture and no sound.

2. *Base true-false items upon statements that are absolutely true or false, without qualifications.*

Poor: If a test is valid it is reliable.

This appears to be an excellent item, but appearances can be deceiving. Responses to the item will depend upon one's definition of validity. A test may have been judged to possess a high degree of content validity, but when administered be found to lack reliability. If, however, one defines validity correlationally, a high validity coefficient will also mean that a test is reliable.

Improved: If a teacher obtains a correlation of .90 between a test and a criterion, he knows the test is highly reliable.

3. *Avoid negatively stated items when possible, and eliminate all double negatives.*

Poor: It is not infrequently observed that copper turns green as a result of oxidation.

Improved: Copper will turn green upon oxidizing.

4. *Avoid the use of unfamiliar or esoteric language.* Comprehension of an item is determined by its difficulty. It is always best to keep its language simple and straightforward and not to confound the student with five-dollar words when fifty-cent ones will do.

    Poor: According to some peripatetic politics, the *raison d'etre* for capital punishment is retribution.

    Improved: According to some politicians, justification for the existence of capital punishment can be traced to the Biblical statement, "An eye for an eye."

5. *Avoid complex sentences with many dependent clauses.* Highly involved sentences and compound sentences tend to distract the student from the central idea of the item. It is a poor practice to make one of the dependent clauses in a true-false item false. It is likely the student will not focus on such seemingly unimportant parts of the statement, and the item becomes a "trick" or "catch" question. With compound statements, the student does not know which elements to judge true or false.

    Poor: Jane Austen, an American novelist born in 1870, was a prolific writer and is best known for her novel *Pride and Prejudice,* published in 1920.

There are so many details in this item that the student does not know which to focus on. The item is false for many reasons (Austen was a British novelist, 1775–1817, and the book was published in 1813), and different students will get credit for different amounts of knowledge.

    Improved: Jane Austen is best known for her novel *Pride and Prejudice.*

Writing Changing-Alternative Selection Items (Multiple Choice)

1. *The items should pose a clear, definite, explicit, and singular problem.*

    Poor: Salvador Dali is
        a. a famous Indian statesman.
        b. important in international law.
        c. known for surrealistic art.
        d. the author or many avant-garde plays.

    Improved: With which of the fine arts is Salvador Dali associated?
        a. Surrealistic painting
        b. Avant-garde theater
        c. Polytonal symphonic music
        d. Impressionistic poetry

2. *Include in the stem any words that might otherwise be repeated in each response.*

    Poor: Milk can be pasteurized at home by
        a. heating it to a temperature of 130 degrees
        b. heating it to a temperature of 145 degrees
        c. heating it to a temperature of 160 degrees
        d. heating it to a temperature of 175 degrees

Improved: The minimum temperature that can be used to pasteurize milk at home is:
a. 130°F
b. 145°F
c. 160°F
d. 175°F

3. *Make all responses plausible and attractive to the less knowledgeable or skillful student.*

Poor: Which of the following statements makes clear the meaning of the word "electron"?
a. An electron tool
b. Neutral particles
c. Negative particles
d. A voting machine
e. The nuclei of atoms

Improved: Which of the following is a description of an electron?
a. Neutral particle
b. Negative particle
c. Neutralized proton
d. Radiated particle
e. Atom nucleus

4. *Make options grammatically parallel to each other and consistent with the stem.*

Poor: As compared with the American factory worker in the early part of the nineteenth century, the American factory worker at the close of the century
a. was working long hours
b. received greater social security benefits
c. was to receive lower wages
d. was less likely to belong to a labor union
e. became less likely to have personal contact with employees

Improved: As compared with the American factory worker in the early part of the nineteenth century, the American factory worker at the close of the century
a. worked longer hours
b. had more social security
c. received lower wages
d. was less likely to belong to a labor union
e. had less personal contact with his employer

Writing Test Items for Junior and Senior High School Students

Junior high school students can use commercially available (e.g., IBM) answer sheets. A commercial scoring template may be used for hand scoring. If the answer sheet is teacher-made, a fan, strip, or cut-out key (see chap. 11) may be used. The following series of test items aims at measur-

Figure A.1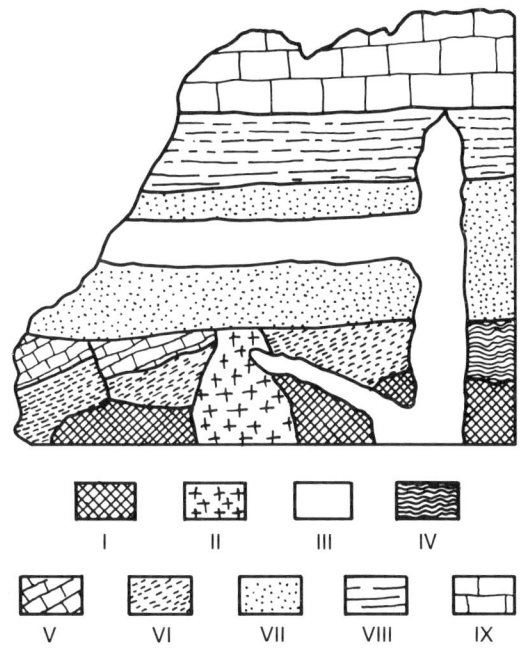

ing the junior high school student's understanding of land-feature diagrams. The test item should not be one previously studied in the class.*

Items 1–5 refer to the cross-sectioned land-feature diagram in Figure A.1. Formations are indicated by Roman numerals.

1. Fossils would be least likely to occur in
   a. III
   b. V
   c. VII
   d. VIII
   e. IX

2. An unconformity exists between
   a. I and III
   b. III and VI
   c. V and VII
   d. VII and VIII
   e. VIII and IX

---

*The material in this section is based on Dr. Clarence Nelson's monograph *Improving objective tests in science* (1967), pp. 18–21. Sample items reproduced by permission of the National Science Teachers Association, 1742 Connecticut Ave. NW, Washington, D.C., 20009.

3. The youngest formation is
   a. I
   b. II
   c. III
   d. V
   e. IX

4. The oldest formation is
   a. I
   b. II
   c. III
   d. V
   e. IX

5. Which formation is made up of igneous rock?
   a. III
   b. V
   c. VII
   d. VIII
   e. IX

Similarly, the student's interpretation of a chemical formula not previously encountered can reveal whether or not she understands the symbols and conventions she has studied in class.

6. The number of atoms of oxygen in the formula $2Al_2(SO_4)_3$ is
   a. 4
   b. 7
   c. 8
   d. 12
   e. 24

Summarizing, Analyzing, and Reporting Student Achievement Data (Chapter 13)

Figures A.2 and A.3 extend our remarks on elementary school reporting and marking by illustrating report forms for sixth and tenth grades. Both report forms use letter grades and indicate the student's separate courses and teachers. The sixth grade form has spaces for brief comments from each teacher. Both forms provide for an attendance record, usually not reported for elementary students. The combined letter-number grading on the tenth grade form indicates the increased importance of marks in high school.

Classroom Management and Discipline (Chapter 14)

The high school principal or vice-principal often has major responsibility for managing student discipline because of the shift from the self-

CLARKE COUNTY SCHOOL DISTRICT
Mid-Quarter Progress Report

STUDENT NAME	HUBERTY, KURT D
HOMEROOM	06-
STUDENT NUMBER	023620
TERM	FOURTH REPORTING PERIOD

DATE 5/09/86

SCHOOL NAME	HILSMAN MIDDLE SCHOOL
& ADDRESS	870 GAINES SCHOOL ROAD
GUIDANCE PHONE	548-7281

C J HUBERTY
KURT D HUBERTY
120 PLANTATION DRIVE
ATHENS GA 30605

COURSE	INSTRUCTOR	GRADE	ATTENDANCE Present	ATTENDANCE Absent	COMMENTS
0640/61 SCIENCE	CORNELIUS, R	B			
0634/12 MATHEMATICS	MADDOX, KATHLEEN	B			FREQUENTLY LACKS ASSIGNMENTS
0620/13 SOCIAL STUDIES	BUMGARTNER, K	C			FREQUENTLY LACKS ASSIGNMENTS
0612/24 LANGUAGE ARTS	VARNEDOE, J	B			FREQUENTLY LACKS ASSIGNMENTS
0662/25 ART	HENRY, CAROLE	A			
0682/16 READING	ARTHUR, T	C			OCCASIONALLY COMES TO CLASS UNPREPARED
0656/37 PHYSICAL EDUCATION	BUFFORD, H	A			

CONTACT GUIDANCE OFFICE FOR MIDDLE SCHOOL GRADING INDEX

Figure A.2
Middle School Report Form, Sixth Grade

Note: Reproduced by permission of Clarke County School District, Athens, Georgia.

CLARKE COUNTY SCHOOL DISTRICT
GRADE REPORT

CEDAR SHOALS HIGH SCHOOL

Any questions pertaining to the student's performance, please contact the guidance office.

PROGRESS REPORT FOR FOURTH REPORTING PERIOD   85-86

CARL J HUBERTY
JEFFREY N HUBERTY
120   PLANTATION DRIVE

ATHENS   GA 30605

1st Reporting Period Ends	October 8, 1985
2nd Reporting Period Ends	November 20, 1985
3rd Reporting Period Ends	January 17, 1986
4th Reporting Period Ends	March 5, 1986
5th Reporting Period Ends	April 25, 1986
6th Reporting Period Ends	June 10, 1986

STUDENT NUMBER..: 015703   HUBERTY, JEFFREY N

HOMEROOM TEACHER: MCWHORTER

GRADE - SECTION.: 10 - H

GUIDANCE PHONE..: 546-5375

*** - PARENT CONFERENCE REQUESTED

"I" CONVERTS TO "F" AFTER 10 DAYS

Instructor	Course Title	1st Report	2nd Report	3rd Report	Mid Year Exam	4th Report	5th Report	6th Report	End of Year Exam	Final Grade	Credit Unit	Cumulative Absences
GIBBS	ADVANCED ENGLISH II	86/B	90/A-	81/B-	86/B	83/B						
	ATTENDANCE	30/	30/	30/		29/ 1						1
COLEY	ADVANCED ALGEBRA II	92/A-	92/B+	95/A	92/A-	94/A						
	ATTENDANCE	30/	30/	30/		29/ 1						1
BROWN	BSCS, ADVANCED BIOLOGY	95/A	88/B+	88/B+	79/C+	83/B						
	ATTENDANCE	30/	30/	30/		29/ 1						2
POWELL	ADV. POLITICAL & ECONOMIC SY	95/A	93/A	92/A-	74/C	84/B						
	ATTENDANCE	30/	30/	30/		29/ 1						1
KELLY	LATIN II	93/A	95/A	90/A-	95/A	89/B+						
	ATTENDANCE	30/	30/	29/ 1		29/ 1						2
GUNTER	PHYSICAL ED.	99/A+	99/A+	94/A	91/A-	93/A						
	ATTENDANCE	30/	30/	30/		30/						
	ATTENDANCE											
	ATTENDANCE											
	ATTENDANCE											
	ATTENDANCE											

Students will not receive credit for any class in which they are not in attendance for at least 160 days or class periods.

Your son(s) / daughter(s) absences to date are reflected in the appropriate column.

Please contact your school counselor if you have questions.

LEGEND:
  Attendance
  Days Present / Days Absent

The final grade is determined by averaging seven figures. These figures are the six 6-weeks reports and the average of the mid-year and end-of-year examinations.

Index To Grades

A+ = 97-100
A = 93-96
A- = 90-92
B+ = 87-89
B = 83-86
B- = 80-82
C+ = 77-79
C = 73-76
C- = 70-72
D+ = 67-69
D = 63-66
D- = 60-62
F = 0-59
WP = Withdrawn Passing
WF = Withdrawn Failing
I = Incomplete
     [converts to F (50) in ten days]

Figure A.3
High School Report Form, Tenth Grade

Note: Reproduced by permission of Clarke County School District, Athens, Georgia.

contained classroom of the elementary school to departmentalization. Although high school teachers are expected to be able to maintain a classroom environment conducive to learning, they may send students who are disruptive to the school office if things get out of control.

Kingston and Gentry (1977), reporting a statewide study in Georgia, list the ten most common discipline problems in order as follows: (1) truancy, (2) failure to do assignments, (3) impertinence and discourtesy, (4) use of profane language, (5) smoking in the building or on school grounds, (6) stealing small items, (7) obscene scribbling on walls, (8) congregating in halls and lavatories, (9) destruction of school property, and (10) lying of a serious nature. The most frequently used strategies for dealing with discipline problems at the secondary level included parent conferences, suspension, corporal punishment, extra assignments, restriction, and detention. Ratliff (1980) reports that frequent use of corporal punishment is contrary to recommendations by adolescent psychologists.

Levine and Kozak (1979) report that use of narcotics, gang fighting, violence against teachers, sex offenses, and drinking occur in urban and suburban schools in both working-class and middle-class neighborhoods. However, the National Institute of Education (1978) notes that 26 percent of urban schools, as compared with 6 percent of rural schools, reported serious discipline problems. As a result of a U.S. Supreme Court case decided in 1975 *(Goss* v. *Lopez),* students must be given a formal hearing before suspension. The concept of "in-school suspension" has been developed to keep disruptive students isolated from peers in a closely supervised room where they work on assignments. When they display appropriate behavior they are returned to the mainstream (Meares and Kittle 1976; White 1977; Harvey and Moosha 1977; Seyforth 1980).

Two excellent resources on discipline at the secondary level are *Effective Classroom Management* and *Discipline,* in the Hot Topic Series (1984–85), Phi Delta Kappa, Box 789, Bloomington, Indiana 47402.

Applications (Chapter 15)

The following activities apply the principles of chapter 15 to high school instruction:

1. Write an instructional objective appropriate to a secondary school topic for each of Gagne's learning types (see p. 258).
2. Design a lesson for a high school age student that will foster creative problem solving.
3. Try the Prisoner's Dilemma game, described in chapter 2, with some high school students.
4. Develop a problem-solving grid, as presented in chapter 15, that incorporates evaluation criteria and possible solutions for selecting an appropriate instructional design for high school curricula.
5. Evaluate secondary textbooks and teacher's manuals using the list of features presented on pages 270–272.

Coping (Chapter 16)

Issues discussed in chapter 16 (economics, unions, professional development, computing) are of concern to all educators. People's strength is not in what they encounter, but in how they deal with what they encounter. Write a position paper addressing how you feel about these and other professional concerns. Describe how the issues affect your becoming a teacher, how you will deal with these concerns, and where you want to be in your career in five years.

Suggested Reading

The following books will provide food for thought for those who are becoming teachers, especially in grades 9–12.

Elbow, P. 1986. *Embracing contraries: Explorations in learning and teaching.* New York: Oxford Univ. Press.

A nation prepared: Teachers for the 21st century. 1986. Report of the Task Force on Teaching as a Profession. New York: Carnegie Forum on Education and the Economy.

Useem, E. 1986. *Low tech in a high tech world: Corporations and classrooms in the new information society.* New York: Free Press.

References

Bonney, M.E., and R.S. Hampleman. 1962. *Personal-social evaluation techniques.* Washington, D.C.: Center for Applied Research in Education.

Harvey, D.L., and W.G. Moosha. 1977. In-school suspension: Does it work? *National Association of Secondary School Principals Bulletin* 61 (405): 14–17.

Kingston, A.J., and H.W. Gentry. 1977. Discipline problems in Georgia secondary schools: 1961 and 1974. *National Association of Secondary School Principals Bulletin* 61 (406): 94–99.

Levine, E.M., and C. Kozak. 1979. Drug use and vandalism among upper-middle class adolescents. *Journal of Youth and Adolescence* 8 (1): 91–101.

Meares, H.O., and H.A. Kittle. 1976. In-house suspension. *National Association of Secondary School Principals Bulletin* 60 (397): 60–63.

A nation prepared: Teachers for the 21st century. 1986. Report of the Task Force on Teaching as a Profession. New York: Carnegie Forum on Education and the Economy.

National Institute of Education. 1978. *Safe school study.* Washington, D.C.: Department of Health, Education, and Welfare.

Norton, P. 1985. Problem-solving activities in a computer environment: A different angle of vision. *Educational Technology* (Oct.): 36–41.

Phares, E. 1957. Expectancy changes in skill and chance situations. *Journal of Abnormal and Social Psychology* 54: 339–42.

Ratliff, R. 1980. Physical punishment must be abolished. *Educational Leadership* 37: 474–76.

Rotter, J. 1966. Generalized expectancies for internal versus external control of reinforcement. *Psychological Monograph* 80 (1).

Seyforth, J.T. 1980. Achieving equity and restraint in in-school suspension. *High School Journal* 61: 200–202.

White, B. 1977. In-school suspension: No panacea, but the impact is positive. *Phi Delta Kappan* 58: 497–98.

Glossary

ability to acquire knowledge. Ability to learn.

abstract. Describes a quality that is apart from any particular material or object that has the quality.

action verb. Used in instructional objectives to specify the terminal behavior because it names an observable or measurable behavior and thus describes how learning is to be demonstrated.

advance organizer. Summary introduced before new learning tasks to provide anchoring structures for the new learning.

affective response tendency. Consistency in emotional responses to a specific stimulus situation.

alternative. See *distractor*.

battery. A group of tests standardized on the same population, so that results on the several tests are comparable. Sometimes loosely applied to any group of tests administered together.

behavioral objective. See *instructional objective*.

choice item. Requires the test taker to select an answer from among two or more alternatives. Examples are multiple choice, true/false, and matching items.

coaching. See *probing*.

cognitive influences on learning. Factors having to do with mental activity.

cognitive monitoring. Being aware of one's thinking.

cognitive response tendency. Consistency in manner of perceiving, remembering, and thinking.

cognitive style. Characteristic and consistent manner of processing and organizing what one sees and thinks about.

competency-based education. Involves mastering agreed-upon learning objectives and demonstrating use of these abilities.

complex thinkers. Tend to look at situations in multidimensional or abstract ways.

concept. A thought, an idea of a class of objects; general notion.

conceptualizing ability. Ability to form abstractions (e.g., color, shape, size, texture, function, number).

concrete. Real-world, manipulative.

concrete thinking. Reasoning tied to immediate and tangible information.

construct validity. The degree to which a test measures given psychological qualities. Arguments for construct validity must be based on theory and empirical evidence.

content validity. The degree to which the content of the test samples the subject matter, behaviors, or situations about which conclusions are to be drawn. Content validity is especially important in an achievement test and is determined with reference to the table of specifications and objectives.

convergent questions. Questions that ask pupils to move toward closure, draw conclusions, or recall facts. Convergent questions allow for just one correct answer or end result.

convergent thinking. Coming to a single point or answer; opposed to *divergent thinking*.

correlation. Degree of relationship between two sets of data.

covert. Concealed.

criterion-related validity. The degree to which test scores correlate with measures of criterion performance.

critique. The evaluation teachers conduct of their own teaching performance during and after instruction.

cues. Hints, signals.

culture. Concepts, habits, skills, art, instruments, institutions, etc., of a given people in a given period.

curricular validity. Success of test in measuring given curricular goals.

curriculum guide. A guide developed by curriculum consultants and administrators in cooperation with teachers. Sets goals for the program or subject area, may or may not include instructional objectives and learning activities, and may cover the whole range from kindergarten through twelfth grade. A curriculum guide provides a large structure within which teachers can organize their own units and lessons.

diagnostic test. A test used to identify specific areas of weakness or strength and to determine the nature of deficiencies. Diagnostic achievement tests are most commonly developed for the skill subjects—reading, arithmetic, and spelling.

didactic instruction. Telling, lecturing, as compared to *discovery learning*.

difficulty level. Percentage of students getting a test item correct.

discovery learning. Learning through exploration.

discriminating power. Number of high-scoring testees getting an item correct versus the number of low-scoring testees responding correctly.

distractor. Any of the plausible but incorrect choices provided in a multiple choice or matching item. Sometimes called a *foil, alternative,* or *option*. The choice is "distracting" and appears attractive to the less knowledgeable or skillful student, thereby reducing the efficiency of guessing.

divergent questions. Questions that allow pupils to arrive at unique responses, with no single correct response required. Divergent questions generally require a higher-level response, allow for more creative and critical answers, and ask for new thinking. See *convergent questions*.

divergent thinking. Thinking different from the typical; open-ended.

double-entry researcher log. Strategy for recording one's thinking in problem solving.

emotional influences on learning. Feelings that affect ability to learn.

essay test. See *written test*.

ethnicity. Designation of people by customs, characteristics, language, etc.

ethnography. Set of field research methods used by anthropologists to study culture.

evaluation. The process by which quantitative and qualitative data are processed to arrive at a judgment of effectiveness, value, or worth.

field. Surrounding context or background.

field dependent. Affected by background variables.

field independent. Not affected by background variables.

foil. See *distractor*.

formal test. The four most frequently used formal tests are oral exams, essay tests, teacher-made objective tests, and standardized tests.

formative evaluation. Ongoing evaluation throughout a lesson or instructional unit for the purpose of revising or modifying instruction during its early stages for an individual or the class. See *summative evaluation*.

gender. Identity with social sex roles.

generic influences on learning. A class or group of factors that affect learning.

heuristics. A method of education in which pupils are trained to find out things for themselves; include strategies for problem solving.

iconic. Pictorial.

identify. Individuality; sameness.

impulsive. Acting on sudden inclination without conscious thought.

infer. To decide from something known or assumed.

inference. Conclusion, deduction.

informal test. A test in which the student is unaware that data are being gathered and is not involved in recording responses.

inquiry. Seeking information by asking questions.

inservice. Describes either certified teachers or educational experience that occurs after one has entered teaching; opposed to *preservice*.

instructional objective. A statement describing a task students should be able to do after completing instruction that they could not do before instruction. Also called a *behavioral* or *performance objective*.

instructional strategy. Method of teaching.

instructional validity. Appropriateness of teaching methods to the goals of the lesson.

language. Any means of expressing or communicating, as gestures, sounds, signs, etc.

LD. Learning disabled.

learning style. Characteristic and consistent manner of acquiring knowledge, especially in processing and organizing what one sees and thinks about.

left brain dominance. Tendency toward analytical and sequential thinking.

lesson plan. An outline of teaching procedures for one to five days of a particular class, developed from the teaching unit. The level of specificity depends on the teacher's needs at the time. A daily plan may include a title, goals, objectives, procedures, evaluation, and critique.

LOGO. A programming language, developed by S. Papert, which is a collection of procedures.

mastery test. A test of the extent to which a student has mastered a specific set of objectives or met the minimum requirement set by a teacher.

matching item. A test item calling for the correct association of each entry in one list with an entry in the second list.

measurement. Systematic collection, quantification (i.e., the assignment of numerals to represent things), and ordering of information.

mediated learning. Learning aided by techniques such as organizational strategies or cues for recall.

metacognition. Reflective self-awareness; capacity to think about one's own cognitive process.

minimum competency testing. Testing to assess basic academic skills (e.g., reading, arithmetic) and their applications to "real-life" demands (e.g., keeping a checkbook, calculating the cost of purchases, interpreting a train schedule or map).

mode of representation. Level of presenting learning tasks (e.g., concrete, iconic, symbols).

motivation. Reasons for acting; desires and aversions, goals or intentions, moods and emotions, etc., that could move people to act in one way instead of another.

multiple choice item. See *choice item*.

normal curve. A graph that represents a symmetric distribution of scores.

norms. Statistics that describe the test performance of specified subgroups, such as pupils of various ages or grades, in the standardized group for a test. Norms are often assumed to be representative of some larger population, such as pupils in the country as a whole. Norms describe average or typical performance; they are not to be regarded as standards or desirable levels of attainment. Grade, age, percentile, and standard score are the most common types of norms.

objective item. Item to be answered by a choice among specified alternatives, thus providing relatively consistent and comparable responses.

observation. Act or practice of noting and recording facts and events.

option. See *distractor*.

oral test. A test that allows the pupil to respond to test questions aloud, commonly used with (1) elementary school children, (2) graduate students, and (3) students physically unable to take written tests.

overt. Open to view, public.

pedagogy. The art or science of teaching; instruction in teaching methods.

performance objective. See *instructional objective*.

perseveration. Inability to stop an action.

physical influence on learning. Sensory limitation, low vitality, fatigue, physical impairments.

power test. A test intended to measure level of performance and to sample the range of a student's capacity, rather than the speed of response; hence a power test has either no time limit or a very generous one.

preservice. Occurring prior to entering teaching; student in teacher preparation program.

primary source. In research, an original work or document as opposed to a work *about* a work, document, or historical period.

probing. Technique of encouraging student to add to, improve, or justify their responses when they give partial answers to questions.

product of instruction. The observable or measurable behavior expected after a lesson has been taught, also known as the *terminal behavior*.

prompting. Technique of providing hints or clues to guide the pupil to the correct answer when a question draws either no answer or an incorrect one.

psychomotor influences on learning. Abilities needed to search or produce spoken or written responses; the motor effects of mental processes.

qualitative inquiry. Provides a social science (ethnograhic) perspective using description, interpretation, and appraisal; involves participant observation, field notes, case study, autobiography/biography.

quantitative research. Research in which variables are manipulated and their effect on other variables observed.

redirection. When a question has many possible answers, a teacher directs it to several pupils in turn. This questioning technique increases pupil participation and thus improves student interaction.

referent. The object referred to by a term or word.

reflective persons. Tend to delay in answering test items involving an initial uncertainty, with resulting gains in accuracy.

reliability. The extent to which a test is accurate or consistent in measuring whatever it measures. Consistency can be measured over forms of the text, examiners, scorers, administration times, or sample of items.

resource unit. A sample unit developed for a hypothetical group of students. It may cover an instructional period of weeks or months. A resource unit gives much attention to pupil activities and instructional materials. It is sometimes part of a *curriculum guide* and often aids teachers in planning classroom experiences.

response set. A consistent tendency to follow a certain pattern in responding to test items.

right brain dominance. Use intuitive, simultaneous, holistic thinking.

salient. Standing out from the rest; noticeable, conspicuous, prominent.

schema (pl., **schemata**). Body of knowledge that provides a framework within which to locate new items of knowledge; cognitive frame or structure.

secondary source. A written work about other works, documents, or periods of history.

selection item. See *choice item*.

sensory influences on learning. Perceptual experiences or factors that affect ability to learn.

sequencing ability. Ability to place things in succession.

simple thinkers. Look at situations in single-dimensional or concrete ways.

social influences on learning. Interpersonal effects on learning.

socioeconomic status. Buyer power; e.g., low, average, high.

sociogram. A graphic picture of the social relations among group members.

spatial ability. Handles such tasks as block design (mentally breaking up a gestalt or whole into smaller units), embedded figures (disembedding figures from a larger, more complex figural pattern), or mentally rotating or mirror imaging a figure to match a given figure.

speed test. A test in which performance is measured by the number of tasks performed correctly in a given time. All items are on a similar level of difficulty, generally easy.

standardized test. A systematic sample of performance obtained under prescribed conditions, scored according to definite rules, and capable of evaluation by reference to normative information.

summative evaluation. The use of evaluation data to determine the effectiveness of a unit, course, or program after it has been completed. The purpose is to determine what has been learned. See *formative evaluation*.

supply item. An item that requires students to respond to a simple direct question or an incomplete statement by constructing or supplying their own brief answer.

survey battery. Comprehensive set of tests that measures achievement in given subjects or areas, usually with the understanding that the tests are intended to measure group, rather than individual, status. Survey batteries provide valuable information about the effectiveness of various instructional programs in a school or district.

survey test. A test that measures general achievement in a given subject area, usually with the understanding that the test is intended to measure group, rather than individual, status.

tacit knowledge. Things a person knows or assumes that are not usually conscious or discussed.

taxonomy. Classification scheme.

teaching unit. Unit created by a teacher for a specific group of students. It is more detailed than a *resource unit* and usually covers two to six weeks.

terminal behavior. See *product of instruction*.

test. A systematic method for gathering data in order to make intra- or interindividual comparisons.

validity. Degree of accuracy with which a test measures what it is intended to measure.

variability. Amount of dispersion or spread in a set of scores.

wait-time. The time that elapses between the end of a question and the ensuing response, whether from the teacher or the pupil. Also, the amount of time between one response and the next response or question, whether from teacher or pupil.

written test. A test that allows for direct assessment of the attainment of a variety of goals and objectives and provides latitude for students to express themselves in characteristic ways. Written or *essay tests* may be classified according to the extensiveness of students' responses.

Index

Ability to acquire knowledge tasks, 44–46
Absolute grading method, 234
Adaptive education, 98–99
Adaptive Learning Environment Model (ALEM), 99
Adler, Mortimer, 284n
Adult ego state, 240
Advance organizer, 103
Affective objectives, 65–70
Alderman, D.L., 122, 123
American Federation of Teachers (AFT), 280, 281
Ames, C., 244, 254
Ames, R., 244, 254
Amiran, M.R., 105, 107
Analysis, 58
Analytic method of essay scoring, 206
Anderson, H.O., 126, 140
Anderson, T., 269, 274
Anecdotal records, 153–155, 305

Application, 58
Arlin, M., 243–244, 254
Armbruster, B., 269, 274
Aschner, M.J., 126, 129, 138
Assertive discipline, 241
Assessment, 151. *See also* Test procedures
Associationist theories, 264
Atkins, J., 256, 257, 259, 260, 274
Attendance records, 251
Average (calculation), 211
Axelrod, R., 10, 11n, 15, 275
Ayers, J.D., 59, 75

Bangert, R.L., 98, 107
Bannatyne, A., 26, 27, 29, 30n, 32, 34, 36, 38, 39, 41–44, 46
Barber, L.L., 76
Barker, R.G., 153, 167
Barrows, L.K., 118, 123
Bartholomew, B.R., 238, 254

Basal textbooks
 selection and adaptation of, 269
 teacher's manuals for, 270–272
Bashaw, W.L., 59, 76
BASIC, 113
Bauernfeind, R.F., 231, 232, 236
Beall, D., 114, 115, 123
Behavior modification, 241
Behavioral approach to teaching, 93
Behavioral objectives, 52–53, 63. *See also* Instructional objectives
Belch, P.J., 136, 138
Bellock, A.A., 126, 139
Benthul, H.F., 269, 275
Bentzen, F., 242n, 254
Berliner, D., 99, 107, 140
Berthoff, Ann, 7, 15
Biehler, R.F., 251, 254
Biondi, A.M., 265, 276
Birman, B.F., 290, 293

323

Blind guessing, 187n
Block design, 31–34
Bloom, B.F., 99, 107, 218, 236
Bloom, B.S., 56, 66, 75–76, 127, 139
Bloom's Taxonomy, 56–57, 66, 127–129, 303
Bolter, J.D., 286, 293
Bonney, M.E., 314
Boone, S.M., 126, 139
Borg, W.R., 126, 139
Borich, G., 219, 236
Bork, A., 112–113, 123
Bowler, M., 269, 275
Brain activity, 102, 299
Brainstorming, 102, 266
Branscomb, L.M., 4, 15
Bransford, J.D., 28
Brophy, J.E., 139
Brown, A.L., 92, 107
Brownell, W.H., 257–258, 275
Buffington, A.V., 270, 275
Buggey, J.L., 126, 139
Bunzel, J.H., 285, 293
Busse, T., 265, 276
Buster, C., 206n

Callahan, R., 90
Canfield, J.D., 239, 254
Canter, L., 241, 254
Career ladders, 281n
Carey, Frank T., 285
Carey, L., 9–10, 15, 93n, 102, 107
Carkhuff, R.R., 254
Carlstrom, G., 115, 123
Carroll, J.B., 26n, 27
Chaining, 258
Chan, J.M.T., 119–121, 123
Changing-alternative items, 189–196, 307–308
Chapin, J., 291, 293
Cheating, 246
Checklist, 153, 304–305
Checklist-point-score method of essay scoring, 206
Chicago Mastery Learning Reading Program with Learning Strategies (CMLR/LS), 105
Child-ego state, 240
Chipman, S.F., 92, 105, 107
Choice questions, 159
Class disturbances, 245–247
Classroom interaction, 136–137
Classroom management. *See also* Discipline
  attendance taking and chores, 251–252
  physical environment and, 247
  pupil movement in classroom and, 249–250
  rules and policies of, 250–251
  seating arrangements and, 247–249
  in secondary schools, 310, 313
Classroom rules, 250–251
Closure, 85–86
Coaching technique, 135
Coding tasks, 43–44
Cognitive influences on learning, 22, 24
Cognitive monitoring, 20–26
Cognitive objectives, 49, 56–66
  evaluating effectiveness of, 62–63
Cognitive processes, 5–6
Cognitive response tendency. *See* Cognitive style
Cognitive style, 101–102
Cohen, M.R., 114–115, 123
Communication skills
  discipline strategy and, 239
  studies in, 6–7
Comparative organizer, 103
Complex thinkers, 102
Comprehension, 57–58
Comprehension tasks, 36–38
Computer Applications in Teaching Program (CAITP), 301, 303
Computer hardware, 118
Computer software
  components of, 120–121
  vs. film use, 121
  quality of, 118
  teacher-designed, 119–120
Computer use in classroom
  benefits to, 119
  blocks to, 110–113
  integrating, 288–292
  research on expectations about, 115–117
  research on integrating, 114–115
  resistance to, 116–119
  teacher training for, 7–8, 113–115
Computers in Education survey, 288–289
Concept learning, 258
Conceptual ability tasks
  comprehension as, 36–38
  similarities as, 38–39
  vocabulary as, 39–41
Conover, W.J., 210, 236
Constant error, 219
Constant-alternative selection items, 186–189, 306–307
Construct validity, 221
Content of instructional objectives, 63–64
Content selection of lesson plan, 84–85
Content validity, 220, 222
Conventional morality, 250

Convergent questions, 129–131
Convergent thinking, 102, 298–299
Corey, S.M., 126, 139
CoRT Thinking Program, 105
Cory, G.H., 123, 124
Covert motives, 20
Covington, M.V., 105, 107, 265, 275
Cox, R.C., 160, 167
Creative problem solving (CPS), 267–268
  use of grid for, 268–269
Creativity
  teaching, 265–269
  theories of, 263–265
Criterion-referenced measures, 159–161. *See also* Tests
Criterion-related validity, 220
Critique, 87
Cronbach, L.J., 76
Cruickshank, W.M., 242n, 254
Crutchfield, R.S., 105, 107, 275
Csapo, M., 243n, 254
Cues, 21
Cullinan, D.A., 243n, 254
Culliton, B.J., 279, 293
Culture, 100
Cunnington, B.F., 263, 276
Curricular validity, 222–223
Curriculum guides, 80
Cut-out key, 178, 179

Daines, D., 76, 126, 139
Dalis, G.T., 76
Dare to discipline approach, 241
Darling-Hammond, L., 2, 15
Data. *See* Student data
Dave, R.H., 70, 76
Davies, I., 117, 124
Davies, L.B., 105, 107
Davies, R.M., 275
Davis, O.L., 126, 139
deBono, E., 105, 107
Deese, J., 269, 275
Deno, S.L., 76
DeStefano, L., 100, 108
DeVault, V.M., 291, 293
Diagnostic assessment, 259–260
Diagnostic teaching, 93, 94
  applying, 256–258
  assessment as tool for, 259–260
Diagnostic Teaching Cycle, 257, 259
Diagnostic tests, 143, 163–164. *See also* Standardized achievement tests
Dick, W., 9–10, 15, 93n, 102, 107
Didactic instruction, 104
Diederick, P.B., 205, 208, 213, 236
Digit span tasks, 41–42

Dillon, J.T., 126, 139
Dinkmeyer, D., 254
Dinkmeyer, D., Jr., 254
Discipline
  causes of, 244–245
  definition of, 238–239
  guidelines for classroom, 245–247
  in secondary schools, 310, 313
  strategies for, 239–244
Discovery learning, 104
Distractors, 189
Divergent questions, 129–131
Divergent thinking, 102, 298–299
Dobson, J., 241, 254
Double-entry research log, 7
Doyle, W., 238, 254
Dressel, P.L., 52, 76, 144, 150
Driekurs, R., 239, 254
Duckworth, E., 5, 15
Dulaney, C., 90, 139
duPont, Pierre S., IV, 285

Ebel, R.L., 146, 150, 217, 236
Economic concerns, careers in education and, 279–280
Educational objectives
  affective, 65–70
  cognitive, 56–65
  instrumentation of taxonomy of, 60–61t, 69t
  psychomotor, 70–73
  sources of, 48–50
Edwards, B., 264, 275
Eggen, P., 90, 139
Elementary education objectives, 49
ELIZA program, 135
Elzey, F.F., 210, 236
Emig, J., 260, 275
Emotional factors influencing learning, 23, 26
English, R., 269, 275
Environmental press, 102
Ernst, K., 240, 254
Essay tests, 157–159
  scoring for, 205–206
  suggestions for using, 206
  writing items for, 201–205
Ethnicity, 100
Eurich, N.P., 282n, 293
Evaluation. *See also* Student data, Tests
  definition of, 142–143
  as educational objective, 58–59
  formative, 148
  importance of, 144–145
  lesson plans and, 86–87
  summative, 148
  uses of, 145–146
Evertson, C.M., 139

Expository advance organizer, 103
Extended-response essay items, 202

Fan key, 177, 178
Feldhusen, J.F., 263, 265, 275
Felker, D.W., 244, 254
Feuerstein, R., 104, 105, 108
Field dependent learners, 102
Field independent learners, 102
Field placement, 8–9
Fierson, E.C., 264, 275
Films, vs. educational software, 121–122
Finn, C.E., 280, 281, 293
Flavell, J.H., 20, 28
Floyd, W.D., 126, 139
Foils, 189
Form, of instructional objectives, 64–65
Formal test procedures, 155–159
Formative evaluation, 148
French, J.W., 49, 76
Frequency distribution, 210
Fridell, R., 105, 107

Gage, N.L., 183, 208
Gagne, R.M., 258, 272, 275
Gall, M., 127, 139
Gallagher, J.J., 126, 139
Galloway, C.M., 283, 293
Gardner, David P., 285
Gardner, H., 286, 288, 293
Garr, A.R., 275
Gender, 100
Generic influences on learning, 22–26
Gentry, H.W., 313, 314
Gestalt theories, 264
Giannelli, G., 110–113, 124
Ginott, H., 239, 254
Glaser, R., 92, 98, 105, 107
Glasser, W., 240, 254
Glazer, N., 282–283, 293
Goal cards, 230–232
Goals. *See* Educational objectives
Goodwin, S.E., 242n, 243n, 254
Gordon, E.W., 100, 108
Gordon, T., 240, 255
Gordon, W., 267, 275
Grade equivalents, 212
Graening, J., 275
Graves, D., 263
Griffin, A.H., 240, 254
Grinder, R.E., 98, 108
Gronlund, Norman E., 153, 157, 163, 167, 201, 203n, 208, 218, 236
Gruber, H.E., 264, 275
Grunwald, B.B., 239, 254
Guessing, 187n, 190n

Guide to Creative Action, 265
Guilford, J.P., 26, 28, 264, 275
Guthrie, J.W., 280, 293

Hadamard, J., 264, 275
Hagen, E., 221–222, 236
Hales, L.W., 205, 208
Hallahan, D.P., 242n, 255
Halloran, P.P., 275
Hampleman, R.S., 314
Hand, T., 50, 76
Harder, R., 90
Haring, N.G., 242n, 255
Harrow, A.J., 70, 71–73, 76
Harty, H., 114, 115, 123
Harvey, D.L., 313, 314
Haslem, Elizabeth, 6, 7, 15
Haslerud, J., 264, 275
Hastings, J.T., 218, 236
Havighurst, R.J., 49, 76
Hayward, P., 163, 168
Health, 102
Heffernan, J.J., 118, 123
Hendrickson, G., 257–258, 275
Herber, H.L., 105, 108
Heuristics, 258
Hewes, J.J., 124
Hewett, F.M., 242n, 255
Hlynka, D., 116–118, 124
Hoetker, W.J., 126, 139
Hoffman, M.B., 108
Hollingsworth, P.M., 88, 90, 245, 250, 255
Hoover, K.H., 88, 90, 245, 250, 255
Hoppock, R., 50, 76
Hostility, 246
House, E.R., 117, 118, 124
Howe, L.W., 240, 255
Howsam, R.B., 283, 293
Hudgins, B., 266, 275
Human development, 5–6
Humanistic approach to instruction, 93
Hunking, F.P., 76, 85, 90, 126–128, 139
Hunt, James B., Jr., 285
Hunt, T.C., 117, 124
Hurly, P., 116–118, 124
Husek, T.R., 160, 168
Hutchinson, T., 257, 259, 276
Hyman, R.T., 139

Identity, 101
Inference
  vs. observation, 18, 20, 26
  school related tasks and, 20–46
Informal tests, 143
Information tasks, 44–46
Inman, R.L., 210, 236

Inservice Teacher Microcomputer Implementation Proneness Scale, 114
Inspection grading method, 232–233
Instructional design
　cognitive processing and, 92–93
　definition of, 91
　for secondary schools, 297–300
　task analysis and, 94–97
　tools of, 99–103
Instructional Enrichment Program, 105
Instructional objectives, 51
　and essay items, 202
　of lesson plans, 82
　types of, 52–53
　writing, 52–55
Instructional programs, 105
Instructional strategies, 242–244
　　for different learning types and skills, 258
Instructional validity, 223
Interaction, classroom, 136–137
Internal consistency, 223
Internalization, 66, 67
Isolation, 247
Item data file, 218, 219
Item difficulty, 215–216
Item discrimination, 216–218
Item-analysis techniques, 212–218

Jacobsen, D., 81, 90, 129, 139
Jacobson, L., 133, 140
Jenkins, J.R., 76
Jensen, A.R., 26n, 28, 97, 98n, 108
Jeter, J., 139
Jewett, A., 206n
Jones, B.F., 105, 107

Kaczala, C.M., 115, 124
Kagan, J., 28, 33n, 47
Katims, M., 105, 108
Kauchak, D., 90, 139
Kauffman, J.M., 242n, 254
Kauffman, S.H., 22, 23, 26, 28, 94, 208, 241, 242, 255
Kearney, N.C., 49, 76
Keating, D.P., 265, 275
Kelley, M.L., 139
Keogh, A., 90
Khatena, J., 263, 276
Kibler, R.J., 55, 70, 76
Kingston, A.J., 313, 314
Kirschenbaum, H., 241, 255
Kirsner, D.A., 59, 61n, 68, 69n, 77
Kittle, H.A., 313, 314
Kleinman, G., 126, 139
Klenke, W.H., 118, 123
Kliebard, H.M., 139

Knowledge, 56–57
　modes of representing, 103–104
　tacit, 105
Koestler, A., 264, 275
Kohlberg, L., 250, 251, 255
Kohler, W., 264, 275
Korostoff, M., 119–121, 123
Kounin, J., 134, 140
Kozak, C., 313, 314
Krathwohl, D.R., 66, 76
Kravas, C., 90
Krippner, S., 266, 275
Kris, E., 263, 276
Kropp, R.P., 59, 76
Kubie, L.S., 263, 276
Kubiszyn, T., 219, 236
Kulik, C.C., 98, 109
Kulik, J.A., 98, 107
Kuykendall, C., 269, 276

Ladd, G.T., 126, 140
LaFleur, N.K., 243n, 254
Langer, P., 139
Language, 100
Lasley, T.J., 283, 293
Learners, 100–102
Learning, 257–258
Learning materials, 84
Learning tasks, 97–98
LEAST approach to classroom discipline, 240–241
Lee, B.N., 76
Lee, J.A., 117, 124
Left brain dominance, 102, 299
Lehmann, I.J., 219, 236
Lesson planning, 78–79
　as aspect of teacher preparation, 9–10
　components of, 81–88
　levels of, 79–80
　sample of, 87–88
　for secondary school, 297–298
Levine, E.M., 313, 314
Lindvall, M.C., 98, 109
Lipman, M., 105, 108
Listening, 263
Locus of control, 300
Luria, A.R., 242n, 255

McArdle, R.J., 115, 124
McGuire, C., 62, 76
McLennan, D.W., 122, 124
McNeil, J.D., 76
Maeroff, Gene, 284n
Mager, R.F., 52–55, 65, 76
Mahaffey, M., 275
Mahoney, M.J., 242n, 243n, 254
Manaus, G., 218, 236
Mansfield, R.S., 265, 276
Marks. See also Reporting methods
　dishonest, 234–235

　methods of assigning, 232–234
　philosophy of, 235
　purpose of, 224–226, 230
Masia, B.B., 66, 76
Maslow, A.H., 255
Master teacher plan, 281n
Mastery learning methods, 99
Mastery tests, 143
Matching exercises, 159, 196–199
Materials. See Learning materials
Materials distribution, 252
Mathematics curriculum
　development of, 12–14
　diagnostic teaching for, 256–257, 259–260
　trouble spots in, 94–97
Mathematics teacher shortage, 4
Matrix Outlining and Analysis (MOAN), 105
Maxley, P.F., 139
Mayo, S.T., 160, 168
Meares, H.O., 313, 314
Measurement. See also Tests
　definition of, 143
　importance of, 144–145
　uses of, 145–146
Median, 211
Mediated learning, 104
Medrick, S., 264, 276
Meeker, M.N., 26n, 28, 30, 32, 34, 36, 38, 40, 41–44, 47, 265, 274, 276
Mehrens, W.A., 219, 236
Mercer, J.R., 108
Merrill, M.D., 76
Merrill Mathematics Series, 270
Metacognition. See Cognitive monitoring
Metfessel, W.S., 59, 61n, 68, 69n, 77
Meyers, R.E., 267, 276
Michael, W.B., 59, 61n, 68, 69n, 77
Milen, D.T., 76
Miller, L.W., 272, 276
Miller, R.I., 59, 77
Mills, S.R., 126, 140
Mischel, W., 17, 28
Mishler, E.G., 125, 140
Mogens, R.J., 108
Molner, A., 10, 16, 276
Moosha, W.G., 313, 314
Moral development, 250–251
More, D.N., 117, 124
Morgan, J.C., 140
Morris, C.D., 28
Moskowitz, J.H., 290, 293
Moss, H.A., 28, 33n, 47
Motivation
　definition of, 100
　lesson planning and, 84
Motives, covert, 20

Moyer, J.R., 126, 140
Multiple choice items, 159, 189–196
Multiple discrimination learning, 258

National Education Association (NEA), 280, 281
Natural and logical consequences, 239
Nelsen, E.A., 98, 108
Nelson, Clarence, 199n, 208, 309n
Noller, R.B., 265, 276
Nonadaptive education, 98–99
Nonvolunteers, 134
Nonverbal tests, 143
Normal curve grading method, 233
Normalized scores, 212
Norm-referenced measures, 160, 161. *See also* Tests
Norton, P., 300, 314
Note passing, 246
Nuthall, G., 126, 140
Nutrition, 102

Object assembly, 34–35
Objective teacher-made tests, 158–159
Objectives
 behavioral, 51–53, 63
 choice of, 50–51
 cognitive, 49
 educational, 56–73
 instructional, 51–55
 role of content and form in, 63–65
 social, 49
Observation
 drawbacks of, 155
 vs. inference, 18–20, 26
 instructional decisions and, 26–27
 purpose of, 17–18
 school-related tasks and, 29–46
Olton, R.M., 105, 107, 275
O'Neal, M., 275
Oral exams, 143, 155–157
Organization membership, 280
Orlich, S., 81, 90
Osborn, A., 266, 276
Overdependence of one child on another, 246
Overt behavior, 20
Owings, R.A., 20, 28

Palmer, O., 234, 236
Papert, S., 286, 293
Parent-ego state, 240
Parke, B.N., 264, 276
Parnes, S.J., 265, 267, 268, 276
Payne, D.A., 219, 236

Pearson product-moment formula, 223
Pedagogy, 8
Pendergrass, R., 90
Pennsylvania Retrieval of Information for Managing Educational Systems (PRIMES), 13
Pepper, F.C., 239, 254
Percentile rank, 212
Performance objectives, 52. *See also* Instructional objectives
Performance standard, 52–53, 55
Performance tests, 143
Performance-based certification, 282
Perseveration, 34
Petersen, G.A., 28
Phares, E., 314
Philadelphia Teachers in Industry Program, 285–286
Phillips, E.L., 242n, 255
Philosophy for Children Program, 105
Phinney, S., 17, 28
Physical environment, 247
Physical influences on learning, 23, 25
Piaget, Jean, 250, 251
Picture arrangement tasks, 42–43
Picture composition, 29–31
Pictures, 103–104
Popham, W.J., 62, 68, 77, 160, 168, 201, 208
Postconventional morality, 250
Power tests, 143
Preconscious activity, 263–264
Preconventional morality, 250
Prescott, D.A., 174, 180
Pretest conditions, 54
Principle learning, 258
Prisoner's Dilemma, 10–11
Probing techniques, 135
Problem solving, 258
Productive Thinking Program, 105, 265
Products of instruction, 53
Project TEACH, 241
Prompting students, 133–134
Psychological influences on learning, 22–25
Psychomotor objectives, 72–73
Pupil movement within classroom, 249–250
Purdue Creative Thinking Program, 265
Purkey, W.W., 239, 255

Questioning. *See* Teacher questions

Ragsdale, C.E., 70, 77

Rakow, J., 122, 124
Rand, Y., 108
Rank-order correlation coefficient, 220, 221
Rating method for essay tests, 205–206
Rating scales, 152, 304
Ratliff, R., 314
Ratzenberg, F., 242n, 254
Reading, 263
Reality therapy, 240
Redfield, D.L., 140
Redirection technique, 135–136
Reid, J.C., 122, 124
Reinforcement, teacher questioning and use of, 132–133
Reisman, F.K., 22, 23, 26, 28, 93, 94, 96, 108, 241, 242, 255, 256–259
Relative position, 211–212
Reliability, 223–224
Remmers, H.H., 183, 208
Report cards, 227–229. *See also* Marks
Reporting methods. *See also* Marks
 goal cards as, 230–232
 purpose of, 224–226, 230
Research writing, 7
Resource units, 80
Restricted-response essay items, 202
Rice, C.T., 140
Richardson, Shari, 298n
Right brain dominance, 102, 299
Rogers, C.R., 258, 276
Role play
 definition of, 252
 for distinguishing between observation and inferences, 19–20
Romberg, T.H., 5, 16, 276
Rosenshine, B., 140
Rosenthal, R., 140
Rotter, J., 300, 314
Rousseau, E.W., 140
Rowe, M.B., 126, 131–132, 140
Rule-setting, 250–251
Rummel, J.F., 183, 208

Salomon, 286, 288, 293
Sanders, N., 77
Sandoval, Hugo F., 8, 16
Sarason, S.B., 288, 293
Saunders, J., 115, 124
Scannell, D.P., 62, 77
Schema, definition of, 92
Schmidt, W.H., 223, 236
School-related tasks
 involving ability to acquire knowledge, 44–46

School-related tasks *(continued)*
  involving conceptual ability, 36–41
  involving sequencing ability, 41–44
  involving spatial ability, 41–44
Schretter, Teresa, 88n
Schrieber, J.E., 126, 140
Schuttenberg, E.M., 115, 124
Science teachers, shortage of, 4
Scoring, test, 177–179
  essay, 205–206
Scott, R.O., 62, 77
Seating arrangements, 247–248
Secondary education, 49, 294–296
Secondary students, 296–297
Segal, J.W., 92, 105, 107
Self-concept, 239
Self-control, 253
Self-instruction, 242–243
Sensory influences on learning, 25
Sensory modality preference, 102, 299
Sequencing ability tasks
  coding as, 43–44
  digit span as, 41–42
  picture arrangement as, 42–43
Sequential Assessment in Mathematics Inventories (SAMI), 256–257, 259–260
Sex and gender, 100
Seyforth, J.T., 313, 314
Shipman, S., 100, 108
Sigel, I., 28, 33n, 47
Signal learning, 258
Similarities tasks, 38–39
Simons, S.B., 240, 255
Simple thinkers, 102
Simpson, E.J., 70, 77
Skinner, B.F., 241, 255
Smith, F.L., 139
Social influences on learning, 23, 23–26
Social objectives, 49
Socioeconomic status, 100
Sociogram, 155
Sociometric methods, 155
Solomon, M., 269, 276
Spatial ability tasks
  block design as, 31–34
  object assembly as, 34–36
  picture composition as, 29–31
Spatial problems, 248–249
Spearman rank-difference formula, 223
Speed tests, 143
Speedie, S.M., 263, 265, 275
Standard deviation, 211
Standard scores, 212
Standardized achievement tests, 143, 161–162. *See also* Tests

critical analysis of, 164–166
instructor-made vs., 162–163
types of, 163–164
Stein, B.S., 28
Stellwagen, W.R., 62, 77
Sternberg, R.J., 109
Stevens, D.J., 288, 289, 290, 293
Stevens, R., 126, 140
Stimulus-response learning, 258
Stoker, H.W., 59, 76
Strip key, 178, 179
Structure of the Intellect (SOI), 26–27, 264
Structure environment, 242
Student data
  analyzing, 212–218, 310
  assessing reliability and validity of, 218–224
  marking and reporting, 224–232, 304–305, 310
  summarizing, 210–212, 310
Stumpf, M.K., 6, 12, 14n, 15
Summative evaluation, 148
Summerlin, L., 147, 148n, 150
Supply items, 159, 184–186, 305–306
Survey battery, 143, 163. *See also* Standardized achievement tests
Symbols, 104
Synectics, 267
Synthesis, 58
Systems approach to instruction, 93

Tacit knowledge, 105
Talking, as verbal process, 263
Tannhauser, M.A., 242n, 254
Tantrums, 246
Task analysis, effect of, on instruction, 94–97
Tattling, 246
Taxonomy of Educational Objectives: Cognitive Domain, 56, 57, 258
Taylor, J.G., 239, 255
Teacher education programs, 282–283
Teacher effectiveness training, 240
Teacher preparation, 5–11
Teacher questioning techniques
  calling on students, 133–134
  probing or coaching, 135
  procedures for improving, 136–137
  prompting, 134–135
  redirection, 135–136
  reinforcement, 132–133
  wait-time, 131–132
Teacher questions
  classification of, 126–131
  convergent vs. divergent, 129–131

frequency of, 126
importance of, 125–126
level of, 127–129
quality of, 126
Teacher salaries, 279–280, 282
Teacher unions, 280–282
Teacher-made objective tests, 143, 148, 158–159
Teachers
  district-wide support for, 11–14
  high attrition rate of, 3–4
  motivation to become, 3–4
  need for in-depth knowledge of one's discipline, 14–15
  role in instructional process of, 102–103
  shortage of subject-matter qualified, 4–5
Teaching profession
  computer use in, 286–292. *See also* Computer use in classroom
  economic concerns of, 297–280
  nature of, 283–286
Teaching Reading in the Content Areas, 105
Teaching strategies
  lesson planning and, 84
  types of, 103–105
Teaching units, 80
  goals of, 82
  titles of, 81
Temper tantrums, 246
Terminal behavior, 52–54
Test item construction
  for changing-alternative selection items, 189–196
  for constant-alternative selection items, 186–189
  for elementary school students, 199–201
  for essay tests, 201–205
  guidelines for, 183–184
  for matching exercises, 196–199
  principles of, 181–183
  for secondary school students, 305–310
  for supply items, 184–185
Test scoring, 177–179
  essay, 205–206
Testing condition, 52, 54–55
Tests
  administration of, 174–176
  characteristics of quality, 146–148
  criterion-referenced, 159–161
  definition of, 143
  directions for, 173–174
  formal,
  informal, 151–155
  instructor-made vs. standardized, 162

locating information about, 166–167
norm-referenced, 160, 161
planning for, 169–174
standardized achievement, 161–166
types of, 143–144, 151–159
Textbook industry, 269
Textbooks. *See* Basal textbooks
Thorndike, R.L., 221–222, 236
Tinsley, D.C., 126, 139
Tokar, E., 205, 208
Tomorrow's Teachers, 282
Torrance, E.P., 263, 266, 267, 276
Transactional analysis, 240
Traxler, A., 173, 180
Treffinger, D., 263, 265, 268, 275, 276
True-false questions, 159, 186–189
Turkle, S., 135, 140
Tversky, A., 159, 168, 236
Tyler, R.W., 50, 51, 64, 77

Union membership, 280–282
Units. *See* Teaching units
Usher, R.H., 239, 255

Validity
construct, 221
content, 220, 222
criterion-related, 220
curricular, 222–223
defining and estimating, 219
instructional, 223
Values clarification, 239–240
Variability (scores), 211
Verbal association, 258
Verbal tests, 143
Vocabulary tasks, 39–41
Volunteers, calling on, 134
Vygotsky, L.S., 276

Wagner, R.K., 109
Wait-time, questioning, 131–132
Walberg, H.J., 98, 109
Wall, J., 147, 148n, 150
Wallas, G., 263, 277
Walker, D., 269, 277
Walters, S.A., 263
Wang, M.C., 98, 109
Warming, E., 269, 277
Waycross, Georgia, curriculum guide, 11

Wechsler Intelligence Scale for Children (WISC), 26
Weiner, D.H., 238, 255
Weiss, R.H., 263
Wells, H.C., 239, 254
Wertheimer, M., 264, 277
Whelan, R.J., 242n, 255
White, B., 313, 314
Whitley, T.W., 244, 254
Wilson, J.W., 94, 109
Wolf, R., 189
Wright, C.J., 126, 140
Wright, H.F., 153, 167
Writing
as a process of inquiry, 7
as a skill, 260–263
research, 7
Written tests, 143
Wynn, C., 62, 77

Yelon, S.L., 62, 77
Yost, M., 126, 140

Zlatchin, P.J., 50, 76

The Authors

FREDRICKA K. REISMAN received her bachelor's degree in psychology and sociology, her master of science in elementary education, and her Ph.D. in mathematics education from Syracuse University. She has taught third and fifth grade and high school geometry. She has also taught undergraduate and graduate courses in mathematics education at Syracuse University and developmental psychology at Maria Regina College. She designed and taught courses in diagnostic teaching of elementary school mathematics, special education, and elementary education at the University of Georgia where she was chair of the Division of Elementary Education. Presently, Dr. Reisman is Professor and Director of Teacher Preparation at Drexel University in Philadelphia.

Dr. Reisman is the author of *A Guide to the Diagnostic Teaching of Arithmetic, Teaching Elementary School Mathematics: Method and Content, Teaching Mathematics to Children with Special Needs,* articles and chapters in books and encyclopedias. She has developed a mathematics diagnostic assessment for grades K–8 entitled Sequential Assessment Mathematics Inventory (SAMI). Dr. Reisman works closely with school districts and the Pennsylvania Department of Education.

BEVERLY D. PAYNE is an Associate Professor of Elementary Education at the University of Georgia. She is Program Head of Early Childhood Education. Dr. Payne received her B.A. and M.A. from the University of South Florida and her Ed.D. from the University of Georgia. After working and instructing in day-care settings, Dr. Payne began her current career as an elementary teacher educator. In addition to being a coauthor of *Elementary Education: A Basic Text,* Dr. Payne has contributed numerous articles on teacher education theory and practices to the professional literature. She has served as an advisor to public school systems, social service agencies, state departments, and university personnel. In addition, she has conducted numerous presentations at state, regional, and national association conventions.